Exterior view of the Chestnut
Street Theatre, Philadelphia

Master Burke, the child prodigy,
dancing on a barrel while
playing his violin

Playbill for *The Marriage of
Figaro* with Charlotte Cushman
as the Countess

Charlotte Cushman as a
terrifying Meg Merrilies,
perhaps her most famous role

Edwin Forrest (Othello) with
his lawyer for the divorce trial,
John Van Buren (Iago)

Interior view of the exhibition
saloon at Barnum's American
Museum, New York City

Melodrama Unveiled

David Grimsted

Melodrama Unveiled

AMERICAN THEATER AND CULTURE
1800–1850

THE UNIVERSITY OF CHICAGO PRESS

CHICAGO · LONDON

Library of Congress Catalog Card Number: 68-15575

THE UNIVERSITY OF CHICAGO PRESS, CHICAGO 60637
THE UNIVERSITY OF CHICAGO PRESS, LTD., LONDON W.C.1

Printed in the United States of America

FOR MOTHER AND FATHER

not only because I take the melodrama seriously:

"Would you rest quietly on your pillows after the labour of the day, would you sleep peacefully in the grave when the labour of life is o'er? . . . Honour your father and mother or the church yard will give you no rest."

The Good Neighbor

Theatres are mirrors of nature . . . .
They reflect virtue and vice.

John Minshull (1804)

*

When the Revolution that has changed the social and
political state of an aristocratic people begins to
penetrate into literature, it generally first manifests
itself in the drama. . . . The spectator of a dramatic
piece is, to a certain extent, taken by surprise by the
impression it conveys. He has no time to refer to his
memory or to consult those more able to judge than
himself. It does not occur to him to resist the new
literary tendencies that begin to be felt by him; he
yields to them before he knows what they are. . . .
If you would judge beforehand of a literature that is
lapsing into democracy, study its dramatic productions.

Alexis de Tocqueville (1835)

"There is another class . . . who sit down to a work of amusement tolerantly as they sit at a play, and with much the same expectations and feelings. They look that fancy shall invoke scenes different from those of the same old crowd round the customhouse counter. . . . They look not only for more entertainment, but, at bottom, even for more reality than real life itself can show. Thus, though they want novelty, they want nature, too; but nature unfettered, exhilarated, in effect transformed. In this way of thinking, the people in a fiction, like people in a play, must dress as nobody exactly dresses, talk as nobody exactly talks, act as nobody exactly acts. It is with fiction as with religion: it should present another world, and yet one to which we feel the tie."

Herman Melville (1857)

Preface

"IF THE PLAY were uninteresting in itself, and the performance poor, as is often the case," wrote a Unitarian minister in 1853, "still there is the pit which is a microcosm, an epitome of the world. I must see by what emotions, passions, thoughts it is swayed; what deeds it applauds, which it condemns." The minister's fascination with the drama is essentially mine. This study attempts to use the theater of the early nineteenth century to explain the popularity of that most banal of dramatic forms, the melodrama, and to glimpse that most devious of historical objects, the popular mind of an age.

Perhaps the gravest problem of intellectual history is an unavoidable arbitrariness. A particular theme or special group of writers interests a historian, and he studies the nature and the cultural implications of his subject matter. Yet there remain so many other ideas or people that might have been investigated that it is difficult to know the comparative importance of the particular myth or movement described. The drama in some ways is an equally arbitrary subject, but it has two advantages. Drama was the major form of public entertainment available to all classes and the art form most wholly and immediately dependent on popular appeal. Hence it became an unusually sensitive barometer of the least common denominator of an age's attitudes and concerns. The theater of the period also offers a social unit that a historian can handle whole; hence I could define my study in terms of a topic rather than an answer. I approached the drama, not looking for evidence to support a particular idea, but trying to find as many ideas as the melodrama sugges-

ted and to fit them into a specific setting, emotional context, and relationship with other ideas. These advantages of the theater as subject obviously
do not fully circumvent a certain capriciousness in intellectual history,
where the historian, even more than in his other labors, succeeds perhaps
by the nimbleness of his mind more than by the clear centrality of his
chosen set of facts. I simply hope the subject helps maintain a balance
between my ideas and those of the period about which I am curious.

As the early melodrama offers a path to intellectual history, I think the
social context enriches dramatic history in certain ways. The aesthetic-
ally poor quality of its plays has encouraged stage historians to view the
period's theatrical history as a strange interlude either preparatory to
twentieth-century improvements or simply full of quaint plays, practices,
and anecdotes. Seen as a product of particular intellectual and social preconceptions, the period's theater betrays more clearly its meaning and,
in the context of its aesthetic limitations, its achievement. The melodrama becomes less an inexplicable monstrosity and more an emotionally
valid attempt to dramatize an era's faith.

Clearly there are problems in yoking dramatic to intellectual history.
A tension exists in this study between the two areas of concern: the
intellectual historian may be impatient with the theatrical detail and the
dramatic historian uninterested in some of the cultural connections. My
hope is that this tension remains vital and truly suggestive of the groping tentativeness that properly accompanies the movement from surface
to substance, from incident to idea.

"When the Revolution that has changed the social and political state
of a people begins to penetrate its literature," wrote Tocqueville, "it
generally first manifests itself in drama." In the United States the new
governmental system and the new kind of drama became firmly established at the same time, in the two decades surrounding the beginning
of the nineteenth century. In the following years theatrical history
peculiarly reflected many of the new society's intellectual problems. The
new form of melodrama gave the clearest example of the triumph of "the
romantic mode" in its popular, socially acceptable form. Ministers in
their futile attempts to rout drama suggested the folly of religious
expectations that nineteenth-century man might be led away from "the
things of this world." The frustrations of amateur dramatic critics who,
as men of intellect, wished to promote the improvement of the theater
mirrored the predicament of other natural aristocrats who expected to
give guidance to democratic society. Audiences, with their often
chaotic control of the theater, raised in microcosmic form many of the
difficulties about popular rule and minority rights that perplexed society

generally. The early nineteenth century's use of its dramatic heritage from earlier eras suggested both the period's intellectual peculiarities and their lineage. The motivations and dilemmas of those men who wrote for the stage were akin to those experienced by American artists in other areas. And the melodramatic form itself embodied much of this democratic society's attitude toward morality and nature, its enthusiasm for democracy and domesticity, its tacit separation of the world into spheres of the practical and the transcendent, its desire to see ordinary lives taken seriously and yet be charged with excitement, and its faith in and doubts about progress and providence.

These specific topics are intricate parts of my larger concern, that of suggesting the "vision" of the period, the intellectual assumptions so profound that they seemed less ideas than the inevitable way of looking at things. Alfred North Whitehead stated concisely the notion under-lying this study:

> The intellectual strife of an age is mainly concerned with . . . questions of secondary generality which conceal a general agreement upon first principles almost too obvious to need expression, and almost too general to be capable of expression. In each period there is a general form of the forms of thought; and, like the air we breathe, such a form is so translucent, and so pervading, and so seemingly necessary, that only by extreme effort can we become aware of it.

The melodrama by totally eschewing the controversial, what Whitehead calls "questions of secondary generality," became wholly the vehicle of ideas so translucent that there seemed no ideas at all, of notions so pervasive that they were accepted even by those who were most bored and disgusted by the dramatic form. My hope is that this study can both chronicle a fascinating cultural manifestation and give hint of those first principles "almost too obvious to need expression and almost too general to be capable of expression" that pervaded early nineteenth-century America.

THE STUDY rests on primary sources, but this in no way implies lack of indebtedness to the work done by others. Particularly without the pains-taking research on theatrical activities in various localities, I could never have made the necessary assumption that there existed wide uniformity of theatrical practices and attitudes throughout the United States; nor could I have winnowed out much of the fascinating information culled from local newspapers.

I have other debts as well, particularly to the libraries that proved so accommodating in my search for materials: the university libraries of

Brown, Chicago, California (Berkeley), Princeton, Columbia, and Pennsylvania, the Boston and New York Public Libraries, the Folger and Huntington Libraries, the Library of Congress, and the British Museum. I wish especially to thank Miss Helen Willard and her assistants who made so profitable the two summers I spent in the Harvard Theatre Collection. I am also grateful to The Woodrow Wilson Foundation, the University of California, and Bucknell University, all of which provided funds for segments of the study.

The final form of the study owes much to Henry May, Travis Bogard, William Harbaugh, and especially Charles G. Sellers who read the manuscript, in various stages, to very good effect. I shan't mind at all if anyone is foolish enough to attribute whatever he doesn't like in this study to these men; their academic reputations can better bear it. My wife Patricia wishes to make clear that she had little to do with this beyond the details of bibliography and proofreading, being busy with her own work, bearing children, and even occasionally cleaning the house.

Contents

Melodrama Unveiled

I

The Corruption of an Enlightened Age

WHEN THOMAS JEFFERSON was inaugurated president in 1801, William
Dunlap's New York theater was closing another of its unprofitable seasons. Jefferson's election heralded for many of his supporters a new age;
Jefferson himself looked upon it as a revolution to insure a pure and
democratic society. By 1801 William Dunlap's initial high hopes of
creating a model theater that would edify and improve society had
already faded to a simple desire to avoid impending financial ruin. The
contrast between the success of the two men could hardly have been
greater, but Dunlap, in his failure, was helping to usher in a revolution
as significant as that over which Jefferson presided. For while Jefferson
stood symbol for those eighteenth-century political ideals toward which
America had been groping for several decades, Dunlap, in his stratagems to keep his theater going, did much to advance ideas that were to
become preeminent in the nineteenth century. Dunlap's theatrical revolution both stimulated and illustrated what was essentially, as John
Adams described the rebellion a quarter of a century before, a revolution
in the hearts and the minds of the people.

The revolution that Dunlap ushered on stage was not peculiarly
American. Its ideas were foreign born and had achieved theatrical su-
premacy throughout Europe before they were exported to the new
world. But they came to the United States so opportunely that their
success was immediate, so insidiously that many of their eventual
enemies loudly applauded them on their arrival. Necessity rather than
inclination made Dunlap the main agent through whom revolutionary
dramatic ideas infiltrated the United States. Like his father during the
Revolutionary War, Dunlap could well be termed a moderate loyalist in

the intellectual revolution he fostered. He never fully gave his allegiance to the new ideas, but only used them because they proved helpful in his futile ten-year struggle to keep a theater solvent.

In 1796 Dunlap had become co-manager of the John Street Theatre in New York City. In a way, the job was an admission of defeat by the young artist who at seventeen had painted the portrait of Washington and been complimented by the great man, and who later had studied, though with little application, under Benjamin West in England.[1] When he returned to America, Dunlap had not yet thoroughly learned his art. Finding that he couldn't earn a living by it, he looked around for another occupation. That he looked toward the theater was unusual for someone of his social position. Although aristocratic neither in background nor inclination, Dunlap formed closest friendships with persons of social prominence, such as his father-in-law, William Woolsey and his circle, or of literary prominence, such as Elihu Hubbard Smith, Charles Brockden Brown, and James Fenimore Cooper. And such people, while they commonly went to the theater and sometimes even tried writing for it, seldom welcomed any closer connection. Even after he became a manager, Dunlap made a point of going out to visit his theatrical associates rather than inviting them to his home.[2]

Yet Dunlap turned to the stage not as the last resort of a beaten man but as a field of potential greatness for someone young and very hopeful. In London he had spent much time attending the theater; he had returned to New York in 1787 to hear, and to envy, the praise given to Royall Tyler's American comedy *The Contrast*, praise "which lit up the inflammable material brought from abroad."[3] Certainly great drama could be written in America, and clearly the stage could be a tremendous force—Dunlap often called it "a great engine"—for social improvement if intelligently managed. "If the effects of the stage are as great as its friends and enemies have concurred in representing it," Dunlap noted in his diary, "surely I should have the power to do much good."[4] To a man fascinated by the theater, anxious to contribute to social betterment, and in need of a job, it seemed a perfect opportunity.

Dunlap was an intelligently modest man, little inclined to overestimate his accomplishments. Looking back in later years on his dramatic career, he was to evaluate truly its respectable mediocrity; looking for-

---

[1] William Dunlap, *History of the Rise and Progress of the Arts of Design in the United States* (Boston, 1918), 1: 300–307.

[2] William Dunlap, *Diary*, ed. Dorothy C. Barck (New York, 1930), 1: 55.

[3] William Dunlap, *History of the American Theatre* (London, 1833), 1: 147.

[4] Quoted in Dunlap, *American Theatre*, 1: 287.

ward to it in 1796, he saw mainly its excitingly large possibilities and his own ambition to live up to them. A half-dozen of his plays had been performed earlier with moderate success. Dunlap had no illusions about their greatness, but he was still a comparatively young man of thirty; and who could say that slight, pleasant talents might not develop into impressive merit if given strong theatrical stimulus? The offer for him to become co-manager was baited with the provision that he could select the plays to be given and could produce any plays he wrote. Years later he recalled wryly, "the bait took."[5]

Theatrical illusions vanish quickly backstage, and Dunlap's faded with unusual rapidity during his first few years as a theatrical manager. He began his career with two partners, one of them New York's best actor and an egomaniac, the other married to a dipsomaniac who was one of New York's favorite actresses. These two partners publicly feuded, which led to a number of disturbances among their partisans in the audience. One partner even published a tract justifying his conduct by reporting in detail the public indiscretions of the other's wife, some of which were "too disgustful to remember and too disgraceful to the stage to be dwelt upon."[6] Dunlap had to try to smooth this hostility, a role for which he was temperamentally ill equipped. He also found himself largely responsible for the financial management of the theater, another area in which his talents were limited.

Particularly disturbing to Dunlap was the continued unresponsiveness of the public to all his blandishments. He offered a varied theatrical diet: the old favorites were revived; plays from England were put on the boards in record time; and in his first year he produced two new plays of his own and staged the works of other American dramatists in the hope of developing, as he wrote prior to his managerial venture, "proper exhibitions to set before a free and well-ordered people."[7] He also greatly improved scenic display.[8] But the result was general public indifference and consistent financial loss. At the end of his first season as manager he began to borrow money, which practice was to culminate eight years later in his bankruptcy.[9]

What probably galled Dunlap most, in a career highlighted by defeats

---

[5] *Ibid.*

[6] John Hodgkinson, *A Narrative of His Connection with the Old American Company* (New York, 1797), p. 10; Dunlap, *Diary*, 1: 48–64.

[7] *New York Magazine*, 5 (November, 1794): 654.

[8] Despite Dunlap's artistic training, it was not he, but his scene painter Charles Ciceri, who perfected the machinery and scenic display on which the success of melodrama so heavily depended. *American Theatre*, 1: 210–13.

[9] Dunlap, *Diary*, 1: 69.

and frustrations, was his failure to write plays conspicuous for either literary merit or popular success. In his lifetime Dunlap wrote, translated, or revised about seventy-five plays, over three-fourths of which were turned out in his busy years as manager.[10] Most of these, especially the highly successful ones, were translations or adaptations. Even his original dramas were commonly derived to some extent from other plays, novels, contemporary occurrences, or history. He wrote hurriedly, generally in the interstices of a career filled with other responsibilities and activities. He wrote for a popular audience, his fortune often depending more on the novelty than on the worth of his plays. As a dramatist, he was blessed with several minor merits, principally a sense of humor, adaptability, and a knowledge of stagecraft. These are the merits of the hack writer, yet Dunlap never became simply a hack. In spite of the compromises he was forced to make, and despite his lack of creative originality, he retained his hope of writing and presenting drama that would honor him and benefit society.

Dunlap's personal outlook showed its eighteenth-century origins at many points. He viewed accepted religious forms with quiet skepticism, believing in the existence of a Supreme Ruler but arguing that proper worship only came from living an upright life. Although he accepted Christ as Savior, he interpreted salvation as "nothing more than assurance that eternal life is the consequence of believing in him, i.e., adopting his precepts and following his example."[11] Religions that stressed miracles or claimed God-given prerogatives or scorned man's reason were anathema to Dunlap. The "authority" of the Catholic church and the "enthusiasm" of many Protestant sects equally disgusted him. His account of a visit to a Methodist church, upon the urging of a neighbor, is revelatory of his attitude. Dunlap described the sermon in which "the different degrees of sinfulness were enumerated, the last and greatest (all vices and crimes being mention'd before) being deism—crime of horror! mention'd in a thundering voice accompanied by a blow of vengeance on the cushion." When asked to stay for another service, Dunlap declined, went home, and, as purification rite, read in Hume.[12]

In his last years, while suffering from a painful and prolonged illness, Dunlap often addressed brief prayers of thanks or supplication to "God,

[10] Oral Sumner Coad (*William Dunlap* [New York, 1917], pp. 284–93) gives the most authoritative list of Dunlap's plays, with dates of publication and performance. Coad corrects and clarifies the list given by Dunlap himself in *American Theatre*, 2: 382–83.

[11] Dunlap, *Diary*, 2: 488–99.

[12] *Ibid.*, 1: 96–98.

my creator and incomprehensibly great and good Benefactor," but such prayers marked an intensification of his early ideas rather than a change in them.[13] In a work published shortly before his death, Dunlap offered his fullest public religious testament: "the contemplation of the solar system" most correctly hinted to man the real nature of "the creator, upholder, director, and ultimate perfector of the whole." This paean to a God who was known through the perfectness of the machines he had created, coming in Dunlap's last published work, illustrated how intact his earlier religious views had remained. Contemplation of man and the solar system both led "to a confirmation of that religion which teaches love to God and to our neighbors" and kept "the religion of love" from being perverted into "the idolatry of fear."[14]

Dunlap's list of God's jobs suggests the core of his social faith: God, initially "the creator," was to be finally the "perfector of the whole." For Dunlap this ultimate perfection depended on the application of man's reason to the ills of the world. This was why religious enthusiasm and superstition were so dangerous: they came between man and the correct understanding which was necessary both to know God and to see the best course for achieving His earthly ends. "Thinking gives strength to Reason and before Reason the Passions fade away," he noted in 1798. "Desirable state! from which we are at present far removed."[15] Dunlap's plays frequently showed his own faith that if passions were overcome, if reason held sway, happiness, both personal and public, would result. One of his heroes voiced his constant theme: "Stable happiness awaits the man whose every action is by reason guided."[16] Though a devoted father, Dunlap even chided himself for worrying about his son's illness because "a virtuous man would not be dependent for happiness upon the health or sickness of a puny boy."[17] In his view, spontaneity of feeling never led to better results than a rationally devised plan of action. When an author claimed that the music of ancient Greece was "better adapted to touch the heart" because it "was not of the learned kind," Dunlap strongly dissented: "Why Mr. G. should suppose what he calls learned Music to be less capable of touching the heart than Music in its rude state, I cannot conceive."[18]

[13] *Ibid.* (1819), 2: 494.

[14] Dunlap, *Arts of Design*, 1: 306–7.

[15] Dunlap, *Diary*, 1: 127.

[16] William Dunlap, *Leicester* (New York, 1807), p. 107.

[17] Dunlap, *Diary*, 1: 102.

[18] *Ibid.*, 1: 13. Dunlap remembered a performance of Handel's *Messiah* in Westminster Abbey as one of his most thrilling experiences, and even doubted that "the scientific European ear" was more pleased by the Hallelujah chorus than "my uninstructed Yankee organ." "Yet I ought not to

The "desired state" of a rationally governed, perfected society, though still distant, was closer at hand in America than elsewhere, Dunlap felt. Consequently America's intellectual leaders had particular responsibilities. His efforts in the theater and in fine arts grew in part from this conviction. So did his advocacy of democracy and temperance and his opposition to slavery and dueling. But in all his social opinions, he acted with a measured realization that even perfectly good ends must be advanced undogmatically to avoid evil consequences. For example, both slavery and excessive drink were bad, he argued, but their evils would be more than matched by those arising from the oversimple solutions of immediate abolition or legal prohibition. The argument that slavery was evil and hence intolerable might "satisfy the religionist," Dunlap wrote, "but the unshackled inquirer must do nothing but with a view to consequences."[19] He firmly believed that "common sense and the democratic principle," supported by right-thinking men, would eventually abolish social evils.[20] But the complexity of every situation necessitated circumspection in pursuing good ends and tolerance for those who opposed them. Happiness, Dunlap argued, was always dependent on the "prudence" with which one's goals were encompassed.[21]

Dunlap's circumspection and tolerance showed up well in his relationship with his brother-in-law Timothy Dwight, president of Yale and conspicuous opponent of both deism and drama. In a lengthy essay flaying the stage, Dwight pointedly announced that drama seemed harmless only "to a superficial thinker" and was never justified "but by the man in whose heart evil was the predominating influence."[22] Dunlap publicly turned the other cheek by acknowledging that he had gained "much advantage intellectually" from contact with his brother-in-law.[23] When Dwight insisted on reading him one of his poems—called in Dunlap's diary "a bitter invective against all Frenchmen, innovators and infidels" —Dunlap simply "thanked him and gave no opinion."[24]

---

doubt it," he cautioned, "for knowledge has in all things the advantage over ignorance" (*American Theatre*, 2: 69).

[19] *Diary*, 1: 170–71. See also *ibid.*, 1: 119–21; *American Theatre*, 1: 328; *ibid.*, 2: 43.

[20] Dunlap, *Arts of Design*, 1: 338. Though in temperament a product of Jeffersonian democracy, he approved of Jackson. *Ibid.*, 1: 349; *Diary*, 3: 746.

[21] This doctrine he made the specific moral of his capable biography of the tragedian, George Frederick Cooke. *Memoirs of the Life of George Frederick Cooke* (New York, 1813), 1: xii; 2: 400.

[22] Timothy Dwight, *An Essay on The Stage* (Middleton, Conn., 1824), p. 16; p. 116.

[23] Dunlap, *Arts of Design*, 1: 316–17. Dunlap wrote that he had spent some of his "happiest hours" with Dwight at Greenfield Hill.

[24] Dunlap, *Diary* (1798), 1: 207. For a long while Dunlap worked on a novel, which he never finished but segments of which are preserved in his diary, about a minister with ludicrously exaggerated conceptions of the evils of French philosophy and infidelism.

Dunlap's tolerance and distaste for dogmatism made compromise and accommodation a necessity, almost a virtue, and allowed him to keep his principles intact even when the demands of theatrical management forced him to expedients he disliked. This readiness to compromise was shown in his plays which reflected, as well as haste and the desire to capitalize on public whim, the dilemma of a man caught between antagonistic literary traditions and ideologies without sufficient inventiveness to unite them.

His best original dramas most clearly suggested the mainstream and the side currents of his thought. His first acted play, *The Father of an Only Child*, has two loosely connected plots.[25] The more credible one deals with an unhappily married couple, the husband a rake and the wife a flirt, both of whom learn, through a series of comic complications, the folly of their ways. The tone in this section of the play is that of late eighteenth-century social comedy: a light and wordly-wise look at human folly which concludes with a lesson in conventional morality.

The other part of the plot, constructed on melodramatic lines, is full of heartrending sentiment. A heroine pines for her long-lost love; a kindly old man laments the youthful indiscretion that caused him to abandon the child of a secret marriage; and a villain plots to marry the heroine for money and to seduce her sister for sport. In the end, a beggar arrives who, when his disguise is thrown off, is revealed to be lost lover, abandoned son, and old acquaintance of the villain whose enormities are fully exposed. The play contains two dramatic worlds pasted together with some skill but little conviction. In his epilogue, recited by the actress who played the heroine, Dunlap suggested that he felt the play's melodramatic happenings a little ludicrous:

> Well, we've got thro', and in good truth I'm glad on 't.
> A sorry, whining, canting time I've had on't;
> My true love lost and found, and found and lost;
> Like shuttle-cock my passions pitched and toss'd.[26]

Almost all Dunlap's plays reflect a similarly uneasy union of conflicting ideas and literary models. Not that he always used melodramatic forms in constructing his plays. On the contrary, he borrowed widely

---

[25] The play was written in 1788 and first presented the next year under the title *The Father; or, American Shadyism* (New York, 1789). Dunlap revised the play, mainly improving the plot structure and moral clarity, and published it in 1806 as *The Father of An Only Child*.

[26] Dunlap, *The Father*, p. 57. Dunlap's only novel, *The Memoirs of a Water Drinker* (New York, 1837), shows a similar dichotomy: a fairly realistic and grim picture of an actor's life is engulfed in an implausible "romantic" subplot.

and was most successful when he chose the best models. His *Leicester* is a derivative tragedy, but one intelligently derived from good sources. Based on Elizabethan precedents, its blank verse is adequate, its plot well constructed and dramatic, and its heroine the only character of convincing complexity that Dunlap ever drew. Her strange, uncompromising hatred for her husband, and her tender, womanly love for an irresolute, much less noble man are the emotional poles between which she moves. The play's greatest weakness is that Dunlap couldn't merely tell his story. Drama, he thought, was supposed to contribute to social betterment, and so he ended the play with a moral lecture. The husband announces, over the dead bodies of wife and lover, that the scene illustrates the fruits of illicit passion:

> O that mankind
> Would ponder well this scene, which rightly ta'en
> Shows us how near the ever-open Gate
> Of guilty Pleasure is Perdition's Gulph.

He even assures his listeners that his wife was no true representative of her sex.[27] Dunlap's desire "to present a picture fraught with instruction"[28] went far toward smothering a good play under a simple-minded moral parable.

Leicester had an inauspicious one night run; *André*, Dunlap's other important serious play, lasted for only three performances. Little wonder that the hard-pressed manager turned to translating foreign plays—plays which expressed attitudes that Dunlap did not fully share, but which attained a popularity far surpassing that of his own productions. The great immediate theatrical importance of the man designated "the father of American drama" lay in his speedy importation of currently popular French and German plays.

The mainstay of Dunlap's theater proved to be his translations of the plays of August von Kotzebue, which had already achieved unprecedented popularity throughout Europe. *The Stranger*, the Kotzebue play that Dunlap first presented, was one of the German author's most enduring successes in the United States. Dunlap turned to this play because of its London acclaim, and brought it out as a London play, although he had much revised it from the English adaptations. Dunlap noted how unusually affecting its scenes were on both actors and audiences.[29] After its

[27] Dunlap, *Leicester*, pp. 148, 136.
[28] Dunlap, *American Theatre*, 2: 284.
[29] Dunlap, *Diary*, 1: 354–56.

first performance in 1798, the *New York Commercial Advertiser* reported that "the effect of the pathetic scenes was beyond any former example within our remembrance," and added that, when the play was announced for another performance, "the audience testified their approbation by huzzas."[30] Dunlap admitted that "the success of this piece alone" allowed him to keep his theater open, and it soon achieved similar popularity in other American towns.[31] Enthusiasm for *The Stranger* little abated until after the Civil War, and leading actresses continued to play the heroine with such effect that "never, at once, were so many handkerchiefs in requisition."[32]

The Stranger was followed by a host of Kotzebue dramas which repeated their European success in America. Dunlap perfected his German and adapted at least one a year to keep his theater going.[33] As early as 1800 a Baltimore reviewer claimed that praising Kotzebue's plays was "like telling the world the sun possesses heat"; already they had gained "a celebrity hitherto unequalled except in the case of the immortal Shakespeare."[34] Clearly Kotzebue did not deserve the comparisons with Shakespeare that were lavished on him in his first flush of success; his triumph was one not of genius but of competence in codifying tendencies long emerging in drama for which audiences were eager.

A promptbook used in a Philadelphia theater for one of Kotzebue's plays suggests some of the main elements of his dramaturgy: the heroine is discovered "alone, knitting a child's stockings, her sorrowful looks fixed on the picture of a young officer . . ., sighs, wipes her eyes, and continues knitting." Dropping "her hands on her knees, she again looks up to the picture." While she soliloquizes "in a tone of melancholy," "a servant keeps going to and fro, lays the breakfast cloth, and serves breakfast." The heroine speaks briefly to the servant, and there follows "a pause during which the servant arranges the tea things."[35] The stress

---

[30] *New York Commercial Advertiser*, December 11, 1798, quoted in George C. D. Odell, *Annals of the New York Stage* (New York, 1927), 2: 44–45.

[31] Dunlap, *American Theatre*, 2: 81.

[32] From the *New York Mirror* (10 [April 6, 1833]: 318), describing the effect of Fanny Kemble's personation of the heroine.

[33] Before his theatrical career ended he brought out twenty plays from the German, which he translated, or adapted from earlier English versions. About three-fourths were from Kotzebue, but Babo, Iffland, Zschokke, and Schiller, whom Dunlap considered "the greatest dramatist of his age," were drawn on (Dunlap, *American Theatre*, 2: 97). Henry A. Pochman in *German Culture in America* ([Madison, Wisc., 1957], p. 687) credits the superiority of Dunlap's translations for the greater success of the "Kotzebue fad" in America, but Americans most often saw Kotzebue in translations made by Englishmen.

[34] *Baltimore Weekly Magazine*, 1 (April 26, 1800): 7; 1 (May 3, 1800): 9.

[35] Quoted from a Chestnut Street Theatre promptbook for Kotzebue's *The Corsicans*, in Ruth

on everyday activities in Kotzebue's stage business was clearly an attempt to connect art and the most ordinary things that occupied average people. His characters knitted socks and set the table and swept the floor and trimmed the hedge, and the commonplace character of such occupations apparently helped audiences sympathize with dramatic characters with new closeness. A woman's magazine borrowed from Shakespeare to praise a Kotzebue play in terms that show how exciting the ordinary was to audiences unaccustomed to seeing it on stage:

> In all the incidents and situations, the author has been peculiarly happy; they are all of the most simple, natural, domestic kinds; they are such as come home to men's business and their bosoms; they are such as they may everyday see in the families of others, and tremble for in their own.[36]

Kotzebue's domestic plays presented not just the ordinary, but the ordinary closely involved with the unusually pathetic. While the table was being set and the socks knitted, his heroines were also in the midst of some heartrending experience, such as yearning for the young officer in the picture frame. Kotzebue's plots were set up to give ample opportunity for this kind of sentiment. *The Stranger*, for instance, dealt with a woman who had deserted her husband and children for another man, and then, repentant, returned to the vicinity of her home, and finally to the bosom of her family. The situation gave many opportunities for purifying tears and high sentiment about lost innocence, repentance, mother love, and mercy.[37] The problems were "of the most simple, natural, domestic kind," but emotionally intensified to win the approval of all "those whose hearts are warmed by pity and compassion, whose souls expand with benevolence and friendship." Even in Kotzebue's poorly constructed plays, friendly critics could point out that any loss in schema was made up in sentiment.[38]

Kotzebue used spectacular as well as domestic subject matter. In his two most successful heroic dramas, both concerned with Inca resistance to Pizarro, his stage business concentrated on the exotic and spectacular. The grand procession of Inca worshippers was the highlight of *Virgin of the Sun*, and the most memorable scene from *Pizarro in Peru* saw the

---

McKenzie, "Organization, Production and Management at the Chestnut Street Theatre, Philadelphia, from 1791 to 1820" (Ph.D. dissertation, Stanford University, 1952), p. 253.

[36] *Lady's Monitor*, 1 (October 31, 1801): 87.

[37] This situation, though uncommon in the melodrama, proved appealing. When *The Stranger's* popularity diminished, *East Lynn*, featuring the same basic situation, took its place in the theatrical repertory.

[38] *Boston Weekly Magazine*, 2 (March 10, 1804): 79; *Baltimore Weekly Magazine*, 1 (May 31, 1800): 26.

fatally wounded hero use his last energies to save the heroine's child by leaping a chasm with the boy in his arms. Here the spectacle, much like the ordinary detail of the domestic plays, was primarily a setting for the sentiment. Leaping a chasm provided thrills, but such excitement took its direction from its pathetic involvement with self-sacrificing heroism and tender mother love. The same magazine that praised *The Stranger* for its everyday situations said of *Pizarro in Peru:* "We never beheld a tragedy which interested our feelings in such a great degree, and which, at the same time, did not fatigue by its length."[39]

Kotzebue's "exquisite touches of sympathy and native sensibility which speak to the heart" were enmeshed in a theology of feeling.[40] "Compulsive institutions are no longer necessary to preserve decency," announced the good Inca high priest at the conclusion of the *Virgin of the Sun.* "Let truth and nature prevail."[41] Truth and nature, almost synonymous, would prevail, Kotzebue contended, in every truly feeling heart. No rational argument was needed to prove the rightness of a cause that had enlisted "the pious supplications of the trembling wife and mother's heart."[42] Learning, position, social sanctions of any kind were unnecessary, even obstructive, to the man who would do right. The heart was the sure compass that, if left untampered, would guide toward truth; emotional sensibility was the real criterion for virtue, and crying became its testament. Because tears were the sure sign of inner virtue, Kotzebue's characters, male and female, shed them abundantly:

Charlotte: When anyone does me a service my tears are ever more ready than my words.
Dr. Bloomfield: Tears are the language of the heart.
Charlotte: I would willingly have wept but I was ashamed before Mr. Semblance [the villain].
Dr. Bloomfield: And not before me, dear girl?
Charlotte: Before you? O no! on that dreadful night when my father lost so much blood, I saw that your tears ran freely down your cheek.

At the conclusion of this play, when two long-feuding brothers were finally reconciled, Kotzebue had the entire "good" portion of his cast weeping.[43]

---

[39] *Lady's Monitor*, 1 (December 12, 1801): 134.
[40] *Ibid.*, 1 (January 30, 1802): 191.
[41] William Dunlap, *Virgin of the Sun* (New York, 1800), p. 20. All the quotes from Kotzebue are from Dunlap's translations of his plays.
[42] William Dunlap, *Pizarro in Peru; or, The Death of Rolla* (New York, 1800), p. 49.
[43] William Dunlap, *Fraternal Discord* (New York, 1809), p. 18; pp. 59–60.

Kotzebue preached this sentimental metaphysics in both his heroic and his domestic dramas. People in the audience reacted to characters similar to themselves, yet capable of the highest sentiment and put in situations surcharged with emotion and significance. Audiences saw themselves, not as they were perhaps, but as they conceivably might be. The domestic dramas gave a highly emotional context to themes close to the life of everyone: the problems of courtship, the difficulty of family relationships, or the need for self-sacrificing love. Though certainly not the first to use this subject matter, Kotzebue gave it the dramatic centrality and form it was to keep throughout the early nineteenth century. The appeal of the heroic dramas was similar. They revealed the greatness of people little characterized by mental or emotional complexity but possessed of simple and spontaneous virtue. In short, they were simple people who happened to be in important situations. Anyone, only by being true to his natural self, could possess their kind of greatness if given the opportunity. Audiences attested with plentiful tears the purity and potential greatness of their own sympathetic hearts.

Kotzebue retained his popular appeal, but the more intellectual critics soon turned against him. Kotzebue's characters were said to possess "more German nature than human nature," and managers were urged to present English plays instead of having "recourse to the vile trash of Kotzebue."[44] The harsh criticism that gathered strength in the early years of the nineteenth century was in part a healthy reaction to the enthusiasm with which his plays were initially greeted. As Dunlap wrote in his diary in 1813, he felt no desire to join critics in denouncing Kotzebue because he had never made the mistake of rating him as the equal of truly good playwrights like Shakespeare and Sheridan.[45] But the reaction against Kotzebue was not simply, nor even mainly, a truer evaluation of his literary merits. The attacks usually included condemnation of Goethe and Schiller as well; all three men, labeled as practitioners of "German" or "teutonic" drama, were denounced principally for their immorality. Even a reviewer aware of the "genius" of Schiller and Goethe found *The Robbers* "a monstrous production" and condemned Goethe's plays on the basis of "the rules of just morality."[46] The abuse

---

[44] *American Monthly Magazine and Critical Review*, 1 (April, 1817): 206; *Companion and Weekly Miscellany*, 1 (November 10, 1804): 14. This critical detraction was of course not universal. On December 13, 1823, the *New York Mirror* (1: 158), for example, still lumped together "Shakespeare, Kotzebue, and other immortal names."

[45] Dunlap, *Diary*, 2: 460.

[46] *American Quarterly Review*, 4 (September, 1828): 183–89. See also *American Monthly Magazine and Critical Review*, 1 (April, 1815): 205; *Emerald*, 3 (April 16, 1808): 310.

heaped upon *The Robbers* paralleled closely that lavished on Kotzebue's more popular efforts.

Kotzebue's lachrymose sentimentality tended to hide his cantankerous, iconoclastic streak. Some of his plays were too fantastic to have any popular appeal, but even his frequently staged dramas contained sentiments and attitudes which critics felt morally dangerous. Dunlap himself came to feel that Kotzebue's work was vitiated by "his own false philosophy and false estimate of the foundation on which society ought to rest."[47] Kotzebue's highly popular *Lovers' Vows* provides a good sampling of his "immoral" tendencies. The play begins with an extraneous attack on Christianity. An elderly woman, on the point of starvation, announces: "But here comes a Jew. Ah, if I could only beg, of him would I ask relief, for Christians do but profess humanity."[48] Kotzebue dotted his plays with such passing attacks on religion, that "cloud of superstition between man and his god."[49]

Having criticized Christianity, Kotzebue presented his idea that impetuous feeling rather than reason or custom was the proper basis of conduct. His hero, a young man who "can only feel," gives the old woman his last few pennies because his heart tells him that "to perform a good action satisfies both hunger and thirst."[50] When he learns the woman is his mother who years ago had been seduced and abandoned by a nobleman, the stage is set for the delivery of jibes against nobility and civilization. Needing money to save his mother from starvation, the hero looks "where insultingly glitter the stately towers of the Prince's residence," but concludes that benevolence would not be found there— "the cottage of the poor is her palace—the heart of the poor her temple."[51] Indeed, an impoverished peasant couple does care for his mother while the hero goes off to beg help.

Desperation finally leads the hero to justify very antisocial behavior, even robbery. A man in need, he argues, would be right "should he instinctively grasp at a small share of those bounties, which nature presents to all. Such a man does not plunder, he rightly takes his own from the wretch who unjustly usurped it." When a friend warns him that such

---

[47] Dunlap, *American Theatre*, 2: 86–90. Dunlap gave the plots of some of Kotzebue's more extravagant plays, in one of which the hero proposed marriage to his sisters, but when they refused him, settled for the family maid. After she bore an illegitimate child, the whole family—brother, sisters, maid, and baby—went to live in the Pelew Islands.

[48] William Dunlap, *Lovers' Vows* (New York, 1814), p. 8.

[49] Dunlap, *Virgin of the Sun*, p. 49.

[50] Dunlap, *Lovers' Vows*, pp. 47, 8.

[51] *Ibid.*, p. 32.

principles, if widely accepted, would "cut asunder every tie that binds society and change us soon into Arabian hordes," the hero not only admits the possibility but welcomes it: "Amid the hospitable Arabs my mother would not have been suffered to starve on the highway."[52] Distinctions in rank and social codes, Kotzebue argued, weaken the promptings of man's benevolent heart. And virtue was to be found, most purely, among the lowly or among uncivilized groups like the "hospitable Arabs."

Critics found these occasional expressions of preference for non-Christians, savages, and the poor and uneducated upsetting. But their attack centered on the happy ending that Kotzebue gave to this play and to some others that dealt with people who had sinned. In *Lovers' Vows*, for instance, the baron learned of the hard lot of the woman he long ago seduced, repented, married her, and made the hero his legitimate heir. This culmination, like that in *The Stranger* where the adulterous wife was forgiven by her husband, inspired untempered moral condemnation. Critics felt that not only occasional statements, but the very structure of Kotzebue's plays, contained "wild and pernicious views of manners and morals" and suggested that all conventional social restraints be battered down by the impetuous poundings of the individual heart.[53] For if adultery were so pleasantly rewarded at last, what was the premium on behaving in a moral fashion? And who could judge the social dangers if people's sympathy was given to noble brigands like Charles de Moor or fair adulterers like Mrs. Haller? Americans had to be warned about "the seducing dramas of Germany" which threatened "the peace, the virtue, nay the very existence of civil and religious society."[54]

Most vigorous and frequent in its attack on this "constant rumble of dramatick high Dutch" was the most intellectually respected periodical of the day, Joseph Dennie's *Port-Folio*. "Morality, principle, virtue all fade," Dennie predicted, "before this new philosophy of the passions."[55] No doubt remained among "lovers of sense, and Shakespeare, and the

---

[52] *Ibid.*, p. 43.

[53] Dunlap, *American Theatre*, 2: 88.

[54] *Literary Magazine and American Register*, 7 (March, 1807): 215; *Companion and Weekly Miscellany*, 1 (December 1, 1804): 35.

[55] *Port-Folio*, 1 (September 5, 1801): 287; 2 (May 23, 1802): 166. Most of the theatrical columns in the *Port-Folio*'s early years were written by Dennie and John Edmonds Stock (Randolph C. Randall, "Authors of the *Port-Folio* Revealed by the Hall Files," *American Literature*, 11 [January, 1940]: 392–410). If the words were not always Dennie's, the sentiments certainly were. H. M. Ellis reprints a letter Dennie wrote to his parents on May 20, 1800, in which he said that he seldom went to the theater because the players "were so much in the habit of acting the vile trash of one Kotzebue, a jacobin German philosopher and atheist" (*Joseph Dennie and his Circle* [Austin, Tex., 1915], p. 120).

advocates of truth and virtue" about the "noxious tendency" of German drama:

> To villify greatness, to calumniate clergymen and lawyers, to taint the imagination of youth, to "loosen the rudder hands of society," to invent wild scenes, and describe them in rumbling language, appear to be the cardinal objects of this jacobin playwright.[56]

Dennie, very dubious anyway about the course of American society, only hoped that "the voice of reason . . . will prevail against this Teutonic taste in literature," and exhorted managers to "join the contest against the corruption of an *enlightened age*."[57]

The danger of "German ideas" undermining social morality was hardly acute. The lack of popularity of plays by Goethe and Schiller, and the quick decline of Kotzebue's fame, indicated, if indication was needed, that audiences were not anxious to do away with social conventions. Kotzebue's success had resulted from the dramatic dignity he gave to common people and from his sentimental theology rather than from his social protest. Yet, in another sense, critical fears were well taken: Kotzebue's vogue did mark "the corruption of an enlightened age," against which the "voice of reason" was to prove powerless. After him, drama was to be clearly grounded, if not in a "philosophy of the passions" as Dennie feared, at least in a philosophy of feeling.

Hardly had Kotzebue's star risen than it was dimmed by the gaudier glow of other playwrights. These authors, most notably the French manufacturers of melodrama, turned out a dramatic commodity carefully measured to popular taste. They presented plentiful theatrical thrills and much emotion-rousing action stitched together with sentimental dialogue into a sampler whose moral was a platitude. Kotzebue was largely displaced by authors who, without any particular convictions of their own, could devote all their energies to inventing new claptrap of plot and trimmings for their audiences. The American stage was inundated by plays of French melodramatists who, like French cooks, one critic complained, got a lot out of "very slender materials."[58]

Dunlap translated from the French almost as industriously as from the German, and his theater was responsible for the initial staging in the United States of many French melodramas.[59] The elements of these

[56] *Port-Folio*, 1 (September 5, 1801): 283.

[57] *Ibid.*, 2 (May 29, 1802): 166; 2 (January 23 1802): 18.

[58] *New York Mirror*, 6 (June 6, 1829): 382.

[59] Coad attributes nine translations from the French to Dunlap, including the play that ushered melodrama into the United States in 1803, Caignez' *The Voice of Nature*. *Dunlap*, pp. 194–204; 289–91.

plays—their character types, plot structure, and themes— were standardized very quickly; and the setting, decorations, and particular incidents of the plot became the only areas in which ingenuity was employed. The person who went to see an early melodrama witnessed the stratagems of a villain, the innocence of a young maiden, the courage of her true love, the kindness of her old and well-loved father, and the comic antics of some rustic or servant types. The plot almost invariably centered on the efforts of the villain to rob the girl of her virtue, her fortune, or both, and on his finally being foiled by Providence and the exertions of the hero. Into the course of these events some full-scale spectacle was worked, possibly a huge procession or festivity, a thrilling fight or escape, or some tremendous cataclysm, either natural or man-made. Such stage effects, the work of the scene painter and machinist, were the most striking feature of these plays.[60] All the while the orchestra played appropriate background music to heighten the suspense in periods of danger and sweeten the sentiment in moments of lull.

Dunlap also tried his hand at the third type of drama which gained great popularity at the turn of the century. In 1795 he wrote *Fontainville Abbey*, based on the novel by Mrs. Radcliffe, and the following year he produced his original play *The Mysterious Monk*. Both dramas employed the usual trappings of Gothic horror—terrible visions, secret passageways, dankly unwholesome settings, weird figures with awesome power, clanking chains and old bones and flickering candles, all wrapped in an aura of ancient crime and guilt, with the supernatural elements explained away in earthly terms in the end. The effect of these plays was completely dependent on establishing an aura of horror, so Dunlap set his scene carefully:

> . . . her tottering turrets, yielding to the blast, . . .
> Give more impressive warning of decay
> Than sculptur'd skulls on monumental tombs,
> Or all the churchyard pageantry of death.
> At every step I take, increasing marks
> Of awful solitude awake my heart.
> Hail, horrors! suiting to my sadden'd soul . . .
> None other sound I hear, save when the bat
> Flits by my head.

The subsequent action was fitted to the scene; the same character later in the play exclaimed, "Horror on horror heap'd!"[61]

---

[60] William S. Dye, Jr., *A Study of Melodrama in England, 1800–1840* (Philadelphia, 1919), gives a good summary of these constant elements.

[61] William Dunlap, *Fontainville Abbey* (New York, 1807), pp. 155–56; 205.

By channeling Gothic, German, and French drama into the United States, Dunlap gave its theater a salty taste of the tide that was to engulf the stage for over half a century. But his efforts were not limited to variations on foreign themes. He wrote brief patriotic interludes and long, and even more patriotic, songs. He also wrote the stories and lyrics for several operettas. One of his most profitable ventures was a disjointed travelogue about national types visiting in America, which was supposed to give coherence to a display of 50,000 square feet of painted canvas scenery.[62] He also wrote one tragedy—many critics think it was his best work—based on an incident in American history in which the ideas of an older America, to which he spiritually belonged, clashed with those of nineteenth-century America, which he had done so much to foster theatrically. Had Dunlap been fully conscious of his theme, *André* might stand as the most intellectually arresting drama of the period. As it was, Dunlap showed in his play, almost unwittingly, two ways of thought in conflict, and his choice between them.

André is Dunlap's simplest, most tightly constructed play. It begins after André has been condemned for treason; it ends with his death on the gallows. The conflict arises from various efforts to save the noble André made by virtuous, right-feeling people. But all these warm-blooded appeals congeal before Washington's rational, almost godlike sense of justice. The characters who plead for André's life offer an impressive cross-section of nineteenth-century dramatic types: the gentleman of such character and generosity that he wins the love even of his enemies, the dashing and warm-hearted patriot soldier, the beautiful sweetheart separated by parental injustice from her true love, the doting wife and mother, the innocent and angelic children, the old soldier gladly sacrificing self for his country's good. The plot is so manipulated that the happiness of each of these sentimental types depends on Washington's freeing André. In typical nineteenth-century plays only a complete villain, a Baron Trevasi or a Simon Legree, could be deaf to such pitiful and virtuous pleas. Certainly only a monster could refuse André's modest request that he be shot instead of hanged. But in this case the monster, impervious to every plea of the human heart, is the great and noble Washington, whom Dunlap and his fellow countrymen so deeply revered. The reason for Washington's refusal is, of course, neither callousness nor lack of sensitivity, but a deep sense of duty and a realization that in this instance the promptings of wise policy and personal

---

[62] *A Trip to Niagara; or, Travellers in America.* Dunlap said of this, his last play: "The main intention . . . was to display scenery" (*American Theatre*, 2: 280).

kindness diverge. The tears and emotions of even the best of people prove of no avail against a mind that knows that sentiment may be misguided and that sense must hold sway if good is to triumph.

The play was not as good as its theme. The characters were all one dimensional, and the blank verse was smooth but uninspired. Without a line particularly memorable for either brilliance or badness, it went its five-act course with unobtrusive competence. The intellectual conflict was the core of the play seemingly without Dunlap's fully realizing it. He apparently intended to write a drama of character rather than of theme, and the flatness of his cast was not an intentional foreshortening designed to give clarity to an idea, but the resort of someone who lacked sufficient originality, or who spent too little time on the play, to develop anything but smooth stereotypes. Despite its weaknesses, *André* displayed the uninventive integrity of Dunlap, who wrote it with ready-made characters but, abetted by historical fact, managed to manipulate them to express his own convictions.

André was a theatrical failure, in part because of a bad production, in part because of its theme. After three performances, only the first of which drew a large house, its stage career ended. A few years later Dunlap resurrected it in another form which won greater popular success and critical disdain. *The Glory of Columbia—Her Yeomanry!* retained the people and plot of the original, but bore little other resemblance to *André*. The main plot was dwarfed by a new subplot designed to demonstrate the unimpeachable honor of simple American farmers. Dunlap relegated characters of high seriousness like Washington or André to the background and instead focused attention on Paulding and Van Vert and David Williams and his sister Sal, all pure and simple American farm people given to singing catchy songs, voicing their patriotism, and producing low humor. Simply because the stage Irishman was popular, Dunlap wrote a whole, and wholly extraneous, act around the shenanigans of an immigrant just arrived from Ireland. Ever willing to compromise, Dunlap cut out most of the idea and structure of his play to make room for low comedy and blatant chauvinism. In performance, usually on the Fourth of July, managers found it advisable to further trim the play's remaining dignified portions.

In 1805 William Dunlap went bankrupt after devoting self and substance to the theater for nine years. It was a galling defeat for a man who had jeopardized his social position by becoming professionally tied to the theater and who had often sullied his ideals in a determined effort to keep the theater running. To one less able to recognize and to laugh at his own misfortune and mistakes, the failure to advance either personal fortune or public taste might have been an embittering tragedy. Dunlap simply accepted it and retired to his farm in New Jersey.[63]

He spent another six years working in a subordinate capacity in the New York theater, but most of the rest of his life was devoted to painting. He specialized in portraiture because this was the one sure way for the American artist to earn money. Later he achieved moderate success with exhibitions of large religious and historical works.[64] Painting paid little better than drama, however, and Dunlap was forced to eke out his income by occasional writings. He wrote biographies of two men he had known well, Charles Brockden Brown and George Frederick Cooke. He wrote a novel, *Memoirs of a Water Drinker*, which presented fictionalized portraits of many of his theatrical acquaintances. And, in his last years, he wrote histories of the theater and of fine arts in America, which two books were perhaps the most important contribution to American cultural life of this "very worthy, amiable, and clever American," who "in his sphere, and up to the measure of his ability . . . was honorably useful."[65]

In his *American Theatre* Dunlap wrote that while he was a manager the New York stage was degraded, much to its financial profit, by "the exhibitions of a man who could whirl around on his head with crackers and other fireworks attached to his heels."[66] This "antipodian Whirligig" exploded vividly the hope Dunlap had cherished when he became manager that he might transform his theater into "a great engine for social good." He had wanted to devote more performances to the classics, especially Shakespeare, but he made little progress here. He had hoped to introduce the best of contemporary plays, but his only translation from the one modern dramatist who won his full admiration, Frederick Schiller, proved a failure.[67] He had dreamed of cultivating an American dramatic flowering which, in point of numbers of native plays produced, he succeeded in doing. But in terms of either quality or popular success, the American achievement remained negligible.

Nonetheless, Dunlap's efforts marked a new dramatic age. When he quitted his managerial position, the type of play that would be popular for the rest of the nineteenth century had been acclimated to the Ameri-

---

[63] In *Arts of Design* (1: 317) Dunlap described the event most simply: "I engaged in theatrical speculations and became bankrupt in 1805."

[64] Dunlap, *Arts of Design*, 1: 344–62.

[65] *American Quarterly Review*, 8 (September, 1830): 161; John Inman's obituary in *New World*, 1 (December 5, 1840): 428.

[66] Dunlap, *American Theatre*, 2: 151.

[67] Dunlap translated *Don Carlos*, but it had only one performance. *American Theatre*, 2: 97.

can stage. This drama made light of the rationality which Dunlap felt to be the hope of society and replaced it with a concept of feeling or intuition. It paid little heed either to poetry or to characterization but rather emphasized stage effect and scenic display. And from Dunlap's time on, the legitimate drama was to share the stage with novelty acts akin to the spinning man with firecrackers tied to his feet. Dunlap had hoped to create a better theatrical world by following his principles, but he ended by ushering America into a new dramatic age by his compromises. He was, as he himself wrote, "one who had on trial found circumstances too strong for his desires of reform, and who, after a struggle of years (with ruined health and fortunes) gave up the contest without giving up the wish or the hope."[68]

His *History of the American Theatre*, written in 1832, testified to the resilence of his hope for dramatic reform. The quotation that prefaced the book suggested its theme: "The corruption of the theatre is no disproof of its innate and primitive utility." He made no defense of the contemporary American theater; indeed, he depicted it primarily as an evil, one too popular to be abolished and too harmful to be left unguided. The theater would inevitably exist and play a central role in educating the people, would either "guide or mislead." If left to "mercenary managers," it would neglect those lessons of morality and patriotism that were essential if America's rulers, the people, were "to qualify for the high office they were destined to fulfill."[69] He proposed, therefore, that either the government or public-spirited "men of taste, literature, and moral standing" set up a theater purged of contemporary excrescences and devoted to social betterment—very similar in intent to the theater he had dreamed of over thirty years earlier as a profit-making institution.[70]

Dunlap's plan, as he should have known, offered no real answer. Even had benevolent and enlightened gentlemen been willing to give money and name to a theater, it was no answer. For people who went to the theater were not primarily concerned with being uplifted, at least in any way that proved unentertaining. A philanthropic theater could probably have done little more than Dunlap or other conscientious managers did in inculcating a preference for better plays. The fault was not simply audience stupidity or bad taste; Shakespeare continued to be year after year the most frequently performed playwright. But nineteenth-century

---

[68] *Ibid.*, 1: 276.
[69] *Ibid.*, 1: 129; 2: 360.
[70] *Ibid.*, 1: 131.

audiences understandably craved a drama reflective of their own situations and standards. Dunlap might well have asked himself why audiences patronized the high tragedy of *André* only when it had been transfigured with the low-comedy antics of David Williams and sister Sal, their "father and the cows; and the children, and the pigs, and the rest of the livestock" into a play whose only intellectual point was to show that "somehow or other there is sort of something here (*touching his breast*) that we yankees don't choose to truck for money."[71]

---

[71] William Dunlap, *The Glory of Columbia—Her Yeomanry!* (New York, 1817), pp. 15, 21.

2

Men of God and Intellect

OTHER AMERICANS besides Dunlap urged a publically subsidized theater. Perhaps the most elaborate proposal was worked out by a Bostonian, William Haliburton, in 1792, the year that the Massachusetts law against theatricals was repealed. He advocated the state's building a community center to house a theater, gardens, legislative offices, an adult education center, and halls for banqueting, town meetings, and militia meetings. The poor were to be admitted to the theater free, and all profits were to go to "promoting manufacturers, employing the able and maintaining the helpless poor." Haliburton stressed that such a theater would help both to draw all classes in the community together and to provide the educated and virtuous populace so necessary to a democracy. Certainly such an establishment would produce, Haliburton concluded, "truly astonishing" effects "on the manners of the people" and on "the intellectual powers of man."[1]

By the 1840's problems connected with incipient industrialization, especially growing uneasiness about class disparities and about the moral callousness inculcated by the pursuit of the dollar, inspired renewed interest in the theater as agent of social policy. In 1847 Frederick Sawyer provided an extensive historical and sociological justification of the theater. He propounded theatrical subsidization for the traditional reason that this would insure wholesome control by "the moral and religious part of the community," but also on the more interesting grounds that widespread participation in public amusements was

---

[1] William Haliburton, *Effects of the Stage on the Manners of the People; and the Propriety of Encouraging and Establishing a Moral Theatre* (Boston, 1792).

necessary for both the emotional and social health of a people.[2] His basic argument was taken up by a group of liberal clergymen in the 1850's who urged their congregations to support and hence influence the commercial theater[3] and by a few individuals who revived the idea of a governmentally supported drama. Most outspoken was Edward Everett Hale, who contended that America's greatest failure was not corruption or immorality but the brutishness inculcated by the primacy of its doctrines of hard work and profit making. The rich and poor both needed the theater to give them broader and more humane sympathy and understanding, and free drama was desperately important for poorer urban groups who were in danger of being brutalized less by immoral entertainments than by lack of amusements. The government had a responsibility to provide recreation, he concluded, "just as it provides education."[4]

Such pleas, although suggestive of widely held fears about the course of American society, never gained broad social backing. In a period when liberals considered negative government as the primary cure for social ills, when vestigial religious objections to drama remained, and when the theater seemed to have forfeited much of its intellectual dignity, only a handful of people supported the idea of governmentally or privately endowed theaters. Only reluctantly and slowly in the decades before the Civil War did local and state governments assume full financial responsibility for police and fire protection and for a modicum of public education; local governments financed internal improvements, and the federal government debated support for railroads and for that "useful" intellectual discipline, science.[5] But drama and the theater remained far beyond the pale of such commitments: Dunlap's "moral engine" was not practical like the steam engine, and the benefits of the theater seemed more vague and less substantial than those of canals. Besides, theaters existed and expanded as a free enterprise; what reason, then, for "unnatural" governmental interference?

Though Dunlap's "the wise and the good" were thus deprived of a chance to control a theater, they nonetheless sought to influence it. Two general groups strove to give direction to the theatrical tastes of the

[2] Frederick W. Sawyer, *A Plea for Amusements* (New York, 1847), pp. 247–48.
[3] See, for example, Henry Whitney Bellows, *The Relation of Public Amusement to Public Morality* (New York, 1857); M. D. Conway, *A Discourse, Delivered in the Unitarian Church* (Cincinnati, 1857); *Amusements: Their Uses and Abuses* (Progressive Friends' tract, New York, 1856).
[4] Edward Everett Hale, *Public Amusements for the Rich and Poor* (Boston, 1857), p. 15.
[5] See A. Hunter Dupree, *Science in the Federal Government: A History of Policies and Activities to 1940* (Cambridge, Mass., 1957), pp. 44–90.

many. One, composed mostly of ministers, argued that the theater was "the Synagogue of Satan," which should be destroyed or, at the very least, avoided by the righteous.[6] The second considered the stage, in the words of America's first dramatic magazine, a potentially "humanizing and instructive academy," and sought to turn it from what it often was to what it ought to be.[7] Both groups, though destined to frustration, exerted some influence; as a vocal minority, they made managers anxious to diminish—when convenient—the faults exposed. Just as important, these critics provided or aroused much of the period's discussion of the methods, standards, and objectives of good drama.

Religious critics of the theater had less influence largely because their criticism was wholly destructive in intent; to them there was great significance in the fact that a principal entrance to every theater was labeled "the pit."[8] Harriet Beecher Stowe, when first asked to adapt her *Uncle Tom's Cabin* to the stage, refused in terms which illustrated the attitude of the stage's religious opponents: "If the barrier which now keeps young people of religious families from theatrical entertainments is once broken down by the introduction of respectable and moral plays, they will then be open to all the temptations of those which are not such."[9] Although Mrs. Stowe was reconciled to "respectable and moral plays" when, hidden under a shawl, she finally attended a dramatization of her novel, other religious figures had no reason for changing their objections to any attempt to bridge "the wide gulph between the drama and the communion table, between the theatre and heaven."[10] Religious periodicals pointed to the example of Alsypius, an early Christian whom pagan pranksters forced to a gladiatorial show where he became so fascinated with blood and splendor that he left the church for the amphitheater.[11] Contemporary Christians were at least as susceptible and had to be repeatedly warned to "shun the theatre. Do not go there even once."[12]

A sameness of argument ran through almost all the religious attacks

---

[6] John Edwards, *Warning to Sinners, or an Address to All Play-Actors, Play Hunters, Legislators, Governors, Magistrates, Clergy, Churchmen, Deists and the World At Large* (New York, 1812), p. 3; James MacDonald, *May I Go to the Theatre?* (New York, 1856), p. 5.

[7] *Thespian Oracle,* 1 (January, 1798): 1.

[8] David Hale, *Letters on the New Theatre by a Father* (Boston, 1827), p. 8; MacDonald, *May I Go to the Theatre?*, p. 22.

[9] Quoted in Montrose J. Moses, *The American Dramatist* (Boston, 1925), pp. 110–11.

[10] William T. Hamilton, *A Sermon on Theatrical Entertainments* (Mobile, Ala., 1841), p. 12.

[11] *Connecticut Evangelical Magazine and Religious Intelligencer,* 5 (February, 1805): 319; *Virginia Religious Magazine,* 2 (May, 1806): 180.

[12] Joseph Parrish Thompson, *Theatrical Amusements: A Discourse on the Character and Influence of the Theatre* (New York, 1847), p. 40; William S. Plumer, *Theatrical Entertainments* (Philadelphia [1837]), pp. 23–24.

on the theater. Catholics and Quakers, Episcopalians and Baptists, Congregationalists, Presbyterians, and Methodists who chose to attack the stage drew on the same arsenal of arguments. Tone and emphasis varied from writer to writer, but the ideas always paralleled those of the two most widely quoted eighteenth-century opponents of the stage, Bishop Tillotson and John Witherspoon. And the oft-repeated parade of authorities opposed to the stage, containing such unlikely clerical supporters as Plato, Aristotle, Ovid, Tacitus, John Hawkins, and Rousseau, was one that had been organized by the Quaker, Lindley Murray, in 1789.[13] Section, like sect, caused little change in the argument; ministers in the South spoke against the stage in the same way as did those in the East and West, and seemingly as often.[14] The religious attack on the stage was made with essentially one voice.

Part of the attack paralleled complaints made by almost all thoughtful observers. The presence in the theater of prostitutes and liquor dealers, "the hyenas of humanity who leap upon the grave of innocence and revel in the very vitals of modesty and worth," was decried by both the stage's supporters and its opponents.[15] But the latter argued that the pure must never go where they could encounter "the most depraved and yet the most enticing companions the community affords," who would inculcate, particularly among the young, "an entire distaste for the quiet and pure enjoyments of the home."[16]

Religious figures also saw grave dangers in certain stage practices that most other people accepted with equanimity. One of their commonest charges was that "the Supreme Being is often addressed profanely" on stage and that plays were frequently "interlarded with oaths and irreverent expressions."[17] Nonreligious critics sometimes cautioned a performer about swearing, but the ministerial argument was much more inclusive. One clergyman proved his point with some examples of profanity on stage usually withheld as "too revolting to the moral feelings"

---

[13] Lindley Murray, *Extracts From the Writings of Diverse Eminent Authors of Various Religious Denominations; and at Various Periods of Time, Representing the Evils and Pernicious Effects of Stage Plays and Other Vain Amusements* (Philadelphia, 1799). The compilation was first published in 1789 and was reprinted at least as late as 1837.

[14] Considering its population and publishing facilities, the South contributed more than its share of extant anti-theater tracts. There seems no evidence for the generalization that the church put a serious curb on the theater in the North but not in the South.

[15] Hamilton, *Sermon on Theatrical Entertainments*, p. 7.

[16] Hale, *Letters on the New Theatre*, p. 12; D. Hayes Agnew, *Theatrical Amusements With Some Remarks on the Reverend Henry Bellows' Address* (Philadelphia, 1857), p. 11.

[17] Thompson, *Theatrical Amusements*, p. 28; *Christian Journal and Literary Register*, 3 (April, 1819): 122.

to repeat: "God God," "Lord have mercy," and "Egad."[18] Ministers claimed that all prayers or references to God on stage, even when given with complete reverence in appropriate places, were blasphemous.

The costumes of the stage were another focus for clerical ire, especially after the successful introduction of the ballet in the 1830's by Madame Hutin whose "gross and scandalous display of her person" was viewed, one pamphlet amazedly reported, even by "respectable females . . . without disgust and even without blushing."[19] Such moral callousness, a Baptist minister opined, clearly foreshadowed the decline of America;[20] and many others painted, obliquely, the horrors of stage costumes. To avoid sullying the imagination of its readers, one periodical said it would "not speak of instances such as the one . . . where an actress danced in flesh-coloured pantaloons"; and moral scruples prevented a minister from elucidating "the principal charm of a female dancer, nor . . . those feats of agility which elicit the loudest applause."[21] Lyman Beecher, dedicating the Tremont Theatre in Boston after a religious group had bought it, exulted in the power of a God who could reclaim for His purposes a building defiled not merely by actors, but also by the impurities of Fanny Ellsler's ballet costume.[22] Even aside from ballet, religious leaders found theatrical costumes "indecorously" revealing. For example, they frequently argued both biblical and natural injunctions were broken by actresses willing to show their "own sex unsexed" by "wearing the breeches," either in young boy parts or in attempts at impersonating some tragic hero.[23]

The clergy emphasized these specific and undeniable charges less than more sweeping and dubious indictments. Their condemnation of players, for instance, was usually unbounded. John Witherspoon declared that actors were "almost universally vicious," and Timothy Dwight announced that "player, vagabond, and maximum of vice and wickedness, be only different names for the same thing."[24] Religious

[18] *Panoplist, or Christian's Armory*, 1 (February, 1806): 412; MacDonald, *May I Go to the Theatre?*, pp. 13–14.

[19] *Address to the Public* [New York, 1833?], pp. 4–5.

[20] Stephen P. Hill, *Theatrical Amusements* (Philadelphia, n.d.), p. 298.

[21] *Christian Journal and Literary Register*, 3 (April, 1819): 124; Thompson, *Theatrical Amusements*, p. 28.

[22] Beecher's speech was reprinted in the *Boston Courier* (July 6, 1843) and is included in an appendix to Harrold C. Shiffler, "The Opposition of the Presbyterian Church in the United States of America to the Theatre in America, 1750–1891" (Ph.D. dissertation, University of Iowa, 1953).

[23] Theodore L. Cuyler, *Sermon on Christian Recreation and Unchristian Amusement* (New York, 1857), p. 15.

[24] John Witherspoon, *A Serious Enquiry into the Nature and Effects of the Stage*, in *Essays on Impor-*

leaders reiterated that to attend the theater was (worded with Episcopalian restraint) to "encourage actors and actresses in a course of life extremely unfavorable to their immortal interests," or (stated with Presbyterian vigor) to "support and encourage a set of performers in a life of vanity, licentiousness and sin."[25]

Attacks on the plays themselves were similarly immoderate. On occasion the clergy contented themselves with measured criticisms of plays. Certainly drama did inculcate a "Natural Religion rather than that of Christian revelation"; uncontestably the first plays, the Greek tragedies, were "somewhat heathenish in their morals."[26] But there was little in modern drama to justify the sweeping charges commonly made that it "sanctions prodigality, deceit, seduction, treachery, and murder," that "piety and virtue are made to appear contemptible, and vice, in the person of some favorite hero, is exhibited as attractive, honourable, and triumphant," or that "in this mirror of nature, vice appears as virtue, and virtue as vice."[27] Not rational consideration, but a complete conviction of evil led ministerial opponents of the stage to conclude "the sentiments contained in plays are either immoral or impure. . . . A good play, did you say? There are none, no, not one!"[28]

The religious conception of the influence of drama was equally horrendous. Opponents of the stage all shared Lyman Beecher's conviction that the theater was "the Centre of the Valley of Pollution," and that "theatres and corruption are cause and effect."[29] They stressed reports linking crime to the drama, especially one made by Professor Griscom of New York which claimed that desire to get money for the theater caused many boys to become thieves and girls to listen "to the first suggestion of the seducer."[30] Others relied on personally gathered information: that three robbers admitted taking to crime after seeing

---

tant Subjects (London, 1765), 2: 100; Timothy Dwight, *An Essay on the Stage* (Middleton, Conn., 1824), p. 101.

[25] *Christian Observer*, 9 (May, 1809): 296; Samuel Miller, *Theatrical Exhibitions: Their Influence on the Character of Individuals and the Community* (New York, 1812), p. 25.

[26] T. Charlton Henry, *An Inquiry into the Consistency of Popular Amusements with Christianity* (Charleston, 1825), p. 46; Robert Turnbull, *The Theatre, in Its Influence upon Literature, Morals, and Religion* (Hartford, 1837), p. 15.

[27] *Christian Observer*, 9 (May, 1809): 296; Miller, *Theatrical Exhibitions*, p. 23; Samuel Gore Winchester, *The Theatre* (Philadelphia, 1840), p. 180.

[28] Robert May, *A Voice From Richmond, and Other Addresses to Children and Youth* (Philadelphia, 1842), p. 24.

[29] Beecher, *Sermon*, quoted in Shiffler, "Presbyterian Church," p. 429.

[30] *Western Luminary* (November 30, 1831), quoted in Mabel Crum, "The History of the Lexington Theatre from the Beginning to 1860" (Ph.D. dissertation, University of Kentucky, 1956), p. 324; Winchester, *Theatre*, p. 199; Turnbull, *Theatre*, pp. 38–39.

the melodrama of *Jack Sheppard*; that in one Boston family "three very promising young men had recently been utterly ruined and their ruin could be traced distinctly to the theatre"; that a "weeping mother" had recently exclaimed "O that *Theatre!* He was a virtuous, kind youth, till that theatre proved his ruin."[31] A poem on the dangers of drama, in the roughness of its idea (not to mention its meter), suggested the vagueness, and the magnitude, of religious fears:

> It would be endless to trace all vice
> That from the playhouse takes immediate rise.
> It is the unexhausted magazine
> That stocks the land with vanity and sin.
> By flourishing so long
> Numbers have been undone, both old and young,
> And many hundred souls are now unblest
> Which else had died in peace, and found eternal rest.[32]

The exaggeration of the clerical argument grew partially from a sense of rivalry with the theater. Because the time, money, and inclinations of men were limited, some ministers clearly felt that what was given to the theater subtracted from what was available to God. They argued that, to the true Christian, amusement for its own sake was a "greater crime" than gross sinning was to other people. Recreation was justified only inasmuch as it was needed "to prepare us for future duties"; its regulation was "precisely the same as the use of sleep; . . . where it is not necessary, it must be sinful."[33] Although man's God-given time might properly be expended, even to "an inordinate degree," on "business and household affairs," which were "appointments of God," theaters, novels, or dances were mere "extraneous things and beyond the pale."[34] Anyway, that amusement necessary "for the more vigorous performance of the duties of life" certainly could "be obtained at a cheaper rate than in the theatre."[35]

The price mattered. Men who spent a lot on worldly pleasures were

[31] Reverend John Clay's *Annual Report*, quoted in *New York Mirror*, 20 (January 29, 1842): 39; Hale, *Letters on New Theatre*, pp. 5–6; Hill, *Theatrical Amusements*, p. 302.

[32] Watts's *On the Mind*, quoted in *Academician*, 1 (June 18, 1818): 107.

[33] *Columbia Magazine*, 1 (March, 1815): 202; Witherspoon, *Serious Enquiry*, pp. 24–25, quoted in *Recorder*, 6 (March 3, 1821): 40.

[34] *Gospel Advocate*, 5 (July, 1825): 228–29. The youthful Ralph Waldo Emerson, still under the influence of his clerical upbringing, commented in his journal (June 10, 1822) on the depraving quality of drama and pictured the tormented soul at judgment confounded by a record of misspent time (*Journals of Ralph Waldo Emerson*, ed. Edward W. Emerson and Waldo E. Forbes [Boston, 1909], 1: 147 n.).

[35] Samuel Aiken, *On Theatrical Exhibitions* (Utica, 1825), p. 13.

likely to be "parsimonious to the claims of Zion," ministers asserted.[36] Surely widows, orphans, and the heathen had better claim on the funds of Christians than profane play actors.[37] For the average clergyman, living on a very moderate salary and perhaps oppressed with church indebtedness, the sight of money being lavished on the theater must have been grating. Statistics affirming that more was spent on plays than on churches and schools in some areas, incorrect or not, bothered Christians.[38] And some grew livid over the fact that Fanny Ellsler had "danced sixty thousand dollars out of the pockets of our fellow citizens," or that Edmund Kean returned to England with eleven thousand pounds while the Reverend Ward was able to collect only ten thousand dollars for charity:

> Oh! that they were wise; and would devote the money now expended on pernicious amusements to any truly charitable establishments. Had our Bible, Education, and Mission societies received the sum squandered on an actor, the increase of much vice would have been prevented and the hearts of thousands would have sung for joy.[39]

Some religious writers pressed the idea that the stage was not only a hindrance to religious philanthropy but an enemy of economic success. A minister pointed out that stage attendance was "unfavorable to the regular pursuit of business," and a Providence, Rhode Island, writer expressed amazement that people in that city would endanger their reputation of being "a very industrious, frugal people" by letting "their hard earnings . . . be spent in such vain shows."[40] A Quaker pamphlet, published to warn Friends against backsliding toward the theater, capped its argument with the conclusion that at the least plays encouraged "a disrelish for that frugality and industry in business, on which even a reasonable degree of success so much depends."[41] A Baptist periodical even approved the argument that, if people got used to hearing actors

---

[36] Henry, *An Inquiry*, p. 169.

[37] *Connecticut Evangelical Magazine and Religious Intelligencer*, 4 (April, 1811): 139.

[38] "The Theatre alone," lamented Thomas Grimké to a group from various religious societies in Charleston in 1829, "swallows up in one year, as in a fearful, mighty Maelstrom, more of our wealth, than all our religious societies in the union" (*Reflections on the Character and Objects of All Science and Literature* [New Haven, 1831], p. 195).

[39] Thomas Brainerd, *Influence of Theatres: A Lecture on the Nature and Tendency of the Stage* (Philadelphia, 1840), p. 7; *Recorder*, 6 (May 12, 1821): 80.

[40] Edward N. Kirk, *Love of Pleasure: A Discourse Occasioned by the Opening of the New Theatre in Boston* (Boston, 1854), p. 9; Martha Clark, *Victims of Amusements* (Philadelphia, 1849), p. 11.

[41] Society of Friends, *An Address on the Subject of Theatrical Amusements, from the Monthly Meeting of Friends Held in New York to its Members* (New York, 1840), p. 5.

recite words they did not mean, the principle of contract would be threatened.[42]

The rivalry between church and stage for time and money was looked on as a specific battle in a larger struggle for the hearts of men. Benedite Flaget, later to become the first Roman Catholic bishop of Louisville, wrote that a single theater "must neutralize the efforts of the most zealous and holy Bishop," and he opposed making St. Louis the seat of the diocese if the report were true that a theater had been erected there. He asked how any prelate could successfully encourage a God-centered life "when the play-actors may preach in principle and in practice, the intrigues, luxuries and vanities of the world? That would be to mingle light with darkness, truth with falsehood, Belial with the God of Israel."[43] Plays were sinful, John Witherspoon argued, from their very nature, for drama depended on stimulating the human passions and affections, and it was the Christian's duty "to endeavor to moderate his passions as much as possible" and "to wean his affections from the world."[44]

The text that "no man can serve two masters" was invoked to suggest the incompatibility of "the pleasures of the world with the pleasures of religion," the essential antagonism between "the lovers of pleasure and the lovers of God."[45] A Presbyterian periodical summed up the dichotomy: "Whoever can join in the world's pleasures and diversions with satisfaction and delight can have no real fellowship or community with God."[46] And to those tempted to ask if the theater might not provide an "innocent amusement," the Episcopalian *Christian Observer* countered with a question: "Are they the works of Satan or of Jesus Christ? For there can be no medium in religion."[47] In varying phrases, with differing intensity, ministers who chastized the drama repeated their plea and their warning to all who must "die and stand at the bar of God": "Men and brethren, fellow professors of the religion of Christ, why waste your

---

[42] *Panoplist*, 2 (November, 1806): 280.

[43] Quoted in William G. B. Carson, *Theatre on the Frontier* (Chicago, 1932), p. 11. There was also a more direct rivalry when revivals and drama competed for audiences in some locality. See Sol Smith, *Theatrical Management in the West and South for Thirty Years* (New York, 1868), pp. 72, 74; Walter Leman, *Memories of an Old Actor* (San Francisco, 1886), pp. 90–92.

[44] Witherspoon, *Serious Enquiry*, pp. 31, 41.

[45] Charles Cleveland, *Theatrical Amusements: Letter to a Professing Christian* [from *Columbian Centinal* (December 9, 1818)] (Boston, 1868), p. 6; Thompson, *Theatrical Amusement*, p. 5; *Christian Observer*, quoted in *Connecticut Evangelical Magazine and Religious Intelligencer*, 6 (February, 1806): 318.

[46] *Massachusetts Missionary Magazine*, 3 (March, 1806): 376.

[47] Masillon, quoted in *Christian Observer*, 9 (January, 1810): 25.

precious invaluable time on tragedy, comedy, farce? Behold who are at our doors—death, judgment, eternity."[48]

One minister claimed that neither faith nor works distinguished "the religious part of society" so much as its "uniform avoidance of what is generally comprehended under the phrase 'worldly amusements.'"[49] Not the theater alone, but also dancing, card-playing, horse-racing, and novel-reading came in for a fair share of denunciation by those who felt that the sole purpose of life was to search out God's way and advance his kingdom. Though the drama was not, as the clergy often charged, hostile to the moral concepts of society, it was indifferent to the ascetic qualities some religious leaders stressed. "The intrigues, luxuries, and vanities of the world" were, as Flaget suggested, its subject and concern. And those persons who felt that such interests opposed a right relationship with God rightly opposed the theater.

The triumphs of the godly were few. Sometimes a theater, abandoned because of age or lack of patronage, fell into religious hands. Occasionally reports circulated that theatrical interest was declining, particularly in the period after the Panic of 1837 when ministers mistook economic decline for spiritual awakening. Theatrical disasters, especially the 1812 fire in Richmond in which some seventy-one people were killed, also warmed some religious leaders in the conviction that a righteous God was at work. But such exaltation was always short-lived. The theater continued to expand in territory and appeal. If many playhouses burned, they were quickly rebuilt, often larger and more luxurious than before.[50] The violence of the religious attack was in large part the result of its ineffectiveness.[51] Desperation much more than exaltation, or even hope, marked the tone of most religious writing about the theater.

A minister in 1812 complained that the "criminal and pestiferous" evil of play-going "has crept under a sort of disguise, into the Church of Christ, and has come to be considered a lawful amusement for Christians."[52] Other Christians throughout the period lamented the failure of their co-religionists to set "a suitable example of self-denial and perse-

---

[48] Kiah Bayley, *Fashionable Amusements Inconsistent with the Design and Spirit of the Gospel* . . . (Wiscasset, Me., 1804), p. 29; MacDonald, *May I Go to the Theatre?*, p. 25.

[49] D. R. Thomason, *Fashionable Amusements With A Review of Doctor Bellows' Lecture on the Theatre* (New York, 1857), p. 18.

[50] *On the Amusement of the Theatre* (Methodist tract no. 11 [New York, 1826]), p. 3; *Baptist Missionary Magazine*, 1 (July, 1818): 390; H. P. Phelps, *Playgoers of a Century* (Albany, 1880), pp. 54, 281.

[51] See Shiffler, "Presbyterian Church," pp. 224–30.

[52] Miller, *Theatrical Exhibitions*, p. 36; *Theatrical Exhibitions* (New York: American Tract Society Publications, n.d.), p. 1.

vering piety" by avoiding theatricals.[53] Church members too poor or too ill to support religious services were reported able to make it to the theater, and even clergymen had to be warned that if they went to plays their congregations would "suspect a want of that holy unction which should distinguish the sacred office."[54] The situation was one in which ministers who saw the drama as highly evil naturally spoke against it, while those who thought it harmless probably said nothing. In small communities, amateurs or strolling companies often presented plays even in churches.[55] In a largely secular society, a religion which allowed "no neutral ground" between God's work and the devil's pastimes demanded greater asceticism than most of its adherents were willing to give. When over eight hundred citizens of Memphis went to a circus while only fifty showed up for an important interdenominational meeting, the local editor was not surprised. "Churches are always here, but circuses we 'have not always.'"[56]

If there was covert disregard for the anti-dramatic position within the church, secular opposition was open and pointed. Religious pamphlets frequently were met with quick replies. When one Reverend Gildersleeve of Augusta, Georgia, attacked the theater and its leading actress, the editor of the local paper wrote a pamphlet asserting that the minister was ": wholly unworthy even to kiss the hem of her garment."[57] Thomas Smyth's pamphlet against the stage brought forth two against him, one making "a distinction between drama, and its abuses, and the sincere follower of Christ and the canting, whining hypocrite," and the other pointing out that Smyth's salary, "were it expended on the heathen, would be the means of converting many a soul to the true faith."[58] Sol

---

[53] *South Western Christian Advocate* (June 15, 1839), quoted in Douglas L. Hunt, "The Nashville Theatre, 1830–1840," *Birmingham–Southern College Bulletin*, 28 (1935): 18.

[54] Thomas T. Skillman's *Western Luminary* (1831), quoted in Crum, "Lexington Theatre," pp. 313–23; Henry, *An Inquiry*, pp. 110–11.

[55] For example, as early as 1795, when drama was legally proscribed in much of New England, a group of amateur thespians from Yale gave some plays in a church in Litchfield, Connecticut, which drew between 1,000 and 1,500 spectators (James Cronin, "The Life of Elihu Hubbard Smith" [Ph.D. dissertation, Yale University, 1946], p. 65). See also Leman, *Memories of an Old Actor*, pp. 212–13; George H. Hill, *Scenes from the Life of an Actor* (New York, 1853), p. 166.

[56] *American Eagle* (November 3, 1843), quoted in Charles C. Ritter, "The Theatre in Memphis, Tennessee, from its Beginning to 1859" (Ph.D. dissertation, State University of Iowa, 1956), p. 44.

[57] A. H. Pemberton, *Calumny Refuted, or A Defense of the Drama* (Columbia, S. C., 1831), p. 7.

[58] Thomas Smyth, *The Theatre, a School of Religion, Manners and Morals* (Charleston, 1838); "Thespis," *A Review of the Reverend Thomas Smyth's Two Sermons Against the Theatre* (Charleston, 1838), p. 13; "Otway," *The Theatre Defended. A Reply to Two Discourses of the Reverend Thomas Smyth* (Charleston, 1838), p. 27. Noah Ludlow urged his son-in-law to reply to a ministerial attack, because such a pamphlet "would sell well." Ludlow to Mat Field, September 14, 1844, Ludlow MSS, HTC.

Smith ended his attack on Lyman Beecher's denunciation of actors with the recommendation that the Congregationalist minister "cultivate Christian charity."[59] The nonreligious press generally showed, in milder language, the same lack of sympathy for the religious argument.[60] The frequent and highly publicized visits to the theater by most of America's political leaders testified that no large part of society shared the strong hatred of the drama expressed by a few clergymen.

The frustration of the clerical attack came not only from opposition and neglect, but also because it tended, in minor ways, to increase the social respectability of drama. Managers tried to discredit opposition by eradicating some of the specific practices condemned. The word "God," for example, was almost invariably transformed into some expression like "heaven," or "divine providence," or "supreme being," which was considered less noxious on the stage. As the century progressed grossness in language and frank sexual allusions tended to be refined. Even the inevitable poetic justice of drama's moral conclusion accorded with the desire to give religious critics no handle for complaint. A few theaters particularly prided themselves on the unquestionable uprightness of all their presentations, doubtless, as one minister charged, the "better to subserve their selfish ends."[61]

This peripheral success of the religious attack formed part of its central defeat. Clerical opposition had focused on the stage more than on other "worldly amusements" not because it was totally immoral and indefensible but because it had moral pretensions and was warmly defended. "The world strongly pleads," complained one minister, "they can learn as much from a good play as from a sermon."[62] The world did so plead. Mark Twain's assertion that the church taught Christian morality to one-tenth of mankind while the stage taught it to nine-tenths—and taught it more effectively—was only an extreme version of an idea voiced regularly.[63] The idea infuriated some clergymen. "Nothing . . . can be more ludicrous than claiming for the theatre the character of a pious institution," thundered Lyman Beecher, and

---

[59] Smith, *Theatrical Management*, p. 177; quoted in *Spirit of the Times*, 13 (August 26, 1843): 312.

[60] The *Cleveland Advertiser* (November 10, 1836), for example, referred to the "crabbed philosophy" of a religious attack on the stage (quoted in Shiffler, "Presbyterian Church," p. 227) and the *New York Evening Post* scored the "inveterate prejudice . . . of the most honest, but mistaken opposition." (Isaac Harby, *A Selection from the Miscellaneous Writings of the Late Isaac Harby, Esquire* [Charleston, 1829], p. 39.)

[61] William Hall Pearne, *Fashionable Amusements, An Address Delivered Before the Preacher's Mutual Improvement Society* (Auburn, N.Y., 1853), p. 13.

[62] George Burder, *Non-Conformity to the World* (Boston, 1810), p. 104.

[63] Mark Twain, *Contributions to the Galaxy*, ed. Bruce McElderry, Jr. (Gainesville, Fla., 1961), pp. 128–29. Twain was incensed by a minister's refusal to bury a comedian.

Timothy Dwight more fully exposed the impiety involved in the stage's pretensions:

> When a finite sinful creature . . . sets up another mode by which the divine instruction and bounty may be received, and another school of morality in which to outstrip his Maker and God, how impious and how base his conduct! Here we discover not only disobedience to God, but an attempt to usurp his place in the universe![64]

The drama's educational and moral pretensions were a hope rather than an impiety for a great many Americans. "Next to the sacred institution of religion, and the almost as sacred establishments of a free press," one periodical wrote, "the theatre possesses the greatest influence over the mind and manners of men."[65] Others omitted the qualifications, and called it, at least potentially, "the most powerful moral agent in society" whose "benefits would be unequalled by any other institution."[66] " A moral lever," "the sheet anchor of refinement," " a school where manners may be polished and everything learnt which distinguishes us from barbarism," "a great public school in which all classes may assemble," "a Promethean art that shall breathe life into the impassioned marble of history, and upon the cold beauty of the moral code"—such were the phrases used to illustrate the theater's importance.[67] Especially for people who could not, or would not, read, but who "will receive the lessons of wisdom when impressed by the exertions of others," the theater was to be "the School of Virtue, the School of Manners, the Great School of Society."[68]

John Howard Payne, at the time still a mercantile apprentice in New York, listed in his short-lived magazine some specific goods to be gained from drama's "glowing and impressive" representations:

> The Tyrant is induced to relax his wonted severity; the hand of avarice is opened to the tender influence of Benevolence; the wantonness of the profligate is succeeded by philosophic thoughtfulness, the asperity of

---

[64] Beecher, *Sermon*, quoted in Shiffler, "Presbyterian Church," p. 426; Dwight, *Essay*, p. 90.

[65] *Cynick*, 1 (September 28, 1811): 19.

[66] *Mirror of Taste*, 1 (January, 1810): 51; *Kentucky Gazette* (May 12, 1812), quoted in Crum, "Lexington Theater," p. 127.

[67] Harby, *Miscellaneous Writings*, p. 256; John Howard Payne to *Troy Gazette*, October 28, 1806, "Letter Books," HTC, 1: 166; *Lady's Monitor*, 1 (October 31, 1801): 86; Robert Treat Paine, *Works in Prose and Verse* (Boston, 1812) p. 366; Robert Dale Owen, *Pocahontas* (New York, 1837), p. 18.

[68] Dunlap, *American Theatre*, 2: 118; *Theatrical Censor*, 1 (December 9, 1805): 2. The importance of the theater to the illiterate in a democracy was often stressed (*Emerald*, 3 [April 2, 1808]: 282).

Misanthropy is softened into charity and cheerfulness; the conscience of the criminal is struck to repentance.[69]

If more mature critics did not fully share this faith in the easy reformation of confirmed tyrants, profligates, and criminals, they felt that among more ordinary citizens the drama could discourage such proclivities and encourage virtuous conduct. "All—every age and every condition in life," Walt Whitman contended, "may with profit visit a well-regulated dramatic establishment, and go away better than when they came."[70]

"Well-regulated" was the key term. Few enthusiasts wholly defended the drama as it existed; rather they were excited by what it might become under "proper regulations and supervision."[71] Because those with effective control of the drama did not always exert it in the proper direction, the responsibility for guidance fell on critics, "men of letters" who were "the natural guardians of public taste and morals."[72] If the drama had grave faults, there was no reason why they couldn't be removed by equally grave critics, "persons better educated and of a more refined taste" to give "a better direction to the public taste."[73]

America of the early 1800's was not lacking in men of some literary pretensions willing to speak out as "the voice of an enlightened audience," and a great many publications opened their columns freely to dramatic news and reviews.[74] The plight of one St. Louis editor suggested that the country was rife with embryonic stage critics. "Gentlemen, just stand back and give us room," he pleaded shortly after a new theater opened. "We have now on our table nine communications on the subject of the Theatre, all sent to us within the two days last past. . . . And such a compound of eulogies, complaint, admiration, and approvals as they present! We would as soon attempt a description of Pandora's box, as decipher the half of them."[75] Despite such complaints, newspapers and especially periodicals devoted a large portion of their space to serious dramatic criticisms.

The critic's life was not an easy one, partly because of the inevitable "delicacy and arduousness" of the task. "The office of a reviewer is, in a republic of letters," one of them concluded, "as beneficial and neces-

[69] *Thespian Mirror*, 1 (December 28, 1805): 1–2.
[70] *Brooklyn Eagle* (February 12, 1847), reprinted in *The Gathering of the Forces*, eds. Cleveland Rodgers and John Black (New York, 1920), 2: 314–15.
[71] *Critic*, 1 (November 22, 1828): 62.
[72] *Mirror of Taste*, 1 (January, 1810): 54.
[73] *American Quarterly Review*, 1 (June, 1827): 334.
[74] *Theatrical Censor*, 1 (December, 1809): 3.
[75] *Missouri Republican* (July 28, 1837), quoted in Carson, *Theatre on the Frontier*, p. 195.

sary, though as odious and unpleasant, as that of an executioner in a civil state."[76] The critic must "act as judge, and pass sentence according to dramatic laws without fear or favor"; hence he had "to avoid, as much as possible, all human passions," but to remember that "the Judge is condemned if the guilty is absolved."[77] Especially in the early 1800's the responsibilities of critics, in their own eyes, were so great that most protested their reluctance to take up the task. But the "always irksome, and, too often, thankless" duty could not be shirked: "Where is he that loves the stage and knows its proper end, who can see the abuse with which it is covered and surrounded, without striving, by serious censure, or the force of ridicule, to restore it to the state of happier days?"[78]

The air of self-sacrificing virtue that writers assumed when they took on the role of critic had some justification. Though martyrdom was not the critic's lot even in the early nineteenth century, strongly stated criticism often provoked counterattack. Usually this was verbal. The most frequent charge was that critics condemned works to show their own "conscious superiority" and that this "untimely cloud of carping calumny" put "Drama in a greater jeopardy from its pretended guardians than it possibly could be from its open and avowed enemies."[79] Sometimes the critic was even accused of "wanton cruelty," of being "an assassin who stabs in the dark."[80] His motives and his intellect, too, were suspect. The Boston critic, Robert Treat Paine, in defending a friend's play, wrote:

> Streams, when neglected, sink to common sewers,
> And disappointed authors—turn reviewers.[81]

And a Philadelphia actor wrote a farce in which a critic was put on a magical "wheel of truth" and came out a goose.[82] Critics also faced more direct attacks. Some actors filed damage suits against critical

[76] *Critic*, 1 (April 18, 1829): 386; *Monthly Anthology*, 4 (February, 1807): 85.

[77] *New York Mirror*, 7 (June 26, 1830): 407; Harby, "Essay on Criticism," *Miscellaneous Writings*, p. 174; *Monthly Register, Magazine, and Review of the United States*, 2 (May, 1807): iv.

[78] *American Monthly Magazine and Critical Review*, 1 (July, 1817): 221.

[79] *New York Mirror*, 7 (March 13, 1830): 286; *Port-Folio*, 1 (June, 1809): 513; *Ladies' Visitor*, 1 (January 6, 1807): 18.

[80] *Mirror of Taste*, 3 (January, 1811), prospectus; Matthew Carey, *Desultory Reflections Excited by the Recent Calamitous Fate of John Fullerton* (Philadelphia, 1802). Fullerton was allegedly driven to suicide by unjust critical hostility, as was the tragedian William Conway (Wood, *Personal Recollections*, pp. 85, 312–13).

[81] Robert Treat Paine, "Epilogue" to William Charles White's *The Clergyman's Daughter* (Boston, 1810).

[82] James Fennell, *An Apology for the Life of James Fennell* (Philadelphia, 1814), pp. 364–65; Dunlap, *American Theatre*, 2: 170–72.

detractors and others resorted to physical assault. One mediocre actor properly named John Savage became famous for his violent guardianship of his wife's acting reputation. When a Boston critic summarily dismissed her stage abilities, Savage challenged him. When the critic, wounded in the duel, persisted in his opinion, Savage publicly thrashed him with a horsewhip.[83]

Despite the hardships of the job, plenty of Americans were willing to become critics to help save the drama from its abuses. At times these abuses were quite specific, as when a Philadelphian, who couldn't get his letters to the editor published, began a periodical of his own solely to protest a change in ticket purchases which, he felt, would benefit the aristocracy. For five weeks almost every article in the journal from a "letter from the manager's dog" to a review of the history of the drama in heroic couplets protested the new plan to "cheat the sovereign people":

> Alas! the stage
> Now feels the horrors of an iron age.
> An iron age when wealth alone commands
> Obsequious boots and curst rapacious hands;
> When Nature is expelled, and managers vend
> Shakespeare and Otway to their richest friend;
> Acknowledge wealth alone can sanction taste,
> And count all acting but to it as waste:
> Who spurn the public pleasure, nor e'en stop
> To turn great nature's temple to a banking shop.[84]

In the sixth issue, shortly before suspending publication, the editor included a broader group of subjects—and a short notice complementing the public on the spirit they had shown in opposing the plan and thanking, rather backhandedly, the managers for acceding to the public will.[85]

The *Boston Weekly Magazine* (1816–18), a periodical of broader interests, exemplified the more common kind of critical concerns. Its editor gave space to three "correspondents" on the theater. These critics, apparently

---

[83] Charles Blake, *Historical Account of the Providence Stage* (Providence, 1868), pp. 204–6. Sol Smith told of another actor who severely caned an editor for publishing unfavorable reviews, but the most notorious case was Thomas Hamblin's mauling of the editor of the *New York Herald* (Smith, *Theatrical Management*, p. 140; Francis C. Wemyss, *Theatrical Biography of Eminent Actors and Authors Compiled from the Standard and Minor Drama* [New York, n.d.], p. 4).

[84] *Cynick*, 1 (October 5, 1811): 53–54.

[85] *Ibid.*, 1 (October 26, 1811): 94. The editor blamed William Wood for the plan of renting large boxes for a whole engagement, though the latter, in tracing popular dislike for the plan, said he had always opposed the idea. Wood mentioned no incident in 1811 (*Personal Recollections*, pp. 338–43).

friends, began their work with a joint statement about having "the highest opinion of the attracting powers and general usefulness of the stage—and the lowest opinion of the manner in which, under its present conductors, those powers are cultivated and that usefulness exerted." As representatives of the "only competent judges," "the intelligent and virtuous part of the community," it was their obligation to judge drama by "a permanent standard of taste and a constitution of approved principles for the government of the thespian . . . world."[86]

Their range was wide. They discussed the character of the audience, the quality of the stock company, the interpolations of some of the actors, the types of costumes and properties used, the calibre of plays presented. But while ranging over a diverse group of dramatic evils, they kept their eyes on the central villains of their piece, Messrs. Dickson and Powell, the theater's co-managers. Their criticisms were specific, clear, and pressed with an invective that gave barb to every charge. They lost no opportunity for sweeping attack: after a brief engagement by Thomas Cooper, the popular tragedian, they wrote, "We deem it . . . our duty to console with the managers upon the temporary suspension of the reign of dulness and indecency, which they have been so long labouring to establish." Nor was any detail too mundane for their attention, not even the quality of oil used for lighting: "If they cannot light up the stage with Genius, let us at least have it illuminated with Oil!"[87] Their remarks, like those of other critics, seem honest, intelligent, biting, and, in regard to their hopes for general theatrical reform, futile.

Although critics had no doubts about specific stage failings, they had more trouble defining the "permanent standard of taste" to be invoked in weighing a play. Most often they turned to Shakespeare and dotted their criticism with phrases borrowed from Hamlet's advice to the players. Actors were not to "tear a passion to shatters," "to split the ears of groundlings" to "overstep . . . the modesty of nature" or "make the judicious grieve"; both plays and players were, critics repeatedly asserted, "to hold, as 'twere, the mirror up to nature." A certain lack of precise meaning in the phrase doubtlessly enhanced its popularity. It had all the failings and the advantages of the more modern terms "real" or "true to life." It sounded unobjectionable; it could be applied to any aspect of the drama that the writer supported or disliked; and it was very vague unless more exactly defined. In short, the phrase was a convenient verbal tool used to give an aura of intellectual respectability to almost

---

[86] *Boston Weekly Magazine*, 1 (October 12, 1816): 2; 1 (June 7, 1817): 139.
[87] *Ibid.*, 1 (November 23, 1816): 26; 1 (November 30, 1816): 30.

any observation. For example, when the editor of a St. Louis paper thought that a singer, seven months pregnant and in the manager's words "as big as a small hogshead," should not have the lead in an opera, he could tactfully point out that Mrs. Bailey was not "in a condition to hold the mirror up to nature" as Cinderella.[88]

If the theater as reflector of nature was not an exact critical concept, it did convey a generalized meaning. Used with commonsense fairness, the concept was applied to attack common abuses: oversimplified or inconsistent characterizations, gross improbabilities of plot, and highly inflated dialogue. If the phrase did not mean, at least it implied, that drama should have a plot developing from conflicts between conceivable human beings in language truly expressive of human feeling. The theatrical mirror was, then, to reflect reality. But Shakespeare had added that it "show virtue her own feature;" nineteenth-century critics also emphasized, usually with more simplistic implications, the moral quality of the stage's reflection. The masthead of a periodical edited by the youthful Samuel Woodworth and John Howard Payne, both soon to become important playwrights, paraphrased Shakespeare:

> Plays are mirrors where mankind may see
> How bad they are, how good they ought to be.[89]

The drama was, at once, to present truth and to inculcate accepted standards of morality.

The stage as mirror and the stage as moral educator need not be contradictory; the drama by reflecting well the world around it would presumably teach. Yet a mirror with a moral purpose was one in which certain distortions were permissible, even desirable. Because man was "a creature of imitation," the theater was a particularly good educator; but for the same reason the material presented in the dramatic classroom had to be carefully culled. Because men to some extent became what they saw on stage, critics felt that the theater had special obligations to say nothing which "savours of indelicacy" or "tends to loosen the ties of morality or lessen . . . attachment to pure virtue."[90]

Such limitations sometimes conflicted with the desire for dramatic realism. One critic's definition of tragedy showed how concern for social morality often warped critical judgment. "The tragic muse should love to sing of successful virtue, of triumphant heroism, and of

---

[88] Sol Smith to Richard Corré, October 8, 1837; *Missouri Republican*, both quoted in Carson, *Theatre on the Frontier*, p. 210.

[89] *Fly*, 1 (November 27, 1805): 14.

[90] *Polyanthos*, 1 (December, 1805): 61; *Observer*, 2 (October 31, 1807): 283.

defeated iniquity," he concluded.[91] What was to be tragic about such themes the critic, in his eagerness to promote morality, did not say. Clearly, if virtue must invariably be successful and iniquity inevitably defeated, mirrored nature was going to have to be severely distorted before the audience, "principles undebauched," could go home "with a greater love of virtue and abhorrence of guilt stirring within them."[92] "On the part of a lady performer, in particular," concluded William Leggett, "we would rather see a slight deviation from nature, where nature requires immodesty, than a rigid adherence to it."[93]

To most critics any discrepancy between the requirements of accurate reflection and of moral instruction went unheeded. They generally treated the two aims as being perfectly compatible. If conflict was noted, critics remained unwilling to sacrifice either of their convictions. A Boston reviewer, for example, while advocating "the final triumph of persecuted virtue," admitted that "the wicked sometimes prosper and the innocent suffer" in this world, and that "the poet by representing life in this aspect may represent it truly." But he concluded, "yet according to their merits or demerits, they must be punished or rewarded. If this is not done there is no impartial distribution of divine justice, no instructive lecture of a particular providence, no imitation of the divine dispensation."[94] Why there was no "imitation of the divine dispensation" if the author represented life truly the critic did not consider. Obviously, it was more pleasant for "every feeling bosom when virtue and constancy are rewarded."[95]

Theatrical reviewers of the early nineteenth century believed in a moral law or dispensation as sure and all-encompassing as those that guided the solar system or guarded natural rights. If virtue did not insure a kind of success or happiness, the world must be morally governed by luck or some equally fickle force, and not by a perfectly just universal providence or law. When in specific cases life seemingly did not work out this way, there had to be some mistake, and the occurrence was not so important as what ought to happen, or indeed what must happen, in a world guided by immutable principle. Critics of the period aligned themselves with Job's comforters.

Since most critics, when forced to choose, felt it better for drama to distort life than to blur its moral teaching, they might have been expected

[91] *Aeronaut*, 2 (September 1, 1816): 321.
[92] *Port-Folio*, 1 (July 11, 1801): 222.
[93] *Critic*, 1 (November 15, 1828): 48.
[94] *Emerald*, 2 (March 21, 1807): 137.
[95] *New York Mirror*, 1 (May 29, 1824): 350.

to accept melodrama. No one argued that melodrama was true to life; but the moral was always there, writ large and obviously. Every spectator knew who was good and who bad and how the final chips of poetical justice would fall. Yet critics were completely convinced of the worthlessness of " the childish geegaws yclep'd Melo-dramas."[96] The most popular form of drama throughout the period was the form most vigorously and constantly denounced by critics. A performance of an old play might inspire moral quibbles, but these paled to insignificance before the laments over the livid stupidity of a modern melodrama. "These good old plays—these transcripts of life and true exemplars of human character are compelled to give place to caricatures of nature," moaned one critic suffering from a surfeit of melodrama, "to dramatic performances which, instead of being the mirrors of life, exhibit a medley of reflecting surfaces, . . . in which nothing is seen but distortion."[97] Much better imperfect lessons in a schoolroom, critic after critic averred, than a badly cracked mirror in a fun house.

No twentieth-century critic surpassed his brethren of the early 1800's in scorn of the melodrama. They hurled epithets of every sort at it: "the monstrous progeny of a union of pantomime and tragedy," "the bastard issue of caricature and show," "the blue-blazes-and-bloody-ruin school of drama," "humbugs . . . of pointless dialogue and empty verbiage, set off by tinsel and the poor accessories afforded by glaring and preposterous scenery."[98] And they understood exactly the literary flaws of the genre and attacked regularly "the monstrous productions of modern dramatists" which could only "debase our intellect, and degrade the ranks of literature which must always stand depreciated where the artificial thing is stamped with a value."[99]

The *Boston Weekly Magazine* gave especially full display to all the failings of melodrama. Characters "made for the plot," false and bombastic language, plays that were "mere sugar plums of show" or "geegaws" for the "full-grown babies of the town" and which did honor only "to Mr. Worrall's paint pot"—all were repeatedly scorned. In one particularly apt article, the critics stated well the central concerns of contemporary playwrights:

---

[96] Robert Ewing, *Theatrical Contributions of "Jacques" to the "United States Gazette"* (Philadelphia, 1826), p. 9.

[97] *American Monthly Magazine and Critical Review*, 2 (February, 1818): 299.

[98] *Emerald*, 3 (October 1, 1808): 598; *Spirit of the Times*, 15 (June 7, 1845): 176; *Yankee*, 2 (August, 1829): 58; *Corsair*, 1 (March 30, 1839): 45.

[99] *Country Courier*, 2 (December 5, 1816): 13.

Our modish writers . . . appear to be extravagantly fond of Aristotle's maxim, that "the marvellous is always delightful." Accordingly a plot is made up in their hands of a very ingenious snarl of perplexities, the unravelling of which constitutes the great interest of the piece. These dramatic storytellers lead their readers into paths well "puzzled with mazes," and the argument consists in extricating their heroes and heroines from what, in real life, would be unpoetically considered as inextricable difficulties. Their fable is a labyrinth of delightful perplexities: and if they succeed, by the imminent dangers of their situations, and the dexterity of their "nick of time" escapes—to raising the reader's curiosity to such a pitch of intensity as to prevent any scrutinizing attention to the utter barrenness of the road over which they hurry him—the design is answered.[100]

As long as playwrights furnished plentiful excitement, audiences seemed to forget or forgive all else. The intended guardians of the stage could only denounce "the sickening degradation" which marked drama's retreat "from the solid to the shell; from the substantial to the ephemeral; from the giant to the dwarf."[101]

In the last decades of the half-century, critics showed decreasing concern with broad formulations about what drama should be. The reason was not only that the stage neglected their counsels, but that the development of professional publicity techniques tended to discredit criticism and lessen its public influence. By the 1820's it had become established practice for managers to give season tickets to editors, and for papers in return to insert press releases—descriptively called "puffs"—at the behest of the theater.[102] A magazine in 1821 reported that London reviewers were paid "in a more exact manner" than in America where it is only customary to present the editor "with a season ticket for himself and family."[103] Even for editors who wrote independently about theatrical events, free tickets, advertisements, and gifts—even a tactfully presented "seegar"—might influence their views.[104] There is perhaps reason to believe, though the editor heatedly denied the charge, that the support given by the *Spirit of the Times* to Josephine Clifton was not totally unconnected with the basket of champagne the actress gave to the editor.[105] An intendedly private letter written by the manager of

---

[100] *Boston Weekly Magazine*, 2 (January 24, 1818): 63; 1 (October 19, 1816): 6; 1 (February 1, 1817): 66; 2 (February 28, 1818): 83.

[101] *Spirit of the Times*, 11 (January 22, 1842): 564; *Aeronaut*, 7 (October 21, 1817): 97–98.

[102] Wemyss, *Twenty-Six Years of the Life of an Actor and Manager* (New York, 1847), pp. 367–72; Noah Ludlow, *Dramatic Life as I Found It* (St. Louis, 1880), p. 499; *Dramatic Mirror* (Boston), 1 (February 10, 1829): no. 11.

[103] *Recorder*, 6 (June 23, 1821): 103.

[104] *Figaro*, 1 (November 23, 1833): no. 6: Whitman, *The Gathering of the Forces*, 2: 319.

[105] *Spirit of the Times*, 9 (June 15, 1839): 169.

the Chatham Theatre, a Frenchman, illustrated the pressure that was generally applied with more subtlety: "I send you free admis to my theatre to praise my acturs, you no prase my acturs you shall not have free admis anymore."[106]

By 1825 the art of theatrical publicity had come to be more refined. Charges were made that many critics pronounced favorably only if properly bribed; and some newspapers came to sell space for puffs, which they printed as news, at the same rate they charged for advertisements.[107] When New York's Bowery Theatre opened in 1826, it employed a "very capable man . . . at a handsome salary, to 'write up' the merits of the theatre, and such members of the company as the management desired to be advanced."[108] For those critics who could not be influenced by the press agent, the theater set up a "Cold Cut Room" on one side of the refreshment bar where writing materials and food and drink were provided "exclusively to editors and magistrates." "As the offering will be gratuitous," concluded the periodical's account, "it will no doubt call forth the thanks of the fraternity."[109] Such policies helped make the Bowery one of America's most prosperous theaters for many years and opened the way to stardom for many American players who began their careers there, most notably Edwin Forrest. When the Bowery refused to give some money to William Leggett, at the time editor of a magazine devoting much space to the drama, Forrest personally donated $50, less to relieve "a necessitous, virtuous friend" than to "exalt our national drama."[110]

Theatrical people quickly learned the lesson: success was as much a matter of preparing an audience as pleasing it. By the 1840's publicity techniques were well developed; most of the later great theatrical sensations built their triumphs on the talents of a press agent as well as on their own. Harry Wickoff, for example, early attached his talents to Edwin Forrest's wagon and had even greater success as the promoter of Fanny Ellsler, while P. T. Barnum's handling of Jenny Lind made notorious the press agent's techniques.[111] By the late 1840's almost all

---

[106] Quoted in *Prompter's Whistle*, 1 (August 31, 1850): 15. The magazine argued that the free admission given to the editors really was an "implied contract."

[107] All Philadelphia newspapers sent out an announcement demanding exact payment for printing this kind of theatrical "review." Francis C. Wemyss, *Twenty-Six Years*, p. 368. A New Orleans theater even gave a benefit performance for its pet newspaper critic. Smith, *Theatrical Management*, p. 231.

[108] Joe Cowell, *Thirty Years Passed Among the Players* (New York, 1844), p. 74.

[109] *New York Mirror*, 3 (December 17, 1825): 162; *ibid.* 10 (April 20, 1833): 331.

[110] Edwin Forrest to Prosper Wetmore, August 8, 1828, in Forrest MSS, HTC.

[111] Edwin Forrest, "Diary," HTC. Nathaniel Parker Willis, *Memoranda of Jenny Lind* (Phila-

newspapers were "slaves of the paid puff" system and a good many periodicals were suspect.[112] The situation was such that "only the verdant ones" took theatrical criticism seriously; the public had come to regard it "all as paid for," as "either a puff or a libel."[113]

Just as important to the decline of trenchant criticism was the continual blunting of critics' hopes for a reformed theater. This process on an individual level had gone on from the beginning of the century. Joseph Dennie, for example, instituted a theatrical column in his *Port-Folio*, but gave up the job after a few years because the drama proved impervious to well-argued and strongly stated opinions.[114] Later reviewers experienced similar disillusionment. The critic's acceptance of his failure to reform the theater marked essentially a recognition of theatrical democracy. The critic had always been slightly better educated than the average theatergoer and, good democrat and proud American that he generally was, he expected that the public would defer to his more seasoned judgment and his sincere concern for social betterment. By the time of "Tippecanoe and Tyler too" the theatrical audience's natural aristocrats, though they continued to attend the theater as they continued to vote, had relinquished expectations that good intentions and high cultural ideals would entitle them to a position of effective guidance.

The theatrical critic was not alone in his failure, as he was not alone in his faith that he might aid human betterment. To many men of the early nineteenth century the spread of knowledge was the beginning of reform. And part of that complex of motives which impelled some men to write temperance pamphlets or give abolition speeches prodded others to turn out theatrical criticisms with the expectation of doing "the state some service."[115] Nothing was more necessary or noble than removing the several remaining blights on the most advanced country in a progressing world. And dramatic ills, like other social flaws, would fade if intelligently exposed and determinedly fought.

---

delphia, 1851), and the scrapbook of Jenny Lind clippings (HTC) suggest well the incredible campaign Barnum mounted.

[112] Whitman, *Brooklyn Eagle* (February 8, 1847), in *The Gathering of the Forces*, 2: 310. On October 7, 1846, Whitman noted the appearance of a "long cut and dried puff in yesterday's *New York Herald* of the Keans' acting in a play *which accidentally didn't come off!*" and added that it was not the only "awkward blunder of this kind" that had recently occurred (*ibid.*, 2: 341).

[113] *Spirit of the Times*, 12 (April 16, 1842): 84; Wood, *Personal Recollections*, pp. 454–55; *Arcturus*, 1 (February, 1841): 149.

[114] *Port-Folio*, 1 (January 3, 1801): 4; 5 (December 21, 1805): 393.

[115] Richmond *Compiler* (April 4, 1838), quoted in Martin S. Shockley, "A History of the Theatre in Richmond, Virginia" (Ph.D. dissertation, University of North Carolina, 1938), 1: 43.

The activities of these dedicated, harassed, and usually unpaid critics were quixotic only in respect to the completeness and immediacy with which they expected to encompass their goals. They fought not windmills, but real enough evils—bad plays, bad productions, bad theatrical customs. Despite minor successes, they failed in their long-range purpose of creating a theater dedicated to intelligent and moving drama and to moral improvement. The reason for their failure was neither lack of effort nor lack of intelligence. Their problem in part was that their goal was double: their concept of what a moral theater should be impinged at times on what honest drama must be. But mainly their defeat signified that they upheld higher standards than could be realized in the period's theater. Setting themselves against a dramatic trend that was popular and suggesting little alternative but plays written in other periods, they could only fail. But even long-run failure did not mean their efforts were useless. Their consistent advocacy of the "good old plays" against "modern trash" accounted partially for the fact that audiences in the first half of the nineteenth century saw more of *Richard III* than of *Rosina Meadows, the Village Maiden*; more of the passions of *Othello* than the derring-do of his fellow military leader, *Putnam, the Iron Son of '76*.

The opinions of religious leaders and would-be cultural guides about the theater shared a similar defeat. The theater paid them only passing heed: one was the unsuccessful enemy, the other the well-intentioned friend whose advice was, in most cases, to be politely disregarded. One discouraged critic concluded, "It may be a question whether a regeneration can take place on our stage without a national convulsion to alter the complexion of national character."[116] In a very real sense the "complexion of national character," or perhaps of international character, did determine the course of drama. The theater was acutely sensitive to the wishes of the people, and these people wanted something from life which the strictest of ministers found un-Christian, something from the theater that its serious critics felt a "total debasement of a polite and elegant source of rational amusement."[117]

---

[116] *Aeronaut*, 7 (October 21, 1817): 108. The article ended on the note of hope frequently sounded in the period: "but the genius of our own country yet slumbers; happily we may live to behold its resurrection."

[117] *American Quarterly Review*, 8 (September, 1830): 154.

3

Gods, Gentlemen, and Groundlings

CRITICS frustrated by the drama's resistance to their verbal pressure offered one explanation, one excuse—frequently by quoting a couplet of "that great rock of criticism," Dr. Samuel Johnson:

> The Drama's laws the Drama's patrons give
> For they that live to please, must please—to live.[1]

Everyone who wrote seriously on the drama of the early 1800's accepted Johnson's idea about audience control. Managers were declared "guiltless" when they presented bad plays on the grounds that they, too, were hapless victims of "the perversion of public taste."[2] Playwrights excused literary failings by saying that their plays were intended not to augment literature but only to attract an audience.[3] A few critics exhorted the people to use their sovereignty to correct dramatic abuses; "the only prompter" who could ring up the curtain on a better stage, one editor concluded, was "Public Opinion."[4] Critics more wary of "the depraved taste of a corrupt multitude" urged managers and actors to satisfy "the judicious few" rather than "the noisy rabble that gapes at every puppet show and yells in every ale house."[5] Even so strong a

---

[1] *Mirror of Taste*, 4 (July, 1811): 55–56.

[2] *New York Mirror*, 1 (October 11, 1823): 86; *Theatrical Censor*, 1 (December 9, 1805): 2; William Pelby, *Letters on the Tremont Theatre* (Boston, 1830), p. 11.

[3] Mordecai M. Noah, *Marion; or, The Hero of Lake George* (New York, 1822), p. 5; James Rees, *Dramatic Authors of America* (Philadelphia, 1845), p. 128; Anna Cora Mowatt, *Autobiography of an Actress* (Boston, 1854), p. 203.

[4] *St. Louis Pennant* (July 9, 1840), quoted in William G. B. Carson, *Managers in Distress: The St. Louis Stage, 1840–1844* (St. Louis, 1939), p. 82.

[5] *American Quarterly Review*, 15 (June, 1834): 353; *Boston Weekly Magazine*, 1 (June 7, 1817): 139.

democrat as Walt Whitman chided managers for their "fallacious idea that it is necessary to please the million" when it would be much wiser "to please the select few who guide, (and ought to guide,) public taste."[6] But whether praising or deploring or simply accepting the rule of the audience, all observers admitted its potency. For good or ill, the people who attended gave "the tone to every part of the theatre"; they became to a large extent the effective managers.[7]

These audiences who controlled the theater were not confined to a particular geographic area. Even after 1825 when New York became recognized as the country's theatrical center, its hegemony was far from complete. The Park and the Bowery, unlike Broadway today, were not absolute monarchs in determining theatrical taste, but only the first among equals. In 1833, for example, Fanny Kemble found the company at New York's Park Theatre terrible, the one in Philadelphia somewhat better, and in Boston "the best company I have played with *any where* out of London."[8] Actors came to feel, however, that success on the American stage was partially dependent on a New York reputation; that one had played "at the Park Theatre in New York" was something worth advertising in playbills throughout the United States. Thus New Yorkers usually had a chance to see European plays and players a few weeks before people in other cities. But these were minor supremacies. Each major city had its own company or companies, and each was able to attract both leading "stars" and stock actors regularly.

A nineteenth-century biographer described the popularity of a comedian who specialized in Yankee parts as "co-extensive with the land that gave him birth."[9] This praise, if extravagant, was far from incredible. Drama moved in step with the population across the continent. Behind the first wave of permanent settlers in the West came itinerant performers—ventriloquists, or singers, or magicians—to provide entertainment wherever they could borrow a building and assemble an audience. When any village began to show greater growth than its neighbors, some group of actors would play a brief engagement. If growth continued, either a dramatic entrepreneur or some of the town's leading citizens would build a theater and arrange for regular dramatic seasons.

---

[6] *Brooklyn Eagle* (April 25, 1847), in *The Gathering of the Forces*, ed. Cleveland Rodgers and John Black (New York, 1920), 2: 339. Whitman argued that the theater could be regenerated only by "an entirely new race of managers," a solution akin to the "new race of mothers" he later called for to relieve the bleakness of post-Civil War America's democratic vistas.

[7] William Dunlap, *History of the American Theatre* (London, 1833), 1: 358.

[8] Frances Anne Kemble, *Journal* (Philadelphia, 1835), 2: 132.

[9] William K. Northall, *Life and Recollections of Yankee Hill* (New York, 1850), p. iv.

Cincinnati's theatrical history was typical. Soldiers put on the first play in 1801. An amateur group in 1804 gave a performance at which the village president greeted people and a general read the prologue. In 1805 a professional couple acted with the amateurs, and in 1811 a professional troupe from Pittsburgh visited. The Thespians in 1814 built a theater for their own use and that of any touring professionals, and later gave special performances to honor visits by Jackson and Lafayette. By the 1830's a professional company played there for several months in each year.[10] A Unitarian minister in Cincinnati described the process. "We have seen it out here in the West, where beside our rivers and lakes the town expands; the first petal it puts forth is the Church—the second is the theatre." He added that though the heads of the first organization had prophesied the stage's "entire destruction ... yet God does not side with them, but rather it would seem with the theatre."[11] In Houston, Texas, God even permitted two professional theaters to exist at a time when the town still had no churches.[12]

Growing towns gained their own acting companies, but smaller ones remained dependent on occasional visits from troupes either touring or passing through on their way to major engagements. The catalogue of place names given by touring actors suggested the reach of the drama in the period. Lowell, Worcester, Bangor, Belfast, Orono, and Oldtown comprised one short tour of a Boston actor; and twenty years later on a different coast he acted in Sacramento, Tod's Valley, Cherokee Flat, Rough and Ready, Rattlesnake, Mud Springs, Red Dog, Hangtown, Fiddletown, and Folsom. The first dramatic jaunt of one young actor took him to Cooperstown, Canandaigua, Hercules, Hollow, Skaneateles, Manlius, and Utica. His memoirs, like those of the man who became his co-manager, were full of the problems met in performing in places like Chambersburg, Lockport, Bedford, Niagara Falls, Fredonia, and Westfield; in Haynesville, Cahawaba, Selma, Columbus, Macon, Milledgeville, Athens, and Greenville.[13] Citizens in all these places saw plays performed, if not perfectly, at least by many players who were stars and

---

[10] Ophia D. Smith, "The Early Theatre of Cincinnati" and "The Cincinnati Theatre, 1817–1830," *Historical and Philosophical Society of Ohio Bulletin*, 13 (October, 1955): 231–37, 241–42; 14 (October, 1956): 269–77.

[11] Moncure D. Conway, *A Discourse, Delivered in the Unitarian Church, Cincinnati, Ohio* (Cincinnati, 1857), p. 5.

[12] Edward G. Fletcher, "The Beginnings of the Professional Theatre in Texas," *University of Texas Bulletin*, 36 (June, 1936): 23.

[13] Walter Leman, *Memories of an Old Actor* (San Francisco, 1886), pp. 212–13, 260–61; Noah M. Ludlow, *Dramatic Life As I Found It* (St. Louis, 1880), p. 10; Sol Smith, *Theatrical Management In the West and South* (New York, 1868), pp. 33, 76–86.

favorites in the nation's largest cities and best theaters. And while good companies occasionally came to remote small towns, the most unsettled areas were not safe from the theatrical performances of men like Harry Langton, a somewhat more talented and equally audacious precursor of *Huckleberry Finn*'s King and Duke.[14]

Francis Wemyss listed, in the American section of a book intended to guide would-be stage stars, fifty-eight American communities that had permanent theaters. He pointed out that countless other towns had facilities adaptable to stage uses. His conclusions regarding the spread, if not the effect, of drama seem correct: "Wherever immigration builds up a town or city, there rises a temple of Drama, to hold the mirror up to nature."[15] "Yes, now" ran one theater's dedicatory poem,

> . . . where late the forest stood,
> In Nature's wildest solitude,
> Where all was but a prairie sod
> Which human foot but seldom trod,
> We hail the Drama's spotless page.[16]

One of the classic acting stories in the period, repeated in various forms, dealt with backwoods people who watched, without clapping or laughing, a troupe of strolling actors perform for several nights. In the version of the favorite western manager and low comedian, Sol Smith, when after several nights he finally milked a half-smothered laugh out of someone, a deacon sternly reprimanded the amused person: "Mr. Thompson, you must quit that or leave the meeting."[17] Smith's story suggested that, if dramatic companies penetrated remote areas, they did not get there very often.

Consequently, lightly populated areas often developed amateur theatrical groups. Soldiers in frontier military posts gave the first stage performances in many regions; a traveler in Wisconsin in the early 1830's described in detail a military production with "the lights ingeniously placed in bayonets, prettily arranged."[18] Longer lasting were the countless "Thespian corps" formed to provide drama in towns

---

[14] *Ibid.*, p. 43.
[15] Leman T. Rede, *The Guide to the Stage* (New York, 1858), pp. 13–18. Edward W. Mammen, *The Old Stock Company School of Acting: A Study of the Boston Museum* (Boston, 1945), p. 10, says there were thirty-five permanent stock companies in 1850.
[16] Fletcher, "Beginnings in Texas," p. 45.
[17] Smith, *Theatrical Management*, p. 109. Smith claimed that this happened in Haynesville, Alabama. Variations on the story are found in Northall, *Life of Hill*, pp. 13–14; Jonathan Kelley, *Dan Marble* (New York, 1851), p. 127; P. T. Barnum, *Struggles and Triumphs, or Forty Years' Recollections* (Hartford, 1869), p. 155.
[18] Charles Fenno Hoffman, *A Winter in the West* (New York, 1835), 2: 3.

seldom penetrated by professionals. In rural Missouri, for example, almost all towns populated by a few thousand were occasionally entertained by local amateur efforts.[19] These acting clubs usually comprised many of the town's most prominent young men; to one in Nashville, Tennessee, belonged the future generals John Eaton and Sam Houston, two future United States senators and one congressman, and, as honorary members, Felix Grundy and Andrew Jackson.[20] A few of the Thespian clubs survived for great lengths of time such as the one in Wilmington, North Carolina, which lasted from 1800 until the Civil War. After the man who had played the "more refined female" roles left to become the Anglican bishop of Mississippi, the club hired professional actresses to support the male members.[21] To help in attracting an audience the proceeds from amateur performances were usually allocated to various local improvements—buying books for the library, building a needed bridge, or contributing to a fund to purchase an organ for an Episcopal church.[22]

The extent of amateur enthusiasm for drama was enough to draw out frequent contemporary criticism and warnings, some meant as jokes and others advanced with heavy sobriety. Letters signed with fictitious names denounced the effects of enthusiasm for amateur acting, particularly on young men. For instance, "Richard Heeltap," who claimed to be a shoemaker from a town near St. Louis, said that his young assistants, after forming an amateur acting company, had become utterly worthless in their work.[23] Another merchant discovered the dramatic disease in his own family just in time to prevent them from cutting a hole in the living-room ceiling to let in the ghost of Hamlet's father. The merchant complained that even his clerks had been recruited for the family dramatic company and had begun to write business memos in blank verse. He

---

[19] Elbert Bowen, *A Study of Theatrical Entertainment in Rural Missouri Before the Civil War* (Columbia, Mo., 1959), pp. 71–97.

[20] Douglas L. Hunt, "The Nashville Theatre, 1830–1840," *Birmingham-Southern College Bulletin*, 28 (May, 1935): 7.

[21] James G. Burr, *The Thalian Association of Wilmington, North Carolina, with Sketches of Many of its Members* (Wilmington, N. C., 1871), *passim*. Amateurs frequently employed professional assistance when available. The actor John Gaisford's *The Drama in New Orleans* (New Orleans, 1849) is primarily an account of his paid help to a group of gentlemen amateurs.

[22] *Gridiron* (Dayton, Ohio), 1 (November 21, 1822): 97; *Kentucky Gazette* (August 1, 1809), in Mabel Crum, "The History of the Lexington Theatre From the Beginning to 1860" (Ph.D. dissertation, University of Kentucky, 1956), p. 23; *Virginian* (March 30, 1827), in Richard Hadley, "The Theatre in Lynchburg, Virginia, from its Beginnings to the Civil War" (Ph.D. dissertation, University of Michigan, 1942), pp. 86, 257.

[23] Quoted in William G. B. Carson, *The Theatre on the Frontier: The Early Years on the St. Louis Stage* (Chicago, 1932), p. 30.

concluded that strolling players would soon augment their numbers, for "how could Alexander the Great return to measure yard-wide at his master's shop? How could Macbeth, after being let into the secrets of the infernal cauldron, think of recommencing his soap-boiling?"[24]

Such accounts were exaggerations of real tendencies. Certainly apprentices, made discontented with the humdrum of shop life by a taste of the glories of the theater, did make up a goodly part of theatrical recruits. The rarely serious Sol Smith took time off from amusing people with his memoirs to warn solemnly of the dangers inherent in Thespian corps. "The successful amateur," Smith cautioned, "becomes dissatisfied with his profession or business, whatever it may be, applies to a manager for a first appearance in a regular theatre—appears—fails—takes to drink and is ruined."[25] Probably few who failed as Richard III or Young Norval on such occasions followed Smith's course to drink and destruction. Certainly the labor of amateurs and their service—that of bringing theatrical entertainment to areas seldom reached by professionals—deserved better reward.

The importance of amateur theatricals was slight in comparison to that of professionals wherever the latter were available. And professionals performed in urban centers constantly and in moderately populous areas with regularity. Anyone who lived in or occasionally visited a large town could see good professional drama if he had the price, and admission prices were not generally prohibitive. A dollar was commonly charged for the highest priced seats and a quarter for the cheapest. Over the half-century prices tended to decrease, at first in certain theaters in the most populous cities and, during the 1840's, in most theaters over the country. Managers sometimes complained that lowered prices meant decreased profits, but perhaps a truer explanation for this loss was that managers reduced prices only in times of crisis when competition was keen and the theater's financial position precarious.[26] By the 1840's many theaters made large profits by pursuing a low-price policy. Most notably, the Boston Museum, which combined high moral tone with low admission rates, and William Mitchell's Olympic Theatre, with its pit filled with apprentices and newsboys, seemingly expanded

[24] Reprinted from *Bouquet* in *Huntington Literary Messenger*, 1 (March, 1810): 114.

[25] Smith, *Theatrical Management*, p. 22.

[26] William Wood, *Personal Recollections of the Stage* (Philadelphia, 1855), p. 299; Ludlow, *Dramatic Life*, p. 445; Carson, *Managers in Distress*, p. 160; William W. Clapp, *Records of the Boston Stage* (Boston, 1853), p. 375; Reese Davis James, *Old Drury of Philadelphia: A History of the Philadelphia Stage, 1800–1833* (Philadelphia, 1932), pp. 59–66; George C. D. Odell, *Annals of the New York Stage* (New York, 1927–49), 4: 568–89, 611, 623–38.

the habit of theatergoing.[27] That lowered admission rates succeeded in drawing larger audiences suggests that the prices charged did curb the frequency with which people went to the theater. Yet prices always were low enough to make occasional theatrical attendance possible for most Americans.

Not severely limited in the area it reached nor prohibitive in the prices it charged, the theater drew "all ranks of the people together."[28] Unfortunately observers, convinced though they were that the "Drama's patrons" ruled, were seldom very specific about the makeup of this ruling body. Most theater owners in the early nineteenth century divided their houses into three area and price groups—the boxes, the pit, and the gallery. This arrangement was sometimes modified, particularly in theaters built after 1840 when the pit was frequently turned into a parquet area or the gallery omitted. By the 1840's several theaters had two instead of three price areas, but the triple division remained the one most generally used. With the exception of Negroes and prostitutes, no one was forced to sit in a particular section of the theater, but the price differences themselves served as crude social separators. Those observers who described American audiences claimed to find three groups represented there, corresponding to the physical divisions of the theater. Their class differentiation, artificial and over-rigid as it was, gave sociological precision to their discussion of the theater's audience.

One night in 1820 a farmer from Maine, drawn to Boston by his duties in the Massachusetts General Assembly, decided to break his usual adherence to the rule of "a penny saved is a penny earned" and to squander a few cents on a theatrical visit. Not being familiar with dramatic ways, he inquired about the best place to sit from a friend, who explained to him "the internal situation of the house":

> It appeared that the gallery was the resort of the particoloured race of Africans, the descendants of Africans, and the vindicators of the abolition of the slave trade; that the tier of boxes below it in the center was occupied by single gentlewomen who had lodgings to let, and who were equally famous for their delicacy and taciturn disposition. The remainder of the boxes, I was given to understand, were visited by none but the dandies, and people of the first respectability and fashion; while the pit presented a

[27] Claire McGlinchee, *The First Decade of the Boston Museum* (Boston, 1940); William K. Northall, *Before and Behind the Curtain* (New York, 1851).
[28] The phrase was used by Henry and Hallam in petitioning the Massachusetts General Assembly to repeal its law against theaters. Quoted in Dorothy Bonawitz, "The History of the Boston Stage from the Beginning to 1810" (Ph.D. dissertation, Pennsylvania State College, 1936), p. 30.

mixed multitude of the lower orders of all sorts, sizes, ages and deportments.[29]

Allowing for humorous innuendo, the description of the assemblyman's
friend fitted the pattern that most other observers of theatrical audiences
set up.

The gallery probably contained no abolitionists, and was not, except
in the South, filled only with Negroes, though members of this race were
generally restricted to it. Apprentices and other persons lacking in funds
or abounding in high spirits generally bought gallery seats. In all
theaters the gallery was the place most suitable for rowdyism, the best
point from which to bombard disliked actors, members of the orchestra
who failed to play popular tunes, or even the helpless "middling classes"
ensconced in the pit. During the early years of the nineteenth century,
many people in this section were servants of persons in the boxes;
gentlemen and ladies were told in advertisements that it was necessary
to send someone to the theater an hour or two ahead of time to hold
their seats.

Negroes in northern theaters shared the gallery with Caucasians;[30] in
the South, where theaters had more elaborate gallery arrangements, they
had it to themselves. Boxes were fitted out within the gallery for free
Negroes who preferred the privacy or prestige that these offered, whereas
slaves, "not admitted without a pass from their owners expressing their
approbation," filled up the general gallery area.[31] Perhaps the only place
in the country where persons of known Negro ancestry were allowed to
watch plays from the main part of the house was in the Camp Theatre in
New Orleans. Here "escorted colored women," generally quadroons or
octoroons accompanied by Caucasian men, were given access to all parts
of the theater one night each week. By a kind of tacit agreement, white
women did not attend the theater on these evenings.[32]

"The Rambler," an elderly gentleman who edited a magazine of
theatrical criticism, preferred watching a play from the pit for two
reasons. First, it was close to the stage so expressions could be more

---

[29] *Ladies' Port-Folio*, 1 (February 5, 1820): 46.

[30] There were some exceptions. In Cleveland the theater set up a "Negro gallery" in 1851, which
drew an indignant protest in the *Plain Dealer* from a Negro who pointedly suggested a white gallery
be set up for *Uncle Tom's Cabin*. Gerhard W. Gaiser, "The History of the Cleveland Theatre from the
Beginning Until 1854" (Ph.D. dissertation, State University of Iowa, 1953), pp. 103-4.

[31] Mobile, Alabama, theater program, April 13, 1841, in NYPL. In a few places in the South,
Negroes were excluded from the theater (William S. Hoole, *The Ante-Bellum Charleston Theatre*
[Tuscaloosa, Ala., 1946], p. 8; Fredericktown playbill, July 13, 1818, in Joseph Ireland, *Extra-
Illustrated Records of the New York Stage*, HTC, ser. 1, 5: 77).

[32] John A. Kendall, *The Golden Age of New Orleans Theatre* (Baton Rouge, 1952), pp. 38-39.

exactly determined; and second, it was free from the shouting that came from the gallery and the "whispering as loud as most serious incidents of tragedy" that went on in the boxes.[33] "Honest folks" or "middling classes" were the designations usually given to the occupants of the pit; they were considered "the sterling part of the audience," in contrast to the "fashionables" in the boxes and the "unfashionables" in the gallery.[34] But, as Washington Irving's Jonathan Oldstyle learned, the pit had its disadvantages. The gallery would sometimes rain "apples, nuts and gingerbread on the heads of the honest folks in the pit," and the huge chandelier used for lighting the stage would drip its wax on their coats. Irving chided the people in the boxes to show "less affection, less noise, less coxcombs," and urged that the gallery be given "less grog and better constables," but his advice for the improvement of the pit was only protective: clean benches, umbrellas, and patience.[35]

Obviously America's middle-class theatergoers were not all the frank, dignified, and upright farmers or tradesmen of the Jonathan Oldstyle or Maine assemblyman variety. As early as 1810 a Pennsylvania writer urged managers to raise admission to the pit because "it would to some degree tend to exclude many who, though fit to sit only in the upper gallery, make their way into the pit to the great annoyance of those decent well-behaved people, who go to enjoy and understand the play, not to blackguard or speak loud."[36] Other observers described the "true note of independence" characteristic of pit audiences: "Untrammeled by the chains of fashion, they disdain the confinement of either coat, vest, stockings, and sometimes even shoes—thus evincing their entire contempt for the 'polite company' in the boxes." The writer went on to single out particular individuals in the group: an old gentleman drinking rum, a dandy, a sailor, and an Irishman and his girl.[37] An aristocratic observer, the Duke of Saxe-Weimar Eisenach, was particularly annoyed by a New Orleans pit audience which he said was composed of "sailors and countrymen from Kentucky," who cracked nuts even "during the finest pieces of music."[38]

"A mixed multitude of the lower orders of all sorts, sizes, ages, and

---

[33] *Rambler's Magazine*, 1 (1812): 12–13.

[34] *American Athenaeum*, 1 (November 17, 1825): 307.

[35] Washington Irving, *Letters of Jonathan Oldstyle, Gent.* (New York, 1824), pp. 24–25, 33.

[36] *The Hive*, 1 (December 11, 1810): 201. The *New York Evening Post* (October 26, 1821) offered a similar complaint about the lack of social exclusion in boxes caused by the Bowery Theatre's originally having the same price for both pit and boxes. Theodore Shank, Jr., "The Bowery Theatre, 1826–1836" (Ph.D. dissertation, Stanford University, 1956), p. 26.

[37] *American Athenaeum*, 1 (June 28, 1825): 119.

[38] Quoted in Kendall, *New Orleans Theatre*, p. 37.

deportments"—not a very specific description, but one whose vagueness approximated the unclassified miscellany that made up a pit audience. The people in the pit were easy to ridicule for their lack of elegance or education, or to praise for the relative seriousness and intensity of their interest. Walt Whitman recaptured something of the rough grandeur of such audiences in his reminiscences about "The Old Bowery" of the 1830's, when it was New York's "middle class" theater between the fashionable Park and the disreputable Chatham:

> Recalling from that period the occasion of either Forrest or Booth, any good night at the Old Bowery, pack'd from ceiling to pit with its audience mainly of alert, well-dress'd, full-blooded young and middle-aged men, the best average of American born mechanics—. . . the whole crowded auditorium, and what seeth'd in it, and flush'd from its faces and eyes, to me as much a part of the show as any—bursting forth in one of those long-kept-up tempests of hand-clapping, peculiar to the Bowery—no dainty kid-glove business, but electric force and muscle from perhaps 2,000 full-sinew'd men. . . .[39]

Above the pit physically, and generally socially and financially as well, were the theatergoers in the boxes. Farther from the stage than the pit—an important disadvantage in a theater lit by candles or gas—the boxes had in their favor privacy, prestige, and a kind of social decorum. Most of the women who went to the theater, particularly those who preferred to be called ladies, sat in the boxes; the more respectable northern theaters "in compliance with public opinion" barred women from the pit.[40] With them were their escorts and other gentlemen with pretensions to quality.

The socially respectable did not occupy the third tier of boxes; these were reserved for "the unescorted gentlewomen with lodgings to let." Because no decent woman would go any place where she might come in contact with prostitutes, these women were given a special section. Many vigorously protested this plan which allotted "a distinct portion of the proscenium to those unfortunate females who are the victims of seduction" and which made the drama accessory to "the indecent traffic of impures."[41] Despite protests from observers and noise from the women themselves, most theaters gave them their section.[42] They were

---

[39] Walt Whitman, "The Old Bowery," in *Complete Prose Works* (New York, 1914), p. 429.
[40] Chesnut Theatre (Philadelphia) playbill, January 1, 1840, in Ireland, *Extra-Illustrated*, HTC, ser. 1, 12: 167.
[41] Dunlap, *American Theatre*, 1: 407–9; *Mirror of Taste*, 2 (October, 1810): 296.
[42] The assemblyman from Maine enjoyed his visit to the Boston theater well enough, but left convinced that some law should be passed to stop the "salutations from the third tier of boxes,"

regular patrons not finicky about the entertainment offered and paying
the highest admission price, and this money was "often needful to a
treasury impoverished by the absence of persons of enlightened piety."[43]
Perhaps, too, managers felt that the number of people prostitutes
attracted to the theater as their place of assignation was greater than the
number they kept away. Only in the 1840's did theaters begin to bar
them, usually simply by refusing admittance to any unescorted woman.[44]

As several cities grew large enough to support more than one playhouse the class lines dividing box, pit, and gallery were often trans-
ferred to particular theaters. Thus in New York in the 1830's the Park
Theatre was associated with the upper classes, the Bowery with the
middle, and the Chatham with the lower.[45] In Baltimore, Tyrone Power
found one theater considered the "aristocratic house" and the other the
seat of "the sturdy democracy."[46] In the 1840's the "aristocracy" particularly were connected with the many "opera houses" that opened
and usually quickly failed. In 1848 a lady was overheard at the Park
Theatre explaining that she preferred a more exclusive opera house but
"unfortunately we of ourselves are not sufficiently numerous to support
an Opera, so we have been forced to admit the People."[47] Until midcentury theaters had generally to attract "all ranks of the people together."

Cutting across the lines of pit, box, and gallery were the less distinct
ones between the "taste and discernment" of a few people and "the
depraved palates of the majority"—a distinction insisted upon by both
critics and playwrights who felt their success incommensurate with their
talents.[48] John Howard Payne typically complained of the theater's
dependence on "the idle, profligate, and vulgar," and Robert Mont-

---

for the protection "of every respectable person in the theatre, and particularly . . . females"
(*Ladies' Port-Folio*, 1 [February 5, 1820]: 46). The *Boston Weekly Magazine* (2 [March 14, 1818]: 91)
argued similarly that police should silence "the shameful outcries of the followers of Ate" in the
theater.

[43] Cornelius Logan, "A Defense of the Drama," in Smith, *Theatrical Management*, p. 274.

[44] Ludlow, *Dramatic Life*, pp. 478–79; *Spirit of the Times*, 16 (July 18, 1846): 252; Elaine McDavitt,
"A History of the Theatre in Detroit, Michigan, from the Beginnings to 1862" (Ph.D. dissertation,
University of Michigan, 1946), p. 196. One actress reported that by 1852 all Boston theaters and
some in New York had abolished the "third tier," and in 1869 another said the abolition was
"complete throughout the whole land" (Mowatt, *Autobiography*, p. 445; Olive Logan, *Before the
Footlights and Behind the Scenes* [Philadelphia, 1870], pp. 34–35).

[45] *Spirit of the Times* (9 [May 4, 1839]: 108), for example, argued that the Bowery's main value
was as "a most useful safety valve" to draw undesirables away from the Park.

[46] Tyrone Power, *Impressions of America* (Philadelphia, 1836), 1: 141.

[47] Reported in *Spirit of the Times*, 18 (March 4, 1848): 24.

[48] William Dunlap, *Memoirs of a Water Drinker* (New York, 1837), p. 131; Dunlap, *American
Theatre*, 2: 3.

Theater – ~~United States~~

History:

725.822 M

792.092 F3   792.27 G1

792.0973 C3-2

792.0973 Y2, 54, R1, H1

gomery Bird wrote in his diary that one of the reasons he turned his considerable talents from the drama to the novel was that the theaters were "not at all fashionable." He decided it was no honor, as he learned it was not profitable, "to write for and be admired by the groundlings, villains that will clap when you are most nonsensical and applaud you most heartily when you are vulgar; that will call you 'a Genius, by God—' when you make the judicious grieve and a 'witty devil' when you force a woman to blush."[49] "The judicious few," lamented John Howard Payne, "are very few indeed. They are always to be found in a Theatre, like flowers in a desert, but they are nowhere sufficiently numerous to *fill* one."[50]

These "flowers in a desert" were generally supposed to bloom in boxes. Critics often charged that "the gods" in the gallery and "the groundlings" in the pit demanded the bastard brands of drama that were popular. The division, however, between "the lovers of sense and Shakespeare" and the devotees of farce and melodrama probably reflected only slightly the economic and social cleavage suggested by pit, box, and gallery. The proportion of pit and gallery attendance to that in the boxes of Boston's National Theatre or Philadelphia's Chestnut Theatre remained fairly constant whether *Hamlet* or *The Six Degrees of Crime* was the attraction.[51] Any lack of highly cultivated sensitivity among spectators resulted less from a lack of "fashionables" than from a mass audience where perfect taste was not to be expected among rich or poor.

The excitement caused by the tours of leading performers underlined the breadth of appeal of the drama. Beginning with George Frederick Cooke's visit in 1811, most leading European performers found their way to America and met enthusiastic theatrical and social receptions. Wendell Phillips, for example, remembered that he and his classmates at Harvard Law School trooped to Boston each night to see Fanny Kemble perform when, "if you'd put a cap sheaf down over the theatre, you would have covered about all Boston had to offer in the way of culture and learning." Judge Story, his mentor at law school, being reminded that his Puritan ancestors would not approve of all his theatergoing, replied, "I only thank God I'm alive in an era with such a woman."[52]

---

[49] Quoted in Clement E. Foust, *The Life and Dramatic Works of Robert Montgomery Bird* (New York, 1919), p. 51.

[50] John Howard Payne to Benjamin Pollard (November 13, 1810), "Letter Book," HTC, 1, 66.

[51] William Pelby, "National Theatre Account Book," HTC, *passim*; William Wood's "Account Book for the Arch Street Theatre, 1828," printed in James, *Old Drury*, pp. 438–49.

[52] Quoted in "Thespian," "Famous Playes," HTC, pp. 416–17.

Even more exuberant was Richard M. Johnson, soon to be vice-president of the United States. "By heavens, Adams!" he said to the former president, "She's a horse! She's a horse!"[53]

Under the stimulus of the press agent, enthusiasm became furor. The 1840 tour of Fanny Ellsler, the most wildly popular theatrical event prior to the alliance of Jenny Lind's voice and P. T. Barnum's megaphone, brought out all the trappings of a great star's triumphal tour. Tickets were publicly auctioned off at very high prices; theatres were sold out long before performances; and large crowds that could not get in milled around outside. Crowds met her on her arrival in each town; in Baltimore people even insisted on unhitching her horses and drawing her carriage themselves into the city.[54] "*She* comes!" wrote some early Ogden Nash:

> "Hard times" no man ever mentions,
> The only "pressure's" in the crowded Pit;
> The only case deserving our attentions
> Is to obtain sufficient room to sit.
> I'm sure I love my relatives, and yet I'd rather
> See Fanny's Grand Pas than my own grandfather.[55]

"Ellsler cuffs, Ellsler boots, and even Ellsler bread" could be bought in the United States long after the much enriched danseuse returned to Europe.[56]

Audiences not only attended plays and lionized stars, but often assumed roles as conspicuous as those on the stage. The theater, as well as playhouse, was a social club where people went to be seen, to talk together, and to indulge in other nondramatic pleasures. "The pleasure of seeing and being seen" was an important aspect of theatrical enjoyment; the management of the Bowery Theatre had the back of boxes painted "of the apple-blossom colour, as being most favorable to display the ladies to advantage."[57] Even a playwright complained that one theater allowed "too much light on stage, and too little in the boxes" so it became difficult to "recognize a friend across the house."[58]

---

[53] James Murdock, *The Stage, or Recollections of Actors and Acting from an Experience of Fifty Years* (Philadelphia, 1880), p. 272.

[54] Wemyss, *Twenty-Six Years*, p. 332. Reportedly Ellsler hired people to applaud, and purchased bouquets to be thrown to her (Logan, *Before the Footlights*, pp. 301, 307).

[55] *Spirit of the Times*, 10 (June 27, 1840): 193.

[56] Leman, *Memories of an Old Actor*, p. 138.

[57] *Virginian* (September 17, 1822), quoted in Hadley, "Theatre in Lynchburg," p. 42; *New York Mirror*, 6 (August 23, 1828): 50.

[58] Samuel Woodworth in *New York Mirror*, 1 (May 22, 1824): 342.

Other social pleasures were more disturbing to those interested in the play. Critics complained of "the music of cracking peanuts" as Americans "mouncht and mouncht and mouncht" their way through long theatrical evenings.[59] Despite suggestions that "the honors of maternity are more appropriate to the domestic than the dress circle," the problem of noise from babies remained "coextensive with the existence of the theatre."[60] At New York's Chatham, Mrs. Trollope found not only "a general air of contempt for the decencies of life, more than usually revolting," but also a woman in a dress box "performing the most maternal office possible." More often Mrs. Trollope was upset by the casualness of American audiences and their spitting of chewing tobacco, which was "incessant" in Cincinnati and Washington, "unceasing" in Philadelphia, and occurred "without ceasing," in New York.[61] Others complained of people accompanying the music by thumping their feet or sticks "out of all time, to the great annoyance of the Orchestra, the singers on the stage and those of the audience who possess any taste for music."[62] One critic had to threaten public exposure to make one man in the audience stop singing along with the performers.[63] Perhaps hardest on the actors were "the downright snorings with which the pit is frequently made voluble."[64]

The most frequent abuse was the "buz buz and hum hum of small talk" during the performance. "The din of oaths" from the gallery, "the uproarious state of fermentation" in the pit, "the titter of the impure, and the dull chatter of her stupid wooer" in the third tier, "the loud conversation . . . in the midst of a soliloquy" from the boxes—all sometimes competed with a performance.[65] Even though ladies in the audience were thought to insure decorum, a Virginia editor felt obliged to warn some of his "fair countrywomen" that "speaking louder than

---

[59] *New York Mirror*, 11 (April 5, 1834): 319; Robert Ewing, *The Contributions of "Jacques" to the "United States Gazette"* (Philadelphia, 1826), p. 101.

[60] *New York Mirror*, 20 (October 1, 1842): 319; *New Orleans Daily Picayune* (July 3, 1860), quoted in Joseph P. Roppolo, "A History of the English Theatre in New Orleans, 1845–1861" (Ph.D. dissertation, Tulane University, 1950), 1 : 84.

[61] Frances Trollope, *Domestic Manners of the Americans*, ed. Donald Smalley (New York, 1960), pp. 339–40, 234, 271.

[62] *National Banner and Nashville Whig* (November 8, 1826), quoted in Hunt, "Nashville Theatre," p. 16.

[63] *New York Mirror*, 2 (January 8, 1825): 191.

[64] *Dramatic Mirror* (Boston) (September 19, 1829), no. 5.

[65] *Spirit of the Times*, 16 (March 7, 1846): 24; *Corsair*, 1 (March 16, 1839): 14; *Mirror of Taste*, 2 (November, 1810): 379; *New York Mirror,* 13 (December 12, 1835): 191; 10 (September 29, 1832): 103.

the players during the performance . . . is not the way to excite admiration and respect."[66] Because audiences made so much noise early in a performance, one critic claimed that all dramatists realized they had "to indite a sufficiency of trash to last for half an hour" before getting their plays really underway.[67]

On occasions like Christmas, Thanksgiving, Election Day, or, noisiest of all, the Fourth of July, the staged drama became an almost superfluous excuse for spectator conviviality. Normally audience behavior did not prevent the stage entertainment from being heard, but perfect order usually provoked perfect surprise. "We cannot but remark the quiet and good order that prevailed," said a Natchez newspaper in 1836. The writer was not sure whether "the presence of so many ladies or the vigilance of the police" caused the audience's unusual propriety.[68] Even with the help of ladies and policemen in the audience, managers had trouble keeping their repeated promise that "order and decorum will be preserved throughout the house."[69]

Occasionally members of the audience interrupted a play, not out of indifference to what was happening on stage, but because they became so moved by a story that they mistook it for reality. Many tales of such audience response were circulated—about a sailor's jumping on stage to give aid and money to the dying Jane Shore, of a Worcester woman's pleading with the gamester to stop his criminal behavior, of a Baltimore man's objecting to an assault on Coriolanus because "three on one" was not a fair fight, or of a New Orleans boatman's suggestion to Othello, grieving over the loss of the handkerchief, "Why don't you blow your nose with your fingers and let the play go on."[70] Expressions of political opinion particularly drew forth audience response. For instance, when the hero of *Marmion*, during an 1812 performance, asked his fellow Scotsmen if they would entrust their rights to English justice, an elderly Philadelphian stood up in his box, waved his cane, and shouted, "No, sir, no; we'll nail them to mast and sink with the stars and

[66] *Virginian* (September 13, 1832), in Hadley, "Theatre in Lynchburg," p. 36.

[67] *Dramatic Mirror* (Boston) (September 17, 1829), no. 3.

[68] Quoted in William B. Gates, "The Theatre in Natchez," *Journal of Mississippi History*, 3 (April, 1941): 95.

[69] A notice of the Boston Museum in *Boston Daily Evening Telegraph* (September 2, 1843), quoted in McGlinchee, *Boston Museum*, p. 22.

[70] Charles Durang, *The Philadelphia Stage* (University of Pennsylvania Extra-Illustrated copy, N.S.), p. 204; *Literary Museum* (1797), quoted in Herbert Brown, "Sensibility in Eighteenth Century Drama," *American Literature*, 4 (March, 1932): 49; Charles William Jansen, *The Stranger in America 1793–1806*, ed. Carl Driver (New York, 1935), p. 265; *Spirit of the Times*, 13 (September 30, 1843): 372. See also Joseph Roppolo, "Audiences in New Orleans Theatres, 1845–1861," *Tulane Studies in English*, 2 (1950): 132–33; Logan, *Before the Footlights*, pp. 308–11.

stripes before we'll yield." The audience responded with prolonged applause.[71] Such unexpected acts of audience participation were part of the excitement of theatergoing.

Very often interest in the audience surpassed interest in the play. "The acting on stage was good," reported a St. Louis newspaper in 1844, "and the cavorting in pit, boxes, and galleries was extremely interesting." The reviewer paid special tribute to "a new performer called Peg-leg" who "showed off in the gallery with great applause."[72] If show-offs sometimes entertained an audience, celebrities were sure to attract one. George Washington attending the theater drew better than any of the plays written about him, and more Americans turned out to see a Napoleonic general watching a poor play than came to see the best of actors in good dramas.[73] A manager in Nashville complained that none of his expensive stars drew so large a house as did a visit by Martin Van Buren, whom he would have liked to engage "on his *own terms*, for the season."[74] Of course, managers exploited this curiosity at every opportunity. When Henry Clay attended a performance by William Charles Macready, the American senator was given equal billing with the English tragedian.[75]

When leading personages were unavailable, other "curiosities" could be put in the audience. Watching Indians watch a play, for instance, was as good sport as seeing them do a war dance on stage. One enterprising New York manager, after having some "children of nature" act in a play one evening, promised that they would return the next for "their first performance in any boxes."[76] Sometimes the Indians both watched and performed. A group of Cherokees, at the conclusion of a play in the nation's capital, showered the leading lady with their ornaments and headdresses. Conveniently the star had on hand a bevy of ostrich plumes

[71] Ellis P. Oberholtzer, *The Literary History of Philadelphia* (Philadelphia, 1906), p. 240. The play was James Nelson Barker's *Marmion*, and the patriot who interrupted it was the author's father, who was at the time mayor of Philadelphia and a leading Jeffersonian politician, all of which suggests the nature of some of these "spontaneous" outbursts (Paul H. Musser, *James Nelson Barker, 1784–1858* [Philadelphia, 1929], pp. 6–11, 47).

[72] *St. Louis New Era* (June 4, 1844), quoted in Carson, *Managers in Distress*, p. 260.

[73] Ludlow, *Dramatic Life*, p. 579.

[74] Joe Cowell, *Thirty Years Passed Among the Players in England and America* (New York, 1844), p. 97. Not all politicians were so successful. *The New World* (4 [May 21, 1842]: 337) reported, "Dorr, the pseudo-governor of Rhode Island, was invited to this house [Bowery] and attended in state, but he did not *draw*."

[75] Ludlow, *Dramatic Life*, p. 592.

[76] *New York Post* (February 14, 1806), quoted in Odell, *New York Stage*, 2: 249. William Pelby's "Account Book" for Boston's National Theatre, HTC, showed that during the 1836–1838 seasons, no attraction drew better than performances by "27 Iowa Indians."

to present in return.[77] Other exotic peoples drew equally well. The Turks displayed in a New York theater attracted such crowds (or was it the play of *Blue Beard* which was presented in their honor?) that they were given a benefit for the purpose "of accommodating them with additional clothes."[78]

Audiences in the early nineteenth century controlled, as well as contributed to, theatrical entertainment. Popular entertainment must always take much of its color, chameleon-like, from its environment, but the theatergoing public of the period was peculiarly able to insure that no shading in the presentation deviated from its standards. This closeness of audience control made the drama more than any art form, the theater as much as any social institution, immediately sensitive to public opinion.

Audiences then, as now, ruled the theater basically by their patronage. Any type or piece of entertainment that proved popular was repeated and any which failed to draw was discontinued. But besides this broad economic control, audiences held direct financial power over each actor, manager, and author. Part of every salary contract was a provision for a "benefit" sometime during the year. For the visiting stars the benefit generally came at the close of their engagements, whereas the regular members of the company took benefits at the end of each season. For everyone a benefit consisted of the money taken in for a performance minus a certain sum or percentage deducted for house expenses. Because the salaries of stock actors ran from moderate to meager, their success for the season often depended on a bumper benefit. Many actors, one of them wrote, "must either depend on a successful benefit night or have to struggle with poverty from the time their engagements cease, until nearly the commencement of winter."[79]

Managers similarly had their benefits nights, as did authors if their plays were popular enough, and the manager sufficiently generous, to permit a three-night run. Novelties often ensured a benefit's success— such as the tragedian Thomas Apthrope Cooper's hiring an elephant to perform with him or Mrs. Barrett's displaying "her rotundity of figure" in the tights required for the title role in *Hamlet*.[80] But in general per-

---

[77] Alysius I. Mudd, "The Theatres of Washington From 1835–1850," *Records of the Columbia Historical Society*, 6 (1903): 235–36.

[78] Odell, *New York Stage*, 2: 228–29.

[79] Quoted in *ibid.*, p. 257. The comedian John Bernard said that in the early years of the century benefit performances added about a third to most American actors' salaries (*Retrospections of America* [New York, 1887], p. 263).

[80] *Polyanthos*, 1 (January, 1806): 80; *Ladies' Port-Folio*, 1 (January 29, 1820): 35; Charles Durang, quoted in James, *Old Drury*, p. 33.

formers had to depend for this important part of their income on winning the friendship of their audiences over the season. Any loss of public favor resulted in a direct loss of dollars.

Leading performers were sometimes showered with other presents as well. Groups of spectators appreciative of some performer's activities presented flowers, or gifts, or money at the close of an engagement or season. While some of these tributes were sincere, they soon became an expected part of any successful engagement. Being showered with tokens of respect, usually "paid for by the grateful recipient," became so notorious that one comedian satirized it in an advertisement for his benefit performance in Mobile:

> At the close of the performance, Mr. Cowell will be called out, but if not, he will go out, and have a splendid wreath thrown to him . . . and be addressed from the stage box by one of a committee of gentlemen who have long admired his private worth and public services, and be presented with
>
> AN ELEGANT TIN CUP
>
> to which he will make an extemporaneous reply, prepared for the occasion, after the manner of other distinguished artists.[81]

Audiences rewarded actors with applause as well as money. Instead of clapping only at the ends of acts, or possibly at the entrances or exits of some favorite star, theatergoers applauded whenever they approved a scene, or a bit of acting, or a choice sentiment. A kind of running applause punctuated any successful play or the efforts of any popular player. The actor James Fennell, who, among other sidelines, edited a magazine for a while, suggested the frequency of this applause by cautioning the patrons of drama to refrain from interrupting an actor in midspeech: "The merits of an actor can be sufficiently rewarded by the public . . . by applause bestowed on him at his exit or during such pauses as are naturally occasioned by the complete effusion of passion, the declaration of a moral sentiment, or the termination of declamatory speeches."[82] A Virginia editor suggested that it was not "a duty to applaud at the conclusion of every sentence."[83]

Fennell reported that "the responsible part of a Boston audience never hear a really moral sentiment delivered or see a really moral action performed, without a free and liberal applause," and that only the gallery

[81] Wood, *Personal Recollections*, pp. 261–62; Cowell, *Thirty Years*, p. 101.
[82] *Something*, 1 (December 9, 1809): 57. The editorship of Fennell was mentioned in *The Hive*, 1 (June 16, 1810): 35–36.
[83] *Virginian* (February 9, 1829), quoted in Hadley, "Theatre in Lynchburg," p. 113.

applauded indecorous conduct on stage.[84] Other critics felt audiences
gave their applause with less discernment. Very broadly done bits of
comedy and ad libs with local allusions were likely to draw enthusiastic
responses from audiences indifferent to subtler dramatic beauties. Understandably actors extracted this praise even at the expense of the necessarily
delayed favor of the judicious critic. Also understandably critics frequently expressed their rancor over "the influence of gallery and pit
applause, invading the correctness of that acting which heretofore extor-
ted the applause, even from the most fastidious auditor."[85] The readiness
of the audience to applaud anything they approved had its reverse side:
people hissed if something displeased them strongly. Occasionally this
privilege was used to express moral disapprobation. Thus, for instance,
the final curtain of that "vulgar and licentious burletta," *The Beggar's
Opera*, "dropped amidst the hisses of the audience."[86] But hissing usually
was reserved for a performer who, through his own fault or the machinations of some rival, gained the disfavor of the crowd.

Audiences had still other methods of making their wishes known.
Although the main part of the program was prearranged by the manager,
the audience itself often decided upon the between-act entertainment.
Favorite songs particularly were often demanded, and in the 1820's, the
practices of curtain calls and encores began. In thrifty Boston, one
correspondent wrote:

> We (the sovereigns) determine to have the worth of our money when we
> go to the theatre; we made Blangy dance her best dances twice; we made
> Mrs. Seguin repeat "Marble Halls," . . . and tonight we are going to encore
> Mrs. Kean's "I don't believe it" in *The Gamester*. We hope she'll prove
> agreeable and disbelieve it twice for our sakes. Perhaps we'll flatter Mr.
> Kean by making him take poison twice; the latter depends upon the furor
> of the moment.[87]

The account exaggerated audience tendencies, but some theatergoers
clearly did "consider actors as public slaves, . . . bound to be the
obedient and submissive victims of their caprice."[88]

The brunt of the audience's attempts to determine the program
generally fell on the orchestra. The usual complaint was that musicians
indulged in their own tastes for "sonatas and other airs" instead of

[84] *Something*, 1 (December 16, 1809): 78.
[85] *Emerald*, 3 (January 9, 1808): 136.
[86] *American Monthly Magazine and Critical Review*, 2 (November, 1817): 62.
[87] *Spirit of the Times*, 16 (October 24, 1846): 408.
[88] John Hodgkinson, *A Narrative of His Connection With the Old American Company* (New York, 1797), p. 27.

regaling the audience with " our patriotic airs, or other popular tunes."[89] Few people who objected to the orchestra's choice of music bothered with letters to the editor. More directly and more frequently they shouted out their demands to the musicians in a manner that one periodical described as "tout-à-fait imperieuse";[90] if the orchestra proved recalcitrant, they enforced their will with a well-aimed barrage of "apples, stones, or other missiles." This list was given by a Boston orchestra in a card they had printed in a newspaper begging for more audience consideration and restraint.[91] In their exposed location in front of the stage, the harassed musicians quickly abandoned their beloved Haydn or Handel for "Tod-re-I" and "Jefferson's March."[92] Managers were quick to deny the "monstrous calumny" that they preferred classical music to "National Airs."[93]

The orchestras were not the sole target for gallery bombardment. One critic wrote of a Fourth of July performance: "The audience as was to be expected . . . was riotous and noisy, but excepting the throwing of a fork at Mrs. Oldmixon when singing the bravura song, was not guilty of any striking impropriety." The critic went on to blame the management for the occurrence. "It is well known that our taste is not sufficiently refined to enjoy this style of singing," he argued, "and a New York audience, in their soberest moments, will only listen to it for respect for the performer."[94] The critic's assumption was that the audience was bound to become violent, even against an elderly and popular performer, if its tastes were overlooked. The manager was responsible for any disturbance if he failed to cater to the prejudices of his spectators.

Several times boisterousness broke forth into full-fledged riot. Competition between actors commonly touched off these disturbances, especially when supporters of a particular performer decided not to let a rival of their favorite appear. By being very noisy they could turn a play into a pantomime and by throwing things they could drive even the pantomime from the stage. The most serious riots were touched off by insults, real or alleged, that English stars made against the United States. The worst revolved around England's two great tragedians, Edmund

---

[89] "Letter to the Editor," in *Theatrical Censor*, 1 (December 17, 1805): 32.

[90] *Le Petit Censeur*, 1 (December 5, 1805): 278. This Philadelphia publication, written in French, was particularly annoyed because "quelques partisans anglais" had demanded that the orchestra play "le fameux air, God Save the King."

[91] Quoted in Arthur Hornblow, *History of the Theatre in America From Its Beginnings to the Present Time* (Philadelphia, 1919), 1: 229.

[92] *Theatrical Censor*, 1 (January 15, 1806): 74.

[93] Philadelphia playbill (February 2, 1828), Ireland, *Extra Illustrated*, HTC, ser. 1, 9: 21.

[94] *Rambler's Magazine*, 2 (February 2, 1810): 26.

Kean and William Charles Macready. Kean came and departed first. His original tour in 1820 was generally very successful. In Boston, however, during his second engagement there, trouble arose. He was announced to play Richard III but, seeing his meager audience, refused to perform. This ended his hopes of continuing in Boston; he left the city and soon America. But he also left behind him a residue of disgust that his next visit was to kindle into fury. An announcement from "Peter Public" in the *Boston Gazette* of May 28, 1821, revealed the virulence of the anger his conduct aroused:

> One-Cent Reward!—Run away, from the "literary Emporium of the new world," a stage player calling himself Kean. He may be easily recognized by his misshapen trunk, his cox-comical, cockney manners, and his bladder actions. His face is as white as his own froth, and his eyes are dark as indigo. . . . As he has violated his pledged faith to me, I deem it my duty to thus put my neighbors on guard against him.[95]

Kean returned in 1825 to the scene of his insult. He published a very contrite apology in the Boston newspapers informing the public of his gratitude for its favors and his regret at any offense he had given. This time a packed house greeted him, but this patronage was not a sign of forgiveness. Many—probably the large majority—in the audience were willing to give him a chance to make an apology; Kean indicated his willingness to do this, but those who wished to drive him from the stage were "so loud, that whether they were more numerous or not, they carried their point." After a few minutes spent in trying to make himself heard, Kean "withdrew amid a shower of nuts, almonds, cake, and other inoffensive missiles." A bit later he returned to the stage, this time with the manager, to try to placate the audience. The crowd then began throwing metal balls (as well as the softer effluvia) which, one observer said, "seemed to alarm his fears."

The actor withdrew, but the crowd lingered on until late in the evening. Most of the audience left the theater, but many persons outside pushed their way in to reinforce the rowdy part of the crowd. They were not idle: "Considerable damage was done to the inside of the theatre: the chandeliers were wantonly broken, some of the iron railings torn from their positions, the seats in some of the boxes and in the pit were torn up, some of the box doors removed from their hinges, . . . and other injuries to other parts of the house." The riot act was read, but no other action was taken to curb the rioters.[96]

---

[95] Quoted in *Recorder*, 6 (June 2, 1821): 91.

[96] A résumé of the fracas appeared in *Boston News Letter and City Record*, 1 (December 21, 1825): 16–17; Clapp, *Boston Stage*, pp. 183–93, 228–37.

Kean's difficulties followed the pattern of other theatrical riots. A performer's conduct or opinions would anger some people. The slight in many cases was slight indeed; there were attempted riots over Fanny Kemble's stated preference for the English way of sitting a horse.[97] Then all those who liked a good disturbance—not necessarily those who felt indignation at what was said—would attend the theater to enforce their mandates. For many spectators, the tragedian James Fennell pointed out, "the prospectus of a disturbance, or, as some call it, fun, is the most attractive bill that can be made out."[98] Reportedly the manager Barrière, a Frenchman whose English was poor, attracted a large audience when a prankster talked him into substituting "a grand fracas" for the usual adjectives in his bills.[99] In some places, cliques of "ignorant, self-conceited young despots . . . erected themselves into a body of riot" and caused trouble especially for any English actors who might hold less than adulatory opinions of the United States.[100] Such noisy theatrical demands led easily to mob violence and senseless destruction. The *American Athenaeum* rightly concluded that violence was less owing to a justly aroused "moral and decent class of the community" than to "an infuriated mob—excited by misrepresentations and blinded by the cruel instigations of personal malice and implacable hatred"[101]—and more important, perhaps, motivated by a craving for excitement.

The democracy of the early nineteenth-century theater was highly primitive and easily degenerated into mob rule. The arrangement between audience and performers was extralegal and spectators tended to resent any reference to riot acts or police enforcement. One observer commented: "In speaking of the rights of the public in the Theatre, no one who knows what he is talking about has any reference to the Statute book. There is a tacit convention between the managers and the audience, which an intelligent public knows how to enforce. Custom and common sense regulate the understanding." "Exercising their sovereignty" by applause and possessing the "glorious privilege of hissing," spectators had no real limitation on their "rights."[102] Tyrone Power noted that the American theatrical environment was "purely democratic . . ., each man having a right to evince his taste after his fashion" and restrained only by "opinion."[103] "It is the *American people* who

---

[97] Wemyss, *Twenty-Six Years*, p. 216; Kemble, *Journal*, 1: 102–19.

[98] Fennell, *Apology*, p. 406.

[99] *New York Mirror*, 8 (May 28, 1831): 375.

[100] *Mirror of Taste*, 1 (March, 1810): 268; Blake, *Providence Stage*, pp. 214–18.

[101] *American Athenaeum*, 1 (December 29, 1825): 380.

[102] *American Magazine and Critical Review*, 2 (November, 1817): 62–63; 1 (June, 1817): 133–37.

[103] Power, *Impressions*, 1: 60. A New Orleans district judge ruled that ticket holders legally had

support the theatre," roared one critic; "and this being the case, the people have an *undoubted right* to see and applaud who they please, and we trust this right will never be relinquished. No, never!"[104] The theory had great appeal to a democratic people, zealous of inalienable rights of all kinds. And it would have been harmless, making the spectator a lively and wholesome part of dramatic proceedings, had the restraints of "custom and common sense" been always sufficient. But common sense had little to do with most theatrical disputes, particularly those that degenerated to riot, and theatrical precedent sanctioned a good deal of violence. The Astor Place Riot, with the loss of some twenty lives, was the first precedent to set bounds to the sovereignty of the theatrical audience.

The background of the disturbance, complex in detail, was simple in outline. Edwin Forrest and William Charles Macready were the leading tragedians of the day, the one in America and the other in England. As was common practice, each invaded the other's territory. Despite original overtures of friendship on both sides, neither man was the sort to relish competition. When Forrest played in London a second time he attracted small and partially hostile audiences and received harsh notices, the most virulent of which were written by one of Macready's friends. With no evidence at all he assumed that the persons who hissed him were Macready's hirelings. He revenged himself by attending a Macready performance of *Hamlet* in Edinburgh where he personally hissed his rival in one scene. Forrest, with a self-righteousness that could have fooled only himself (and some of his biographers), printed a card admitting the deed, but claiming his hiss was only the accepted mode of expressing distaste for the way that the scene was acted. Not personal dislike, Forrest claimed, but a disinterested concern for the improvement of the drama had been his motive.[105]

Macready feared trouble when in 1848 he left for the United States once again; his closest friend, Charles Dickens, who had angered Americans with his *Martin Chuzzlewit*, even took the precaution of not going to the boat to see him off.[106] He began his tour in New York, where he was well received, but in November troubles began when the two rivals

the right to hiss and stamp in the theater (*New Orleans Daily Picayune* [March 6, 1853], quoted in Roppolo, "English Theatre in New Orleans," 1 : 85–87).

[104] *Boston Weekly Magazine*, 1 (November 27, 1824): 145.

[105] Forrest's letter to *The Times* (London) (April 4, 1846) was reprinted in Wemyss, *Twenty-Six Years*, pp. 384–85.

[106] Dickens' affectionate letter explaining his reasons was reprinted in William C. Macready, *Diaries*, ed. William Toynbee (New York, 1912), 2 : 403–4.

appeared simultaneously in different theaters in Philadelphia. Both drew large audiences for *Macbeth*, but a few of Macready's hearers shouted for Forrest and threw coins and rotten eggs. Macready made a dignified curtain speech saying he had never, secretly or openly, done anything to harm Forrest's career and had not had any bad feelings toward him until the Edinburgh hiss. Forrest lashed back with his version of the trouble: in London Macready had plotted against him; in Edinburgh he had hissed not a rival, but a desecration of the scene; in the United States he had urged his friends not to attack Macready: "Leave the superannuated driveller alone; to oppose him would be but to make him of some importance."[107]

The fight continued. Forrest published cards full of self-justification and abuse of his rival; the English actor answered him occasionally in print, but usually in the pages of his diary, which best revealed the effectiveness of the American's attack on his morbidly sensitive nature. The different vehicles generally chosen for expressing their feelings— the public press and the private diary—gave clues to the personalities of the combatants. Except for a similar egoism and a comparable unpopularity with other actors or managers, hardly could rivals have been more different. The diary, reeking of self-doubt and condemnation as well as exaggerated scorn for others, was Macready. And the public cards, full of paranoia and complete self-righteousness, were Forrest. The Englishman, mentally a Puritan, constantly examining and condemning his own motives and actions, was often ridiculously harsh, perhaps because of his inner uncertainty, in his estimation of his audience, his friends, and his fellow actors. Forrest was incapable of self-criticism. He had faults, he admitted to his biographer, but "I would not change the honest vices of my blood, for the nefarious hypocrisies, and assumed virtues of my malignant detractors."[108] He considered himself the great American actor; if he was not properly appreciated, some evil and anti-American person must be plotting against him. He was in his own mind King

---

[107] Quoted in James Rees, *The Life of Edwin Forrest with Reminiscences and Personal Recollections* (Philadelphia, 1874), p. 324. Forrest wrote to his wife that Macready had not been hissed from the stage only because he'd packed the theater with English "hirelings." "Englishmen must be cuffed into a proper conduct to us" (November 25, 1848). Printed in *New York Herald, Report of the Forrest Divorce Case, Containing the Full and Unabridged Testimony of all the Witnesses* (New York, 1852), p. 121.

[108] Edwin Forrest to William R. Alger (August 28, 1870), Forrest MSS, HTC. Forrest continued, "Yes, let me own that I have a religion of hate—not Revenge. I have a hatred of oppression . . . a hatred of hyprocrisy, falsehood, and injustice—a hatred of bad and wicked men and women, and a hatred of my enemies, for whom I have no forgiveness excepting through their own repentance of the injuries they have done me."

Lear;[109] and to him King Lear and Edwin Forrest were heroes without flaw, except undue benevolence—men who suffered to the point of madness from their own greatness and magnanimity and the cruel machinations of fate and wicked men.

Both actors, Macready in his diaries and Forrest in letters to a close friend, talked much of their own performances. Macready often castigated his playing and prodded himself to do better, but Forrest spoke of his own acting only to praise it. "I never acted better in my life—I never before achieved such a performance of 'Lear'" he wrote James Oakes in 1867. "What a pity it could not have been photographed! I mean the entire representation of the character, with all its power—with all its changeful passions—with all its unspeakable subtleties."[110] Only a year before his death, Forrest told his friend that the great truths Shakespeare had uttered would be repeated endlessly "not only in his immortal pages—but through the inspired life of all great tragedians through all the coming ages of the world."[111] Forrest, in his own mind, had assumed the grandeur of the characters he portrayed and his "inspired life," like that of Hamlet or Macbeth, was to be one of humankind's great heritages. In this supreme bit of egoism Forrest was in one sense right. His life did reflect those qualities that were paramount in his character interpretations: vitality, intelligence, high seriousness, striking effect shot through with a vitiating lack of deep sensitivity or even moderate self-understanding: "I am King Lear."

Differences in characterization followed differences in character. Macready was intellectual in his approach to acting, correct and restrained to the point of coldness. Forrest, physically powerful, was in all his portrayals passionate and fiery, even to the point of caricature. Most critics agreed that his best parts, excepting or including Lear, were those characterized by simplicity and grandeur rather than by intellectual subtlety. Spartacus and Metamora more than Hamlet or Richard were Forrest's great characters. Thus the two actors appealed to different audiences. People with greater intellectual pretensions were Macready's supporters; audiences who cared little for intellectual subtlety preferred Forrest's more robust and moving style. Macready's closest acquaintances were literary and intellectual figures. Forrest pictured himself as a knight-errant of American democracy and lost no chance to

---

[109] Brander Matthews and Laurence Hutton, *Macready, Forrest and Their Contemporaries* (New York, 1886), p. 47; William R. Alger, *The Life of Edwin Forrest* (Philadelphia, 1877), 2: 780–81.

[110] Forrest to Oakes (December 22, 1867), Forrest MSS, Princeton University.

[111] Forrest to Oakes (November 23, 1871), Forrest MSS, Princeton University.

draw attention to his love of country and love of the people; on one occasion he literally kissed the American flag.[112] A good Democrat, he believed in "simplicity of government," in "the strength and the majesty of the people," and in the Whigs' nefarious plotting to "benefit a few at the expense of the many."[113]

Their rivalry in Philadelphia remained merely funny. The sight of "the two great Thespian rivals making speeches and shooting paper pellets" at each other provided amusement as well as "a pleasant state of excitement" for the Philadelphia public.[114] That this excitement should verge into riot in New York was not altogether unexpected. But that "paper pellets" should be replaced by real bullets was an unprecedented twist in theatrical history. Macready's first night in New York was ruined by the noise and missiles of a small part of the audience. In the third act a barrage of four chairs thrown from the gallery, one of them almost hitting Lady Macbeth, caused him to retreat. He planned to leave New York, but instead complied with the public urging of a large group of citizens to remain.[115] Disturbances at his next performance, two days later on May 9, ended in bloodshed.

By the time of the riot the personal dispute between the two actors had become intertwined with other conflicts. Some of the shouts heard during the May 7 performance suggested these: "Three groans for the English bulldog!" "Nine cheers for Edwin Forrest!" "Down with the codfish aristocracy!" "Huzza for Native Talent!"[116] Both chauvinistic nationalism and class hatred, fanned by the political party struggle, figured in the affair. Posters put up just prior to Macready's visit expressed these themes in inflammatory fashion:

WORKING MEN,
shall
AMERICANS or ENGLISH RULE
in this city?

---

[112] Montrose J. Moses, *The Fabulous Forrest: The Record of an American Actor* (Boston, 1929), p. 124.

[113] Edwin Forrest, *Oration Delivered at the Democratic Republican Celebration of the Sixty-Second Anniversary of the Independence of the United States* (New York, 1838), p. 17; Edwin Forrest to his mother, May 20, 1844. Forrest MSS, HTC. The oration, which came at a time when Forrest was considering running for Congress, was probably written by William Leggett. A glowing review of it appeared in *Democratic Review*, 3 (September, 1838): 51–57.

[114] *Philadelphia Public Ledger* (November 23, 1848), quoted in Richard Moody, *The Astor Place Riot*, (Bloomington, Ill., 1958), p. 78.

[115] The list of forty-seven signers included Washington Irving, Herman Melville, Benjamin Silliman, and the playwrights Mordecai M. Noah and Cornelius Mathews.

[116] Quoted in Rees, *Life of Forrest*, p. 332.

The crew of the *British Steamer* have threatened all Americans who shall dare to express their opinion on this night at the English Aristocratic Opera House !!!

We advocate no violence, but a free expression of opinion to all public men!

WORKING MEN! FREEMEN!
Stand by your
LAWFUL RIGHTS.

American Committee.[117]

The American Committee was headed by E. Z. C. Judson, a notorious rabble-rouser, an advocate of America for Americans, and, under the name of Ned Buntline, a prolific author of dime novels.[118] Judson spent the day going around New York working up support for the disturbance; in the evening some of this support was inside the theater. A few arrests quieted things within the opera house, but news of police action inflamed the large crowd that had been gathering outside. They began throwing stones at the building. Policemen, after making a few arrests, were cowed by the crowd. They requested the aid of the militia which had been ordered to stand by for possible trouble. These came well armed, but the crowd refused to fall back. Macready finished the play and, hidden among the audience, left the theater through a police cordon. As he was leaving, the army fired its first volley—over the heads of the crowd. The mob hung back momentarily, but soon the word spread that the military was using blanks. Only the injuries and fatalities resulting from the next round of fire corrected this mistake. The militia, hesitant to fire directly at their fellow citizens, aimed slightly over the heads of the front line of rioters, so that most of their victims were observers and passers-by on the outskirts of the mob.

The next day posters urged citizens to attend a huge rally in the park "to decide now whether English ARISTOCRATS!! and Foreign Rule! shall triumph in this AMERICA'S METROPOLIS." "Come out!" the placards exhorted, "and dare to own yourselves sons of the true hearts of '76!"[119] A large crowd congregated and accepted several resolutions, all condemning "the most wanton, unprovoked and murderous outrage ever perpetrated in the civilized world." Speakers from Tammany and the Empire Club assured the crowd that policemen had been stationed in the theater only "to revenge the aristocrats of this city against the working

---

[117] Quoted in *ibid.*, p. 337.
[118] Jay Monaghan, *The Great Rascal* (Boston, 1952), pp. 168–82.
[119] Reprinted in Moses, *Fabulous Forrest*, p. 260.

classes" and reminded them that, when opened, the Astor Place Opera House had been "restricted to those who wore white kid gloves, such was the spirit of pride and presumption of the nabobs of the Fifteenth Ward, who, led by the Mayor, have brought troops to fire on the people."[120] The crowd again moved toward the opera house, but police and military readiness this time held them at a distance.

The Astor Place Riot was over except for interpretation. Contemporary periodicals bountifully indulged in this. After the first minor Macready trouble, Greeley's *Tribune* expressed concern with theatrical liberty, and commented on the rioters:

> And yet everyone of the miscreants who practice this atrocious and impudent tyranny will boast of his readiness to fight for Liberty, and is ready to knock any smaller man down who insinuates aught against Democracy. They can't imagine any better Democrat than they are, unless it is Forrest.
>
> When will the stage, that vaunted school of Morality, that fulsome adulator and systematic corrupter of Popular Liberty, begin to teach its votaries clearer and truer ideas of Freedom?

After the second and more serious disturbance, the *Tribune* issued warnings broader in scope: the riot showed the need for a less sensational and more principled press, for increased emigration out of the cities to the unpopulated West, and for greater governmental action to curb inequalities of wealth.[121]

Others read similarly broad meanings into the riot. A Philadelphia paper wrote that the most unpleasant aspect of the uprising was that it showed that "there is now in our country, in New York City, what every good patriot has hitherto considered it his duty to deny—a *high* class and a *low* class."[122] "The White and Red roses of York and Lancaster were never more distinctly divided into antagonistic parties than the 'B'hoys' of New York and the 'upper Ten,'" commented the *Home Journal* after the fray. "Let but the more passive aristocratic party select a favorite, and let there be but a sympton of a handle for the 'B'hoys' to express their dissent, and the undercurrent breaks forth like an uncapped hydrant."[123] The B'hoys found enough handles to use against Macready, "the pet of princes and nobles—the stately, but frigid representatives of

[120] Quoted in Moody, *The Astor Place Riot*, pp. 187–94.
[121] *New York Tribune* (May 9, 1849), p. 2; (May 15, 1849), p. 2.
[122] *Philadelphia Public Ledger*, quoted in Moody, *The Astor Place Riot*, pp. 228–29.
[123] *Home Journal* (May 12, 1849).

kings."[124] He was English, he was highly cultivated, he was not a good fellow, he was a favorite of the "aristocrats," he was acting at the "white glove" Opera House, and he had allegedly tried to drive pure American talent, the "true blue Ned Forrest," from the London stage. He was, in short, the epitome of what American democracy, in its cruder forms, detested. The "uncapped hydrant" had only been held back by the use of force and the loss of life. And while the right to support whom one pleased had been protected, many feared that the method would "generate a hatred of the aristocracy by the lower classes that will be bound to show itself."[125] "We are all responsible, all guilty," concluded the most sensitive account of the riot, because American society had allowed great discrepancies of wealth to exist and thus to embitter those who were poorest and least educated.[126]

There was something ludicrous, perhaps something comforting, in the fact that, a year after barricades had been erected in Europe and while a serious strike was going on in upstate New York, tragedy and class warfare should center in a dispute between playactors. Class conflict it was, but in an area where even the extensive loss of life could make it seem hardly more than a senseless, tasteless opera bouffe. The expression of the conflict, as well as its setting, was peculiarly theatrical.

If the Astor Place Riot raised the curtain to contemporaries on an expression of class conflict, it lowered it on one phase of nineteenth-century drama. It ended the old kind of audience control. Plays did not change appreciably, nor did spectators give up the reins of applause, hissing, and patronage. But something of the edge and imperativeness of audience sovereignty was lost. Never again were America's audiences to play such a prominent role in dramatic presentations. The process had begun which would eventuate in the passive spectator in front of the silver screen. The audience's power had been vital, absolute, and subject to severe abuse by any noisy group. "The idea of minority rights," the *New York Evening Post* concluded, "is as applicable to the case of theatrical performance as it is to the case of public meetings for other purposes."[127]

Just as important, the riot marked an end to the conglomerate appeal of the drama. A process that had begun much earlier in New York was

---

[124] "American Citizen," *A Rejoinder to "Replies from England" Together with an Impartial History and Review of the Lamentable Occurrences at the Astor Place Opera House* (New York, 1849), p. 68.

[125] Maud and Otis Skinner, eds., *One Man In His Times: The Adventures of H. Watkins, Strolling Player, 1845–1863* (Philadelphia, 1938), p. 74.

[126] *Account of the Fatal and Terrific Riot at the Astor Place Opera House* (New York, 1849), p. 32.

[127] *New York Evening Post* (May 16, 1849), p. 2.

now accelerated and solidified. One theater was no longer large enough to appeal to all classes. The early nineteenth-century theater had managed to present tragedy, comedy, opera, dance, farce, melodrama, and miscellany in proportions that, if they did not satisfy, at least attracted all classes. The conjunction of these elements, partially the result of necessity because of the sparsity of population, had always been a little uneasy. The Astor Place Riot intimated that this union was no longer possible. The country had grown, and grown apart. The theater after midcentury followed this development. It expanded and divided—into legitimate drama, foreign-language drama, farce, vaudeville, circus, burlesque, minstrelsy, opera, symphony—each with its separate theater and separate audience. One roof, housing a vast miscellany of entertainment each evening, could no longer cover a people growing intellectually and financially more disparate.

4

The Work of Enchantment

THE KINGDOM ruled by theatrical audiences of the early nineteenth century was an unruly one. Failings in presentation ran through the tapestry of dramatic performances like a bright, untidy thread. They gave the coloring of the unexpected to every pattern, often ruining the design, but sometimes enhancing it in striking fashion. People watched a play not confident of seeing the result of a carefully prepared attempt to bring drama to life, but conscious that all sorts of improvisations were going on at the time, from which surprises, good and bad, would result. Some of these surprises were amusing, giving entertainment completely separated from what was intended. And when there was no discord, when by great talent and sufficient preparation and good luck, the plays came to artistic life, the result was not only the pleasure of seeing art, but the excitement of having been party to its creation. To people first attending the theater "all appeared as the work of enchantment";[1] to those who went often part of the pleasure was watching how the work was accomplished.

Dramatic failings were frequent and glaring in the period partly because of the ambitiousness of dramatic undertakings. Considering the limited physical and human resources of each theater, the number, variety, and scenic elaborateness of productions were great. Audiences appreciated variety and display, and managers did their sometimes awkward best to please them.

Bunker Hill, the first American play popular enough to receive repeated performances in many cities, suggests the dramatist's dependence on

---

[1] William Dunlap, *Memoirs of a Water Drinker* (New York, 1837), 1 : 75.

the stage manager. "The English march in two divisions," the playwright wrote, "from the wings . . . to the foot of hill." At this point American and English soldiers fired rifles at each other "for several minutes: . . . six or seven of your men should be taught to fall." As one English unit retreated and another took up battle, the playwright reminded the manager to open all windows near the stage "to let out the smoke." The Americans finally left their shelter and met the British mounting the hill, which gave "room for effect, if the scuffle be nicely managed." While two or three Englishmen were "rolling down hill," a backdrop "having some houses and a meeting house painted on fire, with flame and smoke issuing from it, should be raised." "Small cannon" were to be frequently fired during this battle scene which lasted "for twelve or fifteen minutes."[2]

Such complexity of stage action and scenic effect became more common as the century progressed, even though the theater of the period was in most ways ill-equipped for lavish scenic effects. The standard stage set was of the drop-and-wing variety—a painted canvas backdrop with curtains or painted flats facing the audience on the sides between which performers entered and exited. Dunlap introduced the drop curtain, which fell in front of the scene catching the actors in tableaux, and the Bowery Theatre was the first to use a draw curtain.[3] Limited lighting facilities especially inhibited easy theatrical effects. In the first quarter of the century oil lamps and huge candlelit chandeliers were the chief means for lighting both the stage and spectator portions of the theater. During the second quarter most larger theaters used gas lighting, but it was not until 1848 that the important Charleston Theatre installed gas lighting fixtures. Even lights of this improved sort could not be raised or dimmed with ease. Houselights had to be left on during the play. If these were sometimes too dim for proper stage viewing, they were too bright and too inflexible for optimal atmospheric effects, though the intensity of light on the stage could be varied by drawing shields over lamp or gas footlights or overheads.

Theatrical buildings were usually hastily constructed and had little mechanical equipment, partially because the wooden structures were so susceptible to fire. A contemporary estimated that an American

---

[2] John Burk to William Dunlap, in William Dunlap, *History of the American Theatre* (London, 1833), 1: 313–14.
[3] George C. D. Odell, *The Annals of the New York Stage* (New York, 1927–49), 2: 225–26; Wesley Swanson, "Wings and Backdrops," *Drama*, 18 (1927): 79. The general practice before Dunlap's borrowing of the French and German drop curtain had been for the actors simply to walk off stage when the act was over.

theater had an average life expectancy of about twenty years because of the frequency of fire, a danger certainly increased by many types of scenic display.[4] Even such basic arrangements as an adequate heating system and some means of ventilation were commonly neglected. Unlike the huge patent theaters in London, whose size almost forced reliance on spectacle, most American theaters were sufficiently small that "the naked eye could thoroughly discern the play of countenance, and the face . . . had its full effect."[5]

Despite the theater's unspectacular physical resources, the ingenuity of stage managers permitted very complex and elaborate staging. During a few months of its 1800 season, long before scenic display reached its height, the theater in Boston showed its patrons: "the storming of the citadel . . ., and the destruction of the Persian fleet"; "an explosion of a volcano"; "Rolla tearing the tree from the supporting rock as the Spaniards crossed, to dash them into the cataract"; and "the ancient broadsword combat, Oscar's leap from the tower 18 feet high, the death of Carroll on the bridge, the conflagration of the whole camp."[6] What was probably done badly in Boston in 1800 came to be done with great effect and finesse as the century progressed. Even without the development of new techniques, sheer practice would have perfected the art of scenic display. Melodrama after melodrama required some sort of exotic setting; dramatists left no corner of the globe unvisited in their search for new homes for old plots, and each managed to work into (or more often stick onto) his story, some impressive pageant, festivity, or great scenic catastrophe as climax.

The fascination of seeing spectacles and cataclysms on stage seemed to change the very nature of drama. Critic after critic complained that legitimate drama was dying because of the success and fascination of beautiful scenery, striking effect, and spectacular pageantry. Delight to the mind was neglected, they complained, while managers busied themselves with appealing solely to the eye;[7] theaters had become degraded to "show shops," specializing in "pasteboard pageantry, conflagrations, bombardments, springing of mines, blowing up of castles and

---

[4] Henry Dickenson Stone, *Personal Recollections of the Drama* (Albany, 1873), pp. 313–14; James Rees, *Dramatic Authors of America* (Philadelphia, 1845), pp. 141–42.

[5] Allardyce Nicoll, *A History of English Drama, 1600–1900* (Cambridge, 1955), 4: 22–25; John Bernard, *Retrospections of America* (New York, 1887), p. 26.

[6] Peter Oliver, "The Boston Theatre, 1800," *Colonial Society of Massachusetts Publications*, 34 (February, 1942): 560.

[7] *North American Review*, 35 (July, 1832): 179; *Emerald*, 2 (January 17, 1807): 31.

such like accumulations of awful nursery horrors."[8] A manager lamented:

> Degraded Drama, nursed by viscious taste,
> Has thrown off diamonds to adorn with paste.
> Huge pots of paint, dutch metal, glittering foil,
> Usurp the stage, its classic boards to soil.
> The poet's gift has proved a sorry failure,
> He's been deposed by fiddler and by tailor.[9]

A New Yorker spoke for many of his fellow critics when he sadly concluded that it was "a waste of toil to point out the hundred thousand anachronisms, impossibilities, and inconsistencies" in a performance when it was "almost impossible to praise in adequate terms the beauty and splendor of the scenery."[10]

A prologue to a successful "mechanical" play, spoken between the author and the theater manager, suggested how scenery could alter the dramatist's role:

> *Author:* Much depends upon the painter's art;
> And how—the plane—and saw—perform their part.
> . . . . . .
> *Manager:*   You mean to say
> With hammer, nail and boards you wrote this play?
> *Author:* Precisely so.
> *Manager:*   And should it chance a hit
> Of course you'll lay a claim to taste and wit.
> *Author:* You're right again.
> *Manager:*   Modest,—but if it fails—
> *Author:* Well! damn the carpenter, the board and nails.[11]

Two fairly typical melodramas, written by "a gentleman of Richmond" and produced in that town in 1828, suggested how writers taxed, more than their own imaginations, those of the stage managers. The first play demanded that at one point the villain be "struck to earth by a flash of lightning, "and required a final scene which showed "the fort of Missolonghi in flames. Island in front. Tomb of Byron. Ocean

---

[8] *St. Louis Pennant* (July 9, 1840), quoted in William G. B. Carson, *Managers in Distress: The St. Louis Stage, 1840–1844* (St. Louis, 1949), pp. 81–82; *American Quarterly Review*, 1 (June, 1827): 334.

[9] Noah Ludlow, "Shakespeare," Ludlow MSS, HTC.

[10] *Albion* (October 27, 1827), quoted in Theodore Shank, Jr., "The Bowery Theatre, 1826–1836," (Ph.D. dissertation, Stanford University, 1956), p. 150.

[11] Richard Penn Smith, "Prologue" to Samuel Chapman's adaptation of J. F. Cooper's *Red Rover*, quoted in Francis C. Wemyss, *Twenty-Six Years of The Life of an Actor and Manager* (New York, 1847), p. 151.

agitated by storm. . . ." The second dramatic offering necessitated even more elaborate preparations. The scenery included:

> Grand view of Scottish Valley, Grand Gothic Hall in M'Donald's Castle, Rocky shore on the seabeach, interior view of cave, Grand view of the Ocean, agitated by storm. Ship of war discovered riding at anchor, fully rigged, and filling the entire back of the stage. The Prince passes in a boat pursued in another by his enemies. He is on the point of being made prisoner, when the ship hoists the French flag, and fires upon the pursuing boat, which with its crew is sunk.[12]

Most of such effects were the work of the painter, but the stage machinist became increasingly important. Elaborate machinery was devised to allow ships to move, fully rigged, on stage in "accordance with the action of the sea," and to "tack sails" and move in another direction.[13] Trap doors and pulley systems were used in the frequent allegorical or patriotic interludes, as well as in more conventional dramas. Crowd and battle scenes were elaborately staged; New York's Bowery Theatre had a special door to the stage installed "to admit cavalry, infantry and artillery."[14] Processions of mechanical figures wended their way down mountains. The box set was developed, as were even more complex structures that let the audience see into several rooms in a building at once. Miles of painted canvas on rollers gave a type of scenic motion picture to some dramas.[15] Huge ramps, extending "to the extreme height of the theatre," allowed the stars of "horse dramas" such as *Mazeppa* or *Timour the Tartar* to perform impressive running and jumping feats. The latter play, for instance, demanded that in the third act "the Georgian Chief, mounted on his Steed, rescues Zorilda from the waters into which she has plunged—then dashes up a *tremendous cataract*, and rescues the Prince Agil, who is about to be thrown from a high tower that projects over a waterfall."[16] "Real water" was sometimes

---

[12] Martin Staples Shockley, "American Plays in the Richmond Theatre, 1819–1838," *Studies in Philology*, 37 (January, 1940): 106–9.

[13] Noah M. Ludlow, *Dramatic Life As I Found It* (St. Louis, 1880), pp. 345–46. In Albany, New York, in 1827, *The Flying Dutchman* was given "with a real brig, thirty feet in length, fully rigged and manned" (H. P. Phelps, *Players of a Century* [Albany, 1880], p. 124).

[14] *New York Mirror*, 3 (December 17, 1825): 162. This theater, famous for its huge casts, advertised for "500 supernumeraries" for one of its productions (Shank, "Bowery Theatre," p. 428).

[15] Dunlap's *A Trip to Niagara* was a very successful example of this kind of entertainment. A criticism from *The Weekly Visitor, or Ladies' Miscellany*, 1 (March 19, 1803): 191, suggests that attempts at similar effects were made from the very beginning of the century: "By the flashes of lightning the mountain torrents are seen descending, while the pines waving and bending to the blast, complete the finest moving picture the American stage ever presented."

[16] *Missouri Republican* (August 14, 1838), quoted in William G. B. Carson, *Theatre on the Frontier: The Early Years on the St. Louis Stage* (Chicago, 1932), p. 255.

promised, but more often watery effects were clever optical illusions; during the performance of one spectacle the waterfall "caught fire and burnt up."[17] Perhaps most lavish in their scenic display were the fairy tale plays such as *Aladdin* or *Cherry and Fair Star*, which had long and repeated runs throughout the period. *Cinderella* was put on so often that, a critic jested, "even rats and mice have become as scarce as pumpkins in the increased demand for the materials whereof fairy coaches and their establishments are made."[18]

One of the most frequent and dangerous types of display was that used in the many "sulpher and blue-fired spectacles." An advertisement for *Masaniello; or, The Dumb Girl of Portici* suggested what was attempted:

> Grand eruption of Mt. Vesuvius. Terrific Explosion!! Forked lightnings rend the Sky! The Burning Lava Impetuously Rolls Down the Side of the Mountain, and the Whole Country becomes Awfully Illuminated!!! Fenella plunges into the Sea! Grand Display of Fireworks; Popular Tumult and Death of Masaniello.

Such a play might be dull, but the weary critic had to admit there was "unquestionably a great deal of *fire* and *flash* about it."[19]

Because of the expense of mounting a lavish piece, some managers came to rent out the sets, costumes, and machinery for their successful spectacles. Thomas Hamblin of the Bowery was the most successful exploiter of this arrangement. The importance of the trappings of drama can be seen in his expectation of a full half of the profits for rent and in his assurance to a prospective customer, "Anybody can play Napoleon who can look anything like him, and who does not with the dress on?"[20]

Volcanoes, waterfalls, battle scenes, rescues on horseback, amazing transformations—all were done often on the stages of the nineteenth century. But the questions of how—and of how well—are more difficult to answer. Certainly the handling of scenic effects was often crude and blundering. A Philadelphia manager famous for his dramatic spectacles almost failed once when a gauze representing rain fell properly on the stage, but had to be removed by drawing it up again. The sight of rain rising offended the audience's sense of reality, but, impressed with the

---

[17] *New York Mirror*, 2 (January 15, 1825): 198. New York's La Fayette Amphitheatre prided itself on its "real tank of water" for nautical effects (T. Allston Brown, *A History of the New York Stage From the First Performance in 1732 to 1901* [New York, 1903], 1: 100).

[18] *Knickerbocker*, 6 (October, 1835): 375.

[19] *New World*, 6 (March 25, 1843): 368; *Missouri Republican* (July 20, 1825), quoted by Carson, *Theatre on the Frontier*, p. 81; *New York Mirror*, 4 (June 23, 1827): 383.

[20] Thomas Hamblin to Francis Wemyss, March 18 [18—], in Joseph Ireland, *Extra-Illustrated Records of the New York Stage*, HTC, ser. 1, 9: 149.

other scenery, they chose to be amused rather than angered. The failure of Vesuvius to erupt on cue, however, totally ruined a lavish production of *The Last Days of Pompeii*. The stage manager ordered the curtain down and managed to get the eruption going, but by the time the curtain was reopened the disappointed audience, already leaving the theater, saw only the last sputters of the cataclysm.[21]

If complete failure was possible, imperfections were common. "The people who have charge of the lightning should not show themselves on stage while in the exercise of their duty," warned a critic in a routine review; "and those who wield the thunder should be more moderate in their claps and let some of the words of the play be heard."[22] Yet theatrical managers succeeded well in creating their scenic illusions. The great popularity of plays almost wholly dependent on scenic display for success testified to their competence. Even serious critics who heartily deplored both melodrama and stress on visual excitement were forced to plead guilty to the charge of

> infatuation, when we see palaces rising before us by enchantment, clouds now enveloping the scene, then suddenly dissipated by the brilliant radiance of a golden sun, or when, initiated into the mysteries of the very depths of the ocean, we behold ourselves transported to palaces of coral . . . while the light from upper regions of air, darting athwart the briny medium, plays fitfully and chequeredly on the radiant pillars that support the deep.

Such "bewitching optical illusion" made critics doubt even "the validity of our own censorial judgment and taste which, heaven forfend, should ever be proved to err or be warped by mere tinsel and glitter."[23] Partly because scenic tricks were difficult given the resources of the theater, even because they might not always come off, critics and audiences alike were intrigued by these attempts at visual illusion and fascinated by their successful execution.

Plays featuring spectacle were generally better performed than their more dramatically coherent competitors. Since they required extensive scenic preparation, they were given more adequate attention in other departments. At least the performers knew well in advance what was to be presented—knowledge often denied them in other presentations. And the management was apt to furnish costumes for these pieces so that actors did not have to adapt some dress out of their own often insufficient

---

[21] Wemyss, *Twenty-Six Years*, pp. 152, 256.

[22] "Queredo" in *Missouri Republican* (August 26, 1828), quoted in Carson, *Theatre on the Frontier*, p. 100.

[23] *American Athenaeum*, 1 (October 6, 1825): 231.

wardrobes. Finally, having fewer lines simplified the actor's job and gave less chance for verbal mistakes, or at least made them less important. As long as the various effects came off on schedule, what the actors said or failed to say mattered relatively little.

Although managers lavished careful and ingenious efforts on getting up scenic pieces, the costuming and staging of most plays were left unsuperintended. Players had to furnish their own costumes, and both the meagerness of their incomes and the number of their roles forced them to depend on clever improvisation in stage dress. Little wonder that critics occasionally complained of "dress belonging to all nations under heaven but the right one" in exotic or historical plays. In reviewing *Alexander the Great*, one noted that Alexander himself appeared in a nondescript suit "worn almost every night" by some performer or other; Hephiston encased himself in the armor usually reserved for the ghost of Hamlet's father; two other Macedonians wore English doublets; and yet another "the costume of a Spanish grandee."[24] Traveling stars were particularly annoyed about the attire of their supporting players. Their concern was understandable when the ghost in Hamlet appeared wearing spectacles or Shakespeare's young and romantic Benedict in *Much Ado About Nothing* was shod in a pair of "red morocco slippers."[25] Such incidents explain the note of one playwright on his title page: "The characters being respectable people, it is hoped the author will not be considered impertinent when he suggests that they should be costumed as such."[26]

Sets in nonspectacular productions were similarly modest. The painting of a backdrop was a major project, and consequently efforts in this line were reserved for scenic pieces. A couple of standard drops—one for outdoor scenes and another for interiors—satisfied all usual requirements. Outlays for properties were no more lavish. Two wooden kitchen chairs with a matching table plus a much worn sofa were the furnishings for any interior setting in the Boston Theatre for several years. They were moved from kitchen to drawing room, from lady's boudoir to gentlemen's tavern, from palace to hovel, from Roman villa to Indian tent—always playing the humble role of something to sit or set upon.[27] Even America's leading theater, the Park, never used any-

---

[24] *Comet*, 1 (November, 1811): 52.
[25] Charles Blake, *Historical Account of the Providence Stage* (Providence, 1868), p. 132; Douglas Taylor, ed., *Autobiography of Clara Fisher Maeder* (New York, 1897), p. 30.
[26] Edward G. P. Wilkins, "My Wife's Mirror," May 10, 1856, HTC.
[27] *Boston Weekly Magazine*, 1 (July 5, 1817): 53.

thing "but kitchen chairs in palace scenes."[28] Frequently the sparsity of "supernumeraries" also injured theatrical realism; one or two boys or old men representing crowds and armies was enough to "produce loud horse-laughs in the most serious and effecting scenes."[29]

Although audiences expected lavish and meticulous staging for scenic productions, they were surprised by elaborate settings for other plays. When the tent scene in *Julius Caesar* "looked like the real thing," audiences responded, as they had to spectacular effects in less worthy dramas, with "thunders of applause."[30] The success of *London Assurance* in the early 1840's owed much to the production's unprecedented duplication of the fittings of a fashionable home. Box sets had been used previously, but this play's popularity made them a standard thing and established a trend toward less careless and more realistic staging for comedies and other nonspectacle plays.[31] Charles Kean in 1846 brought some of his scenically ornate productions of Shakespeare to New York and proved the point of an American critic who had earlier urged managers to stage Shakespeare with as much care as they did melodramas in order to "delight at once both the lovers of drama and the admirers of machinery."[32] The success of such plays helped to divert attention from scenic melodramas, whose popularity had always stemmed in part from the contrast between their elaborateness and the haphazard way in which most plays were staged. Yet Shakespeare was perhaps not the victor. "It is an era," wrote the *Spirit of the Times* of Kean's productions, "not in the history of the legitimate drama, but in that of pageantry and spectacle."[33]

"There is seldom seen a show," wrote one discouraged critic, "which is not productive of some strange absurdity or laughable blunder."[34] Absurdities of setting, costume, and properties were bad enough, but more serious and more frequent, the reviewer went on to illustrate, were blunders by actors. Excellent acting alone could convey all the excitement of theater, while the most perfect display of sets and dresses could do nothing to compensate for bad performances. The actors of the early nineteenth century bore the brunt of dramatic responsibility and

---

[28] *Spirit of the Times*, 9 (February 8, 1840): 588.

[29] *Virginian* (August 30, 1822), quoted in Richard Hadley, "Theatre in Lynchburg from its Beginnings to the Outbreak of the Civil War" (Ph.D. dissertation, University of Michigan, 1947), p. 33; *The Actor; or A Peep Behind the Curtain* (New York, 1846), p. 170.

[30] *New York Mirror*, 4 (December 16, 1826): 167.

[31] Odell, *New York Stage*, 4: 534–36.

[32] *Boston Weekly Magazine*, 1 (June 21, 1817): 145.

[33] *Spirit of the Times*, 15 (January 17, 1846): 560.

[34] *Emerald*, 2 (March 21, 1807): 136.

hence of dramatic criticism. Their faults and their achievements were equally impressive.

The player had problems both on and off stage. Socially his reputation was equivocal. Leading ministerial figures denounced the profession as "almost universally vicious," a few periodicals commented on how reluctant people were to ask players into their homes, and actors themselves showed a great sensitivity to prejudices against "profane play-actors."[35] Young women usually tried to make it seem a matter of necessity when they went on stage. The sentimental fiction of Anna Cora Mowatt and Charlotte Cushman, successful actresses and defenders of their profession though they were, stressed the hardships, trials, and tragedies of life on stage.[36] Even an avowed friend of drama, writing in praise of a popular player, described her as "a young actress as yet undebauched by her profession."[37] Respectable families looked askance at acting as a career; Noah Ludlow's reportedly went into general mourning when they learned of his intended profession: "My mother's grief was very great, my sister drooped and became melancholy, my brother Joseph said but little, and seemed unwilling to talk about me...."[38] Such reactions insured that most American performers were drawn from the ranks of excitable young men who found trade dull, the young women they married, their children, and from a few persons whom either ability or family financial distress propelled toward the stage.

Society most often indicted the acting profession on the ground that it tended toward immorality. Probably the opportunity for immoral conduct was unusually great among a group of people moving from place to place and attracting audiences which included the worst as well as all other segments of the community. Although one of the constant rules of the nineteenth-century theater was that "gentlemen" were not allowed backstage (as "seegars" and dogs were prohibited in the audience), ways were found to try, by charm or gift, the virtue of a pretty actress.[39] But brawling, insolvency, drunkenness, and divorce were the best-attested moral faults of actors.

---

[35] John Witherspoon, *A Serious Enquiry Into the Nature and Effects of the Stage* in *Essays on Important Subjects* (London, 1765), 2: 100; *Portland Magazine*, 1 (October 16, 1824): 123; Ludlow, *Dramatic Life*, p. 159.

[36] Anna Cora Mowatt, *Mimic Life, or Before and Behind the Curtain* (Boston, 1856); *Twin Roses* (Boston, 1857); Charlotte Cushman, "The Actress," *Godey's Lady's Book*, 14 (February, 1837): 70–73.

[37] *Boston Weekly Magazine*, 1 (July 19, 1817): 161. Dunlap's *Memoirs of a Water Drinker* (1: 125, 130–32; 2: 35–38) showed his ambivalent attitude toward professional actors.

[38] Ludlow, *Dramatic Life*, p. 7.

[39] Oliver, "Boston Theatre, 1800," p. 558; Olive Logan, *Before the Footlights and Behind the Scenes*

Some major scandals occurred. One actress gained a measure of fame for the frequency with which she changed husbands, and another for stabbing, during a performance, a fellow player who was presumably her lover.[40] Most publicized were the amorous adventures of Thomas Hamblin and the sensational divorce trial of Edwin Forrest and his wife, in which each charged the other with frequent adultery.[41] Although such conduct was neither common among nor limited to actors, incidents happened often enough to allow people with prejudices against players to retain them. The problem partly was that actors' misconduct was more noticeable than that of people in other professions. Their lives were to some extent public property, and their vices were likely to be given public display. Drunkenness, when indulged in by an actor, was not simply a private failing but a public nuisance to everyone who had paid to see a play properly acted.

Certainly many actors proved themselves capable of perfect respectability. Prominent persons in society, politics, and literature went out of their way to entertain leading members of the acting profession, while lesser actors seemed to have no trouble fitting into middle-class America. The memoirs of theatrical people like Wood, Ludlow, Smith, or William Warren gave no suggestion of social ostracism. On the contrary, once established in their profession, they became solid and respected citizens. Of course, to some extent their background, to a greater degree their modest salaries, limited actors' social success. But if actors succeeded, lived decently, and, perhaps most important, made money, they were socially accepted. No one was upset when President Tyler's daughter-in-law, who had acted all over the nation with her father, Thomas Abthorpe Cooper, became official hostess at the White House, though the French minister was amazed that someone could move so smoothly from the stage to what "serves as a Republican throne."[42] The social scorn for actors was, as the Philadelphia manager William Wood pointed out, more a verbal platitude than a driving conviction in America, one similar to society's oft-stated distrust of lawyers.[43]

(Philadelphia, 1870), pp. 440–42; William K. Northall, *Before and Behind the Curtain* (New York, 1851), pp. 205–15.

[40] Ludlow, *Dramatic Life*, pp. 488–89, 550; Joe Cowell, *Thirty Years Passed Among the Players in England and America* (New York, 1844), p. 75; Sol Smith, *Theatrical Management in the South and West* (New York, 1868), pp. 165, 192.

[41] Lester Wallack, *Memories of Fifty Years* ([New York, 1889], pp. 87–92), presents the Hamblin scandal, and *New York Herald, Report of the Forrest Divorce Case* (New York, 1852), gives a complete transcript of that sordid affair.

[42] Elizabeth Tyler Coleman, *Priscilla Cooper Tyler and the American Scene* (Tuscaloosa, Ala., 1955), pp. 84–107.

[43] William Wood, *Personal Recollections of the Stage* (Philadelphia, 1855), pp. xv-xvi.

Dunlap's thumbnail biography of one American actor expressed, like so much of his writing, popular preconceptions exactly. John Martin, Dunlap began, "made his debut, . . . was favorably received, and his destiny sealed." And he concluded, "He laboured hard, lived poor, and died young."[44] Not an attractive fate certainly, but one decidedly not limited to stage players in the period. Nor was Dunlap's account the full story, for with disadvantages went excitement, camaraderie, public applause, close contact with great fictional creations and famous people —rewards more than enough to compensate the imaginative for a slight decrease in security or assured social respectability. Certainly the stage had enough applicants to keep it well filled.

While an actor had to face a vague social prejudice off stage, his troubles on stage were concrete enough. Even very successful players issued frequent complaints about "this hateful vagabond life," a "lifetime of misery and agitation," the "long apprenticeship to a miserable profession."[45] The itinerant quality of the actor's life was a serious problem, especially for families. Means of travel were often primitive and hazardous, particularly in winter when the theatrical season was at its height, and living conditions had to be makeshift. Most players must at times have seconded Eliza Riddle's complaint: "But I do dislike traveling. I want a Home."[46]

The actor's work was hard. Performances were given in the early 1800's three or four times a week. More common later on was a schedule of six performances each week, one every night except Sunday. What made this schedule formidable was the frequency with which bills were changed. Commonly, each night either a new play or one not recently performed was put on. And on the day or perhaps two days between performances actors had to learn or restudy and rehearse another part. Infrequently a popular success would ease the pressure of constant memorization, but even a "long run" rarely lasted more than a week. In New York, Philadelphia, and Boston during the 1830's and 1840's, a few plays had runs of fifty or more nights, but such successes occurred only about a dozen times in the half-century. A Boston critic, absolving actors for their faults in performing, described the usual situation:

---

[44] Dunlap, *American Theatre*, 1 : 171.

[45] Edwin Forrest to his wife, October 15, 1847, printed in *New York Herald, Forrest Divorce*, p. 124; John Gaisford, *The Drama in New Orleans* (New Orleans, 1849), p. 42; Cornelius Logan to *Cincinnati Daily Times*, October 25, 1843, in Smith, *Theatrical Management*, Extra-Illustrated ed., HTC.

[46] Eliza Riddle Field to Cornelia Ludlow Field, July 25, 1844, in Ludlow MSS, HTC.

They have so often been required to take principal parts on a moment's warning; to play every night during the season, and not uncommonly in the longest characters both in play and farce, that they have seldom had the opportunity to impress the words upon their memory, much less to give life, soul, and vigour to their utterances.[47]

"Such labour!" wrote Edwin Forrest, "God and the actor only know the fatigues of it."[48] Allowing for theatrical exaggeration, Forrest was right, at least for those actors who, unlike himself, never became stars repeating the same dozen or so roles year after year. For example, Eliza Riddle and Eliza Petrie, the two leading ladies of the St. Louis theatre, played respectively—and respectably if one may judge from the gifts their fans showered on them at the end of the season—fifty-one and eighty-one different roles during one four-month season. These were generally not small parts, but leading and secondary roles, mostly in full-length plays.[49] Even under the best conditions an actor's load was likely to be heavy. The comedian William Warren, playing at midcentury when long runs had become more frequent and in the Boston Museum, which early gained a reputation for long-lived successes, appeared in 204 different parts during his first four years there.[50]

The grueling schedule of the actor had its compensations. For popular performers like Warren or the Misses Riddle and Petrie, adulation and fair financial returns probably repaid their exertions. The comedy and camaraderie of very small barn-storming troupes where a performer might have to play a half-dozen characters in one drama or die far enough off stage so he could also play the curtain music gave the actor a fair amount of amusement for his effort.[51] But for a stage player of no special talent in the usual run of a theatrical season, the grind was often wearing. Particularly, for the aging actor with little hope of rising in his profession or of earning more than a subsistence wage and for the beginning player without a backlog of previously memorized parts, the strain was considerable. Many a young actor, "hurried from part to part, from night to night, season to season," did become, as one manager complained, "a careless, slouchy, stupid mumbler of sentences, the substance of which he neither knows nor cares to know."[52] Yet the acting

---

[47] *Ordeal*, 1 (February 25, 1809): 124.

[48] Edwin Forrest to James Oakes, January 11, 1863, Forrest MSS, Princeton University.

[49] Carson, *Theatre on the Frontier*, pp. 214–15. Probably these stars played even more roles during those four months; the newspaper files from which Carson worked were incomplete.

[50] Claire McGlinchee, *The First Decade of the Boston Museum* (Boston, 1940), p. 60.

[51] Smith, *Theatrical Management*, p. 23.

[52] Ludlow, *Dramatic Life*, p. 73.

profession was perhaps no harder than most others on individuals lacking in either experience or hope.

The profession required versatility as well as hard work. The stock-company system limited versatility in some ways because most performers were hired to fill a particular type of role or "line of business" in all plays. One actor would specialize in leading tragedy roles, another in juvenile and romantic leads, a third in sophisticated comedy, and still another in low-comedy parts. Old men, old women, heavy villains, serious fathers, singing chambermaids, and even walking gentlemen and walking ladies were all special lines of business which had their practitioners. Mrs. Mowatt rightly pointed out that "the members of the company, in a well-organized theatre, resemble the men on a chess board. Each has his appointed place and fights his battle for distinction in a fixed direction."[53] Few theaters were sufficiently well-organized, however, to let each actor do only his line of characters; both inclination and necessity caused much odd casting.

The manager's right to assign parts often curbed miscasting owing to inclination. Only in star engagements and on actors' benefit nights, when the beneficiary designated the roles, did gross unsuitability occur. Most common were the oddities of benefit nights when all sorts of casting novelties were used to attract the curious. At times a performer sacrificed both audience and profit to gratify some great theatrical ambition. A minor Philadelphia actor insisted on performing Richard III on his night, as the disgusted manager put it, for "his own pleasure" and no one's profit.[54] And a Mrs. Shaw, "a lady of large figure and somewhat corpulent" and a favorite player in "lively old women" and "bouncy chambermaid" parts, aspired also to tragedy.[55] Whenever she had a chance she took on roles like Lady Randolph or Lady Macbeth, despite critical warnings that her very appearance in tragedy—not to mention her acting—was enough to arouse either scorn or sneers. For her benefit she chose to play Hamlet, and such is the stuff of human tragicomedy that the middle-aged, round-faced, comical Mrs. Shaw became, "for one night only," the Prince of Denmark.

Even more ludicrous were the performances of incompetent amateurs.

---

[53] Anna Cora Mowatt, *Autobiography of an Actress* (Boston, 1854), p. 320.

[54] William Warren's diary, quoted in Reese Davis James, *Old Drury of Philadelphia* (Philadelphia, 1932), pp. 33–36. The actor was a Mr. Herbert whose speciality was "humorous old men." One of Herbert's *Richard* playbills is in Ireland, *Extra-Illustrated*, HTC, ser. 1, 10: 40.

[55] Charles Durang, *The Philadelphia Stage, From the Year 1794 to the Year 1855* (Philadelphia, 1854–60), 1: 42. Mrs. Shaw's Boston career received fascinating critical coverage in successive issues of *Emerald*, 1807–9.

Sometimes people who were thinking of becoming players would buy the right to perform with a professional company for one night. If they did passably well or moderately poorly the event usually attracted only brief interest. But some were bad enough to become national jokes. One Shales created such hilarity in his Boston debut in tragedy—his friends presented him with a tin plate and a vegetable wreath—that he was invited to New York, and Elder Adams of the Mormon church drew crowds by his hilarious incompetence.[56] The sport must have been good at times; the *New York Mirror* gave a detailed account of the singing of one Metz, normally a violinist in the orchestra, whose vocal talents were "not worth a fiddlestick":

> Imagine a broken-hearted lover, stepping forward to the stage lights, his hand pathetically on his bosom, with "Is there a heart,"—*applause*—"that never loved?"—*clapping of hands and laughter*—"or felt soft woman's sigh?" —*peals of laughter and stamping of feet*—"Is there a man"—*applause*—"can mark unmoved"—*peals of laughter*—"Dear woman's tear"—singer pauses, licks his lips, winks, draws in his breath, makes a horrible wry face in an endeavor to execute an embellishment, and trills—*thunders of applause and peals of laughter, so you might count every tooth in the house*—singer ends— "tearful eye."[57]

Little wonder the audience made Shales die twice and Metz sing an encore.

Necessity was a more frequent cause of miscasting. When a company was too small to have someone for each line of business, when a play had several characters of one type, or when illness or inebriation prevented someone's appearing, actors had to leave their speciality to do an entirely different sort of part. In such instances, anyone willing to learn the part quickly was used, so that an ambitious walking gentleman might become Iago or a singing chambermaid Desdemona. Necessity also required a change in roles when a stock company gave a special kind of performance for which it was not fully manned. Because most tragic actors, even those of mediocre abilities, preferred to "star it," stock companies often had trouble filling the highest supporting roles of tragedies with competence. In the 1840's stars began to circumvent such disadvantages by touring with a supporting performer or two, a practice which presaged the traveling companies prominent after the Civil War.

Other types of entertainment required even more drastic casting.

---

[56] *Knickerbocker*, 13 (May, 1839): 461; *Spirit of the Times*, 17 (December 4, 1847): 488; 18 (March 11, 1848): 36; 19 (February 2, 1850): 589.
[57] *New York Mirror*, 11 (August, 1834): 3.

Pantomimes drew actors from all lines of business as, with more excruciating effect, did opera. Stock companies did not hesitate to present such entertainment, especially if stars could be engaged to dance or sing the leading roles. For opera, managers hired to augment the regular orchestra any unemployed or amateur musicians that the community had to offer. And every actor in the company would sing, the most painfully tuneless only in the chorus. Under such arrangements audiences would be treated—or subjected—to performances of *Der Freischutz*, or *The Marriage of Figaro*, or *Norma*. Music critics' complaints that many operas drew "their support from magnificent scenery, processions, and decorations" were doubtless well founded.[58] A citizen of St. Louis probably showed good judgment when, after seeing a highly popular production of Rossini's *Cinderella*, he suggested to the manager: "Cut out the music, Sol; it is tedious."[59]

Finances were another constant problem in the life of an actor. Playing in short and uncertain seasons, actors had incomes that fluctuated greatly even when they were adequate. Conditions were particularly hard on the bit players. Paid only a subsistence wage when they worked, they could not count on working regularly. Low wages partly accounted for the prevalence of whole families on the stage. By aggregate labor enough could be saved to tide them over periods of unemployment. The income of even the best paid performers was likely to be erratic. John Howard Payne, traveling as a juvenile star in 1804, complained, "Sometimes I found my pockets so full of money they would burst, and again my funds would sink so low that I could not scrape together enough to pay for the rents which my affluence had created."[60]

Expenditures for costumes and for the conviviality that usually went with theatrical success cut deeply into the wages of performers. And even when work was available, wages were sometimes not. "We would like Boston professionally very much" wrote a leading actress, "if—there is always an if—if we received our salaries regularly."[61] Even dependable managers in important theaters counted on taking in the money they had contracted to pay out. If audiences failed their expectations, they failed their players. For instance, when Dunlap went bankrupt his actors complained in a card to the public that "while the wind

[58] *Euterpeiad; or, Musical Intelligencer*, 1 (October 21, 1820): 118. Of course, in large cities—most notably New York and Philadelphia—operas were often given with adequate orchestras and supporting players. But even there preparations were commonly makeshift.
[59] Smith, *Theatrical Management*, p. 31.
[60] John Howard Payne to Robert Treat Paine, October 6, 1810, "Letterbook," HTC, 1:46.
[61] Eliza Riddle Field to Cornelia Ludlow, February 23 [1840?], Ludlow MSS, HTC.

blew, and the snow fell," they faced winter with "salaries stopped, purses emptied, credit exhausted." The situation of Dunlap's actors was that of most performers during any of the frequent interruptions of theatrical seasons: "Some few could stand the tug tolerably well in consequence of previous provision for a rainy day. . . . But *rueful* was the prevailing cast of countenance."[62] And such conditions were almost to be expected by players entranced into the troupes led into all sections of the country by charlatans like John S. Potter, "the builder and proprietor of more theatres, and the manufacturer of more professional vagabonds" than any other man. Potter reputedly yelled at one of his actors who requested his pay, "What, ask for a salary when the blackberries are ripe?"[63]

Actors' working conditions as well as wages were sometimes bad. They suffered particularly from the cold in winter seasons, when all the company's stoves were often used to try to heat the auditorium. A group of Philadelphia players impressively demanded their rights on this issue in terms that recalled important precedents:

> When in the course of human events, it becomes necessary for a certain body of men to complain of those wrongs which they have endured . . ., a decent respect for the opinions of the *dramatis personae* compels us to make known to you, our manager, those grievances of which we complain. We hold these truths to be self-evident, that all men are created free and equal; that they are endowed with certain inalienable rights, among which are *light, heat, and the power of keeping themselves warm;* and in order to maintain those rights, *stoves* were instituted among mankind, deriving their powers of heat from the fuel that is placed in them. . . . There is a time when forbearance ceases to be a virtue; *such a time has arrived.* The history of the present fire-maker is a history of repeated injuries towards the honorable supernumeraries. . . .[64]

The star system was often considered the cause of the stock actor's problems. Begun early in the nineteenth century, the system was handled through most of the period by Simpson and Price, managers of the Park Theatre, who controlled the American itinerary of most leading

[62] Card printed in *New York Morning Chronicle* (February 25, 1805), quoted in Odell, *New York Stage*, 2: 227–28.

[63] Jonathan Kelley, *Dan Marble* (n.p., 1851), p. 47; Walter Leman, *Memories of an Old Actor* (San Francisco, 1886), pp. 240–42; Smith, *Theatrical Management*, pp. 230–32; Francis C. Wemyss, *Chronology of American Stage, 1752–1852* (New York [1852]), p. 13. Potter was posted by one spirited actress as "Mr. Potter the Coward" and was exonerated of a $100.25 debt "in consideration of the horse-whipping I gave you." Shortly thereafter Potter died. *Spirit of the Times*, 14 (January 11, 1845): 552; 15 (May 17, 1845): 140.

[64] Wemyss, *Twenty-Six Years*, p. 282.

English stars and who ruthlessly attacked those who refused to cooperate with them.[65] Stars hurt drama, it was argued, by leeching the manager of his money and the stock actor of the honor that otherwise would have gone to him. Hence "the starring or starving system," was to many people "a hydraheaded monster that preys upon theatrical existence."[66] Managerial hatred for "bastard starring" was understandable;[67] handing over half the proceeds of an engagement to a star rankled when they knew that from their half had to come the expenses of a large theater and numerous company.

That the "degradation of drama" resulted from the star system is more dubious.[68] The excitement created by a parade of stars decreased the interest in the stock company when it played without outside support, but that it diminished the stock company's effectiveness is more questionable. Even with an array of stars, managers realized that their success depended equally on a capable company, and they spared no efforts to get one. The star system was also responsible for some positive good. It was the arrival of stars, aiming at greatness and needing great parts, that occasioned the repetition of Shakespeare's best plays. And it was the star system that allowed towns as small as Mobile or Natchez to see every great player of the early nineteenth century in his greatest roles. Audiences of the period liked novelty and excitement; when this was not generated by Forrest or Booth or Macready enacting Shakespeare and the better contemporary plays, managers aroused it by resorting to ever more lavish scenery and banally contrived melodrama. The success of the Bowery's flamboyant spectacles, the *New York Mirror* pointed out, resulted from a temporary public preference for "new plays performed by old actors" rather than old plays brought out with fresh stars.[69]

---

[65] Durang, *Philadelphia Stage*, 1: 71, 84; 2: 169, 244. Simpson wrote to Wemyss about Mrs. Sloman who toured America without Park auspices: "And if I cannot punish Jane for her impudence I will try and punish you. . . . Give orders to discharge Jane or never ask me for a favor as long as you live—for I be ――― if I will." (July 15, 1839, in Ireland, *Extra-Illustrated*, HTC, ser. 1, 5: 124.)

[66] Gaisford, *Drama in New Orleans*, pp. 52–55; Louis F. Tasistro, *Random Shots and Southern Breezes* (New York, 1842), 1: 138.

[67] Wemyss, *Twenty-Six Years*, p. 261; George H. Hill, *Scenes from the Life of an Actor* (New York, 1853), pp. 196–212; Ludlow, *Dramatic Life*, p. 73; Wemyss, *Twenty-Six Years*, pp. 172–73; Wood, *Personal Recollections*, pp. 435–63; *The Actor*, pp. 143–44; "Boston Supernumary," *A Peep Behind the Curtain* (Boston, 1850), pp. 75–88.

[68] Dunlap, *American Theatre*, 2: 149; *American Quarterly Review*, 1 (June, 1827): 336–39; Walt Whitman, *Brooklyn Eagle* (February 8, 1847), in *The Gathering of the Forces*, ed. Cleveland Rodgers and John Black (New York, 1920), 2: 312–13; *New York Mirror*, 9 (August 27, 1831): 63; *Dramatic Mirror and Literary Companion*, 1 (August 14, September 4, 1841): 4, 28.

[69] *New York Mirror*, 12 (July 25, 1835): 426.

Actors had faults as well as problems. Their failings were sometimes visual—Thomas Hamblin playing in "silk breeches with a hole in the hinder parts," William Warren as a famished captive waddling around "in all his obesity," an actress with two parts wearing the wrong costume in some scenes[70]—but they were more commonly verbal. Critics advanced three main complaints: failure to give their lines with feeling, failure to give their lines as written, and failure to give their lines. The first of these faults, of course, grew from want of time and talent. The frequency of play rotation required actors to grasp their parts and the means to convey them quickly. That they should often fail to do this, particularly in the higher walks of tragedy, was to be expected. "How badly this play was performed throughout—how the language was mutilated, the meaning perverted, the action interrupted, the art debased, and passion destroyed by deficiency," lamented a reviewer of a production of *Romeo and Juliet*.[71] Such strictures were regularly repeated. What was meant to be tragic was often, as one reviewer put it, "extremely farcical," and vice versa.[72] The melodramatic style of acting was in part a matter of necessity as well as of taste. The stock actor had too little time to develop realistically the characters he played; he almost had to have a set of mannerisms ready-made with which he could embellish any character. Stars, of course, who repeated, say, a dozen roles year after year had time enough to develop characterizations. But even most stars spent their apprenticeships in stock companies where they developed acting techniques under the pressure of having to present quickly many different characters.

Critics felt that actors should minimally have memorized their lines. They almost vied in thinking up ways of chastising actors for failures in recollection: gently, "Had he not been so intolerably imperfect in his part, we should probably have been able to bestow much praise"; scathingly, "Most of the parts were wretchedly defective—the prompter being the most essential character"; observantly, "It appeared to the audience as if Sir Aspen, Mr. Fairfax, and one or two others, were dressed up and placed on the stage for the purpose of reciting what was first audibly read by the prompter"; encouragingly, "Some of them only needed to study their parts a little better (and the prompter not to speak so loud)"; resignedly, "The audience expects Mr. Newton to be

[70] *Dramatic Mirror* (Boston), 1 (February 25, 1929): no. 22; Robert Ewing, *The Theatrical Contributions of "Jacques" to the "United States Gazette"* (Philadelphia, 1826), p. 161; James Anderson, *An Actor's Life* (London, 1902), pp. 125–26.

[71] *Emerald*, 2 (February 14, 1807): 78.

[72] *Comet*, 1 (November 9, 1811): 50.

imperfect, and are seldom disappointed"; flatteringly, "The prompter's voice has not been more sonorous this season."[73] Sometimes memorization was so poor that the actor might ask the audience's permission to read his role.[74] And occasionally players forgot entrances or skipped whole scenes. If something was omitted that was absolutely essential to the rest of the story, a manager might, between acts, tell his audience what should have been enacted.[75]

The effects of failure of memory were often excruciating. "What a cast! what a play! what botchers! what butchers!" exclaimed Fanny Kemble in her diary after a performance of *King John* at the Park Theatre. Her last scene had been particularly horrible:

> King gazed at cardinal, and cardinal gazed at king; king nodded and winked at the prompter, spread out his hands and remained with his mouth open; cardinal nodded and winked at the prompter, crossed his hands on his breast, and remained with his mouth open; neither of them uttered a syllable![76]

Such pauses, in which "for several minutes there was no voice heard but the prompter's," were common.[77] Even stars of the importance of Thomas Abthorpe Cooper, long the American stage's leading tragedian, often did not know their lines perfectly. Joseph Dennie found "mortifying" the sight of William Warren trailing Cooper around stage "to supply him with words approximate to those forcible gestures and expressions of countenance of which he is so complete a master." Perhaps Cooper's experience as manager, when he decided that an unintelligible prompter forced actors to learn their lines, enforced personal reformation. At least by 1816 he was able to prompt his support.[78]

Actors compensated for what they left out by adding a good deal to the script. "Gross interpolation" almost as much as "verbal imperfection" was a constant source of critical complaint.[79] Much of this was

[73] *Emerald*, 2 (January 10, 1817): 17; *Comet*, 1 (December 21, 1811): 118; *Weekly Visitor, or Ladies' Miscellany*, 1 (May 7, 1803): 246; *Memphis Enquirer* (May 6, 1837), quoted in R. S. Hill, "Memphis Theatre 1836–1846," *West Tennessee Historical Society Papers*, 9 (1955): 50–51; *People's Organ* (November 2, 1842), quoted in Carson, *Managers in Distress*, p. 205; *Polyanthos*, 2 (November, 1806): 275.

[74] James Murdock, *The Stage* (Philadelphia, 1880), p. 262; Tyrone Power, *Impressions of America* (London, 1836), 1: 328.

[75] *Spirit of the Times*, 9 (May 18, 1839): 132; Smith, *Theatrical Management*, p. 137.

[76] Frances Anne Kemble, *Journal* (Philadelphia, 1835), 1: 112–13.

[77] *Dramatic Mirror* (Boston), 1 (October 9, 1829), no. 19.

[78] *Port-Folio*, 1 (March 28, 1801): 102; Dunlap, *American Theatre*, 2: 274; *Boston Weekly Magazine*, 1 (December 14, 1816): 38.

[79] *Emerald*, 3 (December 19, 1807): 100.

verbiage substituted impromptu for words that had been forgotten. Once in a while it was a spontaneous interjection. For instance, a three-year-old child, while being saved from the Spaniards, yelled to his rescuer at the critical moment: "Damn your eyes; don't you let me fall."[80] But most additions were intentional, jokes and local allusions that actors threw in to win the interest or applause of their audience. Serious critics usually deplored the practice because such additions to the part "generally plunge the character in incongruity."[81] True enough, but the incongruity deeply amused less meticulous spectators. As one critic admitted grandiloquently, "Occasional interpolations of original wit and local allusions highly entertain the audience, and raise the song of mirth in every heart."[82] Certainly it must have been good fun for the audience and little harm to the play when an actor grandly exclaimed, "The American eagle!" at the conclusion of a patriotic piece; and then, when the thunder of applause that greeted this toast died down, added on his own, "May we never want one in our pocket."[83] Or when a man in the pit of the Washington, D.C., theater "was seized with a violent fit of vomiting," an actor portraying a doctor remarked, "I expect my services are wanted elsewhere," an ad lib that "elicited shouts of applause" from the audience and disgust about American disdain for "the restraints of civilized manners" from Mrs. Trollope.[84]

If these extemporaneous bits of humor were the joy of many a theatrical evening, they also allowed abuse. Especially low comedians often sacrificed taste and sometimes decency to provoke laughter. The extempore additions of actors alone gave color to the charges of immorality on stage. If the "shameful and most impudent interpolations" were generally mild, they were perhaps extreme for a period when discussion, if not practice, of a good many things was highly suspect.[85] Most critics were circumspect about stating offenses to morality and little of a specific nature was mentioned except "the throwing off of a few volunteer damns" when lines were forgotten.[86] The critics of the *Boston Weekly Magazine*, however, always admirably specific in their remarks, did give, after suggesting females read no further, examples of some of the worst

---

[80] Leman, *Memories of an Old Actor*, p. 41.

[81] *Emerald*, 3 (October 8, 1808): 610.

[82] *Polyanthos*, 1 (December, 1805): 60.

[83] John Howard Payne to Robert Treat Paine, October 6, 1810, "Letterbook," HTC, 1: 46.

[84] Frances Trollope, *Domestic Manners of the Americans*, ed. Donald Smalley (New York, 1960), pp. 233–34.

[85] *Yankee*, 1 (July 23, 1828): 239; *Prompter*, 1 (June 15, 1850): 25; *American Athenaeum*, 5 (May 26, 1825): 47.

[86] *New York Mirror*, 5 (December 1, 1827): 167.

of these offenses "not only to female modesty, but to male decency." One actor always inserted a smirking allusion to what would happen in nine months when stage lovers married. Another performer, walking off stage with a girl, remarked, "Come along, my dear, and I'll show you how man was first created." This same person at another time answered when asked where he was going, "I am going to the colleges." The critic observed, for the benefit of "those who are not so well acquainted with the public institutions of Boston" as the actor, that "the colleges" were "noted bawdy houses."[87]

Such unmoralizing sexual allusion was probably infrequent. That the moral worries of critics generally centered on old plays suggested that such comments, even as actors' additions, were not common in new ones. But unquestionably actors did approach impropriety in their efforts to amuse their more ribald fans and perhaps to titillate more refined patrons. For the entire audience the interplay of the actor's wit with an author's words helped to create an expectation of what might happen next—an expectation most often disappointed perhaps, but occasionally delightfully fulfilled.

The chief means for holding actors in line was a system of forfeits. Theoretically a certain amount could be deducted from an actor's salary for each serious mistake he made during performances. Actually, to the good fortune of the less competent members of the profession, forfeits were primarily a psychological threat rather than a financial weapon. After reminding of mistakes and the right to deduct, managers usually paid full salary to restore good will.[88] The "Forfeit Book" of Boston's Tremont Theatre for the years 1841–42 gave a catalogue of the kinds of errors rife in nineteenth-century theatrical performances. Failure to know lines was the most frequently mentioned fault, but a sampling from the book suggests a multitude of dramatic sins:

Mr. Linden improperly dressed, as a living servant having dirty white trowsers instead of knee breeches and white stockings. . . .

Mr. Haynes absent some time during the 4th act when his scenes were on. . . .

Mr. F. S. Hill dressed Julio in military frock coat and heavy boots for ball room scene, and in addition cut Michael out of an entire scene in the 3rd act. . . . necessary to the development of the plot. . . .

Mr. Fairchild (property man) being reproved by Mr. Gilbert (Stage Manager) . . . left the theatre at the end of third act of play which caused

---

[87] *Boston Weekly Magazine*, 1 (July 19, 1817): 161–62.
[88] Leman, *Memories of an Old Actor*, pp. 32–33.

considerable confusion during the remainder of the night, having two busy pieces to play. . . .

Mr. Hill very imperfect as Tom, not knowing one scene from the other, and not changing his dress. The prompt book of Tom and Jerry was taken from the prompt place, a few minutes previous to the curtain rising. . . .

Mr. Thomas . . . when called on to go on was not to be found; and then being too late to send anyone the scene was in great confusion. . . .

Napoleon, Mr. Leman . . . wearing modern white trowsers, though reproved for it last night. . . .

Mrs. Muzzey cast for Mrs. Trott in Town and Country refused the part. . . .

Mr. Wood (pantomimist) announced for this evening did not arrive. . . .

Mr. Chapman missed his last scene having entirely forgotten it. . . .

The curtain did not rise until twenty minutes after time, Mr. Hacket not being ready. . . .

Mr. C. Howard met with an accident . . . by a wing falling and striking him on the head; he was obligated to be carried off the stage. . . .

Mr. Mullikin refused to go on. . . .

The farce was disgracefully played throughout, Mr. C. Howard being very imperfect. . . .[89]

E. L. Davenport probably had reason for writing from England: "We have more natural talents in America, but not so much application. I mean all concerned from manager to supes."[90]

The magnitude of faults seems almost incompatible with testimonies to audience fascination and enthusiasm. But of course the audience did not always respond favorably, nor did gross mistakes in presentation occur at each performance. In a sense the possibility of bad production and of good response were complementary, because good plays done smoothly by the best of professional talent evoked a particularly hearty response by their relative rarity. Hazlitt's well-known comment on Kean's acting—that it "was like reading Shakespeare by flashes of lightning"—had relevance for the entire theater of the early nineteenth century. A good part of the time lapses in both taste and competence kept the stage in dramatic darkness, but this was rent by flashes of ingenuity and genius that fascinated and deeply moved audiences. It was this erratic theatrical climate, the haphazard, makeshift willingness to try anything, that injected into the theater of this period large doses of both the ludicrous and the wonderful.

[89] "Tremont Theatre Forfeit Book, 1840–1842," HTC.
[90] E. L. Davenport to "F," in E. F. Edgett, *Edwin Loomis Davenport* (New York, 1901), pp. 28–31.

5

This Motley Mixture

Whatever the quality of the entertainment, the nineteenth-century theatergoer got a lot of it for his money. The average theatrical evening featured a full-length play, but this was just the beginning. After the play came the farce or short comic opera to insure that the audience went home happy. Though some objected to the dissipation of mood when a cheerful "comedietta" followed hard on the death of Othello or Hamlet, most critics agreed that these amusing afterpieces were "indispensably necessary": "Like the wine we drank after dinner, to correct the humours and promote digestion, they give a fine relish to the intellectual course."[1] There were also generally other types of entertainment to relish between the parts of the dramatic offerings: always orchestral music and commonly songs, dances, or novelty acts.

This pattern of drama, farce, and interspersed musical numbers was dominant, but during every season drama was forced to give way or accommodate itself to things like animals or acrobats, operas or oddities. After seeing a circus in 1811, John Howard Payne wrote: "Some accidental turn of fashion, or that insatiable thirst for novelty which constitutes a predominant feature in our national character may make the enterprise popular and lucrative." But the young actor, judging from his own feelings as well as those "of all men of taste and sense," was convinced that the legitimate drama would not long be associated with "this motley mixture of amusements that can never harmonize."[2] The

---

[1] Robert Ewing, *The Theatrical Contributions of "Jacques" to the "United States Gazette"* (Philadelphia, 1826), p. 27.
[2] John Howard Payne to J. H. Dwyer, November 2, 1811, "Letterbook," HTC, 1: 10.

next half-century proved him wrong. The greatest drama and the grossest novelty were jointly yoked throughout the period to the task of drawing an audience. The "rigid critic" might deplore these "amalgamations," Isaac Harby pointed out, but only "time and intellect" could end them. "Until then, modern theatres may hold up as a motto the reverse of Shakespeare's 'All the world's a stage,' and rather substitute 'The stage is all the world.'"[3]

No one at the time could better testify to Payne's misjudgment than "Mr. Rannie." Little is known of Mr. Rannie except that there were two of him—perhaps a father and son—who separately gave very similar entertainments. The repertory they, or at least one of them, brought to the larger cities of the eastern seaboard, to the small towns of New England, and even to the Mississippi Valley in the first decade of the century was marked chiefly by its diversity. Mr. Rannie did magical tricks "which had excited the curiosity of the most enlightened characters in Europe"—he specialized in replacing the severed head of a rooster; he juggled; he walked the tightrope; he demonstrated ventriloquism; he imitated bird and beast calls; he exhibited a "philosophic fish" which "wrote with a pen any words or numbers desired" and which "much astonished the scientific observers." And he acted in plays. Indeed he and whatever company he managed to scrape together gave New Orleans and Natchez their first known taste of drama in English. In New Orleans he staged a popular farce apparently before it was played in New York; in Natchez he put on such old favorites as *The Provoked Husband* and *A New Way to Pay Old Debts*.[4] The strangest thing about Rannie's repertory, besides his own versatility, was his inclusion of good plays amid the variety of his offerings. He was essentially a one-man circus, but the circus and the drama were, in the early nineteenth century, closely united. The "serious critic" could only lament:

> Wit cannot fall so fast, as folly rises;
> Witness the circus: filled at double prices!

---

[3] Isaac Harby, "Defense of Drama," *A Selection From the Miscellaneous Writings* (Charleston, 1829), pp. 252–53.

[4] George C. D. Odell, *Annals of the New York Stage* (New York, 1927–49), 2: 143–44, 209–10, 344; Mabel T. Crum, "The History of the Lexington Theatre From the Beginning to 1860," (Ph.D. dissertation, University of Kentucky, 1956), pp. 10–12; Joseph M. Free, "The Ante-Bellum Theatre of the Old Natchez Region," *Journal of Mississippi History*, 5 (January, 1943): 14; Roger P. McCutcheon, "The First English Plays in New Orleans," *American Literature*, 11 (May, 1939): 184; Nelle Smither, "A History of the English Theatre in New Orleans, 1806–1842," *Louisiana Historical Quarterly*, 28 (April, 1945): 362; James Barriskill, "Newburyport Theatre in the Federalist Period," *Essex Historical Collections*, 93 (January, 1957): 8–12.

> While fashion, bright and short-lived as the rocket,
> Flies to hear children squeal in Rannie's pocket.[5]

Because they were popular, the regular theater was hospitable to circus-type performers. One of the most successful theatrical groups in the period, popular enough to make hard-pressed managers throughout the country engage them even at ruinous rates, was the Ravel family. Balancing, tumbling, "Herculean feats," and pantomime were the staples of their repertory.[6] Critics and audiences alike generally expressed great admiration for their talents and for the smoothness that came from performing as a well-rehearsed, self-sufficient ensemble. "Wholly dependent on their own corps," noted a long-time theater manager, "their performances exhibited a perfection unobtainable by those compelled to employ uncertain aid from strangers." And this group, America's most "universally enduring popular novelty," found their audiences not in a circus tent but in the country's important theaters.[7]

Like the Ravels, some "equestrian troupes" traveled as complete acting companies, took starring engagements in regular theaters, and presented their stunts within the framework of dramas especially written to show off the prowess of horse and rider. The original circus in America centered on these equestrian dramas, which were given now and again in most of the country's major theaters with acclaim. A historian of the Philadelphia stage wrote that "no other event in our theatrical annals produced so intense an excitement" as the climax to an early circus's production of *Timour the Tartar*. When the horse with the heroine on its back rushed to the brink of the cataract, "the people rose with simultaneous impulse to their feet, and, with canes, hands, and wild screams, kept the house in one uproar of shouts for at least five minutes."[8]

Because any type of animal on stage was likely to arouse interest at least briefly, theaters did not rely only on traveling troupes for their circus-type attractions. Most simple was the practice of displaying unusual animals in processions or in pens on stage to give an aura of authenticity to some exotic setting. When they could get the beasts, managers found it worthwhile to give top billing to "two full grown

---

[5] Robert Treat Paine, *Works in Prose and Verse* (Boston, 1812), p. 366.

[6] Francis C. Wemyss, *Twenty-Six Years of the Life of an Actor and Manager* (New York, 1847), p. 281; William G. B. Carson, *Managers in Distress: The St. Louis Stage, 1840–1844* (St. Louis, 1949), pp. 30–31.

[7] William B. Wood, *Personal Recollections of the Stage* (Philadelphia, 1855), p. 368; Charles Durang, *The Philadelphia Stage from the Year 1794 to the Year 1855* (Philadelphia, 1854–60), 3:23.

[8] Durang, *Philadelphia Stage*, 1: 113.

African zebras" or to produce plays "for the purpose of introducing the wonderful elephant."[9] Such animals on display were simply a part of the scenery, much like the canvas or mechanical distractions that often insured a melodrama's success. Sometimes, of course, they insisted on taking a more important part in the play. The tragedian Cooper rented an elephant for his benefit performance and the beast, walking across the stage with hero and heroine perched unsteadily on its back, introduced in one actor's words, "an unexpected hydraulic experiment . . . to the great astonishment and discomfiture of the musicians."[10]

Animals on stage played a more integral part in many dramas; one of the staple tricks of the melodrama was to introduce an animal in some leading role. Not only would people be attracted by the appearance on stage of, say, a talking magpie, but also plots could be easily twisted and miraculously resolved by the bird's enigmatic behavior.[11] Lions, elephants, cats, monkeys, and apes were given lead roles in plays. Prices were raised at the Bowery Theatre during the highly successful engagement of an elephant billed as Mademoiselle D'Jick who starred in *The Elephant of Siam; or, The Fire Fiend*; in Philadelphia rival managers went to court in dispute over who was entitled to the services of this, "the greatest of all stars."[12] Men often took the place of real animals. One M. Gouffe, for instance performed extensive starring engagements acting in parts that earned him the title of the "monkey-man," and a Mr. Parsloe impersonated both monkeys and cats.[13] Their popularity declined only when Gabriel Ravel began to play this class of character so successfully that audiences were "bathed in tears at the tragical end of the sentimental ape."[14] Seemingly, authenticity was required from these stars; one paper praised the verisimilitude of an actor's stage depiction of an orangutan: "An ape itself could not do it better."[15]

---

[9] Bowery playbill, quoted in Theodore Shank, Jr., "The Bowery Theatre, 1826–1836" (Ph.D. dissertation, Stanford University, 1956), p. 428; *Boston Daily Advertiser*, March 19 and 21, 1822, in Boston Theatre Clippings, HTC.

[10] Joe Cowell, *Thirty Years Passed Among the Players in England and America* (New York, 1844), p. 64.

[11] John Howard Payne, *Trial Without Jury; or, The Magpie and the Maid*, in *ALP*, Vol. 5.

[12] Odell, *New York Stage*, 3: 520–21; Wemyss, *Twenty-Six Years*, pp. 188–89. In Richmond she played ten consecutive performances and outdrew Edwin Forrest (Martin S. Shockley, "A History of the Theatre in Richmond, Virginia" [Ph.D. dissertation, University of North Carolina, 1938], 1: 133).

[13] Wemyss, *Twenty-Six Years*, p. 264.

[14] *New York Mirror*, 10 (September 8, 1832): 78.

[15] *Missouri Republican*, quoted in Carson, *Managers in Distress*, p. 142. "Jones's monkey is nothing in comparison with that of Coyle, whom nature formed for the part," wrote a Boston critic (*Dramatic Mirror*, 1 [February 19, 1829], no. 19).

Perhaps most popular of all animal stars were those featured in "horse-trionic dramas."[16] Play after play "written to order to suit a man and a horse" proved popular despite constant complaints of this "dangerous perversion of an amusement."[17] Dogs were only slightly less well liked on stage, particularly those handled by Cony and Blanchard. One of them, "the sagacious Dog Bruin, in a skin and covering especially adapted for this purpose," even tried his paw at playing a lion, but his staples were *The Cherokee Chief; or, The Ship-wrecked Sailor and his Dog* and *Murder on the Cliff; or, Love Me, Love My Dog.*[18] The bloodhounds that thrilled audiences in *Uncle Tom's Cabin* had numerous dramatic predecessors.

Theatrical audiences had no prejudices against human novelties, as their liberal patronage of a long line of "infant phenomena" proved. In London Master Betty started the century off in this direction, while in 1809 John Howard Payne became America's rather elderly "infant prodigy." Sometimes, in light plays taken lightly, these performances by child stars were charming. For instance, Miss Meadows—"a sweet little girl about seven years of age, yet would pass very well for not more than six"—sang, in a duet with Sol Smith, "Out of my sight or I'll box your ears." Smith, supposedly her lover, though several feet taller and several decades older, improvised, "You can't reach them for a number of years." The young star found this as amusing as did the audience and laughed so hard she had to leave the stage.[19] Infant prodigies usually won their reputations in roles less suited to juvenile charm, however; Richard III, Shylock, and Macbeth were among the most popular.

Although critics berated the enthusiasm for child performers as an indication of "a vicious taste, or rather an absence of taste," the children themselves were generally praised.[20] After all, who could say that the six-year-old who had learned all these lines and accompanying gestures might not develop into a more than competent player? There was also an intellectual justification of these child stars for people who preferred "natural simplicity" to "complicated art" and who argued that

---

[16] *Knickerbocker*, 21 (April 1843): 373. *Mazeppa* and *Putnam, The Iron Son of '76* were the most successful of these plays.

[17] *Spirit of the Times*, 19 (March 17, 1849): 48; *Mirror of Taste*, 4 (November, 1811): 385.

[18] Bowery Playbills in Joseph Ireland, *Extra-Illustrated Records of the New York Stage*, HTC, ser. 2 3: 76, 116; Philadelphia Playbills (December, 1851), University of Pennsylvania.

[19] Noah M. Ludlow, *Dramatic Life As I Found It* (St. Louis, 1880), pp. 452–53. Ludlow went on to say that Miss Meadows was "as beautiful as an imagined houri," an odd simile for a girl of seven who could pass for six.

[20] William Dunlap, *History of the American Theatre* (London, 1833), 2: 257.

"Genius o'erleaps the cliff, where Labour never soars."[21] A surprising number of them, including Edmund Kean, Clara Fisher, Kate Bateman, and Jean Davenport, did go on to distinguished adult careers.

The regular theater often exploited oddity as well as youth. The "Belgian Giant," the "beautiful Albiness," and "the living skeleton" were some of the stars who gave between-act entertainments and performed in plays in the nation's leading theaters.[22] Perhaps most successful was "Signor Hervio Nano"—one Harvey Leach of Connecticut—a man with stunted legs who played starring engagements in roles featuring him as acrobat, gnome, fly, and baboon. But in a few years "the time was gone by" for Leach's exhibitions. Losing his drawing power in theaters, he was finally killed by an English mob when, dressed in some hair suit, he tried to pass himself off as a newly discovered nondescript.[23] Though a freakish novelty quickly lost its newness, newcomers or new combinations were always appearing. For awhile a giant, a midget, and an infant prodigy all pooled their talents in a melodrama, *The Wonders of The Age*.[24]

Such interests culminated conspicuously in the "museums" that became popular in the 1840's, which mixed deformity with drama and curios. An advertising pamphlet published by the Boston Museum indicated the appeal of these places which reputedly spread the drama's respectability among Americans. Its list of attractions—"admission to the whole is only 25 cents"—including Barnum's Feejee mermaid, Sully's painting of Washington crossing the Delaware, groups of wax figures, "500,000 articles comprising every rare and curious thing," stage performances of "Sterling and Witty Comedies, Thrilling and Ingenious Dramas, Soul-Inspiring Operas, Mirth-moving Farces or Gorgeous Spectacles . . ., the most liberal arrangements being made, both in the old country and this, for procuring living novelties such as Giants, Dwarfs, and Orang-Outangs, etc."[25] Museums of this kind achieved great success largely because they constantly offered at very low prices the miscellaneous amusements that regular theaters had offered only now and again. P. T. Barnum was important to the develop-

[21] Paine, "Address, Delivered on the Occasion of Master John H. Payne's First Appearance on the Boston Stage," *Works*, p. 207.

[22] Wood, *Personal Recollections*, pp. 362–63, 401.

[23] *Ibid.*, pp. 401–2; Odell, *New York Stage*, 4: 368; Carson, *Managers in Distress*, pp. 140–43; *Corsair*, 1 (February 8, 1840): 764.

[24] Alysius I. Mudd, "The Theatres of Washington From 1835 to 1850," *Records of the Columbia Historical Society*, 6 (1903): 239; Durang, *Philadelphia Stage*, n.s., 1:152.

[25] *Tom Pop's First Visit to the Boston Museum With His Grandfather, Giving an Account of What He Saw and What He Thought* (Boston, 1848).

ment of this kind of "orthodox theatre," but was even more significant as a man who helped draw most of these novelty performers away from drama and the theater and into the circus tent.[26]

The theater's nondramatic components often were pleasant enough. The manager of the Charleston Theatre early in the century reportedly remarked, "Give me de prette vimin and I will fill my house."[27] This audience predilection was often quietly exploited. The irrepressible John Neal, in Portland, Maine, commented on one actress's legs which were "the talk of the whole town": "They are very pretty legs—there is no denying that—well-shaped and sufficiently free—but why were they *gratuitously* exhibited? They were not in the bills of the day."[28] The answer was obvious. Reporting on Mrs. Mowatt's success in London, Ellen Kean said, with faint caress of claw, that she could not remark on the American star's acting "progress" because she had not seen her, "but I hear she is *looking very pretty* and *that is a merit not to be overlooked*."[29]

By the 1840's some critics were willing to be franker and more specific about actresses' charms. A correspondent for the *New Orleans Daily Picayune* wrote that one dancer had "the finest leg, the prettiest foot, and the most magnificent ankle that I have ever seen; while her arms, neck, shoulders, and bust are grand beyond description."[30] And some managers became bolder in their exploitation. Thus Francis Wemyss understood that the great success of *The Naiad Queen* was due to its "50 Female Warriors" led by Eliza Petrie and Charlotte Cushman (the latter soon to become America's great queen of tragedy): "Such a display of ladies' legs, no mortal man could resist the opportunity of seeing." The "*leg*-itimate drama" had begun.[31]

Not popularity alone testified that audiences were responsive to such talents. A student at the University of South Carolina noted in his diary one evening:

> One Mary Ann Lee, a dancer, has a benefit tonight. There was a great impatience manifested in the society tonight so anxious were the members

---

[26] *The Actor; or, A Peep Behind the Curtain* (New York, 1846), p. 27. Odell says that by the 1842–1843 season the circus "no longer stuck like a leech to the regular plays." Odell, *New York Stage*, 4: 664.

[27] Alexander Placide, manager of the Charleston Theatre, 1795–1812, quoted in a letter from Mordecai M. Noah to Sol Smith, reprinted in Sol Smith, *Theatrical Management in the West and South* (New York, 1868), p. 205.

[28] *Yankee*, 1 (July 23, 1828): 239.

[29] Ellen Kean to Sol Smith (1850), in William G. B. Carson, ed., *The Letters of Mr. and Mrs. Kean Relating to their American Tours* (St. Louis, 1945), p. 73.

[30] Quoted in *Spirit of the Times*, 15 (January 10, 1846): 548.

[31] Wemyss, *Twenty-Six Years*, p. 344; *Spirit of the Times*, 14 (January 4, 1845): 540.

to see the last exhibition of this pretty little actress in Columbia. . . . All of the students, no not all either, but some of the most lascivious, have fallen dreadfully in love with her, and another here called Mrs. Skearet, both pretty women.

The student, having stayed in his room to study, concluded piously, "But who can reflect one moment and say he loves one of these women, whose virtue is as uncertain as a weathercock."[32] And a twelve-year-old Michigan girl wrote of a Detroit actress: "All the young men fall in love with her . . . she is so pretty especially Major Whipple for he goes every night to the play and he is afraid the people will see him and he sits behind the curtain."[33]

Music and dance, often integrated into plays, were also a regular part of the miscellany of a dramatic evening. Each company employed an orchestra and included a few members whose speciality was singing or dancing. The value of any player was increased by musical talent, and leading performers in dance and vocal and instrumental music regularly appeared in leading dramatic playhouses. The Jenny Lind furor capped a half-century of such appearances, but other performers in nondramatic fields won similar success. The Austrian dancer Fanny Ellsler, the Norwegian violinist Ole Bull who pleased Americans by featuring an "Adagio and Grand Bravura Observations upon the National Air of Yankee Doodle," the Hutchinson family vocal group, "charming Humanity singers . . . who would sunder the chains of the bondsman, shatter the inebriate's cup, send the rickety gallows out of the sight of civilized man and reform the world"—all filled theaters as successfully as the best-liked actors or plays.[34]

Critics objected off and on to the jarring incongruity of dramatic and musical offerings. One magazine asked in 1802: "What would be Shakespeare's astonishment . . . to hear from the orchestra immediately after his inimitable dagger scene, the mysterious solemn strains of Yankee Doodle to please the gallery? Or after the mournful death of his Desdemona, a horn pipe or a country dance?"[35] But real controversy centered

[32] Giles J. Patterson, *Journal of a Southern Student, 1845–1848*, ed. Richmond C. Beatty (Nashville, 1944), p. 38.

[33] Laura Mason to Catherine and Emily Mason, August 10, 1833, quoted in Elaine McDavitt, "A History of the Theatre in Detroit, Michigan, from its Beginnings to 1862" (Ph.D. dissertation, University of Michigan, 1946), p. 45.

[34] Odell, *New York Stage*, 5: 17–18; *Spirit of the Times*, 15 (March 8, 1845): 20; *Minneapolis Falls Evening News* (October 24, 1857), quoted in Donald Z. Woods, "A History of the Theatre in Minneapolis, Minnesota, from the Beginning to 1883" (Ph.D. dissertation, University of Minnesota, 1950), p. 13.

[35] *Lady's Magazine and Musical Repository*, 3 (January, 1802): 3; *New World*, 5 (November 26, 1842): 351.

on the growing popularity of grand opera and ballet. Early in the century some had desired to banish "all unintelligible Italian airs, trills, affected squeaks and quavers," and a few critics like Whitman continued to lash "the stale, second-hand, foreign method with its . . . anti-republican spirit and its sycophantic tainting the young taste of the nation."[36] But by the 1830's critics noted with surprise that audiences had begun "to relish the Italian school of singing," and by the 1840's it seemed that "everybody except flatboatmen and steamboat hands love the opera."[37] Ballet scored a similar triumph. When French ballet stars first appeared in relatively scanty costumes some ladies in Boston "turned their backs to the stage and tried hard, but unsuccessfully, to blush," and William Leggett in New York began a crusade against the immoral thoughts "occasioned by the immodest pranks of half-naked dancers" whose "allurements" threatened to sap America's moral strength. But the "vicious and baneful mummery" of ballet proved continually popular.[38]

Despite this wealth of variety, drama remained the central feature of the great majority of theatrical evenings. Of course, the plays, like the miscellaneous entertainment they competed with, varied considerably. Within a week a theatrical company might offer as the evening's feature play a melodrama, a Shakespearean tragedy, an opera, an eighteenth-century comedy, and a fairy-tale play. Because even successful plays customarily ran only for a few days and then were revived for one or two nights season after season, it is difficult to determine their popularity with much exactness. Performance records compiled by historians of the theater in particular cities permit some rough statistics about play popularity, however. Tabulation of the "top twentyfive" plays, to apply modern modes of numerical exactness to a problem given only vague verbal consideration during the period, gives some clue to the best-liked plays during the half-century.

Philadelphia was one of the major Eastern theatrical centers, Charleston the most important one in the South, and St. Louis and New Orleans the home base for most troupes acting in the Trans-Appalachian region. By tabulating play popularity in these cities during segments of the half century—using the War of 1812 and the advent of Jackson as chrono-

---

[36] William Haliburton, *Effects of the Stage on the Manners of the People* (Boston, 1792), p. 11; Walt Whitman, *Brooklyn Eagle* (December 4, 1846), in *The Gathering of the Forces*, ed. Cleveland Rodgers and John Black (New York, 1920), 2: 346–49; *Yankee*; 1 (September, 1829): 146–50.

[37] *Dramatic Mirror* (Boston), 1 (February 13, 1829), no. 15; letter from New Orleans in *Spirit of the Times*, 12 (July 16, 1842): 229.

[38] *Dramatic Mirror* (Boston) (September 16, 1829), no. 2; *Critic*, 1 (November 15 and 22; December 13 and 20, 1828): 48, 63–64; 111–12, 128.

logical divisions—one gets a rough idea of those plays most often seen by Americans. (See Appendix 1, Tables 1–6).

Perhaps the most striking feature of these lists is the high quality of those dramas of most sustained popularity. Of the plays that qualified on over half the lists, three were by Shakespeare: *Richard III* (which appeared on 8 of the 9 lists), *Hamlet* (7), and *Macbeth* (6). Kotzebue's *Pizarro*, along with *Richard*, appeared on all but one list. Two of the best comedies presented in the period—Sheridan's *School for Scandal* and John Tobin's *The Honeymoon*—qualified on six lists, as did the story of Cinderella, in various forms.

Although the general pattern of performance is similar, slight variances in emphasis in different cities emerge. In the periods after 1815, for example, Charleston had fewer performances of melodramas and more of high comedy and of opera than the other cities—a sign perhaps that its theatrical audiences were slightly more aristocratic than those elsewhere. On the other hand, the lists for New Orleans and St. Louis give greater prominence to melodrama and slightly less to Shakespeare and eighteenth-century plays, suggesting that a more westerly situation did work to loosen the ties of the old and to quicken acceptance of the new. All the American plays on the lists, except for the Dunlap translations from the German, qualified in New Orleans only: Mordecai M. Noah's *Wandering Boys* and *She Would Be a Soldier*, Payne's adaptation from the French, *Thérèse*, and Henry Wallack's dramatization of a Cooper novel, *Paul Jones*. The most exotic of American cities was seemingly the most enthusiastic about native drama.

Changes in the kind of play most popular in different periods of the half-century were also slight. Kotzebue's vogue at the beginning of the century and the great success of *Uncle Tom's Cabin* in 1853 marked intellectual epochs for the American theater. In the interim the public expended its greatest enthusiasm on performers of special merit or fame. The one major shift of interest is toward opera and ballet in the later period. Bellini, Auber, and Rossini wrote six operas that qualified on the lists for the 1830–50 period.[39] Other composers such as Mozart, Weber, Donizetti, and later Verdi also achieved conspicuously frequent hearings. Certainly, the public's musical understanding had advanced greatly since the early decades of the century when an actress faced insult and even injury from the audience when she sang a "bravura song" on the New York stage. By mid-century, however, as audiences became more

---

[39] Opera's position on these lists is a little low because the Roppolo lists for New Orleans exclude operatic performances.

experienced and demanding, performances by regular acting companies became less feasible. Consequently opera was more and more left to a few companies that gave increasingly satisfactory and expensive performances to a more limited group of patrons.

Another tendency was a change in the most prominent type of melodrama. In the earlier periods those of the exotic and fairy-tale variety were played most often, while on the post-1830 list the leading melodramas concentrated more on domestic situations and contemporary settings. The change from *Blue Beard* and *Cinderella* to *Lady of Lyons* and *Black-Eyed Susan* suggested the trend toward greater "realism"—though realism still encased in the melodramatic framework—that was to accelerate in the second half of the century. The shift in popularity of the two important Kotzebue plays underlines this change of emphasis. The exotic *Pizarro* was at the top of the list for the two earlier periods while the domestic drama, *The Stranger*, was played less often. But in the final period *The Stranger* gained in popularity and was performed more frequently than the heroic play.

One of the greatest weaknesses of such statistics is that, while they fairly suggest the most popular plays, they do not give a reliable picture of the type of play most often seen. No specific melodrama held its popularity so well as the best Shakespearean tragedies, but the melodramatic form in which new plays were easily cast showed great and increasing attraction. To give some sense of the number of performances of different kinds of plays in given years, the productions during each tenth year were categorized for the cities of Charleston, Philadelphia, New Orleans, and St. Louis, and the percentage of feature productions offered in each category calculated. (See Appendix 2, Tables 7–9). Particular circumstances influence the results strongly—for instance, the great preponderance of Renaissance plays in Philadelphia in 1811 largely reflects George Frederick Cooke's presence—but some trends of taste can be deduced despite these circumstantial fluctuations. The only figures available for 1800, those for Charleston, suggest the enthusiastic early reception of Kotzebue and the turn-of-the-century comedies, which were the immediate precursors of melodramatic plays. In later periods the percentages point up the gradual increase in melodramas presented, with an accompanying decline in popularity of older plays, except in Charleston. In the westerly cities of New Orleans and St. Louis, both melodramatic and native plays were given comparatively often. The musical entertainments of ballet and opera also took up an increasing proportion of theatrical evenings until the 1850 totals.

*   *   *

William Dunlap had felt that the New York theater in 1802 was degraded by the "antipodian whirligig"; by 1851 Philadelphia playbills steadily repeated their promise: "Novelties are in constant preparation and will be produced in Rapid Succession."[40] Between Dunlap's report of an unusual and degrading innovation and the playbill's assumption of novelty as the desire of theatergoers occurred a change, not so much in the taste of the many, as in acceptance by the few. In the interim even the most critical reluctantly accepted the theater as the home of a great variety of oddities, as well as of all types of drama from the most maudlin to the most elevated. It was indeed, in Payne's phrase, a "motley mixture of amusements," a mixture only separated when population increase and growing class differentiation encouraged a complete division between kinds of entertainment, between the legitimate theater, the opera, the ballet, vaudeville, and the circus.

The separation, given impetus in the forties by the growth of highly successful "minstrel houses," and increasing rapidly after the Civil War, gave a consistency to dramatic presentations that was desirable. Critical complaint against the drama's contamination with horses, dogs, monkeys, fireworks, acrobats, deformed persons, and precocious children was well taken. One need not be a purist to feel that an evening of *Hamlet* is not best capped off with a display of tumbling, tightrope walking, or even with a mirth-provoking farce. Yet the change incorporated loss as well as gain: the loss of a primitive vitality in the legitimate theater and the loss of all intellectual content and seriousness of purpose in the circus and vaudeville houses. In 1828 James Fenimore Cooper could write that American theaters were generally superior to those in England partly because they were "not yet sufficiently numerous (though that hour is near) to admit of a representation that shall not be subject to the control of a certain degree of intelligence."[41] By midcentury that hour had come: the long uneasy union of drama and entertainment miscellany was ending in divorce and in the assumption of separate lodgings.

---

[40] Philadelphia Playbills (September 10, 1852), University of Pennsylvania.
[41] James Fenimore Cooper, *Notions of the Americans: Picked Up by a Travelling Bachelor* (London, 1828), 2: 149.

6

The Good Old Plays

"THE DRAMA of one period can never be suited to the following age if in the interval an important revolution has affected the manners and laws of a nation," wrote Alexis de Tocqueville. Because of the great democratic revolution which had gone its unobstructed course in America, Tocqueville concluded, "the great authors of a preceding age may be read, but pieces written for a different public will not attract an audience." Yet several generations of American playgoers belied Tocqueville's idea that in democratic countries "the dramatic authors of the past live only in books."[1] Throughout the first half of the nineteenth century audiences attested their continued enthusiasm for the "good old plays."[2]

Both the theater's need for a constantly changing bill and the lack of quality in contemporary productions caused the stage to be a treasure trove of the best of earlier drama. These plays were given not as literary museum pieces, but because they retained their ability to move and to amuse. Because old plays were numerous, managers and audiences had a wide selection; because they were in no way protected, they could be altered freely; because they were presented alternately with contemporary productions, they gave audiences and critics alike a chance to judge them comparatively. In all these ways—selection, alteration, and criticism—the nineteenth century revealed something of its own attitude in its handling of the dramatic heritage of the sixteenth, seventeenth, and eighteenth centuries.

On the scenic curtain of Ludlow and Smith's New Orleans theater was

---

[1] Alexis de Tocqueville, *Democracy in America*, ed. Phillips Bradley (New York, 1957), 2: 89.
[2] *American Monthly Magazine and Critical Review*, 2 (February, 1818): 299.

a picture of "Shakespeare borne in a halo of light on the pinions of the American eagle."[3] Critical acclaim and frequency of performance, as well as the curtain painting, attested Shakespeare's dramatic divinity. And a few of the Shakespearean alterations that were presented on the American stage of the early nineteenth century gave truth to the image of the bard in the claws of the American eagle. Shakespeare, as James Fenimore Cooper noted, was "the great author of America."[4] The crudest of dramatic groups—a circus in Davenport, Iowa, or a theatrical cart in Portland, Maine—gave his plays, and all social groups responded to their witchery.[5]

No one disputed that Shakespeare was the greatest dramatist who had ever written. Americans of the nineteenth century shared, or perhaps borrowed, the enthusiasm of writers like Schlegel and Madame de Staël on the Continent, and probably more directly of Hazlitt and Lamb and Coleridge in England. Seventeenth- and eighteenth-century complaints about Shakespeare's breaking classical rules regarding the unities or the separation of comedy and tragedy were in general forgotten. His poetic power, his breadth of understanding, his inclusiveness, indeed his lack of concern for classical standards endeared him to romantic critics.[5] Here was a writer too great to be bound by the "common shackles" of literary conventions.[6]

Although some thought Shakespeare could do little wrong, others, less wholly concerned with aesthetic considerations, felt his works possessed great weaknesses. Religious writers especially insisted that Shakespeare, in tragedy and comedy alike, had a fatal flaw: an imperfect sense of morality. Shakespeare's genius was admirable and his knowledge of human nature great, but "what heart affected with a deep concern for religion or even a pure morality, does not wish that his genius had been directed in a better channel?"[7] "His licentious witticisms—his lascivious insinuations—his corrupt allusions" all rendered his plays "in a moral light, the objects of indignation and disgust."[8] The dramatic statue that

---

[3] John S. Kendall, *The Golden Age of the New Orleans Theatre* (Baton Rouge, 1952), p. 210.

[4] James Fenimore Cooper, *Notions of the Americans: Picked Up by a Travelling Bachelor* (London, 1828), 2: 148–49.

[5] Joseph S. Schick, *The Early Theatre in Eastern Iowa* (Chicago, 1939), pp. 34–35; *Dramatic Mirror* (Boston), 1 (February 18, 1829), no. 18. The *New Orleans Daily Picayune* (March 14, 1844) wrote, "the play-going portion of our negro population feel more interest in, and go in greater numbers to see, the plays of Shakespeare" than any other. Quoted in Joseph Roppolo, "Hamlet in New Orleans," *Tulane Studies in English*, 6 (1956): 74.

[6] *North American Review*, 38 (January, 1834): 173–74. See Augustus Ralli, *A History of Shakespearean Criticism*, vol. 1 (London, 1932), for a competent précis of developing critical attitudes.

[7] *Recorder*, 3 (February 10, 1818): 28.

[8] *Alice, the Negro* (New York, n.d.), p. 3.

Shakespeare had carved, the youthful Ralph Waldo Emerson noted in his diary, "is colossal, but its diabolical features poison our admiration for the genius which conceived . . . it."[9] In Mrs. Trollope's only literary conversation in Cincinnati an American informed her: "Shakespeare, Madam, is obscene, and, thank God, we are sufficiently advanced to have found it out!"[10]

Even persons with "an ardent desire for the prosperity of the theatre, as a school of nature and a mirror in which mankind are seen" shared many of these qualms. "Not even Shakespeare, all-powerful as is his name," wrote a critic in a common vein, "should sanction vulgarity and coarse allusions." Fanaticism and bigotry had no place in dramatic criticism, but neither had anything "which tends to loosen the ties of morality, or lessen our attachment to pure virtue" a place in drama.[11] A leading Shakespearean actor asked rhetorically: "But if we are devoted to Shakespeare's excellences, why should we preserve his blemishes? Cannot . . . some omissions be permitted especially when we are not assured whether they are original mistakes, errors of copyists, or the interpolations of intruding editors?"[12] The answer was not only that theater managers could remove, but that they had a moral obligation to pare away what marred Shakespeare's creations. "Why should passages be retained on the stage," queried one manager, "which no well-bred man would venture to read to his sister, daughter or female visitor?" "Cannot the manager erase?" asked one critic. "Why then must innocence blush and modesty hide her face?"[13] Some even argued that the more "indelicate" plays like *The Merry Wives of Windsor* should be banished from the stage as "attempts to destroy the morals of our mothers, our wives, and our daughters." The critic hoped that the comedy's unwholesomeness was counteracted by the afterpiece, "a melodrama calculated to instruct the heart to shun vice and cherish virtue."[14]

[9] Ralph Waldo Emerson, *Journals* (1821), ed. Edward W. Emerson and Waldo E. Forbes (Boston, 1909–14), 1 : 59.

[10] Frances Trollope, *Domestic Manners of the Americans*, ed. Donald Smalley (New York, 1960), p. 92.

[11] *Polyanthos*, 1 (December, 1805): 61; *Observer*, 2 (October 31, 1807): 283. The critic felt that *The Merry Wives of Windsor* did tend to loosen ties of morality and pure virtue.

[12] James Fennell, *An Apology for the Life of James Fennell* (Philadelphia, 1814), p. 460. Fennell was bothered not by Shakespeare's "indecencies, as they are in this age of refinement termed," but by his historical inaccuracies.

[13] William Wood, *Personal Recollections of the Stage* (Philadelphia, 1855), pp. 432–33; *Polyanthos*, 1 (December, 1805): 61.

[14] *New York Mirror*, 1 (May 29, 1824): 350; 2 (November 13, 1824): 126.

Nineteenth-century America's problem with Shakespeare was profounder than mere concern about his occasional "grossness and vulgarity" in language or situation.[15] An American housewife and sometime playwright wrote about how as a girl she " went to school to Shakespeare, and absorbed his teachings into my pilgrim blood": " Macbeth, Lear, how the world needed those chaotic, appalling experiences, and how women needed just such a creation as Richard III to set them thinking."[16] Mrs. Smith didn't say about what Richard set her thinking, but her response was perhaps typical. People were moved by the " vastness " and seeming honesty of the " chaotic, appalling experiences " in Shakespeare, while they were committed to the faith that the universe was ordered, benevolent, and morally progressive.

This conflict showed itself clearly in the lessons which were read into Shakespeare's plays. The colonial device of advertising plays as "moral dialogues in five parts," illustrating for instance in *Othello* "the evils of jealousy and other bad passions, and proving that happiness can only spring from the pursuit of virtue,"[17] was not solely a means of circumventing restrictions on dramatic representations. Such maxims people wanted to find. Thomas Jefferson argued that the worth of *Lear* was that it encouraged "a lively and lasting sense of filial duty" better than "all the dry volumes of ethics and divinity."[18] John Quincy Adams, to take the best known of the nineteenth-century critical dabblers, illustrated this tendency at its worst in his discussion of *Othello*. After rejecting "the common explanation" that Shakespeare was saying "beware of jealousy," Adams proffered his own idea: "The great moral lesson . . . is that black and white blood cannot be intermingled without a gross outrage upon the law of Nature, and that, in such violations, Nature will vindicate her laws."[19] Other critics went to even more trouble in finding moral lessons. One writer typically felt obliged to protect Shakespeare

[15] *Emerald*, 1 (June 21, 1806): 86–87.

[16] Elizabeth Oakes Smith, *Selections from the Autobiography*, ed. Mary A. Wyman (Lewiston, Me., 1924), p. 56.

[17] Quoted in Alfred Westfall, *American Shakespearian Criticism, 1601–1865* (New York, 1939), p. 56.

[18] "Such moral teaching," he concluded, "is my idea of well-written Romance, of Tragedy, Comedy and Epic Poetry." Letter to Robert Skipwith (August 3, 1771), in *The Writings of Thomas Jefferson*, ed. Andrew Lipscomb (Washington, D.C., 1903), 4: 237–39.

[19] Adams to Hackett, in James H. Hackett, *Notes, Criticisms, and Correspondence Upon Shakespeare's Plays and Actors* (New York, 1863), p. 225. Written in 1839, shortly before he began to lead the abolition wing in Congress, Adams' letters expressed strong contempt for the "thick-lipped, wool-headed Moor" and for Desdemona, who "has been false to the purity and delicacy of her sex." "Upon the stage," Adams felt, "her fondling with Othello is disgusting. Who, in real life would have her for a sister, daughter, or wife?"

from the charge that Macbeth savored "more of a daring imagination than of moral utility." This misconception, the critic held, arose from lack of consideration of "the state of public opinion, at the era in which it was written." If this historical context were remembered, the play clearly became an exposé "of the doctrines of witchcraft and demonology" and "their pernicious influence on mankind." The reviewer felt that "the incurable attachment of mankind to superstition" made the message still meaningful.[20]

John Quincy Adams complained that when he said he "studied Shakespeare chiefly as a teacher of morals," he was told that "this was degrading Shakespeare to the level of Esop."[21] That the charge was made suggested that these explanations of moral utility were not universally accepted, at least in such simplistic form. Persons who discussed Shakespeare were neither simpleminded nor literarily insensitive. Yet the desire to prove Shakespeare "virtue's friend" caused even capable critics to reduce his moral complexity to the level of the moral clarity which they felt ought to exist.[22]

Desire for moral parable and qualms about Shakespearean impurities partially explained why early nineteenth-century audiences saw "the plays of this great bard" in "considerably altered, mutilated, or retrenched" form.[23] The acting editions published in the nineteenth century gave fairly clear indication of what theater managers felt it wise to change. The Inchbald edition of acted drama of 1808, that of Oxberry about 1820, and those of Lacy which were issued beginning about 1835 all gave plays "as acted at the Royal theatres, Drury Lane, and Covent Garden." These were essentially the versions given in America. The less complete American editions of acting drama gave plays "as presented at" both British and American theaters, and a leading American manager claimed he followed exactly the omissions made by the English licenser of plays for his Philadelphia presentations.[24]

The changes made in Shakespearean plays were of many kinds. Often minor characters were consolidated—the many servants and subordinate roles in *Macbeth* were all given to "Seyton"—both to cover any

[20] *Town*, 1 (January, 1807): 2.
[21] To Hackett, in Hackett, *Notes Upon Shakespeare*, p. 213.
[22] John P. Tansur, *A Poem on the True Use of the Drama* (Boston, 1838), p. 90.
[23] *Cabinet*, 1 (January 26, 1811): 58.
[24] Wood, *Personal Recollections*, p. 208. David Longworth in New York in the first decade of the century and William Turner in Philadelphia in the 1820's both began ambitious publishing projects of acting editions. More extensive editions followed later, most notably William Taylor's *Modern Standard Drama*, edited by Epes Sargent, and those of Samuel French. These all followed the British editions without significant variations.

shortages of actors and to lard minor roles so that they were attractive to capable performers. Thus the editor of one acting edition praised the blending of Rosse and Angus with Lennox and Macduff "to make them more worthy the attention of good performers and the audience."[25]

The majority of changes, however, were made to suit the tastes of audiences. Perhaps most important were omissions to meet time limitations. Although theater evenings were long, the variety of entertainment demanded that each part be reasonably short. Consequently, most of Shakespeare's plays were shorn of some of their more extraneous speeches and scenes. Most of these cuts were sensibly made. In *Hamlet*, the Fortinbras scenes were omitted as were the casket scenes in *The Merchant of Venice*—certainly the best major amputations that could be made to shorten the plays. A large number of other lines were also pared away, some of them, though not central to the plot, among the play's best passages. Both the Oxberry and Inchbald versions of *Hamlet* omitted the King at prayer and Polonius's catalogue of moral maxims for Laertes. These passages were both given in the later Lacy edition, as were most of the best known lyric parts that had earlier been left out. By midcentury the scholarship and adulation bestowed on Shakespeare came to make poetic considerations as important as those of plot in trimming these dramas.

Cuts because of time limitations were often indistinguishable from those made for other reasons. Often, but not invariably, sexual allusions were cut or changes were made to soften phrasing; "whores" sometimes became "wenches," and "maidenheads," "virtue." And passages not susceptible to such easy modification were frequently left out. But perhaps the amount of ribaldry and sexual allusion that remained was more surprising than what was cut. The remnant of "objectionable Shakespeare phrases in acting editions" could be "omitted or included as the star prefers."[26] The later Lacy editions tended to be more careful in disguising sexual allusions, often by substituting archaic or meaningless words for those that were immediately intelligible to the audience. Thus "cuckoldry" became "wittoldry" and "urinals" transmuted to

---

[25] A note on *Macbeth* in Bell's *Shakespeare* (1773), quoted in George C. D. Odell, *Shakespeare from Betterton to Irving* (New York, 1920), 2: 37. Most of the material and ideas on changes made in Shakespeare prior to the nineteenth century are drawn from this work and from Hazleton Spencer, *Shakespeare Improved* (Cambridge, 1927).

[26] Anna Cora Mowatt, *Mimic Life; or, Before and Behind the Curtain* (Boston, 1856), p. 155. Mrs. Mowatt claimed that by the 1850's "passages, even in Shakespeare, which were listened to by audiences a few years ago without manifestations of displeasure, are now entirely omitted by actors, and if spoken, would inevitably be hissed." *Autobiography of an Actress* (Boston, 1854), p. 441.

"medicals" or "pottels."[27] Such tendency to purify verbally did little damage to the plays. If the speeches of Mercutio and Sir John Falstaff were a bit less earthy in nineteenth-century adaptations, their general attitudes remained intact. Only complete impurists could much object to most of the changes.

Cuts were also made to purify heroines and heroes of any dross in their characters. For instance, Juliet, besides advancing to the respectable age of eighteen, no longer let Romeo kiss her at their first meeting and was less impatient while waiting for Romeo and less petulant to the nurse. And she was allowed to grieve at word of Romeo's banishment, but not to the point of saying that her parents' death would have saddened her less. The dimension which Romeo's initial love of Rosaline gave to his character was also taken away; the hero's having just given up his assault on another girl smudged for nineteenth-century viewers the outline of the tragedy of noble, pure, and star-crossed lovers.

Hamlet similarly suffered improvement. Passages where Laertes and Polonius warned Ophelia against Hamlet, those where Hamlet most cruelly bantered Ophelia, the queen's remark about his growing fat, the soliloquy where he spoke most specifically of his character flaws, beginning, "O what a rogue and peasant slave am I"—all were removed.[28] Even in the Lacy edition where the scene of the King trying to pray was kept, Hamlet's reasons for not killing him at that time were omitted. About this removal an eighteenth-century editor of acting editions commented, "The speech is here commendably thrown aside, first as being unnecessary and next as tending to vitiate and degrade his character," and the Philadelphia manager, William Wood, argued that the whole scene should be omitted because it was "great but repulsive."[29]

Another kind of omission was that of the "quiet endings" Shakespeare attached to his plays. Nineteenth-century audiences and particularly actors preferred strong curtain lines. Thus the scene ended quickly after Macbeth died, and in *Hamlet* the curtain fell on the hero's line, "The rest is silence." Bombastic death speeches however, which had been added in earlier centuries, were mostly dropped. Both Oxberry and Lacy, for

---

[27] Lacy edition of *The Merry Wives of Windsor*, Act II, scene ii; Act V, scene v.

[28] A correspondent to the *Richmond Compiler* (March 10, 1838) severely criticized an actor for making Hamlet seem cruel to the Queen and Ophelia in places (Quoted in Martin S. Shockley, "Shakespeare's Plays in the Richmond Theatre," *Shakespeare Association Bulletin*, 15 [April 1940]: 91).

[29] Bell's *Shakespeare*, quoted in Odell, *Shakespeare*, 2: 32; William Wood, *Personal Recollections*, p. 382.

instance, cut the Macbeth speech which Mrs. Inchbald in her 1808 edition retained:

> Tis done! The scene of life will quickly close;
> Ambition's vain delusive dreams are fled.
> And now I wake to darkness, guilt, and horror
> . . . .
> It is too late!—hell drags me down—I sink,
> I sink; my soul is lost forever. Oh!—Oh![30]

Some measure of the respect for Shakespeare can be seen in the removal of such appendages to his plays while similar passages, heavily underlining the moral lesson, were usually tacked on to contemporary productions.

Other seventeenth-century additions stuck more tenaciously to the Shakespearean repertory of the first half of the nineteenth century. This was especially true of songs and mechanical effects which had been added earlier. Thus the Macbeth witches floated on and off stage on machines, singing ditties like:

> Oh what a dainty pleasure this—
> To sail in the air
> While the moon shines fair,
> To sing, to toy, to dance, to kiss. . . .

The witches also kept some non-Shakespearean verses for their songs and new ingredients for their pot including things like "three ounces of a red-haired wench." Several songs were also warbled by Lorenzo and Jessica in *Merchant of Venice*.[31] And *Romeo and Juliet* featured a spectacular death procession for the heroine where a dirge was sung:

> Rise, rise!
> Heartbreaking sighs,
> The woe fraught bosom swell
> For sighs alone
> And dismal moan
> Should echo Juliet's knell. . . .[32]

In *The Tempest*, both the Inchbald and Oxberry editions retained a tasteless subplot—"the squalid brat of feeble Grub-street brains" and a

---

30 *Macbeth*, Act V, scene viii, in Inchbald, *British Theatre*.

31 The Inchbald, Oxberry, and Lacy editions of *Macbeth*, Act III, scene v, and Act IV, scene i; *Merchant of Venice*, Act II, scene v, Act III, scene v, vi.

32 *Romeo and Juliet*, Act V, scene i, in Inchbald, Oxberry, and Lacy editions.

"profanation," in which "hapless Will Shakespeare is unmercifully mutilated," writers called it—simply because it gave added opportunity for song and scenic effect.[33]

Richard III and *King Lear* were the only popular Shakespearean plays that were staged in seriously mutilated form. *Richard* owed its popularity as much to the eighteenth-century actor-playwright Colley Cibber, who adapted it "from a very extensive and settled knowledge of stage effect," as it did to Shakespeare.[34] The poetry for the most part was Shakespeare's, though Cibber pasted to *Richard III* selections from *Henry IV*, *V*, and *VI*, together with some memorable fustian of his own creating. His contribution was primarily to give stage unity and movement to Shakespeare's long and rather meandering drama. He achieved this mainly by making Richard "as odious and disgusting as possible" and by toning down the ambition and callousness of the other characters.[35] Particularly Queen Margaret, who in Shakespeare's play is almost a prophetic witch providing counterpoint to Richard's active demonism, was vastly diminished in importance. Consequently, Richard became not the cleverest and most conspicuously unprincipled of a group of people bloody with ambition and hate, but an embodiment of evil who "discloses the absence of every human virtue" and whose malignancy wreaked havoc among the essentially righteous in a "sort of melodramatic spectacle."[36] To set up a clear dichotomy between good and evil Cibber brought in the murder of Henry VI at the beginning of the play. The contrast between the saintly but weak king and the vicious and strong usurper established the mood of the drama. Structurally stronger and morally more in tune with the views of eighteenth- and nineteenth-century men, Cibber's version was the only major adaptation that lived well into the twentieth century.

The other popular Shakespearean play given in seriously changed form in the early nineteenth century was *King Lear*. In 1681 Nahum Tate altered the play to make Edgar and Cordelia lovers who, with the rescued Lear, lived happily ever after. In the nineteenth century there was some serious defense and much popular liking for this rearrangement. The serious defense took moral grounds. "The moral's now

---

[33] *Mirror of Taste*, 3 (June, 1811): 387; William Dunlap, *History of the American Theatre* (London, 1833), 1: 60; Mowatt, *Mimic Life*, p. 274; *Corsair*, 1 (April 6, 1839): 60–61.

[34] Francis Gentleman, quoted in Odell, *Shakespeare*, 2: 43.

[35] William Hazlitt, "Introduction" to *Richard III*, *French's Standard Drama* (New York, n.d.), 11: iv.

[36] *Virginian* (August 23, 1822), quoted in Richard Hadley, "The Theatre in Lynchburg, Virginia, from Its Beginning to the Civil War" (Ph.D. dissertation, University of Michigan, 1947), p. 30; *Spirit of the Times*, 15 (January 17, 1846): 560.

more complete. . . .," wrote one supporter of the adaptation, "for although Goneril, Regan, and Edmond were deservedly punished for their crimes, yet Lear and Cordelia were killed without reason and without fault. But now they survive their enemies and virtue is crowned with happiness."[37]

Most commentators were less moved by the improvement of the moral than by the "barbarous mutilations" of the poetry and the disembowelment of the tragedy. The wish was often uttered that "this mighty work of genius will no longer be profaned by the miserable, mawkish sort of by-play (I have no other name for it) of Edgar's and Cordelia's love."[38] Audiences, however, liked the mawkish by-play, though even the altered *Lear* was not among the most popular of Shakespeare's tragedies. The actor James Hackett explained that the young people who constituted the larger part of a theatrical audience were too "inexperienced to comprehend the dotage of the aged and tender father, and to sympathize with his consequent afflictions." Probably the fault was not only with the young. At the age of seventy-two John Quincy Adams wrote that the real center of interest in the play was not the disintegration of Lear at all but the woes of Cordelia.[39]

Certainly the main change in the adaptation of *Lear* was to turn attention on Cordelia and her loves. Indeed, in good nineteenth-century fashion, the villainy of Edmond was proved by his foul designs on Cordelia's chastity. One scene suggests the mettle of Tate's improvement. Attacked by Edmond's henchmen, Cordelia screams, "Help, murder, help! Gods! some kind Thunderbolt to strike me dead." The hero is close at hand. "What cry was that?—Ha! Women seiz'd by Ruffians. Is this a place and Time for Villainy? Avaunt, ye Blood Hounds. . . ." When Edgar reveals his identity Cordelia generously forgives him his madman's costume:

> These hallow'd Rags of Thine, and naked Virtue,
> These abject tassels, these fantastick Shreds,
> (Ridiculous ev'n to the meanest Clown)
> To me are dearer than the richest Pomp
> Of Purple Monarchs.[40]

Such situations and sentiments formed the substance of nineteenth-century drama. Yet the revising was done in the late seventeenth century

---

[37] *Emerald*, 2 (March, 1807): 128; Wood, *Personal Recollections*, p. 433.

[38] *Mirror of Taste*, 3 (June, 1811): 385; *Idle Man*, 1 (1821): 41.

[39] Hackett, *Notes Upon Shakespeare*, pp. 93, 228.

[40] Nahum Tate, *The History of King Lear* (London, n.d.), pp. 34–36; Act III, scene i, in the Inchbald and Oxberry editions.

at a time when Shakespeare was considered a barbaric genius who wrote well but crudely, and who could be improved by more civilized, tasteful, and morally correct minds. Nahum Tate, for instance, in the "Preface" to his *Lear* praised the invention and truth of the Shakespearean tragedy, which he found "a Heap of Jewels, unstrung and unpolisht; yet so dashing in their Disorder, that I soon perceiv'd that I had seized a treasure."[41] The stringing and polishing done by these playwrights of the Restoration and early eighteenth century all showed attitudes that approached the heart of nineteenth-century drama. Love of song and spectacle were the incentive for many of the additions, a preference for elevated rather than common or colloquial terminology stimulated most of the minor changes,[42] and a tendency to subordinate all else to a love story became the basic organizational device in Tate's *Lear* and *Richard II*, in Dryden's *All For Love*, in D'Avenant and Dryden's *The Tempest*, and in Cibber's *Richard III*. Even in *Macbeth*, D'Avenant added a scene to introduce the love versus honor theme in which the hero vacillated between staying home to tend Lady Macbeth and going out to lead his army.

Most important, all the alterations tended toward the morally simplistic, evidenced in the heavy-handed underlining of every moral point. D'Avenant was not content to let the story of *Macbeth* speak for itself. He had Macbeth specifically recite truisms as he expired and he fattened the part of Lady Macduff so that she became, with plentiful platitudes on the folly of ambition, the good opposite of Lady Macbeth.

The moral was also italicized by avoiding all nuances of character, by encrusting the bad with every conceivable flaw and removing all dross from the good. Dryden defined a literary character as "a composition of qualities which are not contrary to one another in the same person."[43] In line with this viewpoint society and its playwrights increasingly tended to polarize good and evil and to make their characters fit wholly into one category or the other. Thus Tate justified his Edgar-Cordelia love story in part because it gave "countenance to Edgar's disguise, making that a

---

[41] Tate, "Preface," *King Lear*.

[42] Spencer catalogues this elevation of diction by the Restoration amenders. In *Hamlet*, for instance, "poor wench" became "gentle maid"; "grunt" became "groan"; "buzzers," "whispers"; "popped," "stepped"; and "my inkie," "this mourning cloak" (*Shakespeare Improved*, pp. 181–82). Nineteenth-century editions never tampered so unabashedly with Shakespearean wording.

[43] John Dryden, "Preface" to his alteration of *Troilus and Cressida*, quoted in Spencer, *Shakespeare Improved*, p. 158. Dryden illustrated his contention by saying that a character might be "liberal and valiant but not liberal and covetous." Note that in his acceptable combination of traits, Dryden linked two positive characteristics rather than any morally ambiguous duo such as "valiant and covetous."

generous design which was before a poor shift to save his life."[44] Led by
a desire to promote virtue and refinement, these playwrights strove for
simplicity in moral viewpoint and for clear proof of divine or poetic
justice by the play's end. Edgar's concluding lines to Cordelia in Tate's
Lear summarized the tendency of most of these adaptations:

> Thy bright Example shall convince the World
> (Whatever Storms of Fortune are decreed)
> That Truth and Virtue shall at last succeed.[45]

The record of what an earlier period did to the plays of Shakespeare
shows that the nineteenth century inherited rather than invented the
moral and dramatic conceptions that most enfeebled its own plays.
Even while the nineteenth century released Shakespeare's dramas from
the melodramatic conventions of the revisions, these same conventions
remained inviolate in contemporary plays. The juxtaposition of Shakespeare and melodrama on the nineteenth-century stage, ironic in the con-
trasts of view and quality, was doubly strange in that contemporary
plays remained ever more tightly bound by the particular moral strait-
jacket from which Shakespeare was progressively freed. Time and critical
acclaim pardoned Shakespeare because he had written well, and the profundity of his plays increasingly mocked the concepts the age demanded
of its own playwrights.

Two other Elizabethan plays held the stage into the 1800's: Beaumont
and Fletcher's *Rule a Wife and Have a Wife* and Philip Massinger's *A New
Way to Pay Old Debts*. These plays indicated the two basic types of non-
Shakespearean drama that the early nineteenth century inherited from
earlier periods: comedy sophisticated and licentious and drama increasingly middle class and moral. The early comedies that continued
to be seen were really in a tradition opposed to the standards of the time.
The period's attitude toward its comic heritage was summarized in an
American critic's metaphorical history of English comedy:

> Comedy was then a robust buxom dame, whose fat sides ever shook with
> laughter, who did not permit sentiment to feed upon the damask of her
> cheek, or excessive delicacy to heighten its blushes. . . . In progress of time
> she became a court lady, fashionable and affected—witty and dissolute. . . .
> As she advanced in years she grew sentimental, assumed a more correct
> demeanour, and primmed up her lips at a naughty jest. She has since lost
> much of her portliness, is greatly addicted to punning, fond of caricatures

---

[44] Tate, "Preface," *King Lear*.
[45] *Ibid.*, p. 67.

and ever apes the newest fashion. . . . What is now styled genteel comedy, where fine gentlemen, kneeling, pour forth sentimental effusions to finer ladies . . . would probably have as little suited their tastes as our evening dinners, French cooking and made dishes."[46]

Critics recognized that what the lady had gained in propriety she had lost in real humor. Perhaps the problem was that comedy needed an element of rough vigor or destructiveness in its humor which was lost in plays primarily concerned with perpetuating social standards. Dunlap pointed out typically that from the Restoration period drama had been "rising in purity, though declining in force." "Sparkling wine" had been given up for "milk-and-water."[47]

The "robust buxom dame" of English comedy was represented on the nineteenth-century stage by Beaumont and Fletcher's *Rule a Wife and Have a Wife*. Considering the bawdiness of both plot and subplot and the centrality of sexual looseness to its humor, nineteenth-century acting versions did little to purify it. Some of the explicit sexual discussion was cut away; for instance, the soldiers were given fewer lines about the attractions of loose women and the extent of the heroine's libido was described in slightly less detail. A few changes were also made in word choice—for example, "lusty" was replaced by "comely"—but such verbal improvement was not applied systematically; a whore remained a whore as often as she was upgraded to a wanton. The most important change was that the heroine's newfound virtue rather than a servant's shouting frightened off her would-be seducer in the final act. This last-minute concession to morality, and a few lines added on the sanctity of marriage, seemingly atoned in the early decades of the nineteenth century for the play's acceptance of sexual vagaries as a source of amusement, however unsuited this was to "the refinement of the modern era."[48]

The "witty and dissolute" lady of Restoration comedy was even less in accord with nineteenth-century America than robust dames like Beaumont and Fletcher's heroines or Shakespeare's "Merry Wives." Most of the best drama from what a critic called "England's most dissolute, feeble-minded, contemptible era" was rarely performed.[49] Congreve's "brilliant wit and pungent satire," and Farquhar's "well-

---

[46] *Literary and Scientific Repository*, 3 (July, 1821): 42–43.
[47] Dunlap, *American Theatre*, 1: 127; *New York Mirror*, 6 (March 14, 1829): 287.
[48] Louisa Medina in the *New York Mirror*, 14 (September 17, 1836): 93. After 1820 the play was given infrequently.
[49] *New World*, 2 (February 6, 1841): 92.

drawn characters, happy incidents, and excellent dialogue" were appreciated, but their general banishment from the stage was nonetheless considered "an honour to the morality of the present age" because their literary skill was wasted "in dialogues of licentious ribaldry, and plots outraging every decorum of life and every moral feeling."[50] Their very ability to give wit to the depraved and to make amusing an "unrestrained contempt of principle" increased the danger that "youth, at least will be decoyed into the snare of admiration."[51]

That *The Country Wife*, with its world manned almost wholly by cuckolds and cuckold-makers, continued to hold the stage in the nineteenth century was due solely to its eighteenth-century mutilation by David Garrick, who changed the amoral farce into a conventional romantic comedy. Wycherley's cunning libertine who spread a false account of his impotency to gain free access to London ladies became a wholesome young man who truly loved the Country Girl. And this girl was no longer married to Pinchwife, but was only his ward and fiancée. Considering the total change in tone, a surprising proportion of the incident and dialogue was retained. Most critics realized that the removal of what "an improved taste delicately rejects" hurt the literary quality of the play, but they argued that "the witty dialogue of former times, blended with the purity and happy incidents of modern dramas" was the best compromise that could be tolerated. But even in the purified form, *The Country Girl* possessed enough "licentious vulgarity" to be thought unsuitable to "these modern days of refinement."[52]

More popular in the nineteenth century than any of her contemporaries was the early eighteenth-century playwright, Mrs. Susannah Centlivre. Mrs. Centlivre's comedies, relying more on comic situation than on wit, were more easily freed from what "could give offense to Morality, or force a blush from the cheek of Modesty."[53] And she was a skillful dramatic craftsman. The preface to an acting edition of her play, *The Wonder*, suggested the reason for its continuing popularity: "There is so much unceasing bustle in the plot, the incidents follow each other so rapidly, and the situations are so laughable that it generally pleases. Its motion is so quick, the spectator has no time to discover its defects."[54] With some

---

[50] *Comet*, 1 (October 19, 1811): 6; *American Quarterly Review*, 8 (September, 1830): 149.

[51] Inchbald, *British Theatre*, 8: 3.

[52] *Ibid.*, 16: 5; *Boston Weekly Magazine*, 3 (April 3, 1819): 82.

[53] An advertisement for a new version of *A Bold Stroke for a Wife*, to be presented for the benefit of a popular New York actress in the 1780's, in Joseph N. Ireland, *Records of the New York Stage* (New York, 1866–67), 1: 113. In this instance the play was cut from five to two acts.

[54] Oxberry, *New English Drama*, 11: iv.

of her racier dialogue deleted, nineteenth-century audiences enjoyed the cunning contrivances of her plots. But even Mrs. Centlivre's plays expunged were condemned for "coarse and vulgar allusions, and indecent expressions" that, one Mississippi newspaper opined, were not "calculated for this meridian."[55]

Early nineteenth-century reaction to *The Beggar's Opera*, with its jibes at social, moral, and literary conventions, was similarly uneasy. Gay's comedy was full of the moral maxims dear to the hearts of nineteenth-century playwrights, each of which was turned upon itself by the context. For example, Peachum and his wife worried about their daughter's virtue in perfectly conventional terms, but their concern was not that she save her honor, but that she expend it profitably. Underneath a canopy of moralisms, every character pursued unabashedly money and sex. The charm of the characters was that such complete roguery or obvious self-deception amounted to a kind of honesty. The Peachums and Macheath were not simply crooks and libertine; they were everyman made amusing by the clarity of their selfish pursuits. The genial cynicism of *The Beggar's Opera* created a moral world almost diametrically opposed to that of nineteenth-century plays. Even critics who saw "a moral design" or who enjoyed its "nervous and pregnant vein of satire" decried its "broad licentiousness."[56] That it was played at all is more surprising than that performances often called forth renewed moral objections to this "vulgar and licentious burletta."[57]

Richard Brinsley Sheridan, like Gay, aimed his comic shafts at conventional moralisms, but with enough propriety to give his plays, especially *The Rivals* and *The School for Scandal*, continuing popularity. In *The Rivals* Sheridan attacked exaggerated sentimental feelings by making them keep the young lovers apart until the woman's novel-inspired silliness and the hero's jealousy-induced fretfulness finally gave way to common sense and happy marriages. Common sense remained Sheridan's answer in *The School for Scandal*, though in this play sentimentalism became not ridiculous affection, but a front for vice. Sheridan contrasted a generous, genial reprobate and his scheming, dastardly brother, a "man of sentiment" who had moral maxims ready for every occasion the better to camouflage his nefarious schemes. Sentimentalism was proved guilty by its association with a complete villain, but the very

---

[55] *Mississippi State Gazette* (November 21, 1818), quoted in Joseph M. Free, "The Ante-Bellum Theatre of the Old Natchez Region," *Journal of Mississippi History*, 5 (January, 1943): 18.

[56] *New York Mirror*, 8 (August 14, 1830): 43; *North American Review*, 4 (November, 1816): 33–44.

[57] *American Monthly Magazine and Critical Review*, 1 (November, 1817): 32; *Dramatic Mirror* (Boston) 1 (February 24, 1829), no. 21.

simplicity of the device vitiated the criticism. Sheridan argued that the devil might quote sentimental scripture, but not that these scriptures were invalid; that people should live morally, which had little to do with prating about morality. The ending of the play, in which Charles refused to talk about reform but made clear that his love for Maria would banish all his former vices, was decidedly in line with the standards of moralistic comedies.

Because *The School for Scandal* rejected the husk of sentimental moralizing while retaining much of the kernel, it was at once an attack on the comedy of sentiment and the great model for nineteenth-century moralistic comedies. In the wit of some of his dialogue and the freshness of some of his characters, particularly the Teazles, Sheridan looked back to the older comedy; in the moral propriety he supported, he pointed the direction that his generation and the nineteenth century took. Sheridan was deservedly the most popular comic dramatist in the nineteenth century. He came closest to saving the best while attacking the worst in the moralistic comedy. An occasional nineteenth-century critic was uneasy about the obviously good Charles' carousing among drunkards and gamblers,[58] but taken as a whole the play contained, as one critic with some antireligious bias wrote, "more morality than a whole volume of sermons."[59]

In the late eighteenth century two other playwrights obliquely attacked the tradition of the sentimental comedy in plays of continuing popularity. Oliver Goldsmith's *She Stoops to Conquer* avoided sentiment by substituting eccentricity, mistakes, and comical situations. Perhaps the play's popularity suffered because its comic techniques were easily and frequently duplicated and expanded. Certainly its genial caricatures and farcical plot were borrowed in the nineteenth century by several "clever, bustling, and humorous acting" pieces which were essentially farces "elongated into five acts."[60] John Tobin's *The Honeymoon* was less easy to imitate. First produced in 1800 after its author's death, this comedy reverted in form and mood to Elizabethan models. Tobin wrote it in graceful blank verse and borrowed even his plot from several Elizabethan plays. The end product was an amusing comedy, "more the offspring of reading than of invention," but perhaps as good as any

---

[58] William Dunlap, *Memoirs of a Water Drinker* (New York, 1837), 2: 131; *Yankee*, 1 (July 9, 1828): 224.

[59] *Baltimore Weekly Magazine*, 1 (June 14, 1800): 61.

[60] *Spirit of the Times*, 14 (January 11, 1845): 552. The article was discussing the comedies of Boucicault.

work of literature so derivative could be.[61] In popularity and critical acclaim, *The Honeymoon* remained second only to *The School for Scandal* among comedies in the early nineteenth century.

Sheridan, Goldsmith, and Tobin all wrote in reaction to the kind of comedy that was prevalent in the second half of the eighteenth century. That period's faith in human improvement and man's amenability to right reason, its belief that human failure was a matter more of folly than of sin, underlay a series of comedies aimed at delineating and hence reforming the foibles of the day. Some of these were related in tone and manner to Restoration comedies, despite their greater propriety and overt moral concern. The comedies of Colman the Elder and Mrs. Cowley, for example, welded wit to mild moral purposiveness fairly successfully, despite complaints that the plays had "too many of the attributes of a homily."[62] At the same time, other dramatists, Richard Cumberland with special success, created a kind of comedy that was almost "all sentiment and no humor."[63] In the 1790's a group of successful comedies written by Holcroft, Reynolds, Morton, Colman the Younger, and Mrs. Inchbald united many of these strands: remnants of earlier wit, a good deal of sentiment, the friendly eccentrics of Goldsmith, and objectives of moral improvement. They served as a bridge between the comedies that predominated in the eighteenth century and the melodrama that usurped popular favor in the early nineteenth.

Many of these more or less sentimental comedies remained very popular. Critics generally expressed ambivalence toward them, compounded of moral approval and intellectual disdain. A typical opinion was that of a reviewer who concluded that although "in the eyes of literature" a sentimental comedy could "exhibit but few pleas for approval," it did offer "a happy medium for the exercise of manly taste without doing violence to female virtue." Admittedly, he argued, the plays of Congreve and Farquhar were much superior; "yet when its simple solidity has been opposed to the seductive brilliance of their immoral flights, we learn the value of humble purity."[64]

The lingering on the nineteenth-century stage of comedies written between Shakespeare's time and about 1750 was a triumph of "seductive brilliance" over the outlook prevailing in the period. On the other

---

[61] Robert Ewing, *The Theatrical Contributions of "Jacques" to the "United States Gazette"* (Philadelphia, 1826); *Mirror of Taste*, 4 (October, 1811): 296; Ireland, *New York Stage*, 1: 127.

[62] Ewing, *Contributions*, p. 62.

[63] *New York Mirror*, 2 (September 4, 1824): 47.

[64] Oxberry, *Acted Drama*, 11: iii.

hand, those serious post-Shakespearean plays that nineteenth-century audiences continued to see revealed the developing intellectual and dramatic trends which culminated in the melodrama. These plays both point toward the tastes of the nineteenth century and point up how long the melodramatic tradition had been in the making.

The interest in Philip Massinger's *A New Way to Pay Old Debts* centered in its hero-villain, Sir Giles Overreach, a grasping corrupt businessman who with fiendlike intensity and ingenuity pursued his one object, that of marrying his daughter into the high nobility. Like Richard III, Sir Giles was an evocation of total evil, made more terrifying by his strength of purpose and subtlety of stratagem. The character was an early stage representative of the businessman and one of the few attempts to give heroic dimensions to someone of this class. Both its concern with the avarice of the self-made man and its moral tone of virtue rewarded and vileness punished tied the play to the nineteenth century.

Qualms about mixing the sterling qualities of courage, industry, and forthrightness with the evil components of Sir Giles' character were assuaged because "every circumstance that occurs is a highly finished moral and almost every speech bestows some valuable instruction."[65] A few minor passages that impugned religion and a few longer ones that argued the impassable gulf between the merely wealthy and the truly noble were omitted, as were some of Massinger's most unctuously poetical speeches and his more archaic or earthy phrasing. The only other conspicuous omissions were several references to an impoverished hero's having lice and smelling bad. The nineteenth century preferred even its most oppressed heroes without lice or odor.[66]

Thomas Otway's Restoration tragedy *Venice Preserv'd*, which was frequently played in the nineteenth century, engrafted sentimental principles onto the stalk of traditional tragedy. Ostensibly a political tragedy which chronicled the defeat of a revolutionary plot against the Venetian senate, the play revolved around more personal problems. One hero was a completely apolitical revolutionary who joined the conspiracy in personal pique at his father-in-law, a senator. His motivation for betraying the revolution was equally frivolous politically; one of the revolutionaries had propositioned his wife. He was even surprised that his friend remained upset when he explained that, before betraying the

---

[65] William Hazlitt's "Introduction" in Oxberry, *New English Drama*, 1: viii.

[66] Inchbald and Oxberry editions, Act II, scenes i and iii. To the credit of the nineteenth century let it be said that the lines where Lady Allworthy pointed out the significance of Overreach's name were cut (Act V, scene i).

cause, he'd made the senate promise to spare the friend's life. Thus the real conflict was not over political issues or ideals but between conflicting demands of love and friendship. It was as loyal husband and friend that the hero took on pathos. The political plot simply enhanced the importance of the love-friendship relations by putting them in a life-and-death context. At times of extreme political turmoil like the French Revolution, so adamantly anti-democratic a critic as Joseph Dennie spied in the play "seditious babble, . . . the execrable cant of the moody malcontents of every age," and "the fruitful source of revolutions, a hideous and hateful brood, disturbing the order and marring the felicity of mankind."[67] But less excitable persons in less politically conscious eras concerned themselves with the expressions of conjugal affection and manly friendship with which the "tender Otway" had so bountifully garnished his play.

Nicholas Rowe, two of whose plays survived into the nineteenth century, looked back with admiration to both Shakespeare and Otway. He considered Shakespeare a great natural genius and wrote his most popular play, *Jane Shore*, "in imitation of Shakespeare's style." Yet he also admired Otway's ability to move all people possessed of "tenderness and humanity." Rowe argued that the proper end of drama was to produce in audiences "pity," which he defined as "a sort of regret proceeding from good nature."[68] This desired dramatic result was to be promoted by a change in the social classes with which drama concerned itself. In one of his prologues, Rowe propounded that "the fate of kings and empires" was no longer suitable for audiences, because "we ne'er can pity what we ne'er can share." Hence "a melancholy tale of private woes" was preferable on the modern stage.[69]

In *Jane Shore* the title character had deserted her husband to become the king's mistress. Throughout the play she lived in virtuous penitence over her former sins, and at the final curtain she harshly died, which gave the story a perfectly moral resolution calculated to discourage female unchastity. For any spectator who might miss the point, a character suggested after the heroine's death:

> Let those who view this sad example know,
> What fate attends the broken Marriage Vow;

---

[67] *Port-Folio*, 1 (March 28, 1801): 103; Ewing, *Contributions*, p. 177.

[68] Nicholas Rowe, Dedicatory Epistle to *The Ambitious Step-Mother*, quoted in Aline Taylor, *Next to Shakespeare* (Durham, N.C., 1950), pp. 250–51.

[69] Prologue to *Fair Penitent* (London, 1703). Early in the nineteenth century this play's popularity plummeted because of moral objections to the plot. Even the writers of the *Salmugundi Papers* (1 [September 19, 1807]: 142) argued that if fewer women saw the play, "the number of 'Fair Penitents' [would] in all probability diminish."

And teach their children in succeeding Times,
No common Vengeance waits upon these Crimes
When such severe repentance could not save
From Want, from Shame, from an untimely Grave.[70]

Such a conclusion clearly presaged nineteenth-century dramatic conventions, as did a great many speeches in the play. Because Rowe wrote at the beginning of the eighteenth century and because his strength lay in ability to "express popular and obvious sentiments," some ideas from his *Jane Shore* suggest with particular clarity the long lineage of melodramatic conventions.[71] The heroine, for example, has a speech about one false step ruining a woman:

If poor weak woman swerve from nature's rule,
If strongly charmed she leave the thorny way,
And in the softer paths of Pleasure stray,
. . . .
In vain with tears the loss she may deplore,
In vain look back to what she was before,
She sets, like stars that fall to rise no more.

Another character attacks the coupling of virtue and rank in a tone that was repeated constantly in the more democratic nineteenth century:

Though no gaudy titles grac'd my birth,
Titles, the servile Courtier's lean reward,
Sometimes the Pay of Virtue, but more oft
The Hire which greatness gives to Slaves
                                    and Sycophants.
Yet Heav'n that made me honest, made me more
Than ever King did, when he made a Lord.

There was even a long section about escape from the vanity and viciousness of court and city life to "a peaceful little retreat, . . . a lowly but a healthful dwelling."[72]

The sentiments of such extracts could fit into almost any nineteenth-century play, but even more significant in connecting these dramas with the melodramatic tradition was the centrality in their plots of women and the problem of female chastity, connected with the desire to arouse pity in an increasingly bourgeois audience. The fame and success of *Jane Shore* was indeed, in Hazlitt's phrase, "embalmed in the tears it has drawn from numberless eyes."[73]

---

[70] Nicholas Rowe, *Jane Shore* (London, 1713), p. 63.

[71] Oxberry, *New English Drama*, 2 : i.

[72] Rowe, *Jane Shore*, pp. 11–12, 22, 24.

[73] Oxberry, *New English Drama*, 2 : ii.

John Home's *Douglas*, a tragedy of the mid-eighteenth century repeated often in the early 1800's, followed in the tradition of Otway and
Rowe. The praise *Douglas* won always stressed that it encompassed
modest achievements with grace. "Its plot is simple," wrote an American
critic, "its diction polished, well-sustained, and energetic, and we know
not where to find, in modern tragedy, more genuine pathos or a finer
strain of eloquence."[74] Its "genuine pathos" put it clearly in the tragic
tradition of Otway and Rowe, but with Home the methods and objectives of the tradition had clarified as the plea in his prologue showed:

> A wife! a mother! pity's softest names:
> The story of her woes indulgent hear,
> And grant your supplicant all she begs, a tear.[75]

The "wife and mother" tied together the other characters: a kindly but
jealous and unloved husband, a vicious stepson who had unwholesome
designs on both the lady and the lands, and her noble and long-lost son
by a husband of her youth.

While the pathos and domesticity of the play was much like that of
Otway and Rowe, *Douglas* moved closer to the nineteenth century. The
plot motif of a baby lost in a terrible storm but showing up as a thoroughly
noble young man despite his rearing in a shepherd's cottage was clearly
a preview of coming attractions. And perhaps most important, *Douglas*
not only featured a man with designs on the heroine's chastity as did the
plays of Rowe and Otway, but also turned him into a complete villain
and the main agent for causing the whole catastrophe, a kind of *diabolus
ex machina*. The emphasis on this character lessened Home's sense of
destiny, especially in nineteenth-century versions of the play. The
longest section omitted in these acting editions was Home's major
passage on the destructive power of fate.[76]

This disbelief in a fate unheedful of human justice probably kept the
best of bourgeois tragedies, George Lillo's *Fatal Curiosity*, off the stage.
The stage popularity of Lillo, a merchant and religious dissenter, rested
on *George Barnwell*, a play about a London youth, the purpose of which

---

[74] *American Monthly Magazine and Critical Review*, 1 (August, 1817): 298.

[75] John Home, *Douglas* (London, 1757). The *North American Review* (13 [July, 1821]: 228) pointed
out that the play's power came from its presentation of "the distress of maternal affection."

[76] The passage, occurring in a story told by a shepherd which was extraneous to the play's plot,
concluded:

> There is a destiny in this strange world
> Which oft decrees an undeserved doom,
> Let schoolmen tell us why. . . .

Home, *Douglas*, p. 41.

was explicitly to teach the moral precept that good apprentices must beware of bad women:

> Be warned, ye youths, who see my sad despair,
> Avoid lewd women false as they are fair,
> . . . .
> Ere innocence, and fame, and life be lost,
> Here purchase wisdom, cheaply, at my cost.[77]

Barnwell's life well illustrated his lecture. Apprenticed to a merchant who was wealthy, wise, and affectionate, surrounded by sincere friends, possessed of a wealthy and loving guardian, George was a thoroughly good and fortunate young man until he was seduced by the beautiful and unscrupulous Milwood. Urged on by the diabolic woman, who wanted to get his money and to destroy him in order to revenge herself on the sex and society that had betrayed her, Barnwell was driven to lie, embezzle, and finally to murder his uncle. The play ended with the execution of both the repentant, redeemed Barnwell and the still unregenerate Milwood. Its merits were those that mitigated the moral: Lillo's sense of fate, which nineteenth-century acting versions largely expunged; the sympathy and respect that Milwood's telling complaints against society aroused, which both relieved and deepened the horror of her conduct to Barnwell; and the tragic irony in scenes such as the one where Barnwell's employer stopped his confession out of an unwise but benevolent compassion for him. But these were merely touches of depth in what was intentionally and basically a moral tract.

The tract was a powerful one and its stage success immediate and continued. The custom of giving it at Christmas or Easter each year, at which time merchants supposedly sent "their apprentices, sons and daughters to visit it, for the moral and practical doctrines it inculcates," was long continued.[78] With theatrical tact, a manager even gave it on the eve of a young man's execution in Cincinnati.[79] The play regularly drew forth vigorous and divergent critical opinion. Most critics found its influence "of the most salutary character." "There is no play in our language," wrote one of its admirers, "better calculated to awaken the tender and virtuous sensibilities of our nature, none so perfectly unexceptionable in its moral tendency." Even after midcentury when the play was treated less seriously, a favorably disposed critic warned:

---

[77] George Lillo, *Dramatic Works*, ed. Thomas Davies (London, 1810), 1: 162.

[78] *Something*, 1 (December 30, 1809): 105. The editor described this as the practice in Boston, though the regularity of this procedure quickly broke down in America.

[79] Ralph L. Rusk, *The Literature of the Middle Western Frontier* (New York, 1925), 1: 434.

"Whoever shall despise the moral of this tragedy may, either in himself or his kindred, live to repent his folly and presumption."[80] The story of a real apprentice whose attendance on the play had checked a course of crime was a frequently repeated bit of theatrical lore. It was reinforced by more contemporary evidence of the play's wholesome effect, like the letter printed in a New York magazine which an apprentice had supposedly written to his parents after seeing *George Barnwell*: "I must confess the representation had an influence on my mind in favor of virtue and piety, which I pray heaven may never be erased."[81]

Hostile critics, however, voiced doubts about the play's moral efficacy. Most commonly they complained that the story of Milwood's being seduced "made her an object of compassion, when we ought only to hate her" and that some of her violent speeches struck "at the whole fabric of social order." "It's bad enough," complained a Boston critic, "to meet strumpets in our necessary intercourse with the world."[82] But even these criticisms suggest a basic acceptance of the moral influence of this sort of drama. For some it was "a stupid piece of dull morality," but few were the sceptics who held that George Barnwell's story would have no effect on the tendency to crime among apprentices.[83]

Eighteenth-century moral dramatists found things other than seducing women about which to warn their audiences:

> Ye slaves of passion, and ye dupes of chance,
> Wake all your pow'rs from this destructive trance!
> Shake off the shackles of this tyrant vice:
> Hear other calls than those of cards and dice.[84]

So wrote and spoke David Garrick in his prologue to *The Gamester*, the only other moral-lesson drama of the eighteenth century to last into the next. Its author, Edward Moore, warned against gambling by showing the fate of an essentially good man who was led to destruction by his weakness and by a treacherous friend who had designs on his wife. After cheating the hero of all his money, the villain had him framed for a murder. In the end the culprit was exposed and an uncle died leaving the impoverished family his money, but these events occurred after the hero had taken a fatal dose of poison.

Moore, a merchant and religious dissenter like Lillo, clearly followed

[80] *Boston Weekly Magazine*, 2 (December 27, 1817): 46; *Comet*, 1 (December 7, 1811): 92; Lacy, *Acting Plays*, 79: 6.
[81] *Ladies' Port-Folio*, 1 (March 25, 1820): 102.
[82] *Town*, 1 (January 3, 1807): 2; *Dramatic Mirror* (Boston), 1 (February 18, 1829), no. 18.
[83] *American Athenaeum*, 1 (June 2, 1825): 55.
[84] Edward Moore, *The Gamester* (London, 1756), facsimile edition, ed. Richard Peake, p. 419.

the pattern of *George Barnwell*. But his play strode closer to the nineteenth century, largely because the religious framework, the sense of inner sin contributing to the catastrophe, was lost. Moore's hero did not commit any crime against others. Indeed his trouble was his nobility and the depth of his friendship for the villain. Mrs. Beverley also suffered from an excess of goodness; although she knew her husband was gambling away their home and security, she gives everything to him and "never upbraids him."[85]

The loss of a religious framework reverberated in the change from terror to tears in the general mood of the play. Moore, like Otway and Rowe, wanted to inculcate pity in his audience. However he resorted to the painfully obvious to arouse this sentiment; his characters were innocents oppressed whose own tears flowed freely over their dilemma. In a play in which the hero was merely a dupe of evil rather than an active agent, the tragic ending was gratuitous. Apparently in answer to contemporary complaints, Moore justified his unhappy conclusion partly by saying such was necessary in tragedy, an appeal to literary tradition that suggested how divorced the tragic ending was from the substance of the play. Because evil was purely external, tragedy became outmoded, simply a literary convention. He further justified his ending by saying it increased the horrors of gambling. Moore had, as a nineteenth-century critic said in praise of *The Gamester*, "made drama wholly subservient to the interests of good morals and domestic purity." Because the play was "founded upon the affairs of common life," a critic concluded, "there is not in the whole range of English drama, a play of more excellent moral tendency."[86]

In his preface, Moore justified writing his drama in prose rather than blank verse by pointing out that he wanted it "to be a natural picture of that kind of life, of which all men are judges" and thus "it was thought proper to adapt its language to the capacities and feelings of every part of the audience." To have its low-class characters speaking in verse would be "unnatural, if not ridiculous; if the more elevated characters also speak prose, the judicious reader will observe that it is a species of prose which differs very little from verse."[87] In flowery inflation his prose did differ very little from bad verse, a tendency which the melodrama further developed. Moore's play clearly used most of the literary conventions that almost all serious plays employed in the nineteenth century.

---

85 *Ibid.*, p. 427.
86 *French's Standard Drama*, 13: iii; *New York Mirror*, 3 (June 10, 1826): 367.
87 Moore, *The Gamester*, p. 422.

Through the successive changes of dramatic emphasis in the plays of Otway, Rowe, Home, Lillo, and Moore, the drama of the nineteenth century was being ever more exactly foreshadowed. Even the more classical eighteenth-century tragedies that retained some popularity showed greater emphasis on tender passions and familial relationships. The very titles of some of these most successful in the nineteenth century —*The Fatal Marriage, The Grecian Daughter, The Rival Queens*—suggested the same emphases that were more extensively developed in overtly middle-class tragedies. Nineteenth-century Americans held "no very high opinion" of neo-classic plays like *Cato*.[88]

Americans in the early nineteenth century admired the "good old plays," especially those of Shakespeare, and saw them often—certainly often enough to make them conscious of the inferiority of the contemporary product. The lament over the decline of drama, despite enthusiasms for some plays and approval of drama's increasing purity, was loud in almost all criticism of the early nineteenth century. One critic wailed:

> Throughout all its changes, since the days of Shakespeare, none of which have, on the whole, been for the better, the drama seems at the present day, to be at its lowest ebb. Our theatres are more splendid than they were in the days of our ancestors; the pomp and circumstance of scenic machinery are more imposing; but the drama itself languishes, because the taste which should support it droops.[89]

The frequency of such complaints suggests that it was not solely a dearth of taste which caused the contemporary failure in drama. The taste of the nineteenth century, whetted on the best drama of earlier periods, recognized and desired good plays. There was simply a laudable yen for the new that accompanied respect for the old.

"Not even Shakespeare's plays, grand as they are," Walt Whitman complained, were suitable dramatic expressions for this new American democracy. Shakespeare was the preeminent representative of "the mighty aesthetic sceptre of the past," but something new was needed to represent "America and Democracy."[90] Although no dramatic pleasure was greater for modern man than "the varied beauties of Shakespeare" and "the sturdy old comedies," it was

---

[88] William Dunlap, *Memoirs of the Life of George Frederick Cooke* (New York, 1813), 1: 271.

[89] *Aeronaut*, 7 (October 21, 1817): 105–6.

[90] Walt Whitman, *Specimen Days*, in *Complete Prose Works* (New York, 1914), p. 288; *Good-Bye, My Fancy*, p. 500; *November Boughs*, p. 394.

no disrespect to those glorious old pieces and their authors to say that God's heavenly gift of genius has not been confined to them. . . . We have here in this land a new and swarming race, with an irrepressible vigor for working forward to superiority in *every thing*. As yet, it is true, all seems crude, chaotic, and unformed, but over the surface of the troubled waters, we think we see far ahead the Ararat, and the olive tree growing near. The drama *must* rise.[91]

Whitman and his fellow Americans continued to await the coming of the new drama "in silence and in twilight," convinced that it was "the twilight of the dawn."[92] But this dramatic dawn remained just beyond the horizon. Intellectual and social changes that had been waxing for centuries prevented the development of plays that were at once good and vital to America and democracy.

---

[91] Walt Whitman, *Brooklyn Eagle* (April 19, 1847), in *The Gathering of the Forces*, eds. Cleveland Rodgers and John Black (New York, 1920), 2: 336–37.

[92] Whitman, *Specimen Days*, p. 295.

7

In Search of a National Drama

THE ISSUE of "who reads an American book, or . . . sees an American play" was of burning concern to the nation's writers and critics long before Sydney Smith made his famous taunt. Few Americans doubted their country's political and material superiority, but those with literary inclinations had long felt, as Whitman asserted, that the final test of any truly vital society was its artistic contribution and that someday "a great and original literature is sure to become the justification and reliance of American democracy."[1] Americans had "wants and necessities . . ., which the locomotive and the steamer cannot supply," and which would be satisfied only when America's literature began to flourish like its commerce.[2] "In due time," critics averred, the sturdy edifice of American society would inevitably be crowned "with the entablature of letters and arts," and "the inestimable glory of intellectual greatness."[3] The faith in this notion, and the consequent frustration, was especially clear in drama where no author gained sufficient acclaim to give America artistic credit abroad and confidence at home. Philip Hone, speaking at the cornerstone-laying ceremonies for the Bowery Theatre, voiced the common expectation: "Perhaps at no distant period the latent talents of some native Bard may here be warmed into existence, who shall emulate the growing fame, acquired in other walks, by Irving and Cooper, and

---

[1] Walt Whitman, *Good-Bye, My Fancy* in *Complete Prose Works* (New York, 1914), pp. 489–94; *Democratic Vistas*, in *ibid.*, pp. 197–203, 236–42.

[2] Uriel Wright, *Address Delivered on Laying of the Corner Stone of the Theatre* (St. Louis, 1851), p. 5; Nathaniel H. Bannister, *England's Iron Days* (New Orleans, 1837), p. 3.

[3] *Democratic Review*, 13 (July, 1843): 45; *Knickerbocker*, 2 (July, 1833): 7.

our city become as celebrated for taste and refinement, as it already is for enterprise and public spirit."[4]

The American playwright's desire to contribute "to the cause of a true national literature" reflected literary concepts that were developing in Europe.[5] Even as, for the first time in dramatic history, playwrights were achieving immediate international successes, the idea waxed strong that great literature must be a peculiarly national product springing from the *Volksgeist*. An American periodical reprinted, for instance, Schelling's essay which proclaimed that Shakespeare's genius was universal primarily because it was a manifestation of national character.[6] "The literature of a people, if it be good, will be peculiar," commented the *North American Review*.[7] The Enlightenment ideal of a cosmopolitan intellectual community sharing assumptions and ideas was being replaced by the notion that great genius must "arise from and grow up with the soil with which it may be connected."[8] If the American past was too limited to permit a folk tradition like that represented by *Beowulf* or Grimm's fairy tales, then the United States, being a new nation, had the right and duty to begin one. The seventeen-year-old Anna Cora Mowatt, having read Schlegel's *Lectures on Literature*, patriotically wrote an epic for the new world, as had many Americans before her.[9] The *North American Review* summarized the feelings that inspired much early American literature. The Revolutionary War had destroyed "the monopoly of genius" and people had begun to enter "the sacred ground of poetry, without putting off their shoes." "The great epics of our country" were written because their authors saw "that all other great nations had their distinguished poetical works, and they resolved that their own land should not be without them; if no one else would write them, they would, though they had little leisure for the labor, and for the art itself neither propensity nor vocation."[10]

Critics argued that in drama particularly the "first essential" was "nationality," because it was "addressed to the people immediately" and had to meet "an ardent sympathy, or it is nothing."[11] And America

[4] Quoted in Theodore Shank, Jr., "The Bowery Theatre, 1826–1836" (Ph.D. dissertation, Stanford University, 1956), p. 14.

[5] Cornelius Mathews, *The Politicians* (New York, 1840), p. 8.

[6] *American Register, or Summary View*, 1 (1817): 259–87.

[7] *North American Review*, 19 (October, 1824): 305.

[8] *Knickerbocker*, 2 (July, 1833): 9.

[9] Marius Blesi, "The Life and Letters of Anna Cora Mowatt" (Ph.D. dissertation, University of Virginia, 1938), p. 28.

[10] *North American Review*, 30 (April, 1830): 314.

[11] *Arcturus*, 2 (October, 1841): 281.

had certain advantages that encouraged the development of a national drama. "The Genius of Liberty and the Liberty of Genius," went a toast at a banquet in honor of an American theatrical manager.[12] Many Americans believed in this direct connection between political freedom and literary potential. Sages like John Witherspoon had long taught that liberty was important to society because it alone "put in motion all the human powers," and hence became "the nurse of . . . literature."[13] The same conclusion was sometimes reached from a historical perspective; "the greatest efforts of human genius," Edward Everett assured an audience, "have been made where the nearest approach to free institutions has taken place."[14] America would be the home of great drama, Frances Wright asserted, because it was "the country where truth may lift her head without fear."[15] Certainly the dramatic muse who long had "cast a fondly wistful eye on the pure climate of the western sky," must soon grace the land where her friend, the goddess of liberty, held sway:

> Behold, Apollo seeks this liberal plain
> And brings the thespian goddess in his train.[16]

"The spirit of Democracy and the spirit of Literature are one," concluded the *Democratic Review*.[17]

In brief moments of enthusiasm the transplantation of dramatic art seemed almost an accomplished fact. George Washington Custis, called on stage by a great ovation after a performance of his *Pocahontas*, told his audience that America, which "gallant cavaliers" had found "a wild and savage desert," had become "the favoured seat of Civilization and the Arts." The reason for this "mighty change" was simple Custis concluded: "A single word, and the tale is told—Liberty."[18]

Soberer moments, however, found Americans perfectly aware that drama of genius had not as yet been written in the new world. Consequently self-conscious citizens pointed out aesthetic compensations for America's artistic barrenness. If the United States had produced no Shakespeare or Dante, it still had the Rockies and Niagara Falls "which

---

[12] Quoted in *Boston Weekly Magazine*, 1 (December 18, 1824): 158.

[13] John Witherspoon, *Lectures on Moral Philosophy* (Philadelphia, 1822), p. 120.

[14] Quoted in *North American Review*, 20 (April, 1825): 430.

[15] Frances Wright, *Altorf* (Philadelphia, 1819), pp. iii–iv.

[16] Robert Treat Paine, "Prize Prologue" (January, 1794), in *The Works in Prose and Verse* (Boston, 1812), p. 158.

[17] *Democratic Review*, 11 (August, 1842): 196.

[18] An undated newspaper account in an unnamed newspaper, reproduced in Murray Nelligan, "American Nationalism on Stage: The Plays of George Washington Parke Custis, 1781–1857," *Virginia Magazine of History and Biography*, 58 (July, 1950), between pp. 312–13.

would elicit poetry from Shylock."[19] This scenic splendor, like libertarian political structure, was supposed to produce artistic results; somehow the land of great "prairies, the rocky mountains and of the Mississippi and Missouri rivers" should produce great geniuses.[20] "They should be giants, too," said Fanny Kemble of the men who wrote in the shadow of American mountains:

> Have these glorious scenes poured no inspirings into hearts worthy to behold and praise their beauty? Is there none to come here and worship among these hills and waters till his heart burns within him, and the hymn of inspiration flows from his lips and rises to the sky? Is there not one among the sons of such a soil to send forth its praises to the universe?[21]

Americans with literary inclinations asked these same questions. "There is, there must be," something "within the mind of man" to respond to these external glories, an American playwright answered. His was the common faith: "Some spirit of beauty and truth must haunt us in our walks through scenes like these, and awaken the soul to action and utterance not unworthy . . . of its great inspiration."[22] Someday "America must have her drama, as magnificent as her mountains."[23]

The excuses offered for American artistic failure were legion, and to some extent legitimate. The age and nation were necessarily materialistic because a hard-working pioneer people with a continent to subdue had little time for art. Benjamin Franklin had earlier described America's artistic situation.

> All things have their season, and with young countries as with young men, you must curb their fancy to strengthen their judgment. . . . To America, one schoolmaster is worth a dozen poets, and the invention of a machine or the improvement of an implement is of more importance than a masterpiece of Raphael.[24]

Most critics would gladly have sacrificed a good many inventions for "the passion of one great Poet . . . to purify the national taste and elevate the national intellect," but they made the best of Franklin's argument and

---

[19] *Knickerbocker*, 6 (September, 1835): 273.

[20] Whitman, *Specimen Days*, in *Complete Prose Works*, p. 145.

[21] Frances Anne Kemble, *Journal* (Philadelphia, 1835), 1: 212.

[22] Mathews, *Politicians*, p. 7.

[23] Charles Durang, *The Philadelphia Stage From the Year 1794 to the Year 1855* (Philadelphia, 1854–60), 3: 246.

[24] Quoted in John Bernard, *Retrospections of America* (New York, 1887), p. 78. Bernard also quoted George Washington as saying that American dramatic development must await greater progress in practical matters (*ibid.*, p. 92).

espoused the idea that America's situation required that the development of "useful" arts precede that of "the elegant arts."[25] The day of literary greatness would surely come. After all, America was a young country, whose literary institutions were "yet in their infancy."[26]

Most playwrights, naturally unwilling to defer the possibility of literary greatness to futurity, found more specific reasons for the nation's dramatic failure. Hostile critics were a favorite target. James Nelson Barker claimed in the preface to his first published play that native drama needed "but the wholesome and invigorating breath of favour" to "bid it rapidly arise from its cradle to blooming maturity." But rather than giving needed encouragement "some critic beadle" always beat the bantling drama of American parentage.[27] "'Tis glorious sport, as all allow and say," complained another playwright in his epilogue, "to roast an author, and to damn a play."[28] The belligerently American critic and dramatist, James Rees, penned an epitaph for all American playwrights:

> Here lies
> A Neglected Son of Genius;
> A Native Flower
> which faded, withered, and died in a garden
> made up of
> FOREIGN EXOTICS.[29]

A few critics earned their sadistic reputation. They wrote off bad plays with few qualms: Dunlap's *The Glory of Columbia* was a "catch-penny production," Payne's *Brutus* contained much "foolish and presumptuous imitation," and Richard Penn Smith's *Eighth of January* was "a detestable heap of rubbish."[30] And on occasion critical disdain led to personal abuse: one reviewer claimed that *The Battle of Eutaw Springs* was not such a bad play considering that "the author must have had his brains blown out at this same battle," and another denounced Nathaniel Parker Willis as "a finical and dainty spotter of pure white paper . . . whose frequent puppyisms you often feel in a mood to kick outdoors."[31] Most critical

---

[25] *Arcturus*, 1 (December, 1840): 24; *American Quarterly Review*, 9 (June, 1831): 409.

[26] *North American Review*, 7 (July, 1818): 199; *Monthly Magazine*, 2 (December, 1805): 622.

[27] James Nelson Barker, *The Indian Princess* (New York, 1808), p. iii.

[28] Robert Montgomery Bird, "Epilogue," *Cowled Lover*, *ALP*, 12: 66.

[29] *Dramatic Mirror and Literary Companion*, 2 (March 26, 1842): 52.

[30] *Polyanthos*, 5 (May, 1807): 139; *Literary and Scientific Repository*, 1 (July, 1820): 223; *Yankee*, 2 (March 19, 1828): 92.

[31] *Monthly Anthology*, 4 (March, 1807): 163; *Missouri Gazette*, quoted in William G. B. Carson, *Theatre on the Frontier: The Early Years on the St. Louis Stage* (Chicago, 1932), p. 304. The attack on Willis was attached to a favorable review of his play.

strictures no more than matched the dramatic failings pointed out, however. Getting rid of "the insects of literature" was a worthy undertaking which critics took seriously,[32] and, judged by standards of literary greatness, most American plays deserved to be swatted.

Authors often attributed base and unpatriotic motives to their critics. Mordecai M. Noah mockingly dedicated one of his plays to its severest critic, William Coleman, who had damned the play admittedly without having seen it. Noah asserted that Coleman's condemnation grew from his lack of feeling for his country, whose independence both politically and culturally he was unwilling to acknowledge.[33] Other playwrights similarly blamed unhappy critical handling on subversive foreign influences and implied that any real patriot would like their plays.

Although many playwrights felt that there was an unpatriotic conspiracy afoot to put down American plays, their charges seem substantiated by little but their own testimony. Periodicals generally showed anxiety to find merit in American productions, and critics frequently introduced their disapprobation with assurances that "we have no disposition to underrate the merits of an American work" or "we read this play with a sincere desire of finding something in it worthy of commendation."[34] Among the many native plays, they kept hoping to find some that would "prove worthy of preservation"; when faced with another poor play, they were "glad to be assured that the thing is not of native production."[35] Critical attack testified to high standards rather than cast doubt on a "perfect willingness to encourage native genius and . . . disapprobation of the regular importation of plays from England;" they simply awaited plays that could profoundly arouse "national feeling, the great desideratum of a republic."[36] But certainly the American republic deserved something better than *The Glory of Columbia—Her Yeomanry!* or *Marion, The Hero of Lake George.*

Like critics, audiences and managers were charged with having "an unconquerable prejudice against American plays" and with hyper-respect for European success.[37] Managers, usually foreign born and with reputed "prejudices in favor of the mother country," were particularly liable to these complaints.[38] Occasionally, in the first years of the

---

[32] *Monthly Register, Magazine, and Review of the United States*, 2 (March, 1807): 243.

[33] Mordecai M. Noah, *Marion, The Hero of Lake George* (New York, 1822), pp. 2–8.

[34] *American Review and Literary Journal*, 1 (1801): 66; *Ladies' Port-Folio*, 1 (January 8, 1820): 10.

[35] *New York Mirror*, 8 (January 29, 1831): 239; *New World*, 6 (April 29, 1843): 519.

[36] *Emerald*, 3 (January 2, 1808): 124; *Analectic Review*, 13 (July, 1818): 70.

[37] *Ordeal*, 1 (May 27, 1809): 332.

[38] *New York Mirror*, 4 (January 20, 1827): 207; Walt Whitman, *Brooklyn Eagle* (April 19, 1847), in *The Gathering of the Forces*, ed. Cleveland Rodgers and John Black (New York, 1920), 2: 336–37.

century, managers did try to give foreign coloration to the domestic product. For example, the play *Fraternal Discord* was presented in Charleston as *Fraternal Discord in England*, and in Philadelphia James Nelson Barker's *Marmion* was originally disguised as the work of an English author.[39] Yet such devices were both unusual and of questionable value. *Marmion* was as popular after its American authorship was revealed as before.[40] The general practice was to emphasize, rather than hide, the American origins of plays, managers, and actors. Beginning with *The Contrast*, most native plays that aspired to the dignity of either prologue or epilogue stressed their American origins to arouse support. The manager's address at the opening of the first permanent theater in Boston set the tone of patriotic stress that persisted in theaters throughout the country:

> Let British Lords their haughty birth declare,
> I boast of being born—in Old North Square.[41]

During the War of 1812, patriotism became more strident. In Boston, advertisements announced that the theater was now even "lighted with new constructed lamps of AMERICAN MANUFACTURE" and English plays underwent a sea change: *Incle and Yarico* was subtitled *The American Heroine*; and *The Benevolent Tar* became *The American Tar*.[42] Certainly by the 1820's the advertising stress given to the American nature of plays, actors, and themes was proof that prejudices about "native talent" were generally favorable. Even when productions were belittled, critics expressed gratitude for "Americanisms and American allusions" and for anything which proved an author "no copier of foreign events and foreign ideas."[43] In the early 1830's two managers recently arrived from England, Thomas Hamblin in New York and Francis Wemyss in Philadelphia, based their enterprises on strident puffing of native talent and appeal to patriotism. In the 1840's even those critics most concerned for "American talent" admitted that the term had been made

---

[39] William Dunlap, *A History of the American Theatre* (London, 1833), 2: 296; William Wood, *Personal Recollections of the Stage* (Philadelphia, 1855), pp. 187–88.

[40] In his autobiography, Wood claimed that the play failed when the author's citizenship was revealed, but this simply did not happen. Arthur Hobson Quinn, *A History of the American Drama from the Beginning to the Civil War* (New York, 1943), p. 141; Durang, *Philadelphia Stage*, 2: 107.

[41] "Address," by Col. J. S. Tyler (1795), quoted in William W. Clapp, *Records of the Boston Stage* (Boston, 1853), p. 26.

[42] Lucile Gafford, "Boston Stage and the War of 1812," *New England Quarterly*, 7 (June, 1934): 327–28.

[43] *Analectic Review*, 13 (July, 1818): 69.

"somewhat nauseous by the use it has served for charlatans."[44] Disappointed playwrights continued to suggest that they were victims of unpatriotic feelings, but probably they were more often beneficiaries of a belligerent national pride. The manager, William Burton, didn't begrudge the $250 he had paid James Fenimore Cooper for an unsuccessful comedy lampooning socialism, because the venture had given his theater the financially desirable reputation of "encouraging American dramatic production."[45]

"Prejudices against native productions and particularly to transatlantic literature" were seemingly nothing more than a vague "intellectual cowardice" and acquiescence in accepted authority, which centered at this time in London and Paris.[46] To affirm the quality of something that did not have the approval of accepted authorities required more than common "independence in matters of taste."[47] "We seem to have exhausted our independence in resisting the Stamp Act," lamented a critic, "for we receive every other stamp with exemplary submission."[48] In the epilogue to his first produced play, Dunlap teased the audience:

> But have a care how you adopt the notion
> That genius may be born this side of the ocean.
> Why risk your judgment by your approbation
> Of mushroom products of our mushroom nation?[49]

Managers, whose money was involved, were even less anxious to take risks. The uncertainty of theatrical profits encouraged reliance on tested products, and plays successfully staged in London, bringing with them "a fame that will excite curiosity," were likely to do similarly well in New York or Philadelphia.[50] John Neal summarized the motives that lay behind managerial preferences for English plays: "Our theatres are supplied with all the London pieces for nothing, and what is entitled to yet more consideration, *after they are successful*."[51] Managerial conservatism might have indeed curbed American theatrical output had it not

---

[44] Whitman, *Brooklyn Eagle* (February 8, 1847), in *The Gathering of the Forces*, 2: 313.

[45] James H. Hackett to Cooper, June 28, 1850; Burton to Cooper, June 5, 1850, in James Fenimore Cooper, *Correspondence*, ed. J. F. Cooper (New Haven, 1922), 2: 681–84.

[46] *The Hive*, 1 (June 9, 1810): 26; Elihu Hubbard Smith, quoted in James E. Cronin, "Elihu Hubbard Smith and the New York Theatre," *New York History*, 31 (April, 1950): 146.

[47] *New World*, 5 (September 24, 1842): 209.

[48] *Knickerbocker*, 5 (April, 1835): 320.

[49] William Dunlap, *The Father of an Only Child* (New York, 1807), p. 83.

[50] John Howard Payne, 1835 letter quoted in Montrose J. Moses, *The American Dramatist* (Boston, 1925), p. 89.

[51] *Yankee*, 2 (August, 1829): 58.

been counteracted by the need for a frequent change of bill and the desire for variety. As it was, managers staged a great number of native dramas, certainly the vast majority of those which were both written for the stage and possessed of some merit.

Authors condemned managers for lack of care in staging their works as well as for lack of patriotism in rejecting them. Particularly because American dramatists let their plays be introduced for benefit performances, which were notoriously hastily prepared, the productions were often disturbing. Isaac Harby's description of the first performance of one of his plays showed what might happen on these occasions: "The two principal characters were read! And were I to mark with inverted commas what was omitted, I fancy the reader would be puzzled to account for the shifting of scenes and, upon the exits and entrances of persons, would wonder 'how the devil they came there.'"[52] Even under the best of circumstances plays were often "murdered." Although *The Gladiator* was one of Forrest's prize plays, its author, Robert Montgomery Bird, found the first production "a horrible piece of bungling from beginning to end." Bird sadly concluded: "If there had been a wish . . . to have the play damned, they could not have taken a better course" than staging it so incompetently.[53]

Complaints about staging methods were matched by expressions of gratitude. Even Bird felt that *The Gladiator*'s Philadelphia production "was well got up, considering—new dresses, scenes, etc."[54] Other dramatists, out of gratitude or hopes of future patronage, thanked the manager for the "unremitted care . . . and the anxious zeal . . . for the play's success" or claimed that their drama's popularity grew from "the willing exertions of a company of . . . talent" and "liberal outlay in really new scenery, machinery, and appointments."[55] The same financial pressures which encouraged managers to turn first to established successes prodded them to do as much justice to every production as time and resources allowed. Admittedly such justice was often slight.

If managers had reasons for producing American plays as well as possible, they had no similar motive for paying the dramatist generously. Some playwrights were glad enough to get their plays produced under any circumstances, but others expected remuneration, something

---

[52] Isaac Harby, *The Gordian Knot; or, Causes and Effects* (Charleston, 1810), p. ix.

[53] Robert Montgomery Bird, "A Young Dramatist's Diary: The Secret Records of Robert Montgomery Bird," ed. Richard Harris, *Pennsylvania Library Chronicle* (Winter, 1959), p. 18.

[54] *Ibid.*, p. 19.

[55] James Workman, *Liberty in Louisiana* (Charleston, 1804), p. vi; Joseph S. Jones, *Moll Pitcher* (Boston, 1855), p. 2.

European authors could not demand in this country. John Howard Payne, after his return to America, claimed that theater managers rejected all his plays with the comment, "We can get new plays from England and for nothing."[56] Consequently they hesitated to pay much for American ones, a fact that many observers saw as the great deterrent to the development of native dramatists. "Wait till we have a publisher who will give us 1000 guineas for a work and then————," remarked M. M. Noah in 1815, leaving the reader to fill in the accomplishments which would flow from such incentives.[57] But the printer offered Noah instead "ten loads of wood" for the right to publish one of his best plays, and other dramatists did not fare conspicuously better.[58] In 1846, a periodical repeated the warning that "the first talents in the country" could be attracted to "this, the most difficult of all literary enterprises" only by liberal compensation. Developing an American drama would pay managers in the long run, but to succeed in this objective they would have to "pay European prices."[59] The simple reason for the scarcity of native drama, Joseph Jones concluded, was that "nobody will pay for it."[60] "Why no drama?" asked the *Democratic Review*, and answered, "managers are loath to pay proper prices."[61]

At the beginning of the century a playwright's pay was traditionally a third-night benefit performance if his play was successful enough to be given for three successive evenings. Managers could avoid any payment by allowing only two consecutive performances, though this trick was seldom used. Occasionally they treated authors with generosity, as when James Nelson Barker was given a benefit on a night when Commodore Perry, fresh from his victory on Lake Erie, was in the theater, an event sure to attract a crowd in itself.[62] But the profits of this system were, in John Howard Payne's words, "at best precarious."

By the 1830's other financial arrangements replaced the "now obsolete law of custom."[63] These arrangements were most often a set fee, sometimes to be augmented with a partial benefit if the play succeeded. The prolific playwright, H. J. Conway, wrote a manager that he was leaving

---

[56] Payne, 1835 letter, quoted in Moses, *American Dramatist*, p. 89.

[57] Mordecai M. Noah, *Grecian Captive* (New York, 1822), p. iv.

[58] Noah, *Marion*, p. 4.

[59] *Albion*, 7 (January 29, 1846): 68.

[60] Jones, *Moll Pitcher*, p. 4.

[61] *Democratic Review*, 27 (December, 1850): 520.

[62] Paul H. Musser, *James Nelson Barker (1784–1858)* (Philadelphia, 1929), p. 49. The benefit took in about $950, of which $200 or $300 was probably deducted to cover the theater's expenses.

[63] John Howard Payne to New Orleans Benefit Committee, quoted in Grace Overmyer, *America's First Hamlet* (New York, 1957), p. 295.

seven plays for his perusal. If they were accepted the author wanted for six of them five dollars apiece "to be paid on delivery" plus five dollars per night "for each and every performance." For the other, perhaps a success somewhere else, he wanted fifty dollars right away and fifty dollars at the end of the first week if it succeeded.[64] Such agreements between author and manager by 1840 had commonly replaced the old benefit system.

Conway obviously was not going to make a fortune on his dramatic productions, but if he made such terms with managers in different cities, his profits were probably commensurate with the amount of time he devoted to their writing. The same might be said of most dramatic undertakings in the period. "Poverty, the great foe of genius," did plague those who tried to make their living from writing plays, but the profession usually allowed a moderate profit to its practitioners.[65] John Blake White, a young Charlestonian studying law and supporting a family, managed to eke out his income by writing a few plays. In his journal he noted profits of between three and four hundred dollars on each of his two best pieces, neither of them outstanding successes.[66] A popular hit like John D. Burk's *Bunker Hill*, if the author were wise or lucky in his dealings with managers, could yield several thousand dollars.[67] Profits in some cases were enough even to make authors callous to criticism. A friend reportedly once told Richard Penn Smith that a play he had just seen was "unsufferable trash." Smith readily agreed, and added, "But as they give me a benefit tomorrow night as the author, I hope to have the pleasure of seeing you again."[68]

Because of contemporary copyright laws, a literary success was safer than a dramatic one. Publishers could not reproduce any copyrighted American literary work, but no law prohibited the staging of any play. Thus playwrights who aimed at theatrical rather than literary effect seldom published their plays and usually guarded all written copies. "I have made it a rule never to sell a copy of a manuscript," wrote Bowery manager Thomas Hamblin, "my *Pieces* being what I depend on."[69] Possession was the only means of control, and not a very sure one at that.

[64] H. J. Conway to J. H. Allen, inserted in MS copy of Conway's "The Banker," HTC.

[65] *Democratic Review*, 27 (December, 1850): 522.

[66] John Blake White, "Journal," ed. Paul Weidner, *South Carolina Historical and Genealogical Magazine*, 43 (April, 1942): 60, 110.

[67] Edward A. Wyatt, *John Daly Burk* (Charlottesville, Va., 1936), pp. 6–7.

[68] James Rees, *The Dramatic Authors of America* (Philadelphia, 1845), p. 128.

[69] Hamblin to Wemyss, September 10, 1839, in Joseph N. Ireland, *Extra-Illustrated Records of the New York Stage*, HTC, ser. 1, 9: 148.

Joseph S. Jones, writer of some of the most successful pieces in the period, finally authorized some of his plays to be published because they were being played in botched versions all over the country and in England without his consent or profit.[70] Dramatists continually complained of this lack of stage copyright, and of the people and legislators who were willing to protect industrial manufacturers and human rights but were unwilling "to protect the mind from foreign corruptions" or "to secure to the homeborn offspring of that mind rights of remuneration."[71] One playwright even had his hero inform the public: "The want of an international copyright law enables the publishers to grind the American author to the earth, and plunder the foreign author of the fruit of his toil."[72]

Prize-play competitions, in which a leading performer would give a stipulated sum for the best drama suited to his talents, attracted many aspiring dramatists. Edwin Forrest initiated and most consistently supported these competitions, but many other stars also offered prizes. Initially the prize plays were hailed as assuring "our Garden of Literature a richer and brighter hue," but soon they came to be regarded as more snare than advantage to the dramatist who was "too often 'stuck' by magnanimous stars . . . whose patriotic desire (!) to foster native genius, and all that, was mere leather and prunella."[73] Some of the competitions were rigged or dishonest; William Pelby suggested that John Blake White would be made winner of his prize competition if the author would accept something less than the stipulated sum, and Dan Marble was committed to giving his prize to Robb and Field although he knew Joseph S. Jones' play was better.[74] Because all rights were given to the actor, the writer of very successful plays earned less than he otherwise might have. And, perhaps most importantly, the very nature of the prize competitions forced the writing "of a sort of mono-drama, or play with one absorbing character."[75] Critics frequently attacked "the fatal obsequiousness of authors" who wrote for particular stars, so that "the genius of the author becomes the mere slave of the peculiarities,

---

[70] Jones, *Moll Pitcher*, p. 2. "As 'Moll Pitcher' has often been acted without my leave, no doubt, in time, it would be printed without consent being asked," Jones explained.

[71] Mathews, *The Politicians*, p. 5.

[72] William I. Paulding, *Madmen All!* in *American Comedies* (Philadelphia, 1847), pp. 184–85.

[73] John Howard Payne, *Thérèse; or, The Orphan of Geneva* (Philadelphia, 1838), p. vi; Dunlap, *American Theatre*, 2: 355; Jonathan Kelley, *Dan Marble* (n.p., 1851), p. 170.

[74] Paul H. Partridge, "John Blake White: The Gentleman Amateur in Republican Charleston, 1781–1859" (Ph.D. dissertation, University of Pennsylvania, 1951), p. 230; Kelley, *Marble*, p. 175.

[75] *Corsair*, 1 (March 23, 1839): 28.

perhaps the very defects, of the performer."[76] Nonetheless the bait, in one sizable sum, attracted some of the most able dramatists and encouraged some of the better plays of the period. Writing a play to match the talents of a capable performer could be stimulus as well as limitation.

While prize competitions spurred gentlemen playwrights to activity in the 1830's, another group of dramatists became associated with particular theaters. Often they were actors or managers who turned out plays in conjunction with other theatrical work, but sometimes their only job was to write plays for a particular theater. Louisa Medina and Jonas Phillips at the Bowery, Benjamin Baker and William K. Northall at the Olympic, Joseph S. Jones, Silas Steele, and Charles Saunders in Boston, Samuel Chapman in Philadelphia and H. J. Conway and Nathaniel Bannister in western theaters all turned out scores of plays, some original but many "compiled" from popular novels. Like later movie scenarists, these were capable craftsmen who tailored anything to the physical and intellectual requirements of the stage with "astonishing rapidity."[77] Even more than the writers of prize plays, they carefully "cut the garment according to the cloth" of "available popular talent."[78] Without great literary pretensions, they possessed notable "powers for arranging terrific plots and for disposing spectacles to the best effect."[79] In many instances their plays were not outstandingly bad; the decline was more in pretension than in result. Perhaps these writers' disregard of Shakespearean precedents contributed to the development of a more modern drama. Certainly the American theater's slow movement toward more realistic dramatic treatment in the second half of the century took place under the leadership of actor- or manager-dramatists such as John Brougham, Dion Boucicault, Augustin Daly, and James Herne.

The generally poor quality of plays was sometimes explained by lack of time as well as lack of compensation. Many prefaces to published plays contained elaborate apologies explaining that the piece had been "sketched in a hurry" or was "a hasty production."[80] These excuses were often perfectly true; most plays were written by people engaged

---

[76] *Boston Weekly Magazine*, 3 (May 8, 1819): 96; *American Quarterly Review*, 1 (June, 1827): 336–37; *Analectic Review*, 8 (October, 1816): 351.

[77] *New York Mirror*, 13 (March 5, 1836): 286; 15 (April 28, 1838): 351.

[78] N. M. Field to J. S. Jones, February 11, 1868, in Ludlow MSS, HTC. Field's instructions were explicit: "There should be characters for Mr. Shewell and Miss Clarke, the Frenchman retained for Warren, the Yankee altered if necessary for Hardenberg, the Yankee Girl retained for Miss Meyers."

[79] *Spirit of the Times*, 16 (February 28, 1846): 12.

[80] William Milns, *All in a Bustle* (New York, 1798), p. iii; William Dunlap, *Darby's Return* (New York, 1789), p. 3.

primarily in other business "in the scanty intervals afforded by an ar-
duous profession."[81] Consequently, according to their authors' own
testimony, full-length plays were frequently written in a week's time or
less; George Washington Custis even reported that his moderately long
The Indian Prophecy was "the work of a few hours."[82] Probably these
reports on speed of composition were often exaggerated because some
authors felt that the quickness with which their plays had been written
would "doubtless be an ample defense" for their defects.[83]

The American dramatist's lack of pay or of time was often considered
a less important curb on dramatic writing than his society's lack of
materials. "The very baldness of ordinary American life is in deadly
hostility to scenic representation," wrote James Fenimore Cooper.
Lack of social variety and contrast made tragedy and comedy difficult,
while melodrama, "except the scene should be laid in the woods," was
"out of the question":

> It would be necessary to seek the great clock, which is to strike the por-
> tentous twelve blows, in the nearest church; a vaulted passage would de-
> generate into a cellar; and, as for ghosts, the country was discovered, since
> their visitations have ceased. The smallest departure from the incidents of
> ordinary life would do violence to every man's experience; and . . . the
> passions which belong to human nature must be delineated in America
> subject to the influence of that despot—common sense.[84]

Such charges, pressed repeatedly by Europeans and acquiesced in by
many Americans, aroused heated protest from others that the country
had "no want of sufficient varieties of character . . . for a diversified
drama."[85] When a character in one American play was informed that the
English reviews had decided that "there are no materials for tragedy,
comedy, or romance in this country," he snorted that "no parcel of
envious, carping, criticizing usurpers abroad, and their dunder-headed
blockheads of followers here" would convince him of any lack of dramatic subjects in America: "As if there was a place or a time in the world,

[81] David Paul Brown, *The Prophet of St. Paul's* (Philadelphia, 1836), dedication page; George
Watterston, *A Child of Feeling* (Georgetown, 1809), p. iii.
[82] George W. P. Custis, *Indian Prophecy* (Georgetown, 1828), pp. 3–4. See also Richard Penn
Smith, *The Eighth of January* (Philadelphia, 1829), preface; Bruce McCullough, *Richard Penn Smith*
(Menasha, Wis., 1917), pp. 3–4.
[83] Samuel B. H. Judah, *A Tale of Lexington* (New York, 1823), p. v.
[84] James Fenimore Cooper, *Notions of the Americans: Picked Up by a Travelling Bachelor* (London,
1828), 2: 150–51.
[85] *American Quarterly Review*, 1 (June, 1827): 341.

when there was a lack of tragedy, comedy, or romance to see, if they chose to keep their eyes open!"[86] "The materials of poetry exist every-where," critic after critic asserted; "the poetical resources of our country are boundless."[87] America had a past full of brave colonists, heroic revolutionaries, and fascinating Indians waiting to be put on the stage. And it had a present rife with new heroes such as inventors or schoolmasters, with "local peculiarities . . . for comedy," with lawyers suitable for "facetious knaves," and, most importantly, with "simple, natural everyday circumstances" that if grasped by a sensitive writer would make moving and meaningful drama.[88]

Limited topics, time, or profit certainly did not prevent a goodly number of Americans from taking on the role of dramatist, at least briefly. During the half-century, they turned out many more than the eleven-hundred plays catalogued in the most complete play lists for the period.[89] They were attracted from many different professions. Joseph Hutton, who died a schoolteacher in North Carolina, was a Philadelphia teacher and accountant when he wrote his plays. William Milns taught school in New York. Samuel Woodworth was a New York editor, and Mrs. Mary Carr edited a Philadelphia magazine. Isaac Harby left his native Charleston to become a leading New York dramatic critic. Elihu Hubbard Smith was a Connecticut doctor and literator of all trades. James Nelson Barker and M. M. Noah were locally important Democratic politicians who moved into the customs' house when Jackson moved into the White House. The former was at one time Philadelphia's mayor and the latter was an important editor and early Zionist. Richard Penn Smith, David Paul Brown, and Robert T. Conrad were all successful Philadelphia lawyers. Nathaniel Deering was a Maine businessman and lawyer. Elizabeth Oakes Smith was a housewife who "wrote teaching my children, rocking the cradle, receiving visitors, superintending the house, engaged in all the multifarious occupations of a New England woman in moderate circumstances."[90] Robert Montgomery Bird was a Philadelphia doctor and later a novelist. Epes Sargent was a Boston

[86] William J. Paulding, *Antipathies*, in *American Comedies*, p. 286.

[87] *Arcturus*, 1 (December, 1840): 28; *Democratic Review*, 5 (June, 1839): 541.

[88] *New York Mirror*, 20 (December 10, 1842): 398; *Arcturus*, 2 (October, 1841): 282; William Tudor, *Letters on the Eastern States* (New York, 1820), p. 131; *Critic*, 1 (November 22, 1828): 62; J. E. Heath, *Whigs and Democrats; or, Love of No Politics* (Richmond, Va., 1839), p. v.

[89] Quinn, *American Drama*, pp. 426–97; Irvine Noble Smith, "American Plays and Playwrights of the Nineteenth Century" (Ph.D. dissertation, University of Denver, 1959).

[90] Mrs. Smith to John Neal, quoted in Irving Richards, "The Life and Works of John Neal" (Ph.D. dissertation, Harvard University, 1933), 2: 812.

gentleman and Cornelius Logan, a supercargo agent. George Washington Custis was a Virginia gentleman-planter, Stephen Mitchell, a Richmond editor, Lemuel Sawyer, a North Carolina congressman, and John
Blake White was a Charleston lawyer and painter. Some anonymous plays
were the work of a "New York mechanic." Anna Cora Mowatt was a
New York socialite. John Burk, a student revolutionary in Ireland, became an editor in Boston and a historian of Virginia. Joseph S. Jones was
a Boston actor and later a successful physician. A few men such as Irving,
Paulding, Simms, and Longfellow, prominent in other literary areas,
also wrote plays.

The reasons why such people wrote for the stage and the themes they
stressed are suggested in gross form in the dramatic works of John
Minshull, a New York butcher. Certainly no conspicuous talent led
Minshull to write plays. Even the development of plot by this "transcendent genius" was wholly inconsequent and his prose dialogue, when
distinguished at all, was a crazy quilt of ill-fitted ideas and metaphors.[91]
His description of a critic, understandably not his favorite kind of
animal, was typical: "Elephant-like, resting on his own judgment, his
duplicity as the divided tree gives way, and he falls into the pit."[92] But
despite his literary limitations, Minshull decided to write plays—plays
which reflected in essentials the motivations and concerns of more
competent amateur dramatists. Managers were understandably un-
enthusiastic about his productions which caused Minshull to write in
one of his prefaces: "I sigh! at the depravity of human nature," with
special preference to the human nature of theatrical managers who were
"deaf to the voice of reason." But three of his productions were finally
staged.[93]

The most notable traits of Minshull's plays were their patriotism and
moralizing. Minshull explained in a preface that his characters were not
real but "effusions of the brain, intended . . . to induce us to love virtue

---

[91] *Thespian Mirror*, 1 (February 8, 1806): 58.
[92] John Minshull, *Rural Felicity* (New York, 1801), pp. v–vi. This is the conclusion of a prelude
on critics which is a classic of a kind:
Son: Our excellent Constitution is the base of our freedom—Pray, Sir, did you ever notice in the
  portrait of the Goddess of Liberty, any traits that justify the reviewer becoming the assassin?
Father: Certainly not.
Son: Then why do critics wield the quill and cause its fluids to infuse the destructive spirit of a
  base mind?
Father: Son, you reason like a philosopher, and a man of nature would shudder at the explanation!
[93] John Minshull, *The Sprightly Widow* (New York, 1803), p. iii; George C. D. Odell, *Annals of
the New York Stage* (New York, 1927–49), 2: 178, 217, 244–45.

and despise vice."[94] To attain this end he had his characters emit platitudes like "be moderate in your passions and your love will last," or
"true happiness in republics is obtained by a strict adherence to moral
rectitude."[95] To show the connection between America and high
morality he introduced several national characters—Irish, Scotch,
French, Cockney, English—and demonstrated how they flourished or
reformed in an American setting. His nationalism was also given vent in
frequent eulogies on liberty, rural purity, the American government,
and George Washington.

Minshull's attitudes coincided with those of other early playwrights.
The encouragement of patriotism and morality were the main goals both
stated in prefaces and emphasized in plays. To foster a national literature,
to inculcate pride in American history and traditions, to display favorable American traits and expose dangerous flaws in society—these were
among the oft-mentioned patriotic impulses which led Americans to
write plays. All were connected with the desire to promote pure public
and private morality by impressing on audiences the differing rewards
of vice and virtue.

Personal motives, of course, mixed with social altruism to encourage
playwriting. Minshull did not limit his themes to patriotic and moral
eulogisms, but sometimes satirized personal acquaintances and even
advertised his trade in his plays. His *Rural Felicity* particularly was
dotted with testimonies to the importance of eating much fresh meat.
His hero at one point announced, "The colour of the complexion depends upon the food we eat," and then added the moral, "To feed constantly on salt pork accounts for the sallow complexion." Commercials
were fewer in *The Sprightly Widow*, but it contained a song, one verse of
which concluded:

> Ale, punch, and wine—enough for to swim in,
> And health to our fair American women.

Followed by the chorus:

> O the roast beef of Columbia! O Columbian roast beef!
> O the roast beef of Columbia! O Columbian roast beef![96]

---

[94] Minshull, *Sprightly Widow*, p. v.

[95] Minshull, *Rural Felicity*, p. 68; *Sprightly Widow*, p. 15. Even in Minshull's only play with a
foreign setting, a comedy about an Italian noble's stratagems to get his refined, angelic wife to sleep
with him, the moral possessed patriotic implications: "To possess a fine park without the privilege
of planting an acorn, is against our national interest." *He Stoops to Conquer* (New York, 1804), p. 10.

[96] Minshull, *Rural Felicity*, p. 16; *Sprightly Widow*, p. 30.

Few dramatists tried to sell a product so directly. But they frequently wrote from personal motives—to earn some money, to pass leisure hours, or to help a theatrical friend. Some also realized that in America with its sparse literary population, as an unhappy critic lamented, little was "necessary but the resolution to write and the folly to publish" in order "to secure a comfortable seat in some of the outhouses belonging to the temple of fame."[97] Only one dramatist admitted he wrote "for fame," but certainly others had hopes. It was at any rate pleasant to be considered a "literary lion" who "told the best stories, rounded the best period, and wrote the best plays of all his contemporaries."[98] Most amateur dramatists were theatrically active primarily in their younger years; probably their hopes were blunted by lack of any great popular or financial success. Their dramatic careers paralleled in telling ways William Dunlap's; easy opportunity and early hopes encouraged a dramatic flirtation which, because of lack of encouragement, finally resolved itself into a more distant friendship.

The plays that resulted from these various impulses toward dramatic authorship were often highly derivative. Dramatists borrowed old plays and redecorated them in various ways. Dunlap rewrote Dekker's *The Honest Whore*, and a decade later Richard Penn Smith rewrote the same play, borrowing from Dunlap as well as from the original.[99] A great number of American plays were merely foreign translations or adaptations. A play on Andrew Jackson's New Orleans' victory was largely a French melodrama with the names changed—the same melodrama John Howard Payne had earlier appropriated for another play.[100] Even previously unsuccessful dramas were rewritten. Ellison's *The American Captive* became Joseph S. Jones' *The Usurper*, and Judah's *A Tale of Lexington* was given theatrical life in H. J. Conway's revision, *The Battle of Stillwater*. *The Comet*, an American farce of 1797, was dusted off in 1843 as *The Comet; or, Millerism Bursted Up*, with all the old characters plus some additions headed by "Plotwell Miller."[101] Any well-liked type of play or character stimulated a host of imitations.

Dramatizations from other literary mediums also were frequent. Early in the century plays drawn from the novels and poems of Scott

[97] *Monthly Anthology*, 3 (January, 1806): 19.
[98] Harby, *Gordian Knot*, p. vii; George P. Morris on M. M. Noah in *New York Mirror*, 15 (July 1, 1837): 6.
[99] William Dunlap, *The Italian Father* (New York, 1810), p. 3; Richard Penn Smith, *The Deformed* (Philadelphia, 1830).
[100] McCullough, "Richard Penn Smith," pp. 9–11; John Howard Payne, *Peter Smink* (London, n.d.).
[101] Chatham Theatre playbill (March 18, 1843) in Ireland, *Extra-Illustrated*, HTC, ser. 2, 2: 231.

were especially popular. James Nelson Barker proved Americans' competence at adapting Scott to the stage, and soon Cooper was providing a domestic commodity suitable for theatrical tailoring. Later Dickens' and Bulwer-Lytton's novels provided regular dramatic materials, as did almost any successful book. The best-liked stories— notably in American literature *Rip Van Winkle* and *Uncle Tom's Cabin*— came out in many versions. By 1840 managers were fully conscious that readers of popular novels usually flocked to the theater to see "their fancies realized in a living embodiment."[102]

Even when the framework was original, the content usually lacked freshness. Most writers presented a sameness of character, conflict, and sentiment which, although usually not a product of direct copying, was also not the result of direct observation and understanding. Many of the most impressive passages in the drama of the period were those most directly borrowed from or inspired by the dramatic masters of past ages, especially Shakespeare. The plays of George Henry Boker, considered by Arthur Hobson Quinn and others the best written in nineteenth-century America, suggest particularly well the imitative originality of many dramatists. The comment that Boker's plays were "the work of his poor fancy ingeniously blended with his rich stealings" is too harsh, but one senses constantly an interest in literary precedent more than in personal perception; Boker's literary advice was to read the English classics and "get out of your age as far as you can."[103] A periodical aptly plagiarized from Pope on the period's dramaturgy:

> Your comedy I've read my friend
> And like the half you've pilfer'd best,
> But sure the piece you yet may mend
> Take courage then and steal the rest.[104]

The American dramatist pilfered most heavily from contemporary European plays, which were the chief staple of the American stage. Hundreds of French, English, and Irish plays achieved great success in the United States; and to a lesser degree, American drama succeeded in London and especially in Dublin, where "passionate appeals to liberty"

---

[102] *Corsair*, 1 (March 23, 1839): 30.

[103] A contemporary of Boker, quoted in John D. Reardon, "Verse Drama in America from 1765 to the Civil War" (Ph.D. dissertation, University of Kansas, 1957), p. 56; Sculley Bradley, *George Henry Boker: Poet and Playwright* (Philadelphia, 1927), p. 79.

[104] *American Gleaner and Virginia Magazine*, 1 (July 18, 1807): 204.

and "withering denunciations of oppression" were appreciated.[105] More significant than the mere interchange of plays was the similarity of their stereotypes, situations, and sentiments. The dramatic techniques of the great age of the nation-state were international, and dramatic literature, supposedly rooted in national soil, sprang really from some international common ground.

There were some differences in dramatic emphasis between nations. The French plays tended to be more tightly organized. When Dunlap wrote his theatrical history in 1832, he pointed out the superior dramaturgy of the French school and of the production methods in "the workshop of Scribe and Co."[106] Like other things made by mechanical process, the French drama was calculatedly efficient sometimes at the expense of the personal idiosyncrasy that gave occasional touches of cumbrous charm to Anglo-American plays. The English-speaking drama was also more morally discreet than the French—for instance, less willing to let the heroine be seduced as well as sorely tempted. Basic distinctions between English, Irish, and American drama were largely a matter of setting or of low-comedy character types; both plays and playwrights moved freely among these countries.

"We must look to ourselves for proper exhibitions to set before a free and well-ordered people," Dunlap had warned as early as 1794.[107] But American dramatists had little success in creating a distinct American species of play. Many gave a national character to their plays simply by using American settings or introducing specifically American stereotypes like the Yankee or Indian or Negro. Important American historical events or military victories were dramatized in a large group of "patriotic plays." Several comedies ridiculed contemporary American social foibles, and increasingly various social ills like the dangers of drinking and gambling, the plight of the poor or, in the 1850's, of the slave were displayed in their American setting. Even the western was initiated, but still American plays were generally little different from European ones.

Americans who called for a national drama had in mind something more than European plays set in America or peopled with American characters. Yet the only peculiarly American intellectual trait emphasized by native dramatists was the country's democratic enthusiasms. For

---

[105] *Spirit of the Times*, 16 (June 6, 1845): 180. Payne's comedy *Charles II* and some of his original farces were very successful in England, as was Woodworth's *Forest Rose*, which played in London for one hundred nights. *Armand* proved very successful, as did Epes Sargent's *Velasco*. Some American melodramas were even better liked, especially those of Joseph S. Jones.

[106] Dunlap, *American Theatre*, 2: 289–90.

[107] *New York Magazine*, 5 (November, 1794): 654.

obvious reasons, English and French theaters seldom rang with speeches like those of the stage General Warren on kings:

> They are manichean demons, who undo
> The good which heaven has done.
> . . . .
> The vegetation shrinks at their approach;
> They live by blood, and tears and sweat and groans
> . . . while prostrate at their feet
> Science and freedom downward to the dust
> Point their dishonor'd faces.[108]

Other American dramatists, if less horrendous in their imagery, were no less firm in their support of democracy. Alone of American plays in the period, David Paul Brown's *Sertorius*, which owed much to *Coriolanus*, took an un-American position of contrasting an aristocrat of great courage and ability with a democratic mob composed of cowardly, pretentious braggarts. The play succeeded, but all other American dramatists who introduced a political theme took the more democratic side.

James Kirke Paulding criticized *Sertorius* for expressing a European rather than an American viewpoint. "When the whole character of our literature shall have received the impress of our Republican government," concluded Paulding, "when our writers, wherever they may lay the scene or the plot of their works, shall warn mankind of the evils of government usurped over the people, then our Drama shall be national."[109] Given this definition, plays set in Europe, ancient and modern, in Asia, in the Near East, in Africa were all perfectly American, because geographic adherence to America was less important than agreement with its principles. And these views could be as easily represented in an exotic as in a domestic setting—even more easily because foreign social and political cleavages gave a nexus for dramatizing the conclusions democratic America had reached.

Consequently dramatic heroes of all nationalities proclaimed the primacy of freedom and the glories of democracy. A refugee from Renaissance Florence orated:

> Mark, by what pious frauds they would convince you
> Republics are but anarchies—rebellions
> Against right-divine—O libellers of Nature,
> That made man capable of ordered freedom.[110]

---

[108] John D. Burk, *Bunker Hill: or, The Death of General Warren* (New York, 1797), p. 39.

[109] *American Quarterly Review*, 8 (September, 1830): 155.

[110] Isaac Harby, *Alberti* (Charleston, 1819), p. 18.

"'The King' and 'Freedom' swell from rival tongues," said a Persian revolutionary, and one of his comrades underlined the point, "Fit words to be in competition."[111] Pelopidas, Romulus, Brutus, Spartacus, Joan of Arc, William Tell, Jack Cade—all were heroes of American drama provided with sentiments suitable to any nineteenth-century democrat. Even when the conflict was between two kings or nobles, the villainous one was a tyrant or usurper while the heroic figure stood for freedom, justice, or the general welfare. Such plays were obviously "calculated to inspire the heart of every freeman."[112]

Praise for America tended to be as strident as was condemnation of monarchy or aristocracy. The United States was a land "which never had and never will uphold a tyrant on its breast," a land with "no debauched monarch to cherish," a land "redolent with the fruits of industry," a land that was as pure and modest as a Quaker maid in contrast with that disgusting old courtesan, Europe.[113] American authors gave their decent characters in all corners of the globe similarly pro-American opinions. A German countess wished that the nobles of her land "would visit the new world to improve their manners"; a guilt-tormented hermit fled to America only to find that "those peaceful, free, and happy shores" were "uncongenial" to such a sinful soul; a Renaissance nobleman, persecuted by tyranny, planned to cross "the yet unblemished wave of the Atlantic" to achieve freedom in "some green, virgin spot."[114] Italian robber barons prayed that "the free soul of America" would "ever be purged of nobility"; and John Rolfe, inhaling the "free atmosphere" of the new world pitied his "dull sluggish countrymen" who "still creep around their little isle of fogs."[115] Even characters who antedated America made eulogies to America's greatness. Romulus concluded one play by planning to "show the world a model" that would "transfer to other times the power to rear a greater Rome in regions yet unborn," and Joan of Arc went to the stake not with a vision of heaven but with a vision of "universal justice" to be begun by "English colonists."[116] This prediction of glories yet to come was a staple of

---

[111] Henry F. Harrington, *Bernardo del Carpio* (n.p., n.d.), p. 45.

[112] *Richmond Compiler* (February 25, 1831), quoted in Martin S. Shockley, "American Plays in Richmond," *Studies in Philology*, 37 (January, 1940): 111.

[113] Elizabeth Oakes Smith, *Old New York* (New York, 1853), p. 53; Lewis Deffebach, *Oolaita* (Philadelphia, 1821), p. 27; Nathaniel H. Bannister, *Putnam, The Iron Son of '76* (Boston, n.d.), p. 21; James Nelson Barker, *Tears and Smiles* (Philadelphia, 1808), p. 21.

[114] Samuel Woodworth, *Lafayette* (New York, 1823), p. 25; John Blake White, *Mysteries of the Castle* (Charleston, 1807), pp. 33–34; Harby, *Alberti*, p. 47.

[115] *Rinaldo Rinaldini* (New York, 1810), p. 8; Barker, *Indian Princess*, p. 8.

[116] John Howard Payne, *Romulus* (1839), *ALP*, 6: 244; John D. Burk, *Female Patriotism; or, The Death of Joan of Arc* (New York, 1798), p. 39.

American dramas, the note of hope with which audiences were sent home after seeing most patriotic, colonial, or Indian plays. A melodramatic William Penn typically catalogued America's future glory:

> This is indeed a chosen land of productive soil, the climate of genial and healthful temperature, cut off from the vices of the old world and the influence of political and religious intolerance which have become so onerous as to more than counterbalance the advantages derived from the social compact. Here an empire may be formed and governed by principles best calculated to secure the happiness of man. *May be? Must be* formed, and will go on and flourish until the institutions of Europe are shaken to the foundation by the example of the perfectability of government. Here the poet's dream of Arcadian happiness will at some future period be realized. Here man will walk forth in the majesty of his nature and feel in all its force the startling truth that all men are born free and equal.[117]

American audiences responded to such "smiting rebukes of servility and daring defiance of tyranny," which regularly drew forth "bursts of approbation."[118] Whitman recalled that when Forrest played in Payne's *Brutus* the paeans to liberty "affected me for weeks, or rather I might say permanently filtered into my whole being."[119] Yet the shallowness of such patriotism was recognized. The ideas, "though often noble and vigorously expressed, run as often into clap-traps, and seem expressly written to gather applause from the least discriminating portion of the audience," complained one critic.[120] Patriotic plays might be "necessary pabulum to the nation's energies," but as that good Democrat William Leggett pointed out, it was hard to be enthusiastic about "nondescript polylogues . . . plentifully sprinkled with sounding phrases about Washington, liberty, and glory" turned out "for the edification of the excitable rabble."[121]

People who had urged the development of an American drama had envisioned something beyond bald self-congratulation. "When we speak of nationality in the drama, we do not mean the inculcation of mere patriotism," cautioned Evert Duyckinck. "There are higher habits of thought . . . than this self love."[122] The desire for a national drama had always been implicitly a plea for an American Shakespeare, some

---

[117] Richard Penn Smith, *William Penn* (1829), *ALP*, 13: 91–92.
[118] Epes Sargent quoted in *Prompter's Whistle*, 1 (September 21, 1850): 55; Nathaniel H. Bannister, *Gaulantus* (Cincinnati, 1836), p. 4.
[119] Whitman, *Complete Prose*, p. 428.
[120] On Forrest in *Jack Cade*, in *Spirit of the Times*, 11 (May 29, 1841): 156.
[121] Durang, *Philadelphia Stage*, n.s., p. 277; *Critic*, 1 (November 22, 1828): 62.
[122] *Arcturus*, 2 (October, 1841): 281.

theatrical genius who would find immortal expression for American ideals and who would offer unquestioned proof of American ability—a writer who would justify America to itself and the world. Had genius turned up, something distinctively American might have been created; as it was, American plays were hardly different from the generality of European ones except for a few character types and bits of patriotic or democratic special pleading.

A few playwrights tried to deal with their country's political uniqueness more seriously; their problems and failures suggest why most American dramatists contented themselves with fitting democratic political bias into the framework of the conventional European heroic or domestic drama. Political drama in eighteenth-century America had been a species of blatant propaganda. Just as Jonathan Sewall wrote a pamphlet opposing the Revolution, he produced a play for the same purpose. This wholly polemical playwriting continued into the first decade of the nineteenth century in the form of dramas advocating or attacking the Jeffersonians or the Federalists. Horatio Nichols' *The Essex Junto* was typical of these dramas. In it Hamilton and Adams, as "General Creole" and the "Duke of Braintree," plotted to murder the Old Patriot and to take over the country, but Monticello defeated the villains. The play was given over to dialogue that revealed the avaricious, dastardly, monarchical, immoral nature of the Federalists and the benevolent, courageous, democratic, and righteous sentiments of the Jeffersonians.

In most nineteenth-century plays such wholly polemical allegory was replaced by more dramatically effective stories in which political attitudes were expressed more through character and situation. James Workman's *Liberty in Louisiana*, written in 1804, illustrated the change in emphasis. In his preface, Workman said that he had first intended to write a political pamphlet proving to the newly annexed citizens of Louisiana the advantages of liberty over despotism. "But on considering the superior effect of sentiments embodied in natural character and exhibited in an interesting story" with the advantages of scenery and music, he "determined to make a dramatic representation the engine of enforcing his political principles."[123] Spanish corruption was personified in Don Bertoldo, the colony's governor. One courtroom scene particularly illustrated the corrupt nature of Spanish rule, but most of the play centered on the Don's desire for the money and person of his young ward. His wife, who lusted after an American soldier, hoped that her husband

[123] Workman, *Liberty in Louisiana*, p. iv.

would run off with her rival, but the girl, of course, spurned Don Bertoldo. When the Don attempted to abduct her, he was intercepted by the Americans who had just come to claim sovereignty in Louisiana. The play ended with the American general spouting Workman's political pamphlet: a long and righteous discussion of the beauties of freedom, justice, equality, morality, and other aspects of the American way of life. This appended political dissertation was an extraneous afterthought; the story was over and Workman unnecessarily underlined its point. The real political substance of the play came from Workman's delineation of the personal traits of Don Bertoldo—his avaricious immorality and his doddering senility—which by implication were the traits of Spanish rule. Similarly the American officer who saved the girl and Louisiana from the Don's baseness embodied the protective perfection of American rule.

The change from eighteenth-century political plays to those similar to Workman's was partly a move from closet to stage drama which required characters with sufficiently human qualities to give them theatrical reality. Workman also understood the advantages a play could have over a pamphlet in promoting a cause. By getting the audience either to scorn or to hate the human traits of the antagonist and to identify with the protagonist, people could be emotionally led to accept an argument, even one with which they did not fully agree. Yet the theater's mass audience required that the technique be used warily. Playwrights seldom tried to say anything more questionable to audiences than Workman's notion that Spanish rule was bad and American good. *Uncle Tom's Cabin* was the first play to use these techniques successfully in a really controversial cause, and it probably would have failed, as it did at first, had not the novel readied the public for its message. Even farces like *The Bank Monster; or, Specie and Shin-Plaster*, "an excellent hit at the time," had to keep "free from political allusions."[124] Hackett understood the situation when he asked an author to write a play "spiced with some pungent glances at the present state of affairs without going deep enough to offend any party."[125]

Those few authors who tried to go deeper into the American political situation had a much more difficult task. Both William Gilmore Simms and Cornelius Mathews were upset by many of the qualities of American democracy, particularly the unprincipled and pandering attitudes of the politician toward the voter. Simms presented this criticism in *Norman Maurice*, a serious drama in blank verse. The hero was an impetuous

[124] *Dramatic Mirror and Literary Companion*, 1 (September 18, 1841): 46.
[125] James Hackett to John Neal, March 10, 1834, in Richards, "The Life and Works of John Neal."

young man of noble principles and grand ambitions and abilities. He loved America and its people and wanted to "serve them in high places." To do this he abandoned the East, which demanded base flattery of its politicians, and went West, where:

> There is a simpler, and a hardier nature
> That proves men's values not by wealth and title
> But by mind and manhood. . . .
>   With them it answers
> If each man founds his family and stands
> The father of a race of future men.[126]

The West, however, was not without temptations to test the hero. Powerful interests tried to get him to drop his defense of a widow's suit; thugs tried to intimidate him; his own supporters encouraged him to tell the voters only what they wanted to hear. Maurice had great faith in the virtues of the popular heart and will, but would debase neither the people nor himself by following common political practices. "I will never" he told his backers,

> Become the creature of selfish party,
> Never use wealth or fraud to rise to power.
> . . . .
> Nor can I offer
> One tribute to the vulgar vanity.[127]

To give theatrical form to his political ideas, Simms introduced a conventional melodramatic situation. A diabolic rival of Maurice, who had framed him and tried to keep the heroine from marrying him, showed up in the West to blackmail him, destroy his career, and seduce his wife. In the course of the last enterprise, the wife killed the villain to save her honor and her husband's political future and then went mad—a tragic conclusion wholly at odds with the optimistic ending of the political story. The play's blatant split personality, particularly at the conclusion, suggests psychological interpretation. Seemingly Simms was so desirous of believing in the triumph of decent democracy that he felt compelled to present a happy political ending, while diverting his fears to the personal story. Troubled about American democracy, in which he believed demagoguery was leading toward civil strife, Simms distorted the sense of his play by the incongruity of its two parts, which were pushed together like unmatched pieces of a jigsaw puzzle.

---

[126] William Gilmore Simms, *Norman Maurice* (Richmond, 1851), p. 9.
[127] *Ibid.*, pp. 20–21.

Those writers who handled American politics in the form of a satiric prose comedy fared better. North Carolina congressman Lemuel Sawyer gave a political subplot to his *Blackbeard* in which the hero campaigned against a demagogue who treated freely, promised jobs to incompetents, and bragged about his total lack of education. The voters were a sorry lot, the most amusing of whom refused to vote until the last minute: "No, I ha'nt voted yet. I'm waiting to see who treats me the best—I vote for them that give me the most grog. I have not had but four drinks today. I'm not drunk enough to vote yet." The hero lost the election but finally was appointed to fill a vacancy in the congressional delegation. Either in jest or expiation, seventy United States congressmen headed by Henry Clay subscribed to the publication of this play which suggested that virtue got into the House of Representatives only through near miracle.[128]

A more ambitious and coherent attempt to expose comically the flaws in American democracy was Cornelius Mathews' *The Politicians*. Set during an election campaign, the play derided both party candidates and their retinues. Election practices like lavish treating, playing up to the most ignorant elements of the population, and trying to seem the commonest of common men were vigorously laughed at. One candidate, for example, went out to "talk Dutch with the German voters, and O'hone a little with the Hibernians," while his rival feared losing the election through failure to dress sufficiently shabbily.[129] Both gave drink, dinners, and flattery to anyone, including the town's worst bums: "The man that says a pauper—yea, a vagabond . . .—is not suitable to hold the highest dignities in the gift of the people, is a traitor and a scoundrel." Political graft also was chided—such things as unfit appointments to office, rake-offs on the money designated for poor houses, and the use of public funds to bolster the price of worthless lands. "To make virtue a topic with a professional politican is sure to give offense," warned one of the campaign managers, who added that in the presence of a politician "a worthy man's honor is no more exposed . . . than a sea captain's wife whose husband has gone on the Canton voyage."[130]

The play maintained a lightness of tone with its satirical seriousness. Mathews did not morally condemn the people he wrote of, but let his

---

[128] Lemuel Sawyer, *Blackbeard*, facsimile edition, ed. Richard Walser (Raleigh, N.C., 1952), pp. xvi, 12. J. E. Heath in *Whigs and Democrats* exposed the divergence between the aristocratic private sentiments and demagogic public utterances of a politician.

[129] Mathews, *Politicians*, pp. 95, 48. "They may name me toad, snake, dog, monkey," one of them said, "but not aristocrat" (*ibid.*, p. 13).

[130] *Ibid.*, pp. 40, 78, 17–18.

laughter carry its own judgment. Aside from its rather miscellaneous structure, the play's greatest weakness was Mathews' resolution of his plot. In the election the people finally turned to "a plain honest citizen" to rid themselves of "squabbling office seekers."[131] The desire for such an answer is understandable in a play written during the election campaign of 1840, but it voided the honesty of Mathews' treatment and avoided the problem he had raised. Yet even with this comfortable solution, the satire in Mathews' play was sufficiently trenchant and serious in intent to prevent the play's being performed immediately or ever successfully.

Joseph S. Jones' highly popular *The Silver Spoon* showed the kind of spoof of democracy that Americans did find amusing. Interest in what was actually a conventional melodrama centered on Squire Batkins who had come to Boston to represent his native Cranberry Centre in the state legislature. Although his political knowledge was slight, the squire was unworried, "I can learn my duty to my country as I go along, and do some little chores for myself and relations."[132] Besides, his constituents had given him very specific voting instructions: "First, last, and always vote agin the city members." Most of the squire's time was spent preparing a speech he intended to make to the legislature "about Cuba, Panic, Women's rights, a little touch on rum slantin' ways a leetle to both sides because our town is about equally divided on the liquor question." The other characters never let him get far when he tried to practice this oration, but he got enough out to suggest its nature:

> These aristocrats who go about seeking whom they can devour somebody, do they take us who come up here from the agricultural, moral deestrects to be the ones to barter our freedom of principle like Ne-buk-od-nez-or of old for a miserable mess of potash?[133]

Batkins' incapacity would have been appalling were he not such a thoroughly likable character: honest, kindly, amusing, and canny in his limited way. He was less a satire on democracy than a representative of it. People laughed at Batkins' foibles without fearing for the system, because democracy in the play rested not on great personal abilities, but on something as vague as the general virtue, of which Batkins was an exemplar. He served in the legislature, as he said, "out of patriotic

---

[131] *Ibid.*, p. 58.

[132] Joseph Jones, "The Silver Spoon" (1852), HTC, Act 1: 8.

[133] *Ibid.*, Act 1: 18, 20; Act 2: 19. Batkins' desire to shine in oratory was inspired by "this Mr. Demosthenes" who had been opposed by a powerful speaker but "took the stump agin him, and beat him if he did stutter a leetle" (Act 2: 8).

motives and not for the dollars 'per diem' per day."[134] Jones succeeded where Simms and Mathews failed partly because he followed Hackett's advice of not going "deep enough to offend," or even bother, anyone. Perhaps too he better grasped the nature of democracy, that its failings were more truly related in genial low comedy than in satire or tragedy.

The patriotic stuffing put into a great many plays, the frequency with which dramas used a liberty-tyranny motif, the stage use of a few distinctly American "types," and the few plays dealing specifically with American political problems were the only distinctly American manifestations that got into drama. Yet this treatment offered only slight variation on common European stage practices and platitudes. American drama failed because it did not break away from the conventions borrowed from, or shared with, Europe. If those conventions were as natural to the new world as to the old, they remained inimical to great dramatic expression. The American dramatist's failure is best examined in those who most nearly succeeded. American drama's claim to contemporary fame centered in John Howard Payne; its claims to quality were hinged on the work of Robert Montgomery Bird. Both succeeded in their way, and both failed.

Payne's most impressive successes came early. At thirteen, in 1804, he and the somewhat older Samuel Woodworth edited a Boston weekly magazine for young people. The following year, while serving as a mercantile apprentice in New York, Payne began to publish anonymously a magazine devoted wholly to the theater, the *Thespian Mirror*. He also wrote, in a period of seven nights he said, his first play, *Julia; or, The Wanderer*, which was given a single performance on the New York stage. Although in his preface Payne said "his chief dependence for favor always rested on morals," the most uncommon part of the otherwise conventional melodrama concerned two low-comedy characters who spent most of their time licentiously planning and attempting attacks on the virtue of the female leads.[135] The play was not well received. The day after the performance Payne, always quick to sense popular reaction, advised himself through his *Thespian Mirror* "to expunge some of the offensive passages, and qualify some others which are at present too obscure and unconnected."[136] It was one of Payne's few original full-length plays, and the only one performed with an American setting. In Dunlap's personal copy of his *American Theatre*, he crossed

---

[134] *Ibid.*, 1: 18.

[135] John Howard Payne, *Julia; or, The Wanderer* (New York, 1806), p. 5.

[136] *Thespian Mirror*, 1 (February 8, 1806): 56.

out the list of Payne's dramas with the note "not American plays."[137]

Payne's magazine had attracted the attention of some New York gentlemen, one of whom decided that such talents "if properly directed will do much good in arresting the dreadful evils which await us from the increasing and desolating effect of democracy."[138] To save the country from democracy and the young man from his weakness for the theater, Payne was sent to Union College in Schenectady. There he spent money lavishly, laid out plans for several literary ventures, and wrote and published still another short-lived magazine. His father's indebtedness won him freedom from Schenectady and permission to try acting. His debut occurred when he was seventeen-and-a-half years old, but he said he was sixteen and looked "still younger."[139] Largely because of his supposed youth, he succeeded so well that he became the first American-born "star." When his attraction began to wane in America, he went to London, where still trading on his youthful appearance—though twenty-two, he was billed as Master John Payne—he was moderately successful. He later toured the provinces, and had great success in Ireland which enthusiastically welcomed "the American Roscius." Failing to gain another chance in London, Payne began his long European career as dramatic carpenter and adapter.

The great majority of Payne's plays were facile adaptations from the French popular theater, long a source of plots for second-rate American and British dramatists. When he had a model to follow, Payne's sense of stage construction was good, and the inflation of melodramatic dialogue suited him well. Some of his adaptations were great successes, and Covent Garden and Drury Lane competed for his services, though both proved reluctant to pay him decently. Payne claimed that his adaptations were "liable to all the labour of an original" because of the moral and literary improvements that the English and American stage demanded.[140] What adaptations did not require was what Payne lacked—originality. His plays, as a friendly critic said of his verse, lacked inspiration and vitality but showed "perfect taste and finish."[141] His famous lyric, "Home, Sweet Home," was the true measure of Payne's talent.

Payne never got the financial reward that his popularity deserved.

[137] Dunlap's note in HTC copy of *American Theatre*.

[138] John F. Seaman to Dr. Eliphalet Nott, quoted in Grace Overmyer, *America's First Hamlet* (New York, 1857), p. 69.

[139] Dunlap, *American Theatre*, 2: 256.

[140] Payne, *Accusation; or, The Family of D'Anglade* (Boston, 1818), pp. iii–iv.

[141] John Gorham Palfrey, "A Tribute to John Howard Payne," *Boston Evening Gazette* (May 29, 1852).

From Schenectady he wrote to a friend that a reading of Franklin's *The Way to Wealth* had encouraged him "to become more economical," but he always lived more extravagantly than his means allowed.[142] Because others usually reaped the profits of his popularity, Payne was discouraged from continuing writing after his return to America. But the literary loss was slight. Washington Irving, Payne's lifelong friend and occasional collaborator, once wrote him that he wanted to see the dramatist "swimming without corks."[143] Payne as playwright, however, was dependent on corks, and these, as was proper to the medium, possessed a volume disproportionate to their weight.

The dramatic frustration of Robert Montgomery Bird was a more serious matter. A Philadelphian trained as a doctor, Bird very early showed literary ambitions. While still in medical school, he wrote several able plays. Perhaps the best of them was *News of the Night*, a farce-satire set in contemporary Philadelphia. The characters, likable and amusing, were all frankly mercenary in their motives. Much of the humor in the play came from Bird's using the conventional situation of a harsh guardian opposing a ward's marriage, but substituting financial for sentimental motivation. A Quaker businessman, Agony, wanted to get for himself the money bequeathed to his two wards. By informing the girls that they would not be permitted to marry until thirty, Agony expected to force them to wed without his permission and thus to forfeit their money. The girls were eager to marry but also prudent enough to want to save their funds. When Agony finally concluded that "those young jades" would become old maids rather than sacrifice their inheritance, he sadly moralized, "The world has come to a fine pass, when avarice becomes a passion of youth as well as of age."[144] Of course, Agony was finally tricked into giving consent to the marriages and also into proposing to his horrendous housekeeper, Mrs. Grimalkin. At the play's end, all three couples embarked on a honeymoon trip to Niagara.

Bird's early plays were never staged; his theatrical success began when Edwin Forrest chose his *Pelopidas* for one of his prize plays. Perhaps because the title role in this play was not of sufficient preeminence to suit Forrest, Bird's *The Gladiator* was produced in its stead. It proved a great success, both popular and critical, for many years, but, like the other dramas written for Forrest, it was more conventional than Bird's earlier

[142] Payne to Henry Brevort, quoted in Willis T. Hanson, Jr., *The Early Life of John Howard Payne with Contemporary Letters* (Boston, 1913), p. 82.

[143] Quoted in Overmyer, *America's First Hamlet*, p. 226. Irving apparently collaborated with Payne most closely on *Richelieu* and *Charles II*, his best adaptations.

[144] Robert Montgomery Bird, *News of the Night; or, A Trip to Niagara*, in *ALP*, 12: 152.

plays. With one exception, all these later tragedies pictured heroic fighters for liberty or country and were freighted with bombast about freedom, justice and patriotism. The characters had some complexity; the plots were effectively organized; the blank verse was seldom silly, and occasionally strikingly convincing and natural. But commonplace sentiments and situations mocked these real merits.

The one exception to the pattern was *The Broker of Bogota*, Bird's favorite among his plays. Despite its South American setting, it was—in Mrs. Bird's words—"a mere domestic story, many incidents of which are common; the date is modern, and the manners not widely different from our own." A "purely domestic story . . . of ordinary incidents and passions" adequately described Bird's central theme,[145] the conflict between a proud, strict, and loving father, and a wayward, weak son, but the theme was embroidered with romantic subplots and a villain, who was to blame for all the son's misconduct and whose melodramatic conniving brought on the play's climax. In the old father, Bird created a character of much credibility, but instead of suiting his story to the essentials of this character, the author, with real theatrical skill, wove it into a plot of complicated villainy. Unlike Payne, Bird had perception and ideas of his own, but by the time these had been translated into drama, they became encrusted with the same theatrical paraphernalia that were the whole of Payne's art.

Forrest predicted, after the successful first performance of *The Broker of Bogota*, that the play would "live when our vile trunks are rotten," but he produced the play infrequently.[146] It was essentially "a departure from the starring system," giving equal importance to a large number of characters, which posed problems for a star encouraged by vanity and popular demand to be always the center of things. The friendship of Bird and Forrest was also disrupted by financial disputes. Forrest refused to give Bird any more than the prize money for his plays, disavowed Bird's claim for recompense for revising *Metamora*, and dismissed Bird's wish to publish his plays. Contractually Forrest was in the right, but a sense of fairness or enlightened self-interest should have encouraged him to be more generous to an author whose plays succeeded so well. Forrest clearly made "the encouragement of dramatists conduce to his own interest."[147] Largely because of financial disappointment, the period's most promising playwright became a novelist.

[145] Mary Mayer Bird, *Life of Robert Montgomery Bird, with Selections from Bird's Correspondence*, ed. C. S. Thompson (Philadelphia, 1945), pp. 74–75; *New York Mirror*, 11 (December 7, 1833): 182.
[146] Edwin Forrest to R. M. Bird, February 12, 1834, quoted in M. M. Bird, *Life of Bird*, p. 74.
[147] William Dunlap, *Diary*, ed. Dorothy Barck (New York, 1930), 3: 625; *Prompter*, 1 (June 15, 1850): 47.

"What a fool I was to think of writing plays!" complained Bird in his diary. "To be sure, they are much wanted. But these novels are much easier sorts of things and immortalize one's pocket much sooner."[148] Though still plagued with money worries, Bird made more of a financial success of his novels and magazine articles, which like his plays were a mixture of the original and the commonplace. Bird felt himself a victim of the lack of taste in Jacksonian America and considered his writing both for book and stage injured by the demands of "our Johnny Raws of the States."[149] He liked his Philadelphia and his farm but showed great enthusiasm for American society in general only when in Europe.[150] He might have written better had he castigated the taste he despised instead of catering to it, but he wanted to succeed and had neither James Fenimore Cooper's robust courage nor his cushion of early success to fall back on.

Although Bird was not a great writer, he was a good one, and his career suggests why people of talent generally wrote poetry, essays, or novels rather than plays. Bird himself explained it by reference to the writer's desire for independence. In the first place the dramatist's means of communication had to be filtered through "the rantings and blunderings of illiterate companies." After this degradation, the play was given over to the "arbitration of ignorance and brutality," to "the mercy of the mob."[151] It was, to use Marshall McLuhan's term, a "cool medium" in which the author provided a sketch that was to be filled in by actors, managers, and audiences. Playwrights too had to be careful about offending any segment of the community; Bird feared for the success of *The Gladiator* because he felt its attack on slavery would damn the play at least in the South.[152] Obviously novelists who said uncommon things or developed unfamiliar forms were not the most popular ones, but the line between success and failure was not so sharp in printed literature as in drama. Novelists, poets, and essayists could use subtler effects and still achieve some success by writing for a more limited audience, but the playwright wholly failed who did not "please the many as well as the

---

[148] Bird, "Secret Records," p. 17.

[149] Bird to James Lawson, quoted in Clement Foust, *The Life and Dramatic Works of Robert Montgomery Bird* (New York, 1919), p. 89.

[150] M. M. Bird, *Life of Bird*, p. 83. "I am afraid if I stay here longer," he wrote from London, "I shall become a Jackson man! I begin to feel like a democrat, and for the first time in my life think that God will lead the foot of the poor man to the neck of the rich, and that, in this, there will be justice."

[151] Bird to George Henry Boker, January 31, 1853, quoted in Bradley, *Boker*, p. 121.

[152] Bird, "Secret Records," p. 10. *The Gladiator* was played frequently in the South, but some critics pointed out its contemporary message. Whitman wrote in the *Brooklyn Eagle* (December 26, 1846), "The play is as full of 'abolitionism' as an egg is of meat." *The Gathering of the Forces*, 2: 331.

few"; he had much the most "promiscuous audience for judges and critics."[153] Even posterity was closer to the writer of books.

Early in the century drama was the most respected form of literature; compared to the "story-telling" novel, it was "a different and higher species of composition."[154] But authors quickly saw that other fields freed them from "the limits of the theatre," "the technical trammels" of the drama.[155] Equally important, the themes that interested most great writers in the period were not particularly theatrical. The beauties of natural scenery, the relationships between man and nature, and the effects of a harsh society on the sensitive man could be most easily developed in nondramatic literary forms. Drama traditionally demanded action, action which writers were unable or audiences unwilling to give up, but which was hard to fit realistically with the major concerns of modern life. Drama also demanded in some sense presentations of different characters and views in immediate conflict, whereas most of the great romantics spoke most convincingly only in one voice, or at least through one person at a time. It was, in Emerson's words, "the age of the first person singular." The I-saying author fitted in to the traditions of poetry and essays, but drama, more than any literary form, prohibited the direct intrusion of the author into his work. The dramatist must "so to speak, put off his identity," one critic pointed out, whereas most writers of the period chose "to exert their talents in those walks of poetry which leave them more at liberty to move in the free and natural current of their own feelings and fancies."[156]

The special requirements of drama combined with the most basic interests and conventions of the age to create a melodramatic dye, gaudy, eye-catching, and superficial. The most popular playwrights like Payne wrote plays with little more to them than the colors of these dramatic conventions. Other writers aimed higher, but ended up dipping their ideas in the same theatrical vats. The mottoes beneath an emblematic representation of "America encouraging the drama" on the curtain of the original Chestnut Street Theatre in Philadelphia suggested much that lay behind melodrama's century-long preeminence. The original legend, "The Eagle Suffers Little Birds to Sing," was soon changed to "For Useful Mirth and Salutary Woe."[157]

---

[153] *North American Review*, 11 (October, 1820): 385; George Handel Hill, *Scenes from the Life of an Actor* (New York, 1853), p. 69.

[154] *American Quarterly Review*, 8 (September, 1830): 134.

[155] Durang, *Philadelphia Stage*, n.s., p. 80; Robert Dale Owen, *Pocahontas* (New York, 1837), p. 15.

[156] *North American Review*, 11 (October, 1820): 385–86.

[157] George O. Seilhamer, *The History of the American Theatre*, (Philadelphia, 1888–91), 3: 147.

8

The Melodramatic Structure

IN ONE of his least perceptive observations, Tocqueville lamented the "licence" which would prevail in democratic drama: "If the effect of democracy is generally to question the authority of all literary rules and conventions, on the stage it abolishes them altogether and puts in their place nothing but the caprice of each author and each public."[1] This was the opposite of what occurred in the melodrama. A play highly successful in one locality was generally successful throughout the western world; and so slight was the writer's personal impress on productions that one competent dramatist's plays were scarcely distinguishable from another's, at least in character, structure, and sentiment. What did happen in the nineteenth-century theater repeated the pattern Tocqueville constantly found in American manners generally: democracy freed drama from its literary conventions, but this liberty begot a conformity or voluntary compliance with other conventions that was at least as strict as anything imposed before.

This is not to deny that there was much superficial flexibility in the melodrama. No limits were placed on time or place or type of character, and its subject matter could be heroic or domestic, patriotic or criminal, nautical or western, rural or urban, fashionable or simple, reform or fairy tale. Its tone might be either comic or serious and its conclusion happy or "tragical." But behind its many changes of costume, its façade of variety, lay a heart, like that of its heroines, of undeviating character, purpose, and purity.

---

[1] Alexis de Tocqueville, *Democracy in America*, ed. Phillips Bradley (New York, 1957), 2: 89–90. Tocqueville's error probably marked his aesthetic fastidiousness. In his discussion of drama his only specific references were to a remark by Racine and to the critical canons of the age of Louis XIV.

"The stage paints Virtue," wrote an American dramatist, "in her holiday garments, and though storms sometimes gather around her radiant head, the countenance of the heavenly maid, resigned, serene and meek, beams forth, after a season of patient suffering, with ineffable refulgence."[2] Virtue and the heroine stood almost indistinguishable at the center of the melodrama, the one a personification of the other. The "ineffable refulgence" of triumphant virtue was best embodied in:

> That height of human good, enchanting woman—
> Woman for ever gentle in her nature,
> Sweet solace of our woes, heightener of joys,
> And when not warped from her native virtue
> The perfect type of purity in heaven.[3]

Play after play repeated this apostrophe to "woman, lovely woman wanting only wings to ascend like a perfect angel."[4] Whatever her background or situation, the heroine was always "a miracle of love and delicacy," "a paragon of excellence," indeed, "an earthly angel." "Eternal God," apostrophized a hero, "thy masterpiece is woman."[5]

Sometimes characters in the melodrama belittled the heroine's virtue, but these were either comic personages whose ideas were to be laughed at, or villains whose notions were clearly diabolic.[6] Heroes who doubted female perfections were quickly converted to purer notions. John Rolfe, for instance, arrived in the new world a skeptic:

> Women! They're made of whimsies and caprice,
> So variant and so wild, that, ty'd to a God,
> They'd dally with the devil for a change.

But John Smith, an older and a wiser man, knew better:

> O woman! Angel sex! Where'er thou art,
> Still art thou heavenly. The rudest clime,
> Robs not thy glowing bosom of its nature.[7]

---

[2] Cornelius Logan, quoted in Olive Logan, *Before the Footlights and Behind the Scenes* (Philadelphia, 1870), p. 35.

[3] William Dunlap, *Leicester* (New York, 1807), p. 119.

[4] John Minshull, *He Stoops to Conquer; or, The Virgin Wife Triumphant* (New York, 1804), p. 9.

[5] Charles H. Taylor, *The Drunkard's Warning* (New York, n.d.), p. 8; John Howard Payne, *Adeline; or, The Victim of Seduction* (New York, 1822), p. 25; Nathaniel H. Bannister, "Rookwood" (New York Public Library microfilm), Act II, scene iv. John Daly Burk, *Bethlehem Gabor, The Lord of Transylvania; or, The Man-Hating Palatine* (Petersburg, Va., 1807), p. 28.

[6] David Paul Brown, *Prophet of St. Paul's* (Philadelphia, 1836), p. 15; George W. P. Custis, *Indian Prophecy* (Georgetown, 1828), p. 19; John Howard Payne, *Brutus; or, The Fall of Tarquin* (New York, 1821), p. 18.

[7] James Nelson Barker, *The Indian Princess; or, La Belle Sauvage* (New York, 1808), pp. 24, 30.

And, of course, Pocahontas waited just beyond the edge of the forest to prove the wisdom of Smith and make Rolfe happily repent his libels on "fair woman."

The heroine always was a fair woman, though this "was the least of her attractions," the outward sign of an even greater inner beauty. "Soul, sense, sentiment, sensibility, and a noble mind" all rendered her "an object too dazzling bright for men to look upon with aught but mental adoration."[8] Such a "vision of blessedness" had a definite social role: "angelic woman" was to be a "mansion of peace," " the greatest happiness of man," and "an influence strong of virtue."[9] The best advice to be given to someone with villainous tendencies was to "save yourself by marriage; 'twill redeem you from delirium," and even the American sailor realized that "when cruising about over the shoals of adversity, what leader like a woman's affection to point out the North Star of happiness!"[10] Indeed the whole melodramatic tradition joined in the chorus of a reformed drunkard's song:

> The best advice I give to all
> Of every clime and nation,
> Is to take a wife, short or tall,
> 'Twill be your sure salvation.[11]

Concepts like "salvation" and "redemption" were often affixed to the heroine's role: "angel woman" was a guardian angel, meant to guide, protect, and solace erring man. One hero exclaimed, "Woman, woman, beautiful woman! What would we poor devils do without them?" And poor devils could always count on their good angels. Whether "in the crowded city or the silent desert," the heroine remained "faithful in love, fearless in danger. Man's first and last, his surest, truest friend."[12]

The heroine simply as angel could not fill the center of drama, which required some sort of conflict. "The chaste-eyed angel, bringing peace

---

[8] Mary Clarke Carr, *The Benevolent Lawyers; or, Villainy Detected* (Philadelphia, 1823), p. 21.

[9] William Dunlap, *Ribbemont; or, The Feudal Baron* (New York, 1803), p. 68; George Watterston, *The Child of Feeling* (Georgetown, 1809), p. 57.

[10] John Howard Payne, *Accusation; or, The Family D'Anglade* (Boston, 1818), pp. 20–21; Charles Saunders, *The Pirate's Legacy; or, The Wrecker's Fate* (Boston, n.d.), pp. 10–11.

[11] William W. Pratt, *Ten Nights in a Barroom* (Boston, n.d.), p. 32.

[12] Nathaniel H. Bannister, *Putnam, the Iron Son of '76* (Boston, 1835), p. 6; Louisa Medina, *Nick of the Woods* (Boston, n.d.), p. 28. The element of condescension implicit in this "woman is man's best friend" credo is historically verifiable. In the late nineteenth century, when a younger generation of women somewhat emancipated themselves, mother, in popular culture, became a man's best friend. And in the twentieth century with the full equality of women that position has been usurped by the dog.

and barring out all shape of wrong and discord," though celestial in character, was highly susceptible to earthly dangers.[13] The conflict and excitement of the melodrama grew from the fragility of both the heroine's position and the concept of virtue she represented. Her very angelic nature endangered her, for she excelled in passive qualities like "modesty, patience, and meekness."[14] In a few patriotic plays the heroine briefly disguised herself as a soldier to aid her threatened country, but in each instance she made it clear that this belligerence was only for the duration. Thus the conversation between two of Jackson's soldiers at the battle of New Orleans:

> *Edward:* Is this real? Do I behold in my preserver, my loved, my constant Charlotte?
>
> *Charlotte:* Forgive me, Edward, if unsexed today, you see me here, a soldier by your side. In her dear country's cause, a woman's spirit towers above her sex.[15]

Even Joan of Arc prayed,

> Let me, heaven,
> Sooner resign my laurels in an hour
> Than lose one single thought that's feminine.[16]

When not swept to courageous action by patriotism, vulnerability and a kind of passivity were as characteristic of the melodramatic heroine as her perfect goodness. "I can only wait patiently for the storm to burst on my head and trust to heaven for deliverance," said a typical heroine, while another sighed, "The Fell destroyer comes! Heaven protect thy fainting suppliant."[17] When a bad woman, in this instance a sensuous Turkish virago, began to transform into a heroine under the influence of a good Christian crusader, she noted, "I think I have acquired a new *sense*, which makes me weak and womanish."[18] Her adjectives were essentially synonyms. Indeed the heroine's weakness was such that she had to be carefully sheltered. She was "the innocent wild flower" and "the modest violet panting for the shade" whose vulnerability was more extreme because not only her character but her reputation could bear no hint of stain:

---

[13] Elizabeth Oakes Smith, *Old New York* (New York, 1853), p. 20.

[14] *The Brothers; or, Consequences* (Boston, 1823), p. 14.

[15] Charles E. Grice, *The Battle of New Orleans* (Baltimore, 1815), p. 54.

[16] John Daly Burk, *Female Patriotism; or, The Death of Joan of Arc* (New York, 1798), p. 24. Joan explained that "love of liberty" steeled her to action, but did not curb her "timid, soft and virgin" nature.

[17] John Howard Payne, *Julia; or, The Wanderer* (New York, 1806), p. 50; *Lucinda*, in *Rejected Plays* (New York, 1828), p. 35.

[18] John Augustus Stone, *Tancred; or, The Siege of Antioch* (Philadelphia, 1827), p. 19.

> Virgins' reputations
> Are frail as flowers, more brittle e'en than glass.—
> Be ye as pure as the unblemished snow,
> The slightest speck that hovers o'er your whiteness,
> Needs but a breath to blot it.[19]

"Throughout all nature," the melodrama taught, "there is no plant so delicate as maiden innocence. The dust on the wings of a butterfly is less perishable than her good name."[20] Total goodness and extreme weakness combined to make the heroine the emotional center of the melodrama:

> There is in woman's fall,
> As in an angel's, so much woe and sadness,
> Men must needs weep.[21]

The constant threat of this catastrophe was the emotional core of the melodramatic structure.

As virtue was personified in the heroine so was the threat to it presented in physical, specifically sexual, terms. If melodramatic heroines fell, it was certainly not for lack of warning. Into almost every play some exhortation to chastity was worked. "Be on your guard against the snare that vice lays for unsuspecting virtue," young girls were told. "Arm yourself against the machinations of man; for lull'd by a false security, many have been lur'd into the lap of infamy, and plunged into the gloomy vortex of everlasting ruin."[22] But avoiding the "gloomy vortex" was not easy, because woman's natural enemy took the same form as her natural protector. When a heroine pledged her love she did so "knowing that when a woman puts her trust in man, she risks all, and places her stock of happiness where full oft the principal and interest both are lost."[23] Like "ivy fondly clinging to the tall oak's majestic side," woman's "fond, confiding heart on manly faith reposes." But should "faithless man" betray this confidence, her lot was hopeless.[24] A mother

---

[19] John Howard Payne, *Woman's Revenge* (1832), in *ALP*, 6: 77; Louisa Medina, *Ernest Maltravers* (New York, n.d.), p. 27; Isaac Harby, *The Gordian Knot; or, Causes and Effects* (Charleston, 1810), p. 49.

[20] William Dunlap, *Fraternal Discord* (New York, 1809), p. 39.

[21] Robert Montgomery Bird, *Caridorf*, in *ALP*, 12: 103.

[22] Joseph Hutton, *School for Prodigals* (Philadelphia, 1809), p. 6.

[23] James Kirke Paulding, *The Bucktails; or, Americans in England* in *American Comedies* (Philadelphia, 1847), p. 63.

[24] Samuel Woodworth, *The Widow's Son; or, Which Is the Traitor?* (New York, 1825), p. 64. The hero in this play sang:

> For woman, dear woman n'er traffics by measure,
> But risks her whole heart without counting the cost
> And should the dear youth whom she trusts with her treasure
> Be shipwreck'd or faithless, her capital's lost.

lamented, "One serpent brought ruin upon Eden, but myriads crawl upon earth, and the daughters of Eve are condemned to dwell among them, and are expected to escape the primeval fall."[25]

Virtue, of course, was not to be tempted by undisguised vice. When faced with open attack on her chastity, the frail vessel of woman became an iron virgin. Many a heroine said in effect at some point in her adventures, "But know, vile hypocrite, thy unmannerly arts shall ne'er disarm the virtue of my indignant soul," or "My soul now sickens at all thy artful blandishments."[26] "Unhand me, ruffian," was indeed a common melodramatic command, and often an effective one. In the mouth of a pure peasant girl, it daunted even the autocratic Louis XIV:

> Why should I shrink from one so powerless?
> And can it be that Virtue's presence awes
> Me thus? That virtue which no weapon needs
> Except its own resistless dignity.

Despite the strength of her "conscious virtue" and "icy looks of chastened purity,"[27] the heroine was always in danger and sometimes fell before the baseness of man. When this happened, repentance, madness, and death were all that awaited her, except in a few instances where after long suffering she was allowed a modicum of happiness. Such unhappy fate was inevitable even if the heroine had been "unfortunate, rather than guilty"—if she had been raped or deceived by "a false marriage."[28] These were favorite plot devices because the woman's total purity of intent made her fall more pathetic, but no less inevitable:

> Tear but one pillar from arched Virtue's Temple
> And all the edifice is hurled upon us.[29]

Shattering virtue's temple was the job of the villain. He was the "smooth and subtle hypocrite," "the base deceiver," "the impious fiend," "the lyingest fiend that walks in shapes of man," a "leviathan of infamy"—indeed the snake in the garden, the initial disrupter of innocence.[30] The melodramatic villain took two basic shapes, one for comedy

---

[25] Richard Penn Smith, "The Venetian," HTC, Act IV.

[26] Nathaniel H. Bannister, *The Gentleman of Lyons; or, The Marriage Contract* (New York, 1838), p. 30; Louisa C. Adams, "Captive of Scio" (Microfilms of the Adams' Papers), Act III, scene 1.

[27] Anna Cora Mowatt, *Armand; or, The Peer and the Peasant* (Boston, 1855), p. 55; Harby, *The Gordian Knot,* p. 52.

[28] John Howard Payne, *Richelieu* (New York, 1826), p. 17.

[29] Bird, *Caridorf*, p. 113.

[30] Mordecai M. Noah, *Marion; or, The Hero of Lake George* (New York, 1822), p. 14; J. H. Wainwright, *Rip Van Winkle* (London, 1855), p. 24; James Ellison, *The American Captive; or, The Siege of Tripoli* (Boston, 1812), p. 16; Harby, *The Gordian Knot,* p. 64; Joseph Hutton, *Fashionable Follies* (1809), in *RPAD*, 2: 69.

and one for serious plays. In the former, though wholly despicable and unprincipled, he remained too obviously foppish and ridiculous to pose a real threat; in the latter, he showed enough intelligence or courage to make him frightening, a devil incarnate.

The comic mood demanded humor, but melodramatic conventions made laughter at the hero or heroine difficult; their elevation seldom allowed indulgence even in wit. Hence much of the burden of the fun fell on the comic villain who was generally a votary of "fashion" characterized by "little gold, plenty of brass, and an abundance of tinsel."[31] He was full of external niceties, often exaggerated to a ludicrous extent, but this fashionable façade covered a totally insensitive heart. Often he was a foreigner, and almost always his manners were foreign-tainted. His vileness was proved by his deceit toward women. Much of the humor in melodramatic comedies derived from his ambition in simultaneously promoting various amorous attachments.[32] The course of any man making passionate love to several women in the same house or social set was easily complicated comically. And because the man was a fop or imposter, a fool and a coward, nothing was easier than fooling and foiling him. Comic bad men tended to seem not "villains, but only idiots."[33]

A different and much more ominous character was the villain of the serious melodrama, where an aura of danger was needed. The setting, particularly in Gothic melodramas, helped create an atmosphere of menacing threat, but this effect was generally supplied by the villain:

> I tremble when I see that horrid man—
> He carries on his brow the badge of vice,
> That narrow cheek, that keen, but sunken eye
> That black complexion, all denote the villain.
> His scowl is dreadful as a winter's blast,
> His hate is deadly—O beware that man![34]

In the serious villain, a host of evil traits coalesced with the demonic energy necessary to make possible success in his foul designs—designs which were "indeed the devil's handiwork." He explicitly rejected any moral control: "Away with conscience—justice—all the checks that lie upon my path! The way to rise is to forego all." And he knew no compassion. His heart was "of marble that cannot be softened" and when he

---

[31] William I. Paulding, *The Noble Exile*, in *American Comedies* (Philadelphia, 1847), p. 128.

[32] Sheridan's Joseph Surface in *The School for Scandal* and Billy Dimple of Tyler's *The Contrast* were the prototypes of the comic villain.

[33] *Monthly Register, Magazine, and Review of the United States*, 3 (1807): 50.

[34] John Blake White, *Foscari; or, The Venetian Exile* (Charleston, 1806), p. 9.

had the heroine in his toils he exulted, "Ha! Ha! Ha! How I banquet on every sigh; each tear is nectar to my soul."[35]

The motivation for the villain's demonism was in a few cases non-existent save for a general malevolence, but commonly some human reason was given for his fiendish behavior. Desire for revenge or extreme avarice or ambition were generally at the root of his "heart's deepest, blackest feelings." The villain in *The Drunkard* explained his actions typically in terms of "revenge and avarice, the master passions of my nature." His desire for revenge came from a twisted hatred of the hero's father for forgiving him when "detected in an act of vile atrocity."[36] This kind of vagueness about the villain's motivation often underlined the horror of his character. No specific list of crimes or perverse reasons could be as effective as intimating total baseness while leaving the specifics to be assumed by each spectator.

Yet this was "complicated villainy" for the villain had in almost every instance one fair goal, the heroine, whom he pursued with diabolic subterfuge or violence. Sometimes designs on the heroine were mixed with ambition or avarice or revenge; for example, a lawyer who had de-frauded a virtuous girl of a great deal of money and feared detection understandably wanted to keep her in his clutches.[37] But most often the villain's desire for the heroine was extraneous to his other pursuits. Whatever the other crimes committed, villainy proved itself by its attack on the citadel of virtue. The "miscreant victim of his own ambition" was usually also a devotee of "insatiate and abhorred lust."[38] For this last crime "would render virtuous the basest action of a demon," and gave the villain "precedences above the darkest of the fiends of hell."[39] The villain had human form,

> And yet art not a man. The
> Virtue's wanting that sustains the name.
> None but a dastard of degenerate birth
> Would triumph o'er a wretched helpless woman.[40]

---

[35] Henry Harrington, *Bernardo del Carpio* (n.p., 1836), p. 28; Nathaniel H. Bannister, *England's Iron Days* (New Orleans, 1837), p. 14; Samuel B. H. Judah, *The Mountain Torrent* (New York, 1820), pp. 42, 51.

[36] John Peirpont and W. E. Smith, *The Drunkard; or, The Fallen Saved* (Boston, 1847), p. 49.

[37] The villain explained, "My fortune depends on her possession, but if foil'd in that, my safety claims her death." John Howard Payne, *Thérèse; or, The Orphan of Geneva* (Philadelphia, 1838), p. 27.

[38] David Everett, *Daranzel; or, The Persian Patriot* (Boston, 1800), p. 26.

[39] Watterston, *Child of Feeling*, p. 42; Junius Brutus Booth, *Ugolino* (Philadelphia, 1840), p. 20.

[40] Nathaniel Bannister, *Gaulantus* (Cincinnati, 1836), pp. 46–47.

In the one play where Satan himself took on human form the dramatist made him lust after the heroine.[41]

Not all bad persons, the melodrama admitted, approved of seducing or raping young women. But if they drew the line at this final outrage, no matter what their other crimes, they became somewhat sympathetic characters. Thus a bandit's declaration of principle presumably much allayed the list of crimes that preceded it:

> I understand Robbery, Murder, and Plunder of all kinds. . . . I can in the darkness of night . . . strangle footmen, jailors, turnkeys, soldiers, anything that's a man who would oppose my path. But sooner, than like a snake to strike the peace or honor of a woman, I had rather the dogs should gnaw my skull at the foot of a pillory.[42]

Nineteenth-century audiences did not condemn the man forced to crime "for daring to uplift a vassal's arm, to stop a lordling's lust." Even though he had tried to seduce the captive heroine for two years and was on the point of killing her husband and raping her, he was not truly a villain if he suddenly appreciated the woman's sterling merits:

> Your constancy exceeds my utmost praise;
> Your heroism the brave man must respect;
> . . . .
> I have conquered these tumultuous feelings—
> Humanity has triumphed over love.[43]

Defeat was always the eventual lot of the true villain. "Death and furies!" "Foiled! Hell and Confusion," and "Foiled again!" gained currency from the frequency of their repetition. Villains usually died, sometimes reciting their own epitaph: "Betrayed, my schemes annihilated—myself undone, my enemies triumphant—lost—lost—all is destroyed—all—all [falls]." Often the villain's death speech underlined the play's lesson: "Is all hope excluded? All, all! Slaves of guilt! Votaries of passion! See here the recompense that awaits you." If the villain failed to point out the moral, some other character would: "In this heaven speaks its doom with awful voice."[44]

Between the villain and the heroine, morally and often physically, stood the hero. His mediating role differed. Often he was primarily a

---

[41] James Hillhouse, *Hadad* (New York, 1825).
[42] Joseph S. Jones, "Zafari, The Bohemian" (1842), HTC, Act I, scene i.
[43] John Hodgkinson, *The Man of Fortitude; or, The Knight's Adventure* (New York, 1807), pp. 29, 27.
[44] Bannister, "Rockwood," Act III, scene iv; Joseph Hutton, *The Orphan of Prague* (Philadelphia, 1808), p. 38; George H. Calvert, *Count Julian* (Baltimore, 1840), p. 68.

shield, fending off the thrusts of the villain. Occasionally he was the pawn over whom the forces of good and evil, the heroine and the villain struggled. Particularly if the hero and heroine were married was he likely to be the center of this moral tug-of-war. Most of the reform-oriented dramas in the nineteenth century featured hero-husbands who drank or gambled or were driven toward crime by harsh circumstances. Because these men were basically good, their weaknesses tended to focus attention on the social evil. The hero could take on this role because moral vacillation was allowable in him; his goodness, unlike that of the heroine, need not be untainted.

Of course, the hero often was simply perfect: as undaunted in action, as faithful in love, as appalled by evil, as elevated in sentiment as even the heroine. A villain, one Lord Sindal, gave a fairly typical catalogue of a hero's virtues:

> He is filled to the very brim with the old fashioned principles of virtue, chastity, sobriety and all that sort of stuff. . . . This pious, chaste, virtuous, timid young man has lived all his days in the country. His body has been fed with milk and his mind with sermons.[45]

The imputation of timidity was, as the audience knew, a villainous distortion; the hero's timidity was only manly modesty, to be thrown off in fearless activity as soon as he scented evil. Bravery was a necessary heroic quality because the hero's basic job was to "protect virtue, serve love and rescue innocence."[46] In plays that had political overtones, patriotic responsibilities were his as well as romantic ones. Yet even when the hero was a fighter for freedom or justice, these motives were meshed with more domestic concerns. For the person who held political power unjustly or wielded it unwisely was generally given unwholesome designs on the heroine as well. "To love is the hero's privilege; and his first duty to protect the helpless" and to "vindicate the holy cause of innocence."[47] So, for example, as the hero struggled to gain Poland's freedom from the Russians, patriotism united with romantic concern: "Oh, Heaven! perhaps even now within the foul tyrant's grasp, she vainly shrieks for aid and calls on death to save her from dishonor."[48] Foul tyrants were by melodramatic definition heartless ravishers.

The hero proved his goodness, as the villain his evil, primarily by his

---

[45] William Charles White, *The Clergyman's Daughter* (Boston, 1810), pp. 21–22.

[46] Mordecai M. Noah, *The Fortress of Sorrento* (New York, 1808), p. 21.

[47] John Howard Payne, *Ali Pacha; or, The Signet Ring* (New York, 1823), p. 12; *Trial by Jury*, in *ALP*, 6: 42.

[48] Silas Steele, *The Brazen Drum* (Philadelphia, 1842), p. 8.

attitude toward "defenseless woman, . . . that sex that *nature formed us to defend*."[49] No hero tolerated so much as joking mention of a desire to do any woman wrong; such a thought was sure to drive him, depending on his temperament, either to anger or a sermon. "And can you so calmly, so unfeelingly, and with so much self-complacency," asked a hero of a comic villain, "meditate the ruin of an artless girl, and the consequent misery of everyone to whom she is dear? I can pity the errors of a fashionable education, but. . . ."[50]

A hero nevertheless was allowed certain faults. He sometimes harbored resentment and desired revenge for old wrongs or was impetuous in his conclusions and conduct, even to the point of doubting the virtue of the heroine. Often he had a weakness that endangered him, and even woman's "recreant love" was not always enough to save him, at least until the play's end, if his weakness was for gaming or drink. Yet through all his degradation the hero proved his goodness by his respect for the "loving, forbearing, self-denying angel" that was his wife. "Joe Morgan, fallen as I am, and powerless in the grasp of the demon, has never hurt her with a cruel word," was the only boast of one alcoholic hero.[51] Though his home decayed and his family starved because of his passion for drink and gaming, such a saving remnant of virtue made the character a weak man to be pitied rather than a bad man to be detested.

The fourth major melodramatic character was the old father, who almost always served one of two roles: either to emphasize the moral of the piece through his good advice, or to set up the conflict between the heroine's love and duty around which the plot revolved. He was usually presented as a person of great natural dignity and elevated sentiment, especially if his principal dramatic job was that of moral lecturer. Without me, the wise old father might have asked the audience as he did his daughter, "Who will you have to caution you against the thousand destructive snares that everywhere endanger youthful innocence?"[52] Because the most ominous snare was that of loss of chastity, most of his moralizing was addressed to this point. The old father endlessly expounded the importance of purity, the fragility of the female reputation, and the need to beware of unprincipled men. If the heroine fell, he was the one who most lamented; if she escaped from the tempter, he was the one who welcomed her back; when vice and virtue gained their just rewards,

---

[49] Carr, *Benevolent Lawyers*, p. 17.
[50] Samuel Woodworth, *The Forest Rose; or, American Farmers* (New York, 1825), p. 24.
[51] Pratt, *Ten Nights in a Barroom*, p. 10.
[52] W. C. White, *Clergyman's Daughter*, p. 9.

it was he who exulted, "Heaven has heard our prayers—Triumph, my daughter. Shout all for rescued innocence."[53]

Of course, any child was under infinite obligation to such a noble-hearted parent. Next to sexual purity, no personal merit was so stressed in the melodrama as "the charms of filial piety." One of these wise old men advised a couple considering eloping against her father's wishes:

> Would you rest quietly on your pillows after the labor of the day, would you sleep peacefully in your grave when the labour of life is o'er and the night of death is come—obey your parents. Honour your father and mother or the church yard will give you no rest.[54]

And they did honor him to the point of gladly offering their own happiness to his welfare. A heroine who had been forced to put off her marriage to the hero for several years, gladly delayed it longer when her father became sick and she felt his illness demanded her full attention.[55] Some lesser heroes were upset by such delays, but the best of them were entranced by these displays of loyalty and virtue. When the heroine informed him that she could not leave her father though she "died for love," the best of heroes, realizing that "she that forgets her duty to a parent will never learn it for a husband," loved her "the dearer for that thought." "Charming girl," rejoiced another suitor, "her duty to her mother overpowers every other consideration."[56]

Such filial piety could be the source of much trouble, indeed of enough to keep a whole play going, if a father's essential goodness or basic wisdom had a rift in it so that he forced or wanted to wed his daughter to an undesirable man. The moral flaw of the melodramatic father was often some crime or indiscretion committed as a young man, with which the villain blackmailed him for his daughter's hand. "The gibbet or your daughter" were the alternatives one villain presented to an old man.[57] In comic melodrama the father's fault was likely to be excessive ambition, which allowed him to be taken in by the villain. Still basically good-hearted, this comic father perhaps desired money or position, which blinded him both to the sterling merit of the hero and to the baseness of the villain.

---

[53] Payne, *Thérèse*, p. 45. In this instance Thérèse was an orphan and her "father" was a priest. The father's role was often assumed by some psychological father figure, especially older military heroes in the patriotic plays.

[54] *Mirror of Taste*, 3 (January, 1811): 48; William Dunlap, *The Good Neighbor* (New York, 1814), pp. 6–7.

[55] *The Brothers*, p. 19.

[56] Paulding, *Bucktails*, p. 73; John Minshull, *Rural Felicity* (New York, 1801), p. 36.

[57] Joseph S. Jones, *Moll Pitcher; or, The Fortune Teller of Lynn* (Boston, 1855), pp. 39–40.

In such a situation the heroine swayed between terrible alternatives. She had either to disobey and disappoint a parent or to sacrifice "that which is dearer than life" to an undeserving man. The proper decision in such a difficult case was never clearly agreed upon. Some of the most elevated of heroines could "never act in disobedience to my father's will" and concluded at least briefly to consent "though my grave should be my bridal couch." A father's stern decree might bring "a gentle, obedient daughter to—anything!"[58] But other girls decided, although they were dutiful in all other instances, that "here duty, my honoured father, were a sacrifice beyond my fortitude."[59] No young woman should barter her most precious jewel for any reason; but so long as she only offered it to save her father and everything worked all right before the transaction was completed, her self-sacrificing nobility only enhanced her worth. And by the end of the play every good father realized, even if his child had been undutiful in this respect, that "it is the part of a father to love the purity of the child, to strengthen it, to guard it—but never to tempt it himself or expose it to unnecessary temptations from others."[60]

The mother appeared less often than the father in the serious plays of the period. Perhaps issuing moral platitudes or forcing a daughter to wed against her will was considered man's work; whatever the reason, the mother was often dead—"an angel spirit"—or at least a less centrally important character.[61] In comedies, however, mothers were more active than fathers in trying to mismate their daughters. The mother as a social-climbing parvenu was a common comic character who was usually eager to wed her daughter to some unworthy or bogus European nobleman, while she scorned the unpretentious hero. "The cretur can scarcely support himself with decency, and yet has the presumption for to think for to marry my step-datur," complained one of them, as she ludicrously preened to receive the villain.[62]

Less elevated in principle and sentiment than the heroine were the "lively girl" and low-comedy stereotypes who often played a major role in the period's plays. In European plays the pair were usually servants, but in plays set in the United States they were commonly people of a humble social position, lively, good-natured and often in love with

---

[58] Charles Breck, *The Trust* (New York, 1808), p. 15; Cornelius Logan, *Yankee Land* (Boston, n.d.), p. 21; A. B. Lindsley, *Love and Friendship* (New York, 1809), p. 6.

[59] Isaac Harby, *Alberti* (Charleston, 1819), p. 24.

[60] William Dunlap, *The Italian Father* (New York, 1810), p. 24.

[61] Hutton, *Orphan of Prague*, p. 15.

[62] Watterston, *Child of Feeling*, p. 11. The stepmother or aunt relationship was sometimes used, seemingly to make the total disparity between the vulgar mother and the elevated daughter more believable.

one another. In contrast to the characters in the central structure of the melodrama, they partook more of purely human qualities and less of superhuman virtue or subhuman baseness. The good were likely to be worldly-wise, and the bad to have a roguish charm. If seldom many-sided human beings, neither were they moral abstractions. Separated from the sublime moral preoccupations at the center of the melodrama, they served as spokesmen for most of the wit and common sense these plays offered.

Dunlap's *The Archers* presented a typical pair of low-comedy lovers whose shrewd simplicity allowed them to present ideas which more elevated melodramatic characters presumably never considered and certainly never expressed. The lively girl urged her sweetheart to fight for his country:

> *Cecily:* I shall like you the better for it as long as I live—if you're not killed.
>
> *Conrad:* Why, you should like me better for dying for my country.
>
> *Cecily:* Should I? Well, maybe I should; but somehow I shall never like a dead man as well as a live one.
>
> *Conrad:* Well, I don't know but that your taste is as well founded as your politics.

No hero or heroine was ever so sensible as to express a preference for a living man over a dead patriot. Similarly, Dunlap gave William Tell long speeches emphasizing love of country, liberty, and union, but when he wanted to suggest a governmental idea that was not wholly a moral platitude he put it in the mouth of Conrad, who told Cecily that "from the governor to the basket-girl, we all build on the same broad bottom, *interest*, girl."[63]

The attitude of one lively girl whose father wished her to wed for wealth suggests the differences between her and the heroine. She would heed no "unjust malediction of an avaricious father," because the right freely to pick her own mate was woman's "Magna Charta of Heaven:"

> While each freeman's son
> Boasts of rights a plenty,
> Daughters have but one
> E'en at one and twenty.
> 'Tis the right to choose
> Tom or Dick or Harry
> Whom we will refuse,
> Which we wish to marry.

---

[63] William Dunlap, *The Archers; or, The Mountaineers of Switzerland* (New York, 1796), pp. 11–12.

Chorus: 'Tis our chartered right
       Nature's hand has penn'd it
       Let us then unite
       Bravely to defend it.
       While our fathers fought
       For our Independence
       Patriot mothers taught
       This to their descendants:
       Daughters, guard and save
       Rights too dear to barter.
       Spurn the name of slave
       Freedom is our charter.[64]

The sensible forthrightness of this position contrasted sharply with the soul-rending solemnity with which a true heroine faced such a problem. Both its matter-of-factness and its gaiety proclaimed that the character did not have to uphold the elevation of thought demanded of the heroine.

Even the beauties of married life, to which the rarified parts of the melodrama paid such flowery praise, were given more skeptical treatment in the low-comedy portions. For instance, one heroine recoiled at the "blasphemy" of her servant-girl's opinion that "love conquers reason, and hymen conquers love."[65] Low-comedy sections of plays sometimes featured an elderly couple, the woman usually a hellion, who were constantly at each other's throats. "I'll just go and take a little whiskey, blow up at my fool of a husband, and then I shall be happy," said one Mrs. Cabbagewell. "What a blessing it is to have somebody to quarrel with."[66] Such a notion about the pleasures of marriage never entered the higher echelons of melodrama.

While the central characters were manipulated to impress a moral truth, the minor characters often made light of these moral maxims. Perhaps the lively girl was most charming when blithely mocking sentimental stage conventions. For example, one girl informed a low-comedy character that she was planning to entice a comic villain just for the fun of being rescued: "Think what a chance there would be to immortalize yourself, Jonathan. Just as the ravisher had seized me in his arms, and was rifling these virgin lips of their nectareous sweets, a blow from my lover's hand lays him prostrate in the dust. O wouldn't that be delightful!"[67] A heroine, even the happiest of them, would never have thought

[64] Samuel Woodworth, *Deed of Gift* (New York, 1822), pp. 8–9.
[65] Judah, *Mountain Torrent*, p. 9.
[66] Bannister, *Putnam*, p. 8.
[67] Woodworth, *Forest Rose*, p. 35.

of joking about anything so serious as the "nectarous sweets" of her virgin lips.

The low-comedy man who represented some sectional or national type was even more prominent in American plays. While the lively girl was a tease, the low-comedy man was at once shrewd and simple minded:

> *Jonathan:* I cannot tell the reason, but I really want a wife,
> And everybody tells me, 'tis the sweetest thing in life.
>
> *Harriet:* If you expect to please me, and win me for your bride,
> You'll have to lie and flatter, and swear, my lad, beside—
> So now begin to practice and if you'd have me wed,
> Declare you even love, sir, the ground on which I tread.
>
> *Jonathan:* I'll tell you that sincerely nor think it any harm,
> I love the ground you walk on, for 'tis your father's farm.
> Could that be mine without you, I'd be a happy man,
> But since you go together, I will love you if I can.[68]

This Jonathan was largely an Americanization of the Irishmen and Yorkshireman of the English stage, and clearly both a descendant of the Jonathan in *The Contrast* and a predecessor of the Jedediah Homebreds of the 1830's, the Deuteronomy Dutifuls of the 1840's, and the Hiram Hireouts of the 1850's. In many of these plays the central hero-heroine-villain situation became increasingly superfluous, as the dramatist focused more and more on the escapades and sayings of the Yankee. Clearly audiences enjoyed being amused by "Jonathanisms."

The Yankee was characterized in large part by his simple mindedness and naiveté. When he mistakenly entered a theater, he thought he was watching a quarrel in "the next neighbor's house"; when he wandered into a brothel, he decided it was a woman's sewing circle; he thought a fortress was a "she-fort"; he called rugs floor "kiverlids." Having hired out as a butler, he replied to his first instructions about admitting visitors: "Carry 'em into your study? If they don't heft more than 350 pounds and ain't too constipacious."[69] This naiveté was united with a great deal of canniness, a kind of hardheaded innate wisdom that protected him and other good people. "They don't make bad husbands, or fathers," said a Yankee militia major of his men, "and, with the aid of steam, will be

---

[68] *Ibid.*, p. 21. Though they were both related to the servant types in European melodramas, the lively girl generally occupied a position implicitly above that of the specifically low-comedy man.

[69] Royall Tyler, *The Contrast*, in *RAP*, pp. 64–65; Joseph S. Jones, "The Silver Spoon" (1852), HTC, Act IV; Steele, *Brazen Drum*, p. 11; Lazarus Beach, *Jonathan Postfree; or, The Honest Yankee* (Philadelphia, 1827), p. 20; H. J. Conway, *Hiram Hireout* (New York, 1852), p. 5.

able to arrive at what I call human perfectability."[70] As Jonathan took over more of the attention in these plays, so he gained increased importance in protecting virtue. Jonathan in *The Contrast* was obviously on the side of good, but Tyler saw a certain danger in his naiveté and pointed out that he needed the guidance of the wise Colonel Manly to save him from the folly of Shays' Rebellion. As the nineteenth century progressed Jonathan was purged of any need for guidance. He remained simple, but soon his essential pure-heartedness and his innate good sense were enough to save him from any real danger. His mental simplicity came to imply a kind of superior wisdom.

This wisdom showed itself partially in the popular truisms he spoke: "I notice one thing, the most fashionable people borrow the most money"; "I never knew a man to go to the almshouse that he hadn't rum to blame for his poverty"; or "Pride you know must have a fall."[71] Wisdom also was revealed in his shrewd practicality and his ability to accomplish almost anything. As early as 1798 William Dunlap complained of a play whose main point was that "two yankee boys can beat four mounseers."[72] This idea was endlessly repeated in these Yankee plays, and the number and rank of people outwitted was steadily raised. By the 1840's one Yankee who wandered into Poland selling a hemp-curing machine had no trouble outfoxing all the "Russian rustycrats" who were curbing the nation's freedom and endangering the heroine's virtue.[73]

Yankee characters were often "sharp dealers" in trade without diminishing their essential goodness. One hoped a minister would preach on Sunday, because "if he does, I can let out my pew for double price, and sell lots of new shoes."[74] Even dishonesty in the stage Yankee was usually an endearing trait. Thus a dairyman, Solomon Swillpail, ran off to sea in pique over the activities of a milk inspection committee that objected when he let rain "sort o' kind o' dylute the adulterations."[75] Shady dealing for these comic Americans was simply good business and

---

[70] George H. Hill, *Scenes From The Life of an Actor* (New York, 1853), p. 94.

[71] Jones "Silver Spoon," Act IV, p. 9; Pratt, *Ten Nights in a Barroom*, p. 26; Beach, *Jonathan Postfree*, p. 20.

[72] William Dunlap, *Diary* (June 29, 1798), ed. Dorothy Barck (New York, 1930), 1 : 304.

[73] Steele, *The Brazen Drum*, p. 5.

[74] Jones, *Moll Pitcher*, p. 20.

[75] Silas Steele, "The Right of Search," HTC, Act I, p. 8. Frances Trollope, *Domestic Manners of the Americans*, ed. Donald Smalley (New York, 1960), p. 302, advanced as evidence of the moral corruption of America the pride or amusement of Americans in the "sly, grinding, selfish, and tricking" Yankee whom no one could match "at over-reaching in a bargain."

left morality untouched. One Yankee described his wooden nutmeg business:

> *Yankee:* I made 'em out of pine plank and sold the whole cargo to a grocer in York. Uncle Ben said it was as slick a trick as ever was hatch'd east'ard. Did you ever hear of Uncle Ben?
>
> *Wentworth:* Damn your Uncle Ben!
>
> *Yankee:* Oh no! don't darn Uncle Ben. Darn me as much as you please— but Uncle Ben's a deacon, and it's a kind of blasphemy to darn a deacon.[76]

In business most of them were "pious yet calculating"; one admitted he was "some sharp, I allow. Guess I know beans, when the bag's ontied."[77] Only after 1840 was moral opprobrium sometimes added to the geniality with which the stage Yankee's calculating acquisitiveness was viewed.

Besides naiveté and shrewdness, the Yankee raised laughter by his insatiable curiosity, exaggerated bravado, tall stories, and an "idiom . . . unique, racy, and pungent."[78] He asked questions of everyone, not liking "to pry into anyone's business in particular," but wanting "to keep a running idea of what's going on in general." He might be so modest that he always went "to bed without a candle," but he was not likely to underestimate his attainments. One Yankee was sure that the heroine could not resist him, because

> I'm the boy for a race, an apple-paring, or a quilting frolic—fight a cock, hunt an oppossum, or snare a partridge with anyone. Then I'm a squire, and a country judge, and a brevet offiser in the militia besides; and a devil of a fellow at an election to boot.[79]

The Yankee also had a stock of tall tales which he lost no chance to tell:

> Maybe you've heern of Uncle Josh's dog—got three of the greatest curiosities any canine ever had: his tail curls so tight his hind legs can't reach the ground; fever and ague wouldn't hang to him—he was too lazy to shake; and he's so like Uncle Josh's t'other dog, you can't tell t'other from which.[80]

---

[76] William Dunlap, *A Trip to Niagara; or, Travellers in America* (New York, 1830), pp. 36–37.

[77] *Cleveland Plain Dealer* (January 8, 1847), quoted in Gerhard W. Gaiser, "The History of Cleveland Theatre From the Beginning to 1854" (Ph.D. dissertation, State University of Iowa, 1953), p. 109; J. T. Trowbridge, *Neighbour Jackwood* (Boston, 1857).

[78] *New York Mirror*, 13 (November 7, 1835): 151. "Why don't you know where Tabbyville is?" one Yankee asked a stranger. "Now do tell. Well, may I be smashed into original sin if that ain't the beatamost." Nathaniel Deering, *Clairvoyants*, in *Life and Works of Nathaniel Deering*, ed. Leola Bowie Chaplin, *University of Maine Studies*, 32, no. 2 (Orono, Me., 1934), p. 207.

[79] Pratt, *Ten Nights in a Barroom*, pp. 4–5; Pierpont and Smith, *The Drunkard*, p. 13; Mordecai M. Noah, *She Would Be A Soldier; or, The Plains of Chippawa* (New York, 1819), p. 19.

[80] Conway, *Hiram Hireout*, p. 6.

Even the sweethearts of these vigorous Yankee boys, "real corn-fed gals, I swow," were described with the same hyperbolic humor. "Lucy is a proper nice gal," admitted Jedediah Homebred of his girl. "The only objection I got to her is she snores so distressin' loud. She snored so loud the other night she was obliged to go to the neighbors to sleep to keep from waking herself up."[81]

The Yankee was only the most popular American variety of the low-comedy character. On the stage he competed with transported foreign variants, such as the English farmer and especially the Irishman. In the 1830's the Irishman became even more common on this country's stage than Jonathan, partly because of the highly successful American tours of Irish actors like Tyrone Power. Less crafty in business than Jonathan, Paddy was likely to be more immoral in other ways. "Sure, what Irishman ever sprung from the green sod," asked one of them, "would think of living without the enjoyment of these illigant accomplishments, eating, drinking, loving, and fighting."[82] Dunlap's version of the Irish-American had him leaving his homeland because "I thought I might as well get rid of my *little inconveniences*, for they will be springing up around an Irishman, like mushrooms around a dunghill . . ., debts, and wives, and children, and such like articles."[83] But all these things were merely amusing for the Irishman, who was naive, canny, quaint of speech, and thoroughly good-hearted. With somewhat different external traits, he was basically Jonathan with a brogue.

Jonathan appeared less often with a burr, perhaps because the Scottish stereotype lacked the simplicity and spontaneity that were the charm of the stage Yankee, Negro, or Irishman. There were a few stage Scotsmen, always proverbially careful of money. When he wanted to patch a feud, the Scotsman offered a pinch of snuff, that being "as binding as if we drank out of the same cup together, and the ceremony is more economical." But he was really a good-hearted soul: "Take a generous pinch, man, you're welcome. . . . Ye cannot say that ever Andrew Macklegraith lost sight of the golden rule."[84] The subplot of Workman's *Liberty in Louisiana* contrasted amusingly the Irish and Scottish low-comedy types: the Irishman, a lusty, thirsty, and charming rogue, who justified his occasional thievery by pointing out that America was "a land of liberty, and where else ought a man to make free?" and the Scotsman, a dour, cautious, and moralistic businessman who preferred making

[81] Hill, *Scenes*, p. 95; Joseph S. Jones, *Green Mountain Boy* (New York, n.d.), p. 15.
[82] James Pilgrim, *The Limerick Boy* (New York, 1856), p. 6.
[83] William Dunlap, *The Glory of Columbia, Her Yeomanry!* (New York, 1817), pp. 37–41.
[84] Richard Penn Smith, *The Triumph at Plattsburg*, in *RAP*, 2d ed., p. 171.

money "in the way of fair trade" and who righteously stressed that he'd "never sell anything for gold that is not treble gilt."[85] The ebullient Yankee, the spendthrift Irishman, and the ne'er-do-well Rip Van Winkle, the period's only important stage Dutchman, were much more popular in low-comedy roles.

The frontiersman was seen on the American stage rarely compared to the Yankee or Irishman. Paulding's Nimrod Wildfire, the "yellow flower of the forest" and "a human cataract for Kentucky," was the only stage westerner to appear in a particularly successful play and in the American version of *The Lion of the West* was supported by a Yankee, Deacon Dogwood.[86] Like the Yankee, he was naive, fond of tall stories, and given to "whimsical extravagance of speech." Wildfire's speech "on the tariff"—a rather brutal jest at Davy Crockett—was a compilation of the clichés of western brag. It concluded: "There's no back out in my breed —I go the whole hog. I've got the prettiest sister, fastest horse, and ugliest dog in the deestrict—in short to sum up all in one word on these here tariff duties—I'm a horse."[87] His bluster was wilder in tone and metaphor than the usual stage Yankee's, and he liked to brawl even better than the Irishman. "I am a gentleman and my name's fight!" shouted one Roaring Ralph. "Foot and hand, tooth and nail, claw and mudscraper, knife, gun, and tomahawk. Or anyway you choose to take me I'm your man. Cock-a-doodle-doo-oo." But beneath this violent exterior was a heart "which would scorn to do a mean or dishonest action" and a canny strength that always allowed him to triumph over evil.[88] For the Kentuckian there was "no such word as gin up."[89]

The one American low-comedy stereotype to retain a servant's position was the stage Negro. Like other low-comedy variants, the Negro's humorous qualities grew largely from his odd dialect and his misuse of words. His special characteristic was inflated pride in badges of rank, such as flashy livery "to stonish de coloured population," and his exaggerated scorn for what was "too cheap and makes common niggers too familly-li-ar wid us perlite swash-ci-e-ty."[90] Though not

[85] James Workman, *Liberty in Louisiana* (Charleston, 1804), pp. 25, 28.

[86] James Kirke Paulding, *The Lion of the West*, ed. James N. Tidwell (Stanford, 1954), pp. 55, 23; *New York Mirror,* 9 (October 1, 1831): 102.

[87] J. K. Paulding, *Lion of the West*, pp. 22, 27.

[88] Medina, *Nick of the Woods*, p. 9; J. K. Paulding, *Lion of the West*, p. 22. *The Times* (London) used this same phrase to describe Wildfire in an appreciative review of the play. Quoted in William I. Paulding, *The Literary Life of James K. Paulding* (New York, 1867), p. 219.

[89] Charles Saunders, "North End Caulker" (New York Public Library Theatre Collection acting copy).

[90] Anna Cora Mowatt, *Fashion*, in *RAP*, p. 283; "Yankee Notions," Lord Chamberlain's collection, British Museum, Act I, scene i.

allowed the belligerence typical of other low-comedy caricatures, the stage Negro, commonly "a free gemman of color" who helped "to polish society," maintained a simple canniness and honesty that made light of his foibles.[91] The description by an American sailor of a Negro was close to the basic definition of all low-comedy types: "He is stout-timbered, and carries in his hold a jewel which many a hansomer-looking craft does not possess—an *honest heart*."[92]

A few plays dealt less glibly with the Negro and gave a pathetic dignity to his character and situation, particularly his memories of broken family ties. "Oh Africa, oh my poor moder! when the cruel buckrah man bin steal us, she de most broke she heart," remembered one of them. "But she be happy now, she bin die on de passage wid grief and hunger."[93] However most dramatists reserved pathos for the upper stratum of their plays, and the happy, pretentious Negro remained the standard character:

> O sing chink-a-chink, chink-a-chink
> O sing chink-a-chink cheery,
> Let the poor negro be joy, be dance,
> And never poor negro be weary.[94]

The happy stage Negro received a kind of apotheosis when T. D. Rice began to "jump Jim Crow" in the nation's theaters. Soon Rice developed a group of afterpieces in which low-comedy Negroes were central, much like those that featured Yankees or Irishmen. But the stage Negro was treated with less respect and more condescension as the days of the minstrel show dawned. A New Orleans writer complained that Rice's European success had made him "too anxious to mix *dignatum cum* 'darkey.' They won't mix, not even with *rice* as a basis."[95] The stereotype's peculiar versatility—"he sing well, he dance well, he play fiddle well"—allowed him to become a one-character show, but that character was increasingly only what the Mississippi *Free Trader* called "a genuine specimen of the 'nigger.'"[96] When Christy's Minstrels, "the genuine syrens of our age and country," opened in New York in 1839, it was the beginning of a new type of theater, the theater of jokes and music divorced from a dramatic framework.[97] It was also the

[91] J. K. Paulding, *Lion of the West*, p. 31.
[92] Saunders, *Pirate's Legacy*, p. 14.
[93] Lindsley, *Love and Friendship*, pp. 12–13.
[94] Beach, *Jonathan Postfree*, p. 22.
[95] Printed in *Spirit of the Times*, 12 (March, 5, 1842): 1.
[96] John Murdock, *The Triumphs of Love; or, Happy Reconciliation* (Philadelphia, 1795), p. 34; *Free Trader* (April 8, 1836), quoted in Joseph Free, "The Theatre in Southwestern Mississippi" (Ph.D. dissertation, University of Iowa, 1941), 1: 253.
[97] *Spirit of the Times*, 18 (October 21, 1848): 420.

beginning of a clear division between the essentially respectful treatment of the Negro in abolitionist drama and the basically condescending concept of the minstrel show.

The last of the major low-comedy types to take the stage before mid-century, Mose the fire boy, was the first low-comedy representative of the American urban population. A contemporary stage historian gave a picture of him and his initial audience greeting in 1848:

> He stood there in his red shirt, with his fire coat thrown over his arm, the stove-pipe hat . . . drawn down over one eye, his trousers tucked into his boots, a stump of a cigar pointing up from his lips to his eye, the soap locks plastered flat on his temples, and his jaw protruded into a half beastly, half human expression of contemptuous ferocity. . . . Taking the cigar stump from his mouth and turning half way round to spit, he said, "I ain't a goin' to run wid dat mercheen no more!"
>
> Instantly there arose such a yell of recognition as had never been heard in the little house before. Pit and galleries joined in the outcry. . . . Every man, woman, and child recognized in the character all the distinctive external characteristics of the class.[98]

This shock of recognition quickly led to a long-enduring regard. A whole series of "Mose" plays gave this city low-comedy hero a rank equal to that of Jonathan or Paddy. Mose, like the frontier hero, was tough and ferocious, but his heart was pure. "The fire boys may be a little rough outside, but they're all right here," one of them told the audience touching his heart. "It never shall be said dat one of de New York boys deserted a baby in distress." The play's author later said, "I made Mose a tough melon, but sweet at the core."[99]

An 1852 Philadelphia playbill suggested both the content and the popularity of plays written around low-comedy characters by that time. The bill offered "a New Domestic Drama, from the pen of Mr. Fenno (author of twenty successful pieces) entitled *The Fireman's Daughter*" featuring:

Barney O'Boozle, from Kilmunymacman
John Trueworth, an old fireman
Bill Chisel, a young fireman, one of the b'hoys
    and no mistake
Alfred Shallowpate, one of the Hairystockracy
Caroline, The Fireman's Daughter

[98] T. Allston Brown, *A History of the New York Stage* (New York, 1903), 1: 284.

[99] Benjamin Baker, *A Glance at New York* (New York, n.d.), p. 31; Baker, quoted in George O. Seilhamer, *An Interviewer's Album* (New York, 1881), p. 101. Baker said he put "the pathos about the baby" into the play because he "was afraid the Centre market boys would take offense."

Muriel Merrythought, a good'un
Mrs. Trafford, a lady with delicate nerves, but strong lungs.

After this came another play by the prolific Mr. Fenno, this time an "interesting and patriotic drama . . . entitled *The Siege of Monterey*" featuring one Jedediah Slapjack.[100]

The Fireman's Daughter hinted at the class division that was beginning to make itself felt in the theater in the 1850's. The play divided good and evil along class lines; Shallowpate, whose distinctive trait was that he was a member of the aristocracy, was clearly the comic villain; and there was no hero save the low-class, low-comedy Bill Chisel. What was being created was a theater that aimed only at the lower classes and that, in catering to them, mocked higher levels of society and concentrated on lower-class idiosyncrasies. Slowly the main melodramatic stream ran back toward its earlier course, as those groups that had made the low-comedy elements in it increasingly prominent were drained off into the specifically low-comedy theater.[101]

Low-comedy humor was often brutal when its laughter was aimed at some group considered inferior. Cruelty marked almost all depictions, for instance, of the old maid, who was presented with a total lack of sympathy in early nineteenth-century American plays. Whether she was speaking or others were describing her, she was clearly ugly, gossipy, silly, affectedly prudish, and anxious to grab at any available man. Her ugliness was the subject for endless mirth: every feature from hair (false) to feet (large) was ridiculed. "When she opened her mouth," one Yankee observed, "if it didn't look like a country grave yard with a few mouldy old tombstones in it." She alone put any value on her appearance —in one instance appraising it at exactly "fifty dollars a year, as that is about the sum it costs me for keeping it in repair year by year." She gossiped so incessantly that she was a "feminine newspaper," and a bad one to boot, in which was inserted "an advertisement for herself" whenever an eligible man was around.[102] Her stress on her "romantic sensibilities and virgin purity," her "youthful innocence," her "garb of maiden modesty," and her fear of "seducing men," especially when she was blatantly throwing herself at a totally uninterested prospect, were

---

100 "Philadelphia Playbills", December 6, 1852, University of Pennsylvania.

101 The activities of Harrigan and Hart in the 1870's and 1880's featuring Negro, Irish, and German-American stereotypes were perhaps the best—certainly the best-known—examples of this kind of theater. See Ely J. Kahn, *The Merry Partners; The Age and Stage of Harrigan and Hart* (New York, 1955).

102 Steele, *Brazen Drum*, pp. 37–38; Pierpont and Smith, *The Drunkard*, p. 13; Mowatt, *Fashion*, in *RAP*, p. 294.

constant jokes.[103] When Mrs. Stowe's relatively likable spinster, Miss Ophelia, was brought on stage the dramatist showed her about to get married.[104]

If the old maid was the most conspicuous target for this kind of cruel humor, any person out of the main stream of the socially approved might be similarly laughed at. Religious and racial preconceptions were easily turned to brutal jibes. "I'll wager he got it for next to nothing," said one low-comedy character; "for they are so Jewish those Jews."[105] The main target of the low-comedy frontiersman was the Indian, whom one of them typically called "tarnal, temporal, long-legged, tator headed, pumpkin eating red niggers! . . . coon whelps!"[106] One of Jonathan Ploughboy's favorite expressions was, "Why, I wouldn't do a neger so," and a moralizing father-type entered a play by pushing a footman to one side with a casual, "Out of my way, you grinning nigger." Nimrod Wildfire told one Negro, "Skulk, you black snake!" which caused an Englishwoman to ask if Americans were "averse to freemen of a different skin," "The Niggers? Why, no, madam, but they are such lazy varmints," Nimrod answered. "I had one once myself. The ague wouldn't stay with him for he was too lazy to shake."[107] Physical deformity was often given similarly humorous treatment. Thus Jedediah explained that his sister "died one day, eating artichokes when she had the chicken pox," after she had "had four children, two gals, one boy, and a cripple."[108]

All low-comedy stereotypes were presented on stage with some condescension as well as much affection. Yet the groups condescended to were apparently those who most enjoyed the low-comedy characters. The New York toughs made a hero of Mose; and the urban immigrant population later in the century patronized the low-comedy theater where they were caricatured. Perhaps the amorphousness of American life made persons with no particular social status eager to watch characters who were simple, naive, and imperfect but who at bottom had a wealth

---

[103] Pierpont and Smith, *The Drunkard*, p. 43; Conway, *Hiram Hireout*, p. 15; Hutton, *Fashionable Follies*, in RPAD, 2 : 28; Jones, *Green Mountain Boy*, p. 11.

[104] George Aiken, *Uncle Tom's Cabin* (1853), in *RPAD*, Act V.

[105] John Howard Payne, *Trial Without Jury; or, The Maid and the Magpie*, in *ALP* 5 : 25. The Jew appeared in only a few plays, usually with a heavy accent in his Shylock role of avaricious money-getter: Ellison, *American Captive*, p. 29; Carr, *Benevolent Lawyers*, p. 11; Lindsley, *Love and Friendship*, pp. 36–37; H. J. Conway, "Guiscard the Guerilla; or, A Brother's Revenge," HTC, (1844), Act II, scene 2.

[106] Medina, *Nick of the Woods*, p. 24.

[107] Woodworth, *Forest Rose*, pp. 16, 19; Mowatt, *Fashion*, in *RAP*, p. 288; J. K. Paulding, *Lion of the West*, p. 32.

[108] Jones, *Green Mountain Boy*, p. 9.

of practical good sense and wholesome good sentiments. And the exaggeration of the stereotypes' naiveté and quaintness enabled even the least sophisticated people in the audience to feel safely superior, comparatively worldly-wise.

* * *

The melodrama in its central portion not only created characters "better than saints, or worse than devils," but also provided circumstances "which outrage all probability . . . for the mere purpose of . . . hanging up the feelings of the multitude on the tenterhooks."[109] Such circumstances were commonly provided by the easy expedient of making one or more of the main characters' origins mysterious. A typical hero announced early in a play, "I am the child of a wreck—born on board a ship. . . . My parents were lost with all the crew save a black man." And shortly thereafter the mysterious fortune-teller confided to the audience: "For what am I a priestess? For the world's idol—money! which will give me power to revenge and punish! One lives that I hope to punish for a deed of youth; a helpless girl was his victim."[110] By the play's end all mystery was dissolved: the villain was actually the seducer of the young Moll Pitcher and the hero was their illegitimate child.

Scenes of recognition and reconciliation were a staple of the melodramatic finale:

> *Brace:* Ha! Where got you this pistol?
>
> *Nat:* 'Twas given to me by my mother.
>
> *Brace:* And her name was—
>
> *Nat:* Mary Brown.
>
> *Brace:* O, God! My son.
>
> *Nat:* Father! (they embrace)

Exclamations like "strange coincidence," and "how unexpected and yet how fortunate!" were indeed suitable when the melodrama's final mysteries were revealed.[111]

No situation was too farfetched for complicating and resolving the plot contortions in these plays. Babies switched in their cradles and children thrown into rivers only to be rescued by gypsies, old servants or monks refusing to reveal situations because they were sworn "to twenty years of secrecy," marriages that must be kept secret, princes disguised

---

[109] *Mirror of Taste*, 1 (April, 1810): 345.

[110] Jones, *Moll Pitcher*, pp. 11, 16.

[111] Saunders, *Pirate's Legacy*, p. 19; Harby, *Gordian Knot*, p. 86; *Lucinda*, p. 32.

as peasants, and blackguards masquerading as nobles, "Unknowns" leaving secluded forest retreats only to wreak vengeance and save the innocent, long-separated relatives who met by chance and only slowly learned the other's identity—all these weird events were melodramatic commonplaces.

These conventions gave to the melodrama an aura of unreality, an existence within a world of its own upon which "real life" touched mainly through established channels. Not only were many fairy tales made into melodramas on the nineteenth-century stage, but most melodramas were full of the elements of the fairy tale in their joyous as well as their mysterious moments. The melodramatic world was one in which anything—good or bad—might happen. A playbill's synopsis of one of these plays, "the moral drama in 3 Tableaux entitled *Madeline; or, The Foundling of St. Gervais*," both summarized these plot conventions and suggested their fairy-tale quality:

Act I – Scene i.　The village of St. Gervais! The Bridal! The False Friend! Dissipation! In this act a Beautiful Village Fete and Dance of 16! Arranged by Monsieur Bouxary.

Act II – Scene i.　The effects of Dissipation. Poverty. The Wife's Faithfulness. The Tempter. Robbery. Mother's Resolve.

– Scene ii.　Hospital of Foundlings. Treachery of Appiani.

Act III – Scene i.　The Mansion of the Countess Bassiere! The Meeting. The recognition. The Maniac. The Restoration. Happy Denouement.[112]

The fairy-tale quality of the melodrama tended to blur the image of the social world even when playwrights attempted to approach reality most closely. Critics and authors alike agreed that the main purpose of comedy was to expose the social follies of contemporary man; this the period's social comedies set out to do. Yet even in these the escape from the conventional forms was only slight; so compelling were the moral preconceptions underlying the melodramatic structure that very little social or individual observation intruded even in plays specifically intended as social comment.

Sheridan had provided the comic model in *The School for Scandal*, but the melodramatic comedy was morally purified so that the good people became unspotted exemplars of human nature. This change was worked in the earliest of American "social comedies," *The Contrast*. Here no audience affection was aroused by a teasing Lady Teazle, or a roguish

---

[112] "Philadelphia Playbills," September 8, 1851, University of Pennsylvania.

Charles; the heroine was "a sentimental grave girl" who fell in love with
the "he-angel," Col. Manly, because "he entered into a conversation
worthy a man of sense to speak, and a lady of delicacy and sentiment to
hear; . . . he spoke the language of sentiment and his eyes looked tenderness and honour."[113] There was nothing intentionally funny about these
characters, and hence most of the real humor of the piece, as in later
melodramatic comedies, depended on the low-comedy stereotypes.

Through some of its characters, *The Contrast* exposed, as did almost
all its successors, the folly of pretension and of aping effete foreign
fashions. Such foolishness was not only made ridiculous in these plays,
but was carefully tied to every kind of stupidity and evil. And by play's
end, the dramatist saw to it that people guilty of such affectations were
properly punished or repentant. The moral purpose was always in the
fore. One author even footnoted his comic villain's announcement that
"fashion justifies anything": "This is not written by the author as a
maxim of truth; but is intended as the false reasoning of a deluded imagination."[114] Abigail Adams had complained, that although Molière's
comedies successfully ridiculed vice, they failed to offer any elevated
examples to engage people to virtue.[115] No American social comedy
failed in this way. The social failing exposed—the vulgar attempt to
import evidence of social superiority—was real enough in a highly
mobile society lacking clearly established social distinctions. But playwrights so stressed exemplars of perfect virtue and encrusted their
representatives of fashion with such gross stupidity and vice that all
satirical purpose, all real connection with society and humanity, was
severely abridged.

Some social comedies in the 1840's clearly showed the impress of
Jacksonian rhetoric against speculators and stockjobbers and of the
hardships of the Panic of 1837. The character of the self-made business
man whom the exigencies of trade had forced into malpractices or crime
and to the verge of bankruptcy became common in these plays. His drive
to make money was always scorned by truly good characters, one of
whom pointed out, "Round the hearts of successful money-getters
prosperity winds a golden coil which avarice tightens." Because of this
strangulation of feeling, "at times when thousands are dying of hunger,"
the businessman speculated "on the miseries of his fellow creatures"

113 Tyler, *The Contrast*, in R*AP*, p. 69.
114 Hutton, *Fashionable Follies,* in RP*AD*, 2:28.
115 Abigail Adams to Mercy Warren, December 5, 1773, *Warren-Adams Letters* (Massachusetts
Historical Society, 1917), 1: 19. Mrs. Adams concluded her criticism: "Tho he has drawn many
pictures of real life, yet all pictures of life are not fit to be exhibited upon the Stage."

and filled "his coffers with the price of blood and tears." He also ruthlessly foreclosed mortgages, although this left poor families "homeless and pennyless."[116] Clearly some of the worst effects of the economic order were blamed on business callousness.

Yet in these comedies the businessman was made more victim than victimizer. If "prosperity . . . hardened his heart," it was extravagance, seldom his own, that drove him to cruelty and crime. Behind every man stands a woman, and behind the stage's corrupt businessman of the 1840's stood a fashionable wife. In every case the defaulter or forger or bankrupt's troubles came because he "unwisely made choice of a wife whose fashionable follies and vices drove him to commit a deed he otherwise would never have been guilty of."[117] While the corrupt businessman was a pathetic character, his wife was likely to be despicable: loud, vulgar, stupid, pretentious, and insensitive to anything but gross socialclimbing ambitions. For her, "the order of husbands" was instituted solely "to pay the debts of their wives."[118] One interchange between husband and wife summed up their characters:

Mr. Tiffany: A pretty time to give a ball when you know that I am on the very brink of bankruptcy.

Mrs. Tiffany: . . . There is Mrs. Adolphus Washaway—she gave the most splendid fete of the season—and I hear on very good authority that her husband has not paid his baker's bill in three months. Then there was Mrs. Honeywood—

Mr. Tiffany: Gave a ball the night before her husband shot himself—perhaps you wish to drive me to follow his example?

Mrs. Tiffany: Good gracious! Mr. Tiffany, how you talk! I beg you won't mention anything of the kind. I consider black the most unbecoming color.[119]

The emphasis on a callous, fashionable wife mitigated any economic protest in these plays. Business necessitated hardening the heart to the point of not melting at the plight of widows and orphans, but real evil resulted only from wifely extravagance. The solution to economic ills was to turn away from "fashion," from ways foreign and new-fangled and aristocratic and extravagant, and back to the old, pure, plain, and American way of life. These plays commonly featured a wise old friend or relative who had remained pure of heart and strong of principle back

---

[116] H. J. Conway, "The Banker; or, Fashion and Failure," HTC, Act I, p. 11.

[117] Conway, "Banker," Act I, p. 4; Act III, p. 15.

[118] W. I. Paulding, *Noble Exile*, p. 146.

[119] Mowatt, *Fashion*, in *RAP*, p. 295.

on the farm, and who both contrasted with the harassed businessman and rescued him from financial ruin in the end. When real social problems intruded into the period's plays, their handling was always sentimental and fitted to the melodrama's moralistic constructs. Vaguely uneasy about new events, dramatists simply urged a revitalization of the old virtues that had in fact encouraged the change. Presumably America's business problem was solved when the moralizing friend from the country saved the day:

> You must sell your house and all these gee-gaws, and bundle your wife and daughter off to the country. There let them learn economy, true independence, and home virtues, instead of foreign follies. As for yourself, continue your business—but let moderation in future be your counsellor, and let *honesty* be your confidential clerk.[120]

Perhaps the American playwrights' difficulty in handling social reality in their plays showed most clearly in the employment problems they had with their heroes. If a European setting were used, heroes were kings or nobles, but in America, though every good male was supposed to work, social and moral preconceptions about different professions made no job wholly suitable for the hero. A few occupations were, of course, eminently appropriate for the virtuous. Farming was particularly conducive to that humble and dignified purity dear to the melodramatic heart. "Though rough and little is his farm," sang one farmboy

> That little is his own, sir.
> His hand is strong, his heart is warm,
> 'Tis truth and honour's throne, sir.[121]

Farmers were almost always presented with great approval in plays, often in direct contrast to people of the upper or urban classes. And by the 1830's the workingman began to take his place alongside his rural compatriot. Though he appeared less frequently on stage than the farmer, and usually in less moralizing parts, he was treated with the same kind of veneration. Joseph Jones, the Boston playwright, most strongly emphasized the worth of the "mechanic," the period's term for the urban workingman: "A mechanic, sir, is one of God's noble-men. . . . The Supreme Ruler of the Universe is himself the Great Mechanic."[122] While the melodrama paid obeisance to their virtues, farmers and workingmen were not felt to possess that elevation of sentiment and nobility

---

[120] *Ibid.*, p. 311.
[121] Dunlap, *Glory of Columbia, Her Yeomanry!*, p. 42.
[122] Joseph S. Jones, *The Carpenter of Rouen; or, The Massacre of St. Bartholomew* (New York, 1840), p. 9.

of action required of the hero. In transplanting the aristocrat of European melodrama to the New World, the easiest solution was to make him a soldier. This was a sensible procedure in patriotic plays where fighting for one's country became the central duty of all good men. The opportunity to display bravery and love of country or liberty was quite understandably the soldiers' lot. The soldier on stage was "full of exalted honor so peculiar to his profession," the essential ingredients of which were deep patriotism and respect for female chastity; one heroine asked, presumably rhetorically: "What has a woman to fear when under the protection of an American soldier?"[123] Sailors were equally adamant guardians of their country and of the fair sex. "To an honest American Tar," said one of them, "a woman's honor, like a fair breeze, is always to be cherished."[124] When a heroine was accosted by a nautical character, she announced, "If you are gentleman, sir, a sailor, you will let me pass."[125]

Given their devotion to protecting country and womanhood, the military met the melodrama's moral requirements. The military also presented differences in rank corresponding to the divisions that the melodrama always suggested. Privates, corporals, and sergeants filled roles characterized by simple goodness; and young officers were acceptable as heroes. Though the military was the only completely satisfactory profession that dramatists found for their American heroes, soldiering was presumably only a wartime occupation for the American. Authors often made their heroes soldiers in peacetime, but this was at best a bastard sort of solution, or rather a way of avoiding a solution. None of the semi-aristocratic professions open to an American ever won much melodramatic approval. Intellectuals appeared on stage only in the form of ludicrous antiquarians, or mad scientists. Artists of any sort were mostly introduced as objects for amusement and scorn, like T. Tennyson Twinkle, who argued that "the true test of the poet is the velocity with which he composes," or Pontefract Pinchbeck, a novelist who prided himself on his contribution to the peopling of "every square mile of earth with villainous vagabonds." Since such persons were commonly "as poor as their verses," no one took them seriously.[126]

---

[123] White, *Clergyman's Daughter*, p. 35; Woodworth, *The Widow's Son*, p. 42.

[124] Ellison, *American Captive*, p. 12. In *The City Looking Glass*, Robert Montgomery Bird introduced a sailor whose only job was to appear suddenly on two occasions to rescue the heroines from rape, pp. 44 and 77–78.

[125] Saunders, *Pirate's Legacy*, pp. 19–20.

[126] Mowatt, *Fashion*, in *RAP*, p. 286; William I. Paulding, *Madmen All; or, A Cure For Love* in *American Comedies* (Philadelphia, 1847), p. 186.

Doctors, too, were mainly inflated quacks handled with unaffectionate humor. A fortune-teller read in the palm of a typical stage doctor, "The fates ordain you'll be a great man-killer."[127] Another one summarized his medical principles:

Feel the pulse, smell the cane, look at
the tongue
Touch the gold, praise the old, flatter
the young.[128]

Appearing more frequently was the lawyer, who was generally associated with dishonesty. When a lively girl was asked if her father was a lawyer, she replied indignantly, "Indeed sir! I'll have you know my father is an honest man!" A Yankee who had a barrel of applesauce stolen immediately went "among the law shops—jist the right place to find rogues."[129] Even a member of a criminal syndicate of western brigands scorned the moral level of a "scrub lawyer" who "had the audacity to enter our honourable profession." And one of his drinking companions added, "A common insult to our order."[130]

The truism that "every man to be a thorough villain ought to be a lawyer" was not strictly followed in the melodrama, but the few dramatic defenses of the profession, in their painful self-consciousness, suggested the general attitude.[131] Thus the prologue to Mrs. Carr's *Benevolent Lawyers* declared:

A benevolent Lawyer! the Lady is mad!
A phenomena sure that is not to be had.
. . . .
Well, really I think I must go to this play
To hear what the author is able to say
In favor of Gentlemen's hearts, of the bar,
With whom every writer of plays is at war.[132]

By the 1830's when a popular dramatist wanted to present a lawyer hero, he justified the character's nobility by carefully explaining that his rich but wise father had had him trained originally as a laborer.[133]

Sometimes heroes were connected with farming, law, or business, but

---

[127] J. K. Paulding, *Bucktails*, p. 93. The younger Paulding introduced three doctors into his *Antipathies* apparently only to prove the variety of idiocy to which medical practitioners were prone.

[128] Woodworth, *Widow's Son*, p. 13.

[129] Woodworth, *Deed of Gift*, p. 38; Joseph S. Jones, *The People's Lawyer* (Boston, 1856), p. 27.

[130] H. J. Conway, "The Brigands of the West; or, The Wolf of the Prairies," (1844), HTC, Act I, scene i.

[131] Payne, *Julia*, p. 55.

[132] Carr, *Benevolent Lawyers*, p. 5.

[133] Jones, *People's Lawyer*, in *RPAD*, 2: 423.

such professional ties were always left as vague as possible; sometimes they were made majors or captains without reference to specific military assignments; and sometimes they were victims of melodramatic unemployment. Presumably they were not idle, but because job opportunities in America did not jibe with the melodrama's preconceptions, dramatists generally made little mention of how the American hero earned his living.

The rigidity of the melodramatic structure limited the dramatic life of real persons as well as of real social situations. George Washington alone was honored with repeated representation and compliment on stage. Hardly a patriotic play went its course without verbally saluting "the matchless hero of the western world," "the greatest of heroes and best of men," "the greatest man that ever lived."[134] The stage Washington was always clothed in the rather frigid dignity and total virtue suitable to a "god-like man." "Seventeen times did my rifle pierce that stately form," narrated an Indian chief in the period's longest-running play. "My eye, that never missed, grew dim, for above thy head, a bright light, like unto the sun, descended, and the Great Spirit crowned thee as the deliverer of a mighty nation."[135] The adoration of Washington often approached sacrilege. A playwright, in writing about one of Washington's spies whose true identity was known only "to Heaven and Him," capitalized both *h*'s; in American popular culture Washington was "the second savior of the world."[136]

Although no other leader faintly approached this deification, a great many generals were given leading roles really interchangeable with that of Washington in plays commemorating military victories. Battle after battle in the Revolutionary War suffered melodramatic celebration, and playwrights even glorified the battles of the War of 1812, though here, one of them admitted, it was more difficult to find things to celebrate.[137] The tradition was running low on material when the Mexican War served to replenish the dramatist's stock. In each of these plays, real military leaders were given a central role; the typical general became a kind of military father figure, who was entrusted with most of the moral and patriotic platitudes required, including a prediction of the future greatness of America.

[134] Ellison, *American Captive*, p. 34; Joseph S. Jones, *The Usurper; or, Americans in Tripoli*, in *ALP*, 14: 164; Samuel Woodworth, *La Fayette; or, The Castle of Olmutz* (New York, 1824), p. 6; Steele, *Brazen Drum*, p. 34.

[135] *King's Bridge Cottage: A Revolutionary Tale* (New York, 1825), p. 6; Bannister, *Putnam*, p. 20.

[136] Charles Clinch, *The Spy* (1822), in *ALP*, 14: 94; James Fennell, *Apology for the Life of James Fennell* (Philadelphia, 1814), pp. 342–43.

[137] Noah, *She Would Be A Soldier*, preface.

Andrew Jackson's melodramatic career was at once perfectly typical and peculiarly interesting because of its contradiction to the supposed popular image of him. *The Battle of New Orleans; or, Glory, Love, and Loyalty* was cut from exactly the same pattern as all these patriotic dramas, except that its author's diction was even more stilted than common. There were two pairs of lovers, the central pair being separated by the girl's father, a businessman who thought she should wed for wealth rather than for patriotism. The hero was an officer under Jackson. The female in the other romantic grouping was captured by the American troops primarily to give Jackson ample chance to talk about the soldier's duty to helpless woman. Filling out the cast were an impressed American seaman, a good Catholic bishop, a low-comedy Irish-American, some British soldiers (somewhat weak in mind and principle), and a chorus of American soldiers who sang in some productions, "The Hunters of Kentucky." But Jackson in the play was not one of the rough-and-ready frontiersmen described in the song. Instead he was unimpeachably dignified, and his speech was laden with classical allusion. In his concluding comment he said that the reward of those freemen who protected New Orleans would be the future greatness of America: "To them shall raise a monument more proud than Antigonus to his father raised, when Greece adorned Demetrius' splendid tomb and hung her garland on the sacred vases." Little wonder that the play's hero was led to prophesy "New Orleans may boast her Leonidas, and future times when they relate our story will couple with our chief the Grecian hero."[138] Old Hickory was given no traits of character but those bestowed on all melodramatic military leaders.

What happened to Andrew Jackson in *The Battle of New Orleans* was fairly typical of the melodramatic metamorphosis of contemporary life. Tocqueville had no reason to fear that democratic drama would neglect "the general features of the race" in trying to capture "the medley of conditions, feelings, and opinions, that occurs before their eyes.[139] Even when the setting was modern and local, melodramatic conventions constantly blurred the outlines of any specific observation. The melodrama as mirror of contemporary life disfigured facts ludicrously by forcing and transforming them into the pattern of the moral and intellectual tenets of the age. Distortion of social reality was constant and great because no detail was allowed to impinge on the grand design.

---

[138] Grice, *Battle of New Orleans*, pp. 55, 19. All the other plays on Jackson treated him with similar elevation of character and diction.
[139] Tocqueville, *Democracy in America*, 2: 89–90.

9

The Melodramatic Vision

CHARLES BRECK, a young playwright, objected strongly when the influential critic, Joseph Dennie, condemned his first plays for failing to comply with the accepted dicta that tragedy must show "the calamities of the great" and comedy exhibit "the follies of the lower part of mankind." "Is it then only with the great we can sympathize?" Breck asked. "Can their distresses command our tears, while the misfortunes of persons of the same grade in society with ourselves, whose habits and manners are our own, cannot move our feelings?" A poor clerk's loss of job "through no fault of his own" when his family's support depended upon it, Breck declared, was every bit as deserving of pity and dramatization as a great king's loss of power.[1]

Breck's argument was of a piece with Walt Whitman's plea for a democratic drama. Both men shared the common realization that the nineteenth century demanded, if the stage was to remain vital, a drama suited to the social situation of the day. And both men, Breck implicitly and Whitman explicitly, recognized the great social change to be toward democracy. Society was clearly no longer a background for its kings or heroes; its leaders were increasingly a projection of the people at large.

The need to work drama around the lives of fairly ordinary people, increasingly the center of society, was especially clear in politically democratic America. "Why go to countries for characters," asked one critic, "where every feeling is different, and every thought out of our own way of thinking?"[2] Certainly America should have no particular interest in

---

[1] *Port-Folio*, 1 (May 3, 1806), pp. 267–68.
[2] *Aeronaut*, 2 (September 1, 1816): 334.

the "theatrical foppery of passionate kings, pouting Queens, rakish Princes and flirting Princesses, knavish Ministers, and peevish Secretaries, lamenting misfortunes in which the bulk of mankind are in no way concerned." To the sensible American "the idle distresses of kings and queens" were "ineffably ridiculous."[3] Interest in such trumpery could only corrupt America's rough equality and republican institutions and its innocence about the "plots and contrivances in all manner of wickedness" of the great:

> Why, with blind passion, Europe's scenes explore
> And waft her mimic follies to our shore?
> Baneful to us the servile zeal that brings
> No tragic forms, but warrior chiefs and kings,
> That spreads with tyrant pomp our rising stage,
> Themes of a barbarous, or a slavish, age.[4]

Developing themes for an enlightened and democratic age, in which "the bulk of mankind" was interested, was the problem of the period's dramatists. "Hitherto, poetry has been on the side of power," admitted one critic; "it has drawn its chief images of greatness from the old aristocratic ideas of sovereignty, war, military glory." This did not imply that tragedy was extinct, the critic argued, because "the dignity of life does not need the outward aid of power and station." Certainly "with the emotions of private life, with domestic tragedy on the stage" could be blended "the heroic ideas of the age."[5] Yet the attempt to combine the "emotions of private life" with "heroic ideas" in the nineteenth century led only to melodrama; Breck might argue for a tragedy of the common man, but he wrote wholly conventional melodramas. The melodrama fitted so well the intellectual preconceptions of the period that even those dramatists who scorned the form were unable to escape it far. No dramatic genius appeared to make clear an alternative way of constructing "democratic" plays, and it proved, as one American playwright complained, "quite as difficult for the Stage as for the Bench to act without precedent."[6] The conviction that "the commonest terms in

---

[3] "Letter" to *National Gazette* (March 22, 1793), quoted in Eola Willis, *The Charleston Stage In the Eighteenth Century* (Columbia, S.C., 1924), p. 167; Philip Freneau in *Time-Piece* (September 6, 1797), quoted in Philip Marsh, "Philip Freneau and the Theatre," *Proceedings of the New Jersey Historical Society*, 66 (April, 1948): 104–5.

[4] *Portland Magazine*, 1 (May 18, 1805): 5; Elihu Hubbard Smith, "Prologue" for the opening of the Park Theatre, 1802, quoted in James E. Cronin, "The Life of Elihu Hubbard Smith" (Ph.D. dissertation, Yale University, 1946), p. 294.

[5] *Arcturus*, 2 (October, 1841): 282.

[6] George H. Miles, *Señor Valiente* (Baltimore, 1859), preface.

life, the most hackneyed in use, are the fullest of strange meaning" was difficult to translate into that literary form in which lively "action and situation are the indispensible ingredients."[7]

The prevalence of melodrama was usually blamed on the "depraved tastes of a corrupt multitude" who controlled the democratic theater: the masses had come into their own and proceeded to massacre subtlety, profundity, and beauty and to worship the superficial, glib, and gaudy.[8] A few critics, unsatisfied with the common explanations of audience vulgarity or the starring system or the size of theaters, sought subtler reasons why contemporary drama failed and particularly why the essence of tragedy was so difficult to instill in truly contemporary plays. Some pointed to the way in which the individual's freedom to act was circumscribed in a highly organized and regulated society. "There are too many eyes open, too many minds informed, too many appeals to justice, too many asylums for the persecuted, too much interference, too much dependence," suggested one critic, "to permit those temptations, dangers, deliverances, and triumphs which in their progress, complication and results form the great interest of tragedy."[9] The tragic hero controlled his own destiny with little interference from forces less than those of fate or the gods, but modern man couldn't achieve such independence. Breck's clerk who lost a job "through no fault of his own" was a victim rather than a determiner of circumstances. Breck rightly argued that he was as deserving of pity—as capable of arousing pathos— as any king or hero, but his fate was too little in his own hands to give him the stature that placed the tragic hero beyond mere pity.

Other critics found the reason for the failure of contemporary tragedy less in the situation of modern man than in his attitude toward greatness. Democratic man, they argued, made a virtue of mediocrity and mistrusted those who were obviously superior to the common run of mankind. Occasionally sentiments appeared in plays which testified to a democratic bias against greatness, particularly that of the military conqueror. "Whence came this greatness," asked one hero, "but from the miseries of subjugated nations."[10] And an old father scorned the pretentious "vain glory" that "prompts the hero to the field," and praised

[7] *Arcturus*, 1 (December, 1840): 28; James H. Hackett to John Neal, March 16, 1834, in Irving T. Richards, "The Life and Works of John Neal" (Ph.D. dissertation, Harvard University, 1933).

[8] *American Quarterly Review*, 15 (June, 1834): 353; *Friend*, 1 (October, 1815): 85.

[9] *Literary and Scientific Repository*, 3 (October, 1821): 333.

[10] Robert Montgomery Bird, *The Gladiator*, in Clement Foust, *The Life and Dramatic Works of R. M. Bird* (New York, 1919), p. 316.

in contrast those who bear "the private ills of life with Christian dignity and honest pride" so as to insure "the admiration of the good."[11]

Yet such pronouncements were infrequent and commonly directed against specific villains, whereas the melodramatic hero was bedecked with all kinds of superlative virtues and, particularly if he were a real American military hero, was treated with near adoration. Despite desires to develop a democratic drama, most critics and authors agreed that "if the tragic muse were limited in her selection of character to common life, the effusions would be vapid and bare of interest."[12] The melodrama did not banish greatness, but rather set criteria for it that excluded the tragic hero. At the end of one play, supposedly based on an incident in Shakespeare's life, the bard proclaimed, "I am indeed happy. A poet, a lover, the husband of the woman I adore. What more is there for me to desire?"[13] Such an avowal of contented domesticity made the play's Shakespeare, more than literary genius, just plain Bill. But seemingly the author wanted not to vulgarize Shakespeare's greatness, but to prove his complete excellence by engrafting domestic worth to literary preeminence. Although few playwrights were so completely silly, the great man of the nineteenth century drama always became an amalgam of its social virtues. The democratic hero possessed, in godlike perfection, all the characteristics that society most valued, but, unlike the aristocratic hero, his greatness was never personal or idiosyncratic.

In a few plays the hero was separated from society by banishment or withdrawal for some wrongdoing, real or alleged. But if he had been guilty of some breach of social bounds, there were extenuating circumstances or deep repentance to lessen the trespass; if he were wholly a victim of social injustice, he scorned society in terms that showed he possessed its virtues in abundance and reentered it when occasions for protecting the pure and innocent demanded. These men were "bandits for the sake of virtue" or outcasts "made so by wrongs and wretchedness, not nature."[14] The misanthropic egoism scorning social mores of the Faustian or Byronic hero never appeared in acted American plays. The democratic hero, rather than rising above society either by his nature or in defiance, measured himself superlatively to its standards. Parson

---

[11] John Blake White, *Foscari; or, The Venetian Exile* (Charleston, 1806), p. 39.

[12] Review of Frances Wright's *Altorf* in an unidentified Philadelphia newspaper of December, 1819, in "Philadelphia Theatre Clippings," HTC.

[13] Richard Penn Smith, *Shakespeare in Love*, in *ALP*, 12: 14.

[14] William Dunlap, *Abaellino, The Great Banditti* (New York, 1802), p. 74; Jonas Phillips, *The Evil Eye* (New York, 1831), p. 10.

Weems' caricature of George Washington, specifically intended for the emulation of young boys, was the prototype for the democratic hero.

The melodrama moved obliquely rather than directly away from the royal and noble personages who were the center of interest in great tragedy. Breck's suggestion that drama concern itself with the lives of clerks, with the growing middle class, was seldom taken literally by dramatists. The early melodrama's class structure remained generally feudal and predominantly populated with kings and peasants, lords and ladies. Yet its essential criterion of rank was based on moral sensitivity; and slaves, peasants, and mechanics were all allowed at times its most elevated roles. Indeed the melodrama's feudal structure was erected partially to give an exciting framework to events and partially to be battered down. The presence of rank gave ample opportunity to prove that rank didn't matter. If melodrama worked within a feudal social structure, it was a belligerently egalitarian feudalism. One peasant hero, in love with a highborn lady, typically filled much of a play with soliloquies about his being as good as anyone else:

> Nature's pure element courses through my veins,
> And with a soul . . .
> As spotless as when from God it came,
> A love of country—an untarnished name,
> A life that slander's tongue dare never touch
> I stand a balance in the scale with kings,
> With all their bloated blood.[15]

Every cliché about virtue being the only just claim to superiority and love destroying the barriers of rank was emphasized. Differences in wealth and social position meant nothing, the melodrama argued to the play's end, when some occurrence or disclosure was introduced to make them nonexistent. The peasant in love with a princess, for example, learned that his supposed mother was actually only a nurse who had taken him at birth from his noble parents. Sometimes the melodrama allowed the prince to marry the peasant; but when a princess was inclined toward one of humble station, he invariably had to be proved in the end the aristocracy's as well as nature's nobleman.

Such twists of plot drew the teeth from the melodrama's egalitarian argument. All the talk about nature's nobleman and love leveling all differences in rank rang hollow when the dramatist felt obliged to resort to such absurdities to salvage class distinctions. In part the convention

---

[15] Nathaniel H. Bannister, *Gentleman of Lyons; or, The Marriage Contract* (New York, 1838), p. 12.

showed democracy's ambivalence toward class distinctions, but, perhaps more importantly, the revelation that the peasant hero was really a prince suggested the excitement and surprises that life might have in store for anyone. Audiences wanted to hate their nobility and have it too. Insisting on the natural equality of all was something that appealed to the common man, but he also liked to find the superiority of the simply virtuous made definite by being outfitted with the trappings of aristocratic rank.

Melodramatic feudalism, while it remained the staple social structure on stage, had increasing competition from more democratic situations as the century progressed. This was especially true of American plays, which could not bring in titles without introducing foreigners, who chauvinistically were usually relegated to the roles of fool, fop, or villain. Though there were no titled aristocrats in America, the melodrama reflected the realization that money made gradations of social level, less lasting perhaps than aristocratic rank, but no less important. The differences between the rich and the poor played much the same role in plays set in America as those between peasants and nobles in Europe; they caused false social distinctions rather than judgment on the basis of merit; they interfered with true love; they were repeatedly shown to be of no real importance, and in the end they were carefully regarded by the playwright. Poor American heroes in love with rich heroines were as scrupulously made financially solvent in the finale as European ones were given knighthood. Sometimes a farfetched happening, like discovery of one's true identity or a huge inheritance, might provide affluence, but in America honest hard work and enterprise were a favorite solution for working the change. The hero of Lazarus Beach's *Jonathan Postfree* lived a typical melodramatic life. A poor boy driven away by his true love's socially ambitious mother, he went to sea, made a fortune, and returned to New York just in time to save the heroine from the villain and her family, who had fallen on evil days, from bankruptcy.

Whatever his wealth and social rank at the end of the play, the melodramatic hero's superiority was that of worth alone. He was nature's nobleman. The idea that nature, rather than man, was the only proper distributor of patents of nobility was a dogma which underlay American democracy and paralleled Jefferson's belief in a natural aristocracy. The substance of many of these plays' egalitarian pronouncements accorded with Jeffersonian ideals, even though the emphasis was most often different:

> I bless the generous fate
> That gave no noble blood to swell my veins.

For had I from the hand of accident
Nobility received, I could not prove
My juster title to that high noblesse
No revolutions level and destroy:
That true noblesse of Genius and of Worth.[16]

The central theme of the passage was akin to the Jeffersonian faith: "The true noblesse of Genius and of Worth," was the "aristocracy of virtue and of talent" that Jefferson felt democracy would bring to power. Yet Jefferson would have recoiled at the egotism here, at the stating of the problem in personal terms rather than as a broad social principle. The belligerence of this equalitarianism also went beyond Jeffersonian concepts: there is a difference between arguing that all men are created with equal political rights and opportunity to pursue happiness and saying, "My accomplishments make me more than equal with those above me in social rank because I started lower." Perhaps this reflected the core of the intellectual change in American democracy between the eighteenth and nineteenth centuries. What had been a matter of rational principle became a matter of personal and emotional faith. Both Jefferson and Jackson felt they were fighting foes of self-determination, but Jefferson rested his appeal on "self-evident truths" whereas Jackson believed, "The bank is trying to kill me, but I will kill it."[17]

Other things besides egocentrism and belligerence made the melodramatic nature's nobleman a different species from Jefferson's natural aristocrat. "Genius and Worth," the criteria for both groups, were reached by very different means. Jefferson had planned the development of his natural aristocracy through an elaborate system of free public education, which would gradually select the very best from the universally educated mass and train these to leadership. Such a program was not necessary to develop nature's nobleman, whose genius was not a product of schools, and whose worth might be curbed by excess of formal education. Nature's nobleman was wise and true and elevated, but he seldom showed sign of great learning or rationality. An old father summarized the melodrama's intellectual creed: "Education may varnish hypocrisy; but nature only could mold a heart like this! simple, god-like virtue!"[18]

What happened to the concept of reason is suggested by a song in praise of it from an early nineteenth-century play. It began by saying that

---

[16] Anna Cora Mowatt, *Armand; or, The Peer and the Peasant* (Boston, 1855), p. 21.
[17] Quoted in Martin Van Buren, *Autobiography*, ed. J. C. Fitzpatrick, *American Historical Association Annual Report*, 2 (1918): 625.
[18] Joseph Hutton, *Fashionable Follies*, in *RPAD*, 2: 48.

life would be worthless did not reason, the "best of heaven's blessings," rule the mind. Its advantages were listed:

> When we see capricious fortune
> Striving all the rich to bless,
> Reason tells us envy not them,
> Riches are not happiness
>
> . . . .
>
> And when on our deathbed lying,
> Full of anguish and of pain
> Reason tells us, "Be of comfort,
> Ye shall surely live again.[19]

Morality or religion would be the obvious sources of such truths; reason was used simply as a title for the good, though the author's concept of the good no longer depended upon rationality. The word soon followed the concept out of the drama. Dunlap's plays were dotted with tributes to reason, but the term appeared irregularly in other nineteenth-century melodramas.[20]

Jefferson himself in the early nineteenth century realized the changes taking place in intellectual attitudes that the melodrama reflected. In 1814 he told John Adams that he enjoyed writing him because to him he could talk about books and be understood. "Our post-revolutionary youth are born under happier stars than you and I were," he noted to his old friend:

> They acquire all learning in their mother's womb, and bring it into the world ready-made. The information of books is no longer necessary; and all knolege which is not innate, is in contempt, or neglect at least. Every folly must run its round and so, I suppose, must that . . . of rejecting the knolege acquired in past ages, and starting on the new ground of intuition.[21]

This "new ground of intuition" was what the melodrama substituted for reason and education. "The voice of nature" remained the guide for human conduct, but its language could now be best interpreted by man's spontaneous feelings. "What reason approves," announced a heroine about a match with a wealthy villain, "the heart rejects."[22] And wherever such a discrepancy existed, the heart chose more wisely than the head: it

---

[19] Lazarus Beach, *Jonathan Postfree; or, The Honest Yankee* (Philadelphia, 1827), p. 16.

[20] William Dunlap, *Leicester* (New York, 1807), p. 118; *Ribbemont; or, The Feudal Baron* (New York, 1803), p. 7; *The Archers; or, The Mountaineers of Switzerland* (New York, 1796), p. 44.

[21] Jefferson to Adams, July 5, 1814, *Adams-Jefferson Letters*, ed. Lester Cappon (Chapel Hill, 1959), 2: 434.

[22] Dunlap, *Abaellino*, p. 12. In his translations from French and German, Dunlap usually reproduced the ideas of the originals rather than his own.

could "never be deceived . . . when thus it throbs in confirmation of the truth." The idea that "the voice of nature cannot err," that "there is an instinct in the heart which will not be deceived" was repeated in melodramas.[23] To do what "my heart tells me" or to act "as nature dictates" were synonymous activities that insured the doing of good.[24] And because man could "judge of true affections by the pulsation of the heart," the good person in the melodrama often proved his purity by ready tears, the outward signs of "heart, affectionate disposition, and fond temperament."[25] Few melodramatic characters wept so bountifully as those of Kotzebue, but hardly a serious play passed without the good females and often even the males shedding a few heartfelt "signs of tenderness."[26] Melodramatists felt, as one old father told a suppliant maiden, "That tear is worth ten thousand words."[27]

Nature is a term of sufficiently pliable meaning to cover many concepts. While the melodrama generally used it to mean the intuitive impulse that led right-feeling hearts to truth, the concept became tied in with another meaning, "the bright and beautiful . . . all around us," which included things like "the sweet song of the blackbird and the cry of the whippoorwill, the fresh, green turf . . .; and the breeze which . . . whispers on my ear a most enchanting melody."[28] Such apostrophes to pretty scenery were frequent, especially in American settings where men could see:

> Dame Nature in a garb,
> Such as in other lands she scorns to wear,
> . . . where men
> Unwearied from her, have not yet learned to hate
> The simple lessons their Great Mother teaches.[29]

The lessons of beautiful nature were always as much religious and moral as aesthetic. For instance, one hero pointed out in a common vein the advantages of the country over the city:

> Nature in her holy temple is ever teaching lessons of wisdom and goodness. The sunshine as it ripens the golden grain, the shower as it falls upon

[23] Samuel H. Chapman, *The Red Rover* (Philadelphia, 1828), p. 51; William Dunlap, *The Voice of Nature* (New York, 1803), p. 40; John Howard Payne, *The Italian Bride*, in *ALP*, 5: 110.
[24] Charles Breck, *The Fox Chase* (Philadelphia, 1808), p. 40; William Dunlap, *The Wife of Two Husbands* (New York, 1804), p. 5.
[25] *Knights of the Orange Grove*, in *Rejected Plays* (New York, 1828), p. 96; William I. Paulding, *Antipathies; or, Enthusiasts by the Ears* in *American Comedies* (Philadelphia, 1847), p. 250.
[26] Isaac Harby, *Alberti* (Charleston, 1819), p. 7.
[27] Charles Breck, *The Trust* (New York, 1808), p. 70.
[28] Louisa Medina, *Nick of the Woods* (Boston, n.d.), p. 13.
[29] Robert Dale Owen, *Pocahontas* (New York, 1837), p. 161.

the parched earth, the luscious fruit hanging from the laden bough, and the blue heaven smiling upon all, lead the heart to *One* whose precept and example was good will and charity to all mankind.[30]

By the 1830's most plays took time off from their busy plots to praise "the mighty workmanship of heaven, and read our father's power in the blushing flower of the field." "O! holy nature!" exclaimed one play's Catholic bishop moved at the sight of scenic beauty, "how powerful thy eloquence!"[31]

Nature's eloquence was couched in perfectly simple language that the humblest could understand. Indeed the humblest had great advantage in this regard because the trumpery of rank and wealth and fashion and education would not cloud their primal perceptiveness. Many things interceded between truth and the sophisticated man, but it was difficult "to deceive the simple and the good."[32] Such an attitude could encourage social complacency, could teach the poor or oppressed to be contented with their lot because they in reality possessed something that was even abetted by their lowly position. This was perhaps the tendency in Europe, where the egalitarian elements of the melodrama were generally more muted. Yet, despite the melodrama's careful avoidance of political statements except in the realm of platitudes, the implications of its basic ideas were radically democratic. Certainly in America, where power was in the hands of the people, melodramatic attitudes played their part in creating the tone of self-righteous belligerence that marked such related developments as Jacksonian democracy, spread-eagle diplomacy, and "Young America" patriotism. Telling everyman that, provided his heart was pure, he was as wise as any sage, as good as any ruler, led to both exuberant self-confidence and deep suspicions about the motives and character of anyone who disagreed.

One of *The Politicians* in Mathews' satirical play told a friend that human faults were always blamed on "Nature, for we father on her all the children of our Fancy, that good Sense, the rugged overseer, refuses to provide for."[33] This comment posed a problem the melodrama usually ignored: was not making nature the great teacher of virtue, and the human heart the true interpreter of its lessons, opening the door to anti-social behavior of every sort? If the heart were the only proper regulator of conduct, was not the villain, led by his desire for the heroine or for

[30] H. J. Conway, "The Banker; or, Fashion and Failure," (1844), HTC, Act I, p. 14.
[31] Bannister, *Gentleman of Lyons*, p. 33; C. E. Grice, *The Battle of New Orleans; or, Glory, Love, and Loyalty* (Baltimore, 1815), p. 39.
[32] John Howard Payne, *Mount Savage*, in *ALP*, 5: 76.
[33] Cornelius Mathews, *The Politicians* (New York, 1840), p. 25.

wealth, doing right? Or anyway who could say he was not being true to his nature?

Well, the melodrama could. Dunlap's translation of an early French melodrama showed succinctly the kind of rationale used to keep nature's impulses within the bounds of social propriety. The situation was carefully developed so that the good characters, if they followed the promptings of their hearts, would transgress social laws. The heroine had eloped with a worthless scoundrel, Isadore Fritz, who soon deserted her and their young son. After long contrition over her youthful folly, she learned of her husband's death and married a virtuous count. At this happy juncture, Fritz appeared: he had forged a false death certificate planning to reclaim his wife after the count had ceded to her half of his estate. The count was willing to part with the property, but when Fritz demanded his son, the count refused. "What, my lord," queried the villain, "would you strike at the basis of society?" To which the hero replied, "I uphold society when I support the cause of virtue. Sacred indeed are the rights of society, but those rights only exist in the heart which obeys the voice of nature, and the dictates of honor and humanity."[34]

Such a statement was as far as this melodrama, or any other, went in opposing the rights of the heart to those of society. And the rest of the play demonstrated how the "voice of nature" led the hero and heroine not to scorn social regulations, but to observe them scrupulously. When Fritz was arrested, they decided that "eternal separation" was dictated by "delicacy as well as the laws of society," and when Fritz was sentenced to die, they decided they must help him escape for fear the count's "unsullied name will be branded with having sacrificed the husband to gain unrivalled possession of the wife." Nature dictated to them not compliance with their own just impulses, but a self-sacrificing social probity that could hardly be more fastidious. And before Fritz died in a plot of his own conniving to allow a happy ending, the count congratulated himself, "I have conquered the weak suggestions of passion . . .; my soul subsides into a tranquility which vice can never know."[35] As Dunlap wrote in another play, "The feelings of nature are again alive within you. Man is not man until his passion dies."[36]

This brand of social insurance was always adopted by the melodrama: the voice of nature urged compliance with social standards, whereas the

---

[34] Dunlap, *Wife of Two Husbands*, p. 58.

[35] *Ibid.*, pp. 61–62, 64.

[36] William Dunlap, *The Italian Father* (New York, 1810), p. 12.

voice of passion was the force of evil that scorned society's dictates. Villains were usually driven by "dauntless passion"; heroines feared "vile passions" and longed for "passionless content"; and when woman fell it was because she had been led "step by step till passion triumphs over nature."[37] In the melodrama, though a góod man might feel "righteous passion," passion in general was both unnatural and impure.

The melodrama's problems with nature were epitomized in its treatment of the Indian, who was certainly embosomed in nature and untrammeled by false conventionalities. When asked from what book he gained his knowledge, the Indian replied, "From the universal book of nature, bound by the green-sward of my native hills, paged by the leaves of my native forests, and imprinted on my memory by the God of my people."[38] With such educational credentials, the Indian had to be treated respectfully by the melodrama, if it were to be true to its theories of ennobling scenery and intuitive impulses of wisdom. Central Indian characters were usually endowed with every trait that coincided with the author's ideas of the good. Thus a Jeffersonian author in the early 1800's gave his Massasoit an American Philosophical Society turn of mind: "Tho' unacquainted with the lore of schools," with his "intuitive mind,"

> He traces nature's climax and explores
> The virtues of each vegetable order;
> And oft at night his wondering eyes survey
> The various glittering orbs of Heaven
> Noting the different stations of the stars,
> And revolutions of the wandering planets.[39]

More commonly the distortion emphasized sensibility, as when Pocahontas decided, "I will use my bow no longer; I go out to the wood, and my heart is light; but while my arrow flies, I sorrow, and when the bird drops through the branches, tears come into my eyes. I will no longer use my bow."[40]

Yet there were latent reservations about the Indian's full equality. Even the purest of Indian maidens might be propositioned by merely vulgar characters, whereas only villains were allowed to insult the white heroine. And though these proposals were indignantly scorned—

---

[37] Joseph Hutton, *The Orphan of Prague* (Philadelphia, 1808), p. 22; *Lucinda* in *Rejected Plays* (New York, 1828), p. 27; John Howard Payne, *Richelieu* (New York, 1826), p. 15; Mary Clarke Carr, *The Benevolent Lawyers; or, Villainy Detected* (Philadelphia, 1823), p. 3.

[38] Nathaniel H. Bannister, *Putnam, The Iron Son of '76* (Boston, n.d.), p. 16.

[39] Joseph Croswell, *A New World Planted* (Boston, 1802), p. 15.

[40] James Nelson Barker, *The Indian Princess; or, La Belle Sauvage* (New York, 1808), p. 15.

"Bad man! Indian girl's red cheek grows redder with shame!"[41]—they still showed the position of the Indian heroine to be less elevated than that of the white. If Pocahontas' experience sanctioned interracial marriage, the Indian girls were usually converted to Christianity first and sometimes had their skin lightened.

> I know she's browner than European dames,
> But whiter far than other natives are,
> And modest blushes oft adorn her cheeks.[42]

Whatever the vestigial racial prejudice, the dramatist's problem in handling the Indian was essentially one of determining how to engraft a theoretical belief in the advantages of nature onto a story in which civilized society justly destroys natural man. John Augustus Stone's *Metamora* was the most popular and honest of melodramatic treatments of the Indian. Loosely connected to a perfectly conventional melodramatic plot was the main center of interest in the play, Metamora, who was known to the whites as King Philip. The Indian chief was an amalgam of melodramatic virtues: he was a rescuer of heroines, a doting husband, a tender father, a brave warrior in the cause of freedom, indeed, as the heroine described him, "the grandest model of a mighty man":

> High on a craggy rock an Indian stood, with sinewy arm and eye that pierced the glen. . . . a robe of fur was o'er his shoulder thrown, and o'er his long dark hair an eagle's plume waved in the breeze, a feathery diadem. Firmly he stood upon the jutting height, as if a sculptor's hand had carved him there. With awe I gazed. . . .

He was even incapable of telling a lie and acted as a spokesman for temperance and for religious toleration.[43]

Driven to war by white encroachments and trickery, he fought savagely under his battle cry of "Red men, arouse! Freedom! Revenge or death!" But in the end his followers were slaughtered, his son was killed, and he and his wife were surrounded. After stabbing his wife to save her from being captured, Metamora let himself be shot and died with his wife's name on his lips. But most of his last speech was a malediction upon the whites:

> May your graves and the graves of your children be in the path the red men shall trace! And may the wolf and the panther howl o'er your fleshless

41 Richard Penn Smith, *William Penn*, in *ALP*, 13: 98.
42 Croswell, *New World Planted*, p. 20.
43 John Augustus Stone, *Metamora; or, The Last of the Wampanoags*, in *ALP*, 14: 10, 17, 21.

bones, fit banquet for the destroyers. Spirits of the grave, I come! But the curse of Metamora stays with the white man![44]

The play allotted only a subplot to the Indian-white conflict, but nonetheless *Metamora* was the only sufficiently honest and powerful Indian drama to jar white complacency. In Augusta at the time Jackson and the Georgians were disposing of the Cherokees and their lands, Forrest was roundly hissed in the role; he "believes in that d———d Indian speech," one Georgian concluded.[45] Other Indian plays resorted to intellectual trickery to mitigate the good Indian's destruction. As in *Metamora*, prophecies and dreams were introduced suggesting the inevitability of the Indian's destruction and making fate more than the white man the guilty party; they were men "whom providence has doomed to utter destruction."[46] Sometimes an Indian, commonly an Indian maiden, was converted to Christianity and expounded the advantages of contact with the whites who taught "the benefits of civilization, the blessings of faith, and how to be good and happy."[47] In some instances the Indians became the dupes of bad white men; thus one author tied the Indians slaughtered by the Pilgrim fathers into a plot of some vile High Church Anglicans to spread Royalist control.[48] More frequently the Indians were divided against themselves, so that bad Indians really caused the tribe's downfall.[49] Cooper's device of playing off the noble Uncas against the vile Magua, the heroic Pawnees against the villainous Sioux, was repeated in several melodramas.

Such distinctions not only absolved the whites of essential guilt, but also allowed playwrights to differentiate between nature in its desirable form and nature as the wild antithesis of civilization. Metamora, alone of good Indians, possessed the wildness as well as the gentler beauty of nature. His very first entrance emphasized his savagery and his strength;

---

[44] *Ibid.*, pp. 25, 40. Mordecai M. Noah's *She Would be a Soldier* (New York, 1819), also allowed the Indian, a very peripheral character in the play, a strong statement of his case against the whites. The dignity which Noah gave to his Indian chief was probably influenced by his conviction that the Indians represented the lost tribe of Israel. Metamora probably descended from the Indian in Noah's play: Forrest played in *She Would be a Soldier* when the Indian in it was acted by John Augustus Stone who later wrote *Metamora*.

[45] James Murdock, *The Stage, or Recollections of Actors and Acting* (Philadelphia, 1880), pp. 298–300.

[46] Joseph Doddridge, *Logan, The Last of the Race of Shikellemus* (Buffalo Creek, Va., 1823), p. 8.

[47] George W. P. Custis, *The Indian Prophecy* (Georgetown, 1828), p. 9.

[48] Croswell, *New World Planted.*

[49] George Jones, *Tecumseh; or, The Prophet of the West* (London, 1824); Doddridge, *Logan;* Barker, *Indian Princess*; George W. P. Custis, *Pocahontas; or, The Settlers of Virginia* (Philadelphia, 1830); Lewis Deffebach, *Oolaita; or, The Indian Heroine* (Philadelphia, 1821); Charles Saunders, "Telula; or, The Star of Hope" (1845), Brown University.

he threw a live wolf over a precipice and exulted that the "brave beast" had turned on him and consequently died fighting, "like a redman." The dramatist even explicitly excused Metamora's not accepting Christianity:

> Hero: 'Twould cost him half his virtues. Is justice goodly? Metamora's just. Is bravery virtue? Metamora's brave. If love of country, child and wife and home, be to deserve them all—he merits them.

And when he went on the warpath he expressed not only the conventional desire to save his native land, but also a passionate desire to drink his enemies' blood.[50] Forrest's powerful acting made Metamora a popular success, but the critically minded were concerned that audiences were encouraged to sympathize with the "reckless cruelties of a bloody barbarian." "Let us hope, for the honor of humanity," the *American Quarterly Review* concluded, "that this applause is bestowed on Mr. Forrest, rather than the ferocious savage he impersonates."[51]

Other dramatist's handling of the Indian took a much more equivocal course: the good Indians possessed only socially unobjectionable traits without any particular ferocity. The usual dichotomy between good and evil, nature and passion, was suggested in an Indian girl's description of her two suitors:

> He [Lenape] is all love, all care, and is concerned if the hot wind too rudely pass over me. . . . He [Manta] spoke of love; his voice was fierce; his eyes were inflamed, and his features distorted with passion. He wooed me as the panther woos the fawn. . . .[52]

This convenient dichotomy leached the drama's commitment to nature. The "voice of nature," the intuitive understanding of the heart, was glorified because it spoke, as the good Indian acted, with complete social propriety; where conduct transgressed social bounds it was guided not by nature but by its opposite, passion. The melodrama's problem, and its solution, was close to that of Ralph Waldo Emerson, who also urged men to do what "the heart appoints." Emerson more openly attacked "popular standards," but he too posed "the law of consciousness"—seemingly little different from a law of conscience—that, for example, prohibited gross sensuality, and told one to support one's family

---

[50] Stone, *Metamora*, in *ALP*, XIV: 11–12. When Forrest presented the play in London, the Lord Chamberlain censored this direct defense of Metamora's non-Christianity, as well as some of his more violent speeches. For example, Metamora's talk about wanting to drink blood was changed, with British fastidiousness, to a desire simply to shed blood. March 23, 1845, British Museum Add. MSS 42983, ff. 428, 492.

[51] *American Quarterly Review*, 8 (September, 1830): 145.

[52] R. P. Smith, *William Penn*, in *ALP*, 13: 87.

and be chaste, though in "unprecedented ways," whatever that might mean.[53] Emerson and the melodrama shared a pervasive faith that what the heart and nature dictated would be "holy" and would not lead to social immorality or destruction, to either incestuous love or cataclysmic hatred for a white whale.

The melodrama's appeal to nature and intuition, instead of endangering society's ethical concepts, in reality provided a surer basis for them than reason had. In the melodrama, as in Cooper's novels, Leatherstocking as man of nature might win "the esteem—respect, nay reverence" of author and audience, but when he wanted to marry a nice middle-class girl he came to see that this was somehow "unnatur'l—agin natur."[54] The voice of nature spoke to all, but, if truly heard, it always reiterated social preconceptions. The melodrama's categorical imperative that anyone of unperverted feeling would innately perceive the rightness of accepted moral standards was incontrovertible. Depending on reason to justify morality, on the other hand, not only permitted dispute but had led to some highly questionable results. In the name of reason many people had accepted deism and rejected religious revelation and worship. The Goddess of Reason had presided over that bloody onslaught against conventional standards, the French Revolution. And contemporary radicals like Frances Wright managed to use reason to prove, for instance, that a proper educational system would remove children from parents.[55] Certainly an appeal to nature offered social conventions more secure protection than the rationality which produced deists, the Goddess of Reason, and Fanny Wright. The melodrama provided an emotional equivalent to the "common sense" philosophy of the period; both strove to safeguard accepted norms against a rationalistic and skeptical tradition that had in many instances challenged social and theological convictions.

Physical nature was similarly viewed as truly natural only in its tamer aspects. In the melodrama, as Captain John Smith was made to announce, "Wild nature smooths apace her savage frown, moulding her features to a social smile." It was a nature of singing birds and playful squirrels where "no cruel animal lurks." To use Robert Frost's dichotomy, physical nature in the melodrama was "Pretty Scenery" rather than the "Whole Goddam Machinery."[56] This attitude of melodrama

[53] Ralph Waldo Emerson, "Self-Reliance" in *Selected Prose and Poetry*, ed. Reginald G. Cook (New York, 1950), pp. 181–82.
[54] Jonas Phillips, "The Pathfinder," HTC, Act II.
[55] Frances Wright, *Course of Poplar Lectures* (New York, 1831), pp. 150–70.
[56] Barker, *Indian Princess*, p. 70; Custis, *Pocahontas*, in *RAP*, p. 182; Robert Frost, "Lucretius Versus the Lake Poets," in *Complete Poems* (New York, 1949), p. 558.

and its society toward nature is visually caught in Asher Durand's well-known painting "Kindred Spirits," which shows William Cullen Bryant and Thomas Cole in an American forest scene. The men are surrounded by much of the paraphernalia of the nineteenth-century nature worship. In the foreground is a blasted tree trunk hidden in shadow, while the focus of the picture is on a rushing cataract, gaunt and shaggy cliffs, distant mountains enveloped in warmly glowing mist, and a graceful tree, its delicate foliage carefully etched against the sky. In the midst of this stand the two men, immaculately dressed in long-tailed coats and carefully tied cravats. One of them uses his walking stick to point out something to the other, rather like a teacher pointing to a lesson on the blackboard. They stand close to the edge of a jutting rock, but there seems no danger of their falling into the chasm below. The painting bears witness to a calm perception of nature, and warm affection for it, that is too serious to be called a flirtation, but is certainly too restrained to degenerate into the more passionate involvement of an affair that might question or oppose society's standards. Social man and nature's promptings in the period's plays were just such kindred spirits.

$$*\qquad*\qquad*$$

Like its social structure and intuitional faith, the melodrama's basic plot situation bore the impress of democratic society. Love was the great emotion experienced by all classes, the great leveler that equalized "the prince's palace with the cottage, and the noble with the shepherd." Love was "created by God in heaven, for the happiness of angels," explained one heroine, but He had sent it to earth "to temper the evils produced by war, and the ambition of princes."[57] Certainly the nineteenth-century playwright generally substituted love for all other passions as his plot nexus and theme. The central characters in most plays were in quest of their proper mates. The thin period of sexual adventure and danger sandwiched between the domesticity of childhood and married life was the meat of both the melodrama and the romantic novel. Plays concentrated on the adventures of the heroine and romances on those of the hero, but the theme was almost exactly the same: the victory of the forces of morality, social restraint and domesticity over what was dark, passionate, and anti-social.

Yet plays emphasized less the romantic than the moral elements in the situation. Cupid, "the dimpled god that pure hearts worship," was a

---

[57] Bannister, *Gentleman of Lyons*, p. 40; John Daly Burk, *Bethlem Gabor, Lord of Transylvania; or, The Man Hating Palatine* (Petersburg, Va., 1807), pp. 23–24.

reigning deity on the nineteenth-century stage, but a deity, dramatists always insisted, "whose honied shafts are dipt in honor, and whose plumed pinions virtue guides."[58] The melodrama's hero-heroine-villain triangle and its sharp division between tenderness and passion insured that plays stressed the honor more than the honey of the romantic situation. The search for mate primarily provided the playing field for a moral joust between good and evil.

"It was very dull," noted a Washington matron about an early nineteenth-century play. "It was as good as a sermon."[59] Because of the need to appeal broadly, dramatic sermonizing emphasized the least common denominators of social morality—virtuous platitudes like "be honest," or "honor your parents," or "cherish your country," or, with most insistence, "be chaste," all of which were "sentiments which need only to be expressed to receive the warmest approbation."[60] The drama's lessons of "honesty, patriotism, morality, and good will to mankind" were not only unexceptionable, but the dramatic situation was always arranged so that they could not be misinterpreted.[61] Good characters were sometimes entangled in "contradictory obligations," were torn for a while between two virtuous principles, between filial obedience and chaste affection or the necessity of telling the truth and of aiding a friend.[62] But the situation was always organized so that there was no question where righteousness lay and resolved so that any permanent choice between the two goods was avoided. For the melodrama, as for Kant, "a collision of duties or obligations" was "altogether unthinkable," at least in the long view, because this would mean that the universe was so structured as to prohibit perfectly moral conduct. The period's drama was "so eminently devoted to the cause of virtue" that the dramatist would "suggest no image, nor awaken any thought that does not harmonize with our best propensities and highest duties."[63]

To make its moral lessons perfectly clear the melodrama usually denied a mixture of good and bad traits to the same person. Plays talked not about "good" or "bad" actions, but rather posed "virtue" against "vice" and "guilt" against "innocence," implying that persons were

---

[58] Samuel B. H. Judah, *The Rose of Arragon; or, The Vigil of St. Mark* (New York, 1822), p. 5.

[59] Mrs. William Thornton, "Diary, 1800–1863," *Records of Columbia Historical Society*, 10 (1907): 185.

[60] *Weekly Visitors and Ladies' Miscellany*, 4 (March 1, 1806): 143.

[61] Freneau, quoted in Marsh, "Freneau on the Theatre," p. 104.

[62] *Friend*, 1 (October, 1815): 85.

[63] Immanuel Kant, *Introduction to the Metaphysics of Ethics* (London, 1797), p. xxiv; *Literary and Scientific Repository*, 3 (October, 1821): 336.

either perfectly pure or perfectly vile. "To represent the most contradictory moral qualities as existing together," one critic claimed was "as much an act of mere wantonness, as it would be to describe an individual as laboring in the last stages of a loathsome disease, and exhibiting at the same time all the outward forms and colors of perfect health."[64] The period's plays acquiesced in this verdict. The point of the melodrama—the essence of both its romantic and moral situations—was that "virtue can hold no intercourse with vice."[65]

The melodrama also avoided moral ambiguity by making sin wholly a product of character rather than of situation or society. Circumstances were sometimes used to explain why an essentially good man had done bad things, but generally one's moral stance was cause rather than caused. Beginning in the late 1830's a few plays suggested familial upbringing as reason for a character's faults,[66] and by the 1850's some, most notably *Uncle Tom's Cabin*, tentatively gave a social rather than personal explanation for evil. The growing tendency toward "realism" in the melodrama of the late nineteenth century reflected largely an increasing willingness to see man's character not as a moral abstraction but as a complex product of a particular personal and social environment.

The drama's moral lessons and convictions were bolstered by its belief that the course of life was guided by a providence or Heaven that always vindicated "the holy cause of innocence."[67] The melodrama constantly offered the ". . . assurance based on changeless truth that holy ends shall be by Heaven sustained" and reiterated its faith that "a crafty villain . . . shall not prevail against an innocent man," that "money may oppress honest integrity for a time, but it will soon escape its grasp," that "the reign of vice, though successful, is short and virtue, though long oppressed, will in the end assuredly receive its bright reward."[68] "Whoever perished, being innocent?" lectured an old father. "They who plow iniquity and sow wickedness, reap the same."[69]

Good characters moved through the melodrama needing "no hope but the goodness of Heaven," which did "watch over the innocent," as

---

[64] *North American Review*, 16 (April, 1823): 402.

[65] John Howard Payne, *Clari; or, The Maid of Milan* (Boston, 1856), p. 33.

[66] John Blake White, *The Forgers* (New York, 1899 [1837]), pp. 33–34; H. J. Conway, "The Brigands of the West; or, The Wolf of the Prairies," HTC, (1844), Act I, scene iii, J. T. Trowbridge, *Neighbor Jackwood* (Boston, 1857), p. 67.

[67] John Howard Payne, *Trial Without Jury; or, The Maid and the Magpie*, in *ALP*, 5: 42.

[68] Henry Harrington, *Bernardo del Carpio* (n.p., 1836), p. 29; H. J. Conway, "Guiscard, The Guerilla: or, A Brothers Revenge," HTC, (1844), Act II, scene 4; John Howard Payne, *Julia; or, The Wanderer* (New York, 1806), p. 28; Hutton, *Orphan of Prague*, p. 23.

[69] Joseph Field, *Job and His Children*, in *ALP*, 19: 258.

the hero announced when he arrived in the nick of time "armed with justice to unravel the web, to unfold the deep-laid arts."[70] And when the web was properly unraveled, melodramatic characters revealed their roles in their explanations of "this wonderful and almost miraculous preservation."

> *Hero:* Blessed Heaven!
> *Villain:* Curst chance!
> *Heroine:* The hand of providence.[71]

If the hand of providence benevolently guided the affairs of men, slapping down the guilty and rewarding the innocent, no one could question the importance of being moral. "Be good and be rewarded" was a dictum which both promoted moral conduct and predicated a morally ruled universe. Who could doubt the moral value of a theater, critics asked, where people "beheld tyranny and oppression trampled on by constancy and virtues" and heard sentiments to persuade belief in "the government and providence of a Superior being."[72]

Unfortunately man's experience suggested that often people of little integrity or benevolence reaped worldly rewards, while others of finer moral fiber suffered much and profited little. In an unusually forthright critical comment, Isaac Harby pointed out that "however 'all reasonable beings naturally love the triumph of justice'—all observing 'reasonable beings' know that justice does not always triumph."[73] Many of the elements in the melodrama were attempts to suggest this frequent grimness of life and yet to deny the reality of any apparent victory of evil. The centrality of the villain in these plays, even though he was always eventually defeated, suggested a world where the evil and terror of which he was an incarnation were constant threats. And playwrights heaped incredible difficulties in the path of the virtuous and allowed the long-continued triumph of the wicked until "the almost miraculous" dispensation of justice, the better to prove "the inspiring truth that there is no extreme of danger and affliction which can justify despair."[74] The melodramatic world was one where all things worked out for the good, but where the sin of despair always lurked just behind the scene because

---

[70] John Howard Payne, *Thérèse; or, The Orphan of Geneva* (Philadelphia, 1838), p. 16; Samuel B. H. Judah, *The Mountain Torrent* (New York, 1820), p. 52.

[71] John Blake White, *The Mysteries of the Castle; or, The Victim of Revenge* (Charleston, 1807), p. 65; Payne, *Trial Without Jury*, in *ALP*, 5 : 53.

[72] *Kentucky Gazette* (March 19, 1811), quoted in Mabel T. Crum, "The History of the Lexington Theatre From the Beginning to 1860" (Ph.D. dissertation, University of Kentucky, 1956), p. 57; *New York Mirror*, 1 (October 4, 1823): 78.

[73] Isaac Harby, *A Selection From the Miscellaneous Writings* (Charleston, 1829), p. 285.

[74] Dunlap, *Wife of Two Husbands*, p. 63.

of the deviousness of the process. "The arm of providence is moral justice," playwrights insisted, but man often needed great faith and resignation before that arm began to move:

> *Hero:* And oh, how sweet, when after virtue's struggle
> We lay our hands upon our heart, and cry,
> We suffer'd Heaven's scourge with resignation,
> And resignation is repayed with bliss.[75]

Drama's faith in historical progress, and particularly in the superiority of the American experiment, was the social equivalent of its belief that providence would reward the virtuous individual; it was similarly hedged with latent reservations. For instance, if progress were constant, presumably each new generation would be superior to the previous one, but in plays dealing with contemporary American life, the present was depicted as degenerate and the immediate past as an epoch of great moral superiority. Perhaps faith in progress encouraged people to explain evil as modern deviation from the upward movement. Anyway, good people usually represented old-fashioned virtues and evil characters newfangled fashions. Even in *The Contrast*, written only a few years after the Revolution and in the same year as the Constitution, this separation was stressed. In a play immersed in American chauvinism, the new country might be expected to show new virtues, but instead the hero and heroine's righteous views were "old-fashioned sentiments," whereas the vileness of the villain and the flaws of other characters were attributed to modern corruptions of taste.[76]

No melodramatic comedy broke with this tradition. Social innocence and purity were invariably pictured as having sharply declined since the preceding generation. Especially after 1840 many plays also showed apprehension about modern social ills, such as the evils of the city, the spread of crime, the hard lot of the poor, or the hard-heartedness of the rich. These problems were usually dramatized in wholly personal terms: some villain was oppressing the poor hero, and when he was foiled so presumably was poverty.[77] This personalization of evil drained these plays of overt social criticism, but the impression remained that in this world where all things work out for the good the times were strangely out of joint.

---

[75] Harrington, *Bernardo del Carpio*, p. 64; William Dunlap, *The Africans; or, War, Love, and Duty* (Philadelphia, 1811), p. 169.

[76] Royall Tyler. *The Contract*, in *RAP*, p. 53.

[77] Silas S. Steele, *The Crock of Gold*, in *ALP*, 14; and Jones, *The People's Lawyer*, offered good examples of this technique.

Reservations about the role of providence and progress in man's existence were never allowed to deny the faith itself. For both dramatists and critics "that poetic justice which is founded in natural justice" had to be "obvious in all things" and always attested by the play's conclusion. The melodrama was essentially committed to defending, in personal terms and in a period when the course of natural justice seemed less self-evident, Blackstone's eighteenth-century legal aphorism: "So intimately connected are the laws of eternal justice with the happiness of each individual, that the latter cannot be attained but by observing the former; and if the former be punctually obeyed, it cannot but induce the latter."[78] This idea that personal happiness must directly flow from moral behavior was the melodrama's categorical imperative insisted on, experience sometimes to the contrary, in order to rescue a morally thinkable universe from its sometimes apparent monstrousness. Breck's suggested theme of an honest clerk's losing his job could not be dramatized without restoring him to good fortune in the end. A just universe demanded that clerks who were honest, by the play's conclusion at least, be properly paid.

The melodrama's undeviating emphasis on the workings of heaven justly guiding men's affairs might suggest a religiously oriented drama. Certainly plays often respectfully introduced religious forms. Heroes and heroines in desperate moments prayed for God's protection; good people were said to go to heaven and villains were consigned to hell; the Bible was sometimes quoted or included in the grand tableaux that ended domestic plays; and melodramatic language often showed the influence of biblical incidents, metaphors, and cadences. Yet no melodrama developed a specifically religious theme; when religious conversion occurred on stage it was clearly an adjunct to some other topic like alcohol or the Indian, with which the play was centrally concerned.

The lack of religious emphasis grew in part from the concept of God these plays presented. He was created in the period's image of the good man; indeed He bore close resemblance to the moralizing old father figure and was referred to as "the great judge of hearts," "the Orphan's friend," and "the protector of innocence."[79] Although this God acted directly in man's affairs, by tossing thunderbolts at villains, for example, or diverting bullets from George Washington, He was severely limited

[78] *Literary and Scientific Repository*, 3 (October, 1821): 341; William Blackstone, *Commentaries on the Laws of England* (Oxford, 1768), 1 : 40.
[79] William Charles White, *The Clergyman's Daughter* (Boston, 1810), p. 16; Louisa Medina, *Ernest Maltravers* (New York, n.d.), p. 20; William Dunlap, *The Father; or, American Shandy-ism* (New York, 1789), p. 27.

by His own moral rules. The conduct of a God obliged to befriend orphans and protect innocence was stringently curbed; He was a legislator and judge who in making laws for man also bound Himself by them. And consequently what really mattered were the laws themselves, the moral mechanism that had been set in motion. Melodramatic providence was, in a sense, the opposite of its Puritan counterpart. For the Puritan, God acted and man was obliged to divine his meaning; in the melodrama, as in both liberal and revivalistic religions in the early nineteenth century, man acted, and if he accepted the code, God was obliged to reward him.

Whereas the melodrama's religion required primarily compliance with moral laws, its nationalism stressed more personal commitment. Its most elaborate mythological spectacles were designed to promote patriotic rather than theological fervor. The final scene in the highly successful *Putnam, the Iron Son of '76* was typical of the patriotic pageantry worked into many American plays.

> *Scene:* Three quarters dark. Ethereal firmament filled with silver stars . . . Eagle flying in the air . . . looking down upon a lion, couchant, on trap. . . . The goddesses discovered in various groups, bearing blue wands with silver stars. God of war on . . . small Roman chariot. Goddess of Liberty on trap . . . in small Roman chariot.

> *Chorus:* We will be free, we will be free
> As the winds of the earth or the waves of the sea,
> Will bow to no tyrant, submit to no yoke
> But struggle like men till our fetters are broke.
> Shout, shout! Let it echo on earth and o'er sea!
> Our tyrant shall tremble; we shall be free!

> (Music changes. Eagle ascends and lion descends. Goddesses dance around waving wands. Goddess of Liberty and Mars points to clouds. Clouds ascend . . . and draw off . . . and [lights up] the signers of the Declaration of Independence discovered. Ben Franklin at head of table. Music changes.)

> *Chorus:* No more in useless broils will we
> Engage our hearts in sympathy:
> But manly stand or manly fall
> In the great common cause of all.
> Raise now our banner high in air!
> Behold it floats in Triumph there.

> (Clouds ascend and draw off, and the American flag discovered on flat [painted].)

Chorus: Long may the stars in glory shine,
    The sun of freedom till the end of time
    Guide on our soldiers till the battle's won!
    Hail our chief, the mighty Washington.

(Music changes; clouds descend, etc. The goddesses dance off waving wands; God of War descends on first trap; Goddess of Liberty on trap.)[80]

Generally only military dramas were capped off by such patriotic spectacles, but loyalty and service to one's country were always made primary virtues. "That sentiment is heavenly," the melodrama argued, which held that "all before the sacred voice of country . . . should fly to her relief."[81] Although "patriotic feeling" was stressed as "one of the first of the virtues," American plays avoided pure chauvinism by usually connecting devotion to country with pride in its freedom, justice, and political equality.[82] The goddess of liberty was as central a figure in patriotic pageants as the American eagle, and her presence illustrated that drama's patriotic commitment was as much to a political ideal as to the nation itself. American playwrights and audiences expended political enthusiasm not only on the United States, but on any country or group that acted in the name of liberty to break "the chains of tyranny."[83] If the terms liberty and justice were tarnished when applied to American actions like subduing Indians or fighting the Mexican War, they retained meaning as ideals that kept the period's drama from simply worshipping the golden calf of nationalism.

A good character toasting America wished it "freedom, prosperity, and the sweet comforts of domestic happiness."[84] The last of this trinity of blessings was the one most strongly emphasized. The happiness of everyone, from king to commoner, depended on domestic tranquility. When one playwright wanted to prove the goodness and wisdom of a king, he had him marry to show to his people "an example of that felicity in that state from which alone national prosperity can spring—the state of chaste and virtuous wedlock." Even a Rip Van Winkle, cursed with the nagging wife sometimes allotted to low-comedy characters, was given a song about "what a paradise on earth" his life would be if only his drinking did not interfere with domestic bliss.[85] If

[80] Bannister, *Putnam*, p. 58.
[81] John Daly Burk, *Bunker Hill; or, The Death of General Warren* (New York, 1797), p. 20.
[82] Custis, *Pocahontas*, in *RAP*, p. 173.
[83] Mordecia M. Noah, *The Grecian Captive; or, The Fall of Athens* (New York, 1822), p. 25.
[84] James Workman, *Liberty in Louisiana* (Charleston, 1804), p. 35.
[85] Dunlap, *Voice of Nature*, p. 27; John H. Wainwright, *Rip Van Winkle* (London, n.d.), p. 14.

one possessed a happy home, no difficulty could dim the brightness of that blessing:

> Life may have pains and tears and agonies
> Like sudden clouds that dim the summer skies;
> But the true radiance stooping from above,
> The sun that lights them all—is wedded love.

In the melodrama, "domestic happiness is the wisest philosophy," the purest joy, the greatest of blessings, "a cordial remedy for all the casual ills of life."[86]

The woman was the chief figure in this domestic paradise, the cornerstone of the "quiet house and domestic fireside" and the guardian of "home-born and domestic joy."[87] The centrality of the woman to the religion of domesticity explained why the structure of plays centered on female chastity and why critics were most upset by any allowances for breaches of womanly purity. From Kotzebue's *The Stranger* in 1798 to Laura Keene's *Life's Troubled Tides* in the 1850's, denunciation was heaped on any play that suggested "that an adulterous wife . . . may under certain circumstances, deserve the sympathy and pitying tears of the audience."[88] So strong was the religion of domesticity that not only "domestic happiness" was felt to depend on feminine purity, but indeed the whole of society. Molière perhaps could be defended for treating womanly purity lightly, because in his "time, and in the unrefined nations," the importance of chastity to "the social order had not yet been discovered," but the modern writer could not:

> Any examples of such crimes' being forgiven and the party restored to favor again would have no small tendency to give a sanction that would be inimical to the best interests of mankind. The crime of infidelity in married woman is irreparable, as it respects society: every violation of this nature diminishes the general stock of confidence; confidence of the most sacred nature, for which no atonement can possibly be made; the stain of which no penitence can wash away.[89]

Because woman was "the source of every earthly bliss" and her home "the abode of universal felicity," seduction became "the unpardonable

---

[86] John Howard Payne, *Spanish Husband*, in *ALP*, 5; 264; William Milns, *The Comet; or, He Would Be An Astronomer* (Baltimore, 1817), p. 31; A. B. Lindsley, *Love and Friendship; or, Yankee Notions* (New York, 1809), p. 50.

[87] Conway, "Banker," Act I, p. 6; John Howard Payne, *Brutus; or, The Fall of Tarquin* (New York, 1821), p. 23.

[88] D. R. Thomason, *Fashionable Amusements: With A Review of Dr. Bellow's Lecture on the Theatre* (New York, 1857), p. 70.

[89] *Emerald*, 3 (April 2, 1808): 284; *Companion and Weekly Miscellany*, 1 (December 1, 1804): 34.

sin."[90] To suggest that any forgiveness for this was possible was "obscene and impious morality."[91]

The way in which the domestic paradise imposed itself upon the older religious framework was suggested in the concluding tableau to *The Drunkard*, a play at least partially written by a minister. The wife stands behind his chair and the daughter kneels beside the reformed drunkard-hero, "Edward, who is seated in prayer. Edward's hand on Bible and pointing up." The background music for this climactic scene, however, was not "Rock of Ages," or "A Mighty Fortress is My God," but "Home, Sweet Home:"[92]

> Mid pleasures and palaces, though we may roam,
> Be it ever so humble, there's no place like home!
> A charm from the skies seems to hallow us there—
> Like a love of a mother,
> Surpassing all other,
> Which seek through the world is ne'er met with elsewhere.
> There's a spell in the shade
> Where our infancy played
> Even stronger than time, more deep than despair.[93]

John Howard Payne's lyric was reportedly the most popular song in the period, even surpassing "Yankee Doodle."

The melodrama stressed situations and offered rewards that were perfectly democratic, that were available equally to all men. It urged men to purity, patriotism, and faith in providence, and it promised them earthly happiness from God, home, and country; but the greatest of these was home with its cornerstone of female purity.

*   *   *

"They are sermons in dialogue," an American periodical said in 1787 of contemporary plays. "If they are not a true picture of life, they show, at least, what life itself ought to be."[94] This description was accurate for the whole melodramatic tradition that followed. Its stress on clear

---

[90] Richard Penn Smith, *The Deformed; or, Woman's Trial* (Philadelphia, 1830), p. 84; W. C. White, *Clergyman's Daughter*, pp. 80, 86.

[91] *Ladies' Port-Folio*, 1 (January 1, 1820): 4.

[92] John Pierpont and W. H. Smith, *The Drunkard; or, The Fallen Saved!* (Boston, 1847), p. 50.

[93] This was Payne's first version of the song, written several years earlier, but differing little from that which made such a hit in *Clari*; printed in Charles H. Brainerd, *John Howard Payne; A Biographical Sketch* (Washington, D.C., 1885), p. 28.

[94] *American Magazine*, 1 (October, 1788), quoted in Herbert R. Brown, "Sensibility in Eighteenth Century American Drama," *American Literature*, 4 (March, 1932): 49; *Emerald*, 3 (December 19, 1807): 99.

division between good and bad, on a nature that led only to truth and nobility, on a providence that distributed its blessings on the merit system, and on a home life that was a paradise on earth were all part of a utopian creation. But this utopia was less a conscious imagining of what society might or should become than an ideal that was considered a kind of reality, experience notwithstanding. Throughout the melodrama the mood was that of fantasy and fairy tale rather than of history or myth. In going to the theater in the nineteenth century, people wanted to "view the splendours of a fairy land," to see "what they never did see, and what they never expect to see anywhere else."[95]

Recalling Periclean and Elizabethan precedents, critics argued that tragedy would continue its traditional role of presenting "the pith and marrow of the past," of being "to the illiterate a lecture on history."[96] Yet between the age of Shakespeare and the nineteenth-century, man's sense of connection with the past had changed. The achievements of men like Newton and Linneaus had shown the advances in understanding that grew from experimental and scientific methods of truth-seeking. Great historians of the eighteenth century such as Gibbon, Voltaire, and Hume pictured history primarily as a record of past follies, encouraged by "enthusiasms" of various sorts. The eighteenth century was considered, in John Adam's words, "the most honourable to human nature"; one examined earlier periods carefully mainly to avoid their failings.[97] Drama shared this sense of severance with the past; its use of history was primarily pedagogic, was more the product of literary convention than of any feeling of real connection with the past.

Post-Enlightenment thought restored positive interest in history—and certainly the melodrama constantly exploited it—but the immediacy of its ties with the present had been snapped. The very exploitation of historical setting by melodramatists or writers like Sir Walter Scott gave history a quaintness, an aura of distance and strangeness, that suggested a lack of immediate connection with the present. The melodrama, as did Thomas Jefferson, liked "the dreams of the future better than the history of the past."[98] In a presumably progressing society, people felt closer ties to the future, with what ought to be, than to history, with what had been.

Perhaps even more than its plot contortions, the melodrama's language served to keep realism at bay and to establish a mood of fantasy. Normal

---

[95] *North American Review*, 37 (October, 1833): 445; *Yankee*, 2 (August, 1829): 62.

[96] *Emerald*, 3 (April 2, 1808): 282–83.

[97] Adams to Jefferson, November 14, 1815, *Adams-Jefferson Letters*, 2: 456.

[98] Jefferson to Adams, August 1, 1816, *ibid.*, 2: 485.

word order was constantly rearranged, apparently for no other purpose
than to set its language apart from common speech; archaically "poetic"
expressions like "whither" or "yon" or "thou dost" were frequently
introduced; and word choice and metaphor remained abstract and conventionalized. The melodrama used predominantly generalized terms,
with built-in emotional overtones, rather than specific descriptions of
things. People talked about their "humble garments" or "beauteous
finery" but seldom of their caps and capes and aprons and long coats.
They might eat a "few paltry crumbs" or "costly viands," but never
steaks or stews or French pastry or rhubarb pie. They lived in "poor
hovels" or "humble cottages" or "spacious mansions." They often
lovingly contemplated flowers or the song of the bird, but whether they
were looking at roses or daisies or dandelions, whether they were
listening to nightingales or sparrows or jays, the audience seldom was
told. Even when a specific object was mentioned the reference was
usually both metaphorical and highly conventionalized. Thus the
heroine was frequently a rose, dove, or violet and the villain was almost
invariably a serpent, wolf, or vulture. Grossly typical of the high melodramatic style of conversation were the words of a simple farmer of
Lexington after he'd helped defeat the British: "Thou boasted sons of
Albion, who like wolves had come among us to devour, who thought
to find us the helpless bird on whom the vulture springs, have roused a
lion fierce and tameless as their own."[99] A taste of real life was rarely let
through this language barrier of the melodrama's conventional abstractions. The melodramatic hero called a spade "a menial implement."[100]

The explanation for the peculiarly bloated quality of melodramatic
language was in part that serious plays were traditionally written in
blank verse, while such verse seemed inappropriate for the more democratic themes and characters that were increasingly predominant on the
stage. Yet the melodrama's strangely contrived speech, more than a
transition between poetic and conversational language, was an intentional breaking of the bonds between the real world and that of stage,
not to intensify experience, but to distort it. A youthful Ralph Waldo
Emerson noted in his diary that dramatic language had to be "just far
enough removed from common life to avoid disgust, while it must chain
the attention and elevate the tone of feeling."[101] Elevation was the
primary aim. James Kirke Paulding's question, "Does it ever occur to a

---

[99] Samuel B. H. Judah, *A Tale of Lexington* (New York, 1823), p. 55.

[100] Jones, *Usurper*, in *ALP*, 14: 161.

[101] Ralph Waldo Emerson, *Journals* (1821), ed. Edward W. Emerson and Waldo E. Forbes (Boston, 1909–14), 1: 289.

particular class of dramatic writers that people ought sometimes to talk
common sense even in a melodrama?" missed the point.[102] Common
sense was not wanted in the highest level of the melodrama, but rather
something stylized, refined, elevated above the level of ordinary existence. A Charleston newspaper complained of the "flat and colloquial"
language of one play: "There is a superiority of speech necessary to be
assumed in everything above the level of conversation.—Drama more
particularly requires it; from its excellent effect, in leading the mind
from vulgarism and common discourse."[103]

This escape from "vulgarism" was considered unnecessary in the low-
comedy sections of plays. Here simplicity and individual peculiarities of
diction and dialect were given free vent. Low-comedy language had a
liveliness that was usually exaggerated to the point of burlesque, but that
sometimes had charming vigor and concreteness. For instance, a low-
comedy lover described his girl:

> Kate Rompwell is a funny lass, with lips as sweet as treacle,
> And for a partner in a jig, I never knowed her equal,
> She'll run, and jump, and wrestle too, altho she's fat and weighty,
> And many a time upon the green I've tripp'd the heels of Katy.
>
> Her eyes are blue as indigo, or high-bush huckle-berry
> Her cheek and lip are red as beets, or like a full ripe cherry;
> Her teeth are white, her hair is brown as a rusty coat potate,
> And like two dumplins are the breasts of pretty buxom Katy.[104]

After hordes of heroines who brought to mind only doves, roses, and
violets, one understands the fellow's love for a girl succulent enough to
suggest huckleberries, beets, potatoes, and dumplings.

Differences in language in the melodrama's two sections mirrored its
implicit division of truth into the ordinary and extraordinary. "The
spirit of the age is mechanical and utilitarian," argued the *Democratic
Review*. "Whatever respects the spirit's life is considered by us visionary
and unreal."[105] Ordinary truth was a matter of everyday life, of practicality, of common sense. Extraordinary truth, the "spirit's life," was the
province of serious drama and transcended all this; it was uplifting and
rather disconnected with the regular business of living. A king's descrip-

[102] *American Quarterly Review*, 1 (June, 1827): 344.
[103] *Charleston Courier* (January 3, 1807), quoted in Paul H. Partridge, "John Blake White: The
Gentleman Amateur in Republican Charleston, 1781–1859" (Ph.D. dissertation, University of
Pennsylvania, 1951), p. 73.
[104] Samuel Woodworth, *The Deed of Gift* (New York, 1822), p. 22.
[105] *Democratic Review*, 3 (November, 1838): 253.

tion of a heroine suggested what was aimed at in serious sections of plays:

> I said not beauty . . .
> It was the spirit's loftier loveliness,
> Unseen,—ethereal, and ineffable![106]

Carefully divorced from ordinary truth, the melodrama's elevation represented a higher truth, reflected the spirit's loftier loveliness.

Stephen Crane in his novel *Maggie*, written in 1896, pictured some of New York's most depraved denizens watching a melodrama and rapturously supporting virtue and vigorously hissing vice. "To Maggie and the rest of the audience," he wrote, "this was transcendental realism."[107] The irony that Crane saw was equally strong in the early nineteenth century. Night after night, city-dwellers applauded sentiments attesting rural purity, women in the third tier apparently accepted the melodrama's parable of female chastity, and discontented wives and unhappy husbands presumably acquiesced in the picture of Home, Sweet Home. If this was not the way their everyday world was, it was still transcendently true, the way it ought to be. And the conviction that the "ought to be" was at least as real as actuality, and more to be talked about, was the core of the gentility that the melodrama reflected and fostered.

"We detest the cant of probability," wrote one of the few critical defenders of melodrama. "If we go to the play, we desire not to see the dull old story of this working-day world grumbled over again; but to have our curiosity excited, our sympathy awakened, our eyes and ears feasted with stirring incidents and ravishing sounds."[108] This was what the melodrama did, "omitting what is irrelevant, commonplace, or simply painful."[109] It was a culmination of a growing desire that drama accept the lives and standards of the people who made up its audience, but the "working-day world" was not especially fascinating to those who lived in it. They preferred a stage reality reflecting their ideas of what life should or might be—all charged with excitement and transcendent

---

[106] Mowatt, *Armand*, p. 11.

[107] Stephen Crane, *Maggie, The Child of the Streets* (London, 1896), pp. 63–64. A description of New York's lower-class Chatham theatre and its audience suggests the same situation: "Crammed full of attentive people, again: sailors, country-folks, and a pit full of boys, watchful, silent and on the keen lookout for any brave speech, relief of oppression, triumph of virtue and manhood against odds; and always applauding such successes to the roof" (*Prompter*, 1 [June, 1850]: 3).

[108] George Daniel, quoted in William S. Dye, *A Study of Melodrama in England from 1800 to 1840* (Philadelphia, 1919), p. 33.

[109] Henry Whitney Bellows, *The Relation of Public Amusements to Public Morality* (New York, 1857), p. 16.

fantasy. Nathaniel Parker Willis might have written of the age's drama as he did of one of its actresses:

> The forms that haunt our dreams in youth
> Can never come again;
> Too beautiful and bright for truth
> We seek them still in vain.
>
> So like are thou to these that we,
> When thou dost greet our view,
> Forget life's dark reality
> And deem its day dreams true.[110]

This was what Melville meant when he stated that theater audiences, in rejecting the commonplace, looked "not only for more entertainment, but, at bottom, for even more reality than real life itself can show." Audiences did want nature, "but nature unfettered, exhilarated, in effect transformed,"—transformed to accord with what was simultaneously man's daydreams and the world's transcendent truth.[110]

The melodrama as dramatic form was shot through with flaws. Its language lacked either honesty or poetry or purposive ambiguity. Its characters were devoid of either originality or complexity. Its plot threads formed a Gordian knot of ridiculous complexity which the dramatist finally cut by near miracle. Its structure was seldom thoughtfully worked out. Its ideals were truisms, the more commonplace and widely accepted the better. Its avowed purpose was moral; and to abet this it set up ridiculous opposites of purity and pollution, innocence and guilt, with providence, in accordance with natural and poetic justice, granting the victory to the righteous. All this divorced the melodrama from any realistic tradition and turned it into what H. D. F. Kitto calls "religious drama," that is, drama where any realistic detail is subordinated to a basic world view. Unfortunately the world view that the melodrama supported, particularly when translated into personal terms, denied any complexity in man's character and situation. The power of the melodrama came from the tension it suggested between a threatening common reality and the perfect structure it upheld as a morally necessary transcendent reality.

The banality of the drama of the early nineteenth century was counteracted principally by two of its resources: laughter and music. Humor, because it operated in the sphere of common reality, often served to

---

[110] "To Clara Fisher Maeder," quoted in Clara F. Maeder, *Autobiography*, ed. Douglas Taylor (New York, 1897), p. xxxi; Herman Melville, *The Confidence Man* (New York, 1964), p. 190.

soften the melodrama's rigid moral dichotomy and to question some of its more dubious assumptions. This tendency to deflate melodramatic conventions was carried even further in the afterpieces in which the humor often came from a vigorous twitting of dramatic and social convention. Enthusiasms like phrenology, or bloomers, or spiritualism, or mechanical gadgets, or worthless currency were turned into one-act jokes, and even the most basic of social preconceptions, such as that of the dutiful wife, were ridiculed:

> *Gustave:* As a wife must obey her husband, I trust, Madame, you will not throw any obstacles in the way of my wishes.
>
> *Pauline:* If they agree with mine, Sir, you may count on my obedience.
>
> *Gustave:* That's the way in all well-regulated families.[111]

My Wife's Mirror, a farce of the early 1850's, suggests the genial twitting of dramatic conventions, social attitudes, and contemporary events that marked the course of these afterpieces. The author used as his main comic device the supposed contrast between the fleshly male and the ethereal female. The hero reminisced about his bachelor days as he awaited his wife's coming to breakfast:

> *Mr. Racket:* Great times those, my boy! Club frequently, Station house sometimes—no end of whist and whisky and—well that's all over—*Sic transit.*—Here I am, five days married and to the loveliest of women— I positively adore her—so ethereal— a sort of crinoline angel—She does come it rather strong on Longfellow though—good gracious how hungry I am—I wonder if she thinks I can breakfast of trochaics—I prefer chops.
>
> *Mrs. R.:* Oh my love you are the most faultless of men.
>
> *Mr. R:* Flatterer! (*Aside*) I wish I had my breakfast.
>
> *Mrs. R.:* No, my adored one, I do not flatter, I see you as you really are— of perfect goodness—handsome as Apollo—chaste as Adonis—a mind of angelic sweetness—virtuous as a sermon, poetic as the editor of the *Home Journal*, ethereal as—
>
> *Mary:* Breakfast, Madam.
>
> *Mr. R.:* Thank Heaven.
>
> *Mrs. R.:* Disgusting interruption!

---

[111] John Howard Payne, *The Boarding Schools*, in *ALP*, 5 : 99. Unfortunately most of these afterpieces were never printed and have not survived. Only titles such as *Bumpology, Mysterious Knockings,* and *The Bank Monster; or, Specie vs. Shinplaster* remain to suggest their contents.

At the table Mrs. Racket found in the paper a report about a German:

Mrs. R.: Exiled for his attachment to the popular cause and now he seeks in a foreign land—

Mr. R.: (*to* Mary) Spoons!

Mrs. R.: Seeks in a foreign land that repose beneath the tree of liberty which was denied him in his own—and where he hopes to taste—

Mr. R.: Sausages!

Mrs. R.: Don't you like the German type of character my dear?

Mr. R.: Infinitely. (*Aside*) I can't read a word of it.

Mrs. R.: If there had been no Germany, there would have been no Goethe.

Mr. R.: Nor Lager beer.

Mrs. R.: No Sorrow of Werter.

Mr. R.: Nor Limburg cheese.

After breakfast Racket began to read a cookbook, and Mrs. Racket asked whether he read Longfellow or Whitman; she was sure he would choose "the delicate, heavenly aspirations of the American Tennyson—the sweet bard of fancy—because his inspired mind claims kinship with your own." When his real choice in reading matter was revealed, Racket defended himself: "It is the cookery book—the most useful as well as the most entertaining of publications. After all my love, marriage is a community of desserts—we sit down to eat the dinner of life together—you take the ethereals and I take the solids . . ., you worship Longfellow and I adore Delmonico." Mrs. Racket however would not sacrifice her conviction that concern with eating was "a vulgar repulsive defect which drove Adam and Eve out of their paradise and will drive us out of ours."[112]

To implement this biblical interpretation she decided to assume the characteristics of her husband so he would be repulsed by his own behavior as reflected in her and reform. She became a glutton until he decided food was not so important; she gambled extravagantly until he decided cardplaying was a bad habit; and she became a ferocious hellion until he decided that belligerence was unbecoming:

Mrs. Racket: Oh, Lion, are you satisfied with your lioness?
Mr. Racket: I prefer to lie down with a lamb.[113]

---

[112] Edward G. P. Wilkins, *My Wife's Mirror* (n.p., 1856), pp. 1–11.
[113] *Ibid.*, p. 23.

At the play's end, one character, a Mrs. Torpedo, announced she was "going to the tabernacle to the Anniversary of the Society for the Spread of Sharpe's rifles, Colt's revolvers, . . . and true religion all over the world." But Racket declined to accompany her: "We, not being philanthropically inclined, will go to the theatre." And when another character addressed the audience, "Ladies and gentlemen, the moral of this piece is—," Racket interrupted him, "That'll never do—nobody cares about morals now a days except the Street Commissioner."[114]

By the 1830's a large category of these afterpieces were take-offs on any serious play that became popular. When one theater in Boston put forth "that interesting Melo-Dramatic spectacle," *Undine; or, The Spirit of the Waters*, the rival house travestied it a few nights later in the afterpiece *Undone! or, Spirits and Water.*[115] *La Bayadère; or, the Maid of Kashmir*, won large audiences all over the country, and the same theaters at about the same time also played its farcical offspring, *Buy It, Dear; It's Made of Cashmere*. At the height of enthusiasm for temperance plays, managers also brought out farces like *Departed Spirits; or, The Temperance Hoax* in which local temperance leaders Deacon Moses Grant and Lyman Beecher were ridiculed.[116] When Mrs. Stowe's *Uncle Tom's Cabin* gained unprecedented success in the North, in New Orleans appeared *Uncle Tom's Cabin in Louisiana*, a drama whose northern characters included:

> Mrs. Convention Sympathy, a Higher Law Expounder and a Bloomer of First Class
> Mrs. Harriet Bleacher Straw, a Milliner Authoress
> Mr. Universal Freedom
> Young America, a Fast Young Gentleman from Down East
> Policemen, mob, etc.

This play, "the most popular piece ever produced in New Orleans," improved on the success of the previous month's "satirical, quizzical burlesque," which had featured one "Harriet Screecher Blow."[117]

The creator of Mrs. Blow, J. M. Field, was typical of the school of stage writers who, beginning in the 1840's, specialized in turning out these burlesques. Perhaps the best-known was John Brougham, often credited with ending the Indian drama with his burlesque *Metamora; or, The Last of the Polliwogs*, whose "tact and talent in catching the various

---

[114] *Ibid.*, pp. 34–36.

[115] William Pelby, *Letters on The Tremont Theatre* (Boston, 1830), p. 14.

[116] John B. Gough, *Autobiography and Personal Recollections* (Springfield, Mass., 1869), p. 89. Gough, later a leading temperance speaker, made his Boston acting debut in this farce.

[117] Joseph Roppolo, "Uncle Tom in New Orleans," *New England Quarterly*, 27 (June, 1954): 219–21.

topics of the day, and twisting them into food for merriment" entertained Americans for years.[118] In large cities, certain theaters, most notably Mitchell's Olympic in New York, gained their greatest successes in vigorous burlesques. Audiences, for example, who went to see the steeds Mazeppa or Vulture thunder down a ramp from the balcony to the stage, also came out for Mitchell's "Perilous Descent of Hassarac mounted on his faithful Donkey Dapple! down a stupendous mass of Rocks reaching several inches above the stage, a feat never attempted by any person on a like Spirited Animal!"[119]

These farces attacked not only what was inherently ludicrous; nothing was sacred to them. Opera was a frequent victim of these jokes. The popularity of *The Bohemian Girl* was duplicated by its minstrel take-off "*The Virginian Girl* starring Signorina Luscreachia Poorgoose and Signor Tomatoe." Bellini's *Norma* inspired Matt Field's *Mis-Normer* in which the Druidic priestess was transformed into a New Orleans' coffee vender and the Britons and Romans became rival market gangs. Field's manuscript, which paralleled closely and cleverly an English translation of *Norma*, shows how these farces laughed the grand into the grotesque. The scene was set:

Norma
Shine forth, young moon, beneath thy light
Norma will sacrifice tonight.

Mis-Normer
Shine forth, young sharks, although you're tight
Normer's coffee'll set you right.

Later the heroine enters:
Lo! Norma comes, by virgins awaited
Solemn her pace, her fair brow elated,
. . .
   While her sickle of gold shines afar.
As she advanceth, Rome's glory waneth,
. . .
Still supernal effulgence maintaineth
   Downward hurling oppression's red star.

---

[118] *Spirit of the Times*, 17 (August 7, 1847): 284.
[119] Advertisement quoted in George C. D. Odell, *The Annals of the New York Stage* (New York, 1927–49), 5:122.

My daughter comes—my heart's with joy elated!
Behold her coffee urn—just newly plated,
    Which gracefully she bears upon her head.
When she draws coffee, every midnight roarer
Is quickly cured by Cuba's grand restorer.
    It is so strong 'twould almost raise the dead.

And the climactic battle approaches:

The day approaches slowly
    When hatred kindled ever
By constant wrongs unholy
    Our shameful bonds must sever.
Then every foe shall be our prey.
Oh God of Terror speed the day.

    The sun is rising slowly
        Our dander's getting higher.
    Our pockets are quite lowly
        And we are getting dryer.
    Then leads the way brave Captain Tyler,
    We'll lick the chaps or bust our biler![120]

All the popular Shakespearean plays also produced farcical offspring, such as the *Macbeth Travestie* in which Lady Macbeth urged on her husband:

What a beast you are: when you told me first your plan
I thought you were quite an enterprising sort of man.

And in the dagger scene Macbeth wondered, "Or is that dagger but a false Daguerreotype."[121] A playbill description of the leading characters in "Rice's Grand Shakespearian Burlesque, interspersed with Songs, Paradies, duets, etc." suggests that some of these farces were cruder:

Otello, Moor of Venice, born in Orange street, or somewhere thereabouts —but a Nigger good as a White Man, and a little gooderer—turned General and did the State some sarbice—snatches and catches not at straws, but airs.

Iago, Otello's Officer, from Salem, Massachusetts, at present speculating in the army.

[120] Matt Field, "Mis-Normer," Ludlow collection, HTC, pp. 1–9.
[121] William K. Northall, *Macbeth Travestie* (New York, 1847), pp. 14–16.

Desdamona, one of those nice creatures with everyone to their liking, and so became Mistress Otello in spite of Papa's restrictions—black looks—lucky thing for Otello she hadn't any brother, or he might look both black and blue.[122]

Shakespearean plays and opera could take such ribbing; the melodrama needed it.

If laughter acted as antidote to melodramatic distortions, music often served to give artistic vitality to the melodramatic vision. The term "melodrama" was first used to describe pantomimed scenes accompanied by music to help establish a mood, and in the nineteenth-century music was generally played to underline the emotional feeling at high points throughout a performance. Many plays were printed with musical cues telling where and what kind of music should be inserted, and their climactic tableaux commonly gained effectiveness from the music or songs that accompanied them. While melodrama developed from background music, it often took its life from song. An early critic defined melodrama in part as a dramatic form in which all characters "heroines or heroes, kings or pickpockets, must indispensably know how to sing."[123] The definition was not strictly true; some melodramas had no songs and most had only one or two. But the success of many of them depended on pleasant musical numbers worked into the web of a conventional story line much like one finds in musical comedies today. Melodramatic silliness was often only a prelude to light and agreeable airs, usually comic patter songs with topical allusions and sentimental or comic ones about love.

In music the melodrama found support not only for its lighter moods, but for its great passions as well. The tradition of melodramatic acting centered on "making points," on the actor's rising and carrying the audience with him to heights of emotional outpouring. The successful play tended to be "a succession of dramatic traps, in which the hands of the audience are invariably taken captive."[124] And melodrama was best lifted to these heights by song. The melodramatic tradition, which began by connecting drama and music, reached its fulfillment in the total union of the two in early nineteenth-century opera. Works such as Beethoven's *Fidelio* or Donizetti's *Lucia di Lammermoor* or Verdi's *Aida* were the lasting monuments of nineteenth-century melodrama. Inane plots and

[122] "Philadelphia Playbills" (January 3, 1852), University of Pennsylvania.
[123] *Aeronaut,* 7 (October 1, 1817): 107–8.
[124] Anna Cora Mowatt, "Stella," in *Mimic Life; or, Before and Behind the Curtain* (Boston, 1856), p. 126.

flat characterizations did little to obstruct their power in evoking human emotions. They were pure melodrama.

Laughter and music served to palliate melodramatic weaknesses, but the form itself had two positive strengths: it took human emotion and evil seriously. Late eighteenth-century drama, guided by the conviction that rational adherence to nature's benevolent laws would bring success, had taken its clearest expression in the moralistic comedy which ridiculed silly people and their follies. In reaction to this tradition, and at the same time accepting its main assumptions, grew up the sentimental and Gothic schools of fiction evoking the tender and the horrifying in human existence. The melodrama combined and sharpened these traditions; and around the core of providence and moral law were spun the galaxy of human emotions. In part because of the lack of complexity and ambiguity in situations and characters that the age allowed, these emotions had to be aroused through verbal excesses and life-and-death situations in which were luridly contrasted love and hate, hope and despair, bliss and woe. But the emotional impact remained real. "What do people go to the theatre for," asked a popular melodramatic actress, "but to laugh and to cry?"[125] The melodrama offered frequent opportunity for such immediate emotional responses; and laughter had its point, while crying, if not the deepest of responses, offered a kind of catharsis.

A defender of the melodrama pointed out that the form filled man's "capacity for enjoyment," banished "all sense of want and weariness," and displayed in contrast to the beautifully virtuous "all that is deformed, dark, and hateful in human nature."[126] This last emphasis represented a change from the predominant social comedies of the late eighteenth century which had stressed folly, mistakes to be eradicated by the sensible application of right reason. Obviously moral rectitude and good sense did not end the hardship or the terror of living—things that did not belong in life if it were truly well ordered. The melodrama restored real evil to its picture of existence, without indicating man's nature, society, or providence, by its emphasis on the villain. This explanation of sin was a serious and silly distortion of life, but it nonetheless gave the grimmer aspects of human existence representation and strong emotional reality.

Rosina Meadows, The Village Maid; or, Temptations Unveiled, was written by an actor-dramatist Charles Saunders, who in a short career turned out a great many plays, only two of which were printed. He

---

[125] Maeder, *Autobiography*, p. 92.
[126] *Literary and Scientific Repository*, 3 (October, 1821): 339.

wrote most of them around specific events or for particular occasions or places, hurriedly and without attempt at originality. For *Rosina Meadows* he borrowed from a popular novel based supposedly on a real incident "well-known to the citizens of the vicinity of Boston." The publisher, apologizing for printing the work, said it was "an effective acting piece," although it did "not possess much literary talent." He also reported that it was often played in New York, Boston, and Philadelphia, where "it met with decided approval . . . to the credit of the author and with profit to the manager."[127] In short it was a melodrama without literary pretensions and with strong popular appeal. Its simplicity and adherence to the conventions made it, aside from its "tragical" ending, perfectly typical. It was stripped of all but the essentials of the melodrama in their most commonplace form; its silliness and strength, its conventions, language, and overtones were those of the genre itself.[128]

(The scene is a village green on the first of May. The young people of the village sing and dance a May dance. All is gaiety.) *The spring, the promise of life, the laughter and music; the village green, simplicity, green innocence, May green.* (The dancers are introduced.)—Patience and Jethro: *Old names, unfashionable names, names that suggest the Puritans, the Bible, strong names and a little comical for people strong and a little comical, the salt of earth, full of simple virtues and salty of speech.*

Milton: *Puritanism, purity, Paradise Lost;* George Milton: *the American name, the name of the father of the country, also son of the soil; one of his sons, a simple farmer, but refined in sentiment and elevated in thought; feet in the soil, heart and head in pure country air, pure as his love.* Rosina: *the rose, sweet, and natural;* —ina: *the little one, delicate, fragile; the delicate bud, the fragile rose;* Rosina Meadows: *the May green meadow and its tender flowers, ripe with life, yet all delicate, its grasses easily crushed, its flowers easily trampled; the village maiden, humble and innocent, daughter of the soil, beloved of a son of the soil, simple and natural; rose in a meadow.*

(A stranger appears from the big city.) Harry: *hairy, bestial.* Harry Mendon: *menacing, mendacious; from the large city to the humble village.*

Mendon: Pray, what is the distance from Boston?
Patience: About 20 miles, sir!

---

[127] Charles Saunders, *Rosina Meadows, The Village Maid; or, Temptations Unveiled* (Boston, 1855), p. iv. A short description of Saunders' career, written apparently by a personal friend, was included in the introduction to his other published play, *The Pirate's Legacy,* pp. 4–5. Though only published in 1855, *Rosina Meadows* was written and performed in 1843. On its popularity, see Odell, *New York Stage,* 4: 644, 5: 461–62.

[128] The incidents and quotations from the play are given in order, except for a few near the end which are rearranged slightly for clarity of condensation.

Mendon: Here is a village apparently enjoying its primitive simplicity; but I fear the easy and frequent communications with the city by the railroad's iron arm may even now have tinctured it. . . .

Primitive simplicity, but evil reaches out, from the city, from complexity; the railroad's iron arm reaches out, the heroine tied to the railroad tracks.

Mendon: —have tinctured it with its vices. I dare say the—
Patience: Sir!
Mendon: How! I have made a mistake here. I must apologize! Excuse me, madam, the warmth of my feelings, engendered by the contemplation of the beautiful scenery, has led me to use an expression at which I fear you are offended!

What offensive expression? " Vice"? Virtue shall hold no intercourse with vice; but it does not matter; the simplest are the wisest; they know, they understand the things of the earth; they can handle evil.

Patience: I accept your apology, sir!
Jethro: Here is my hand to welcome you to our village; but if you talk in that way again to my Patience, I shall withdraw it and put the toe of my boot in the vicinity of your coattails.

Kindly, but common sense is quick and true; Jethro is strong, patience is short; they can take care of themselves.

Jethro: I wonder if I had mutton for dinner yesterday, for I feel awful sheepish.

But no one will pull the wool over his eyes.
But the elevated are noble and generous; their virtue is above this earth; their generosity endangers them.

Old Meadows: . . . if you will share our humble repast. . . .

And the wicked are subtle, devious, ingratiating; they quote the scriptures of the virtuous.

Mendon: O, sir! No city noble, sheltered in his proud mansion, feasted so joyously as I do now! Yours is the bread of industry sweetened with content, made doubly so by youth, beauty, and innocence— nature's heaven born handmaids.

The sweet innocence of nature, the bread of industry is sweet; the city noble, the modern aristocrat in the proud mansion, feasts on the sweet bread of industry, the sweet bread of innocence.

Old Meadows: She was cradled in the woods. She has spent her childhood here, and has grown up a girl of seventeen, without being from the sight of this humble cottage.

The woods and the humble cottage, protection and safety, nature and shelter. But Rosina must go to Boston to seek her fortune; not for money, but she must go, leave the garden; go to Boston where there is no village, no cottage, no May-green meadows.

Mendon: So young and innocent a girl will find many snares and temptations in the city. I fear her course is over a wild and tumultuous sea, full of rocks and quicksands.

Snares for the young, temptations for the innocent; tumultuous sea full of quicksands. Danger! Danger!

Old Meadows: But while virtue and modesty are her guides she has nothing to fear from dangers such as these. She has learned both from the great book of Nature, written by the hand of God!

Mendon: His hand is indeed here, and every leaf and blossom invites us to his love. God made the country, man made the town; there vice is clothed in the temptations that misguided our first parents, and brought sin and death into the world. Heaven forfend that so fair a blossom as Rosina Meadows should be untimely nipped!

God's great book of nature, the country where innocence grows, but bitter fruit grows in man's town, the fruit of Adam and Eve; the fair blossom untimely nipped; sin and death, sin—Heaven forfend!

Old Meadows: Amen to that, I love my daughter—words cannot express how much I love her. But I would rather see her a corpse at my feet, and follow her to a cold grave, the headstone marking where the child of virtue sleeps, than harm should befall her.

Child of virtue, a fate worse than death—words cannot express; such purity.

Mendon: (Aside) By Heaven, she's a divinity! What a voice! Music for the gods! What a form! Such beauties were not formed to bless the wondering eyes of country louts! As Richard says, my daring heart's resolved she shall be mine!

(The villagers enter with a wreath to crown Rosina.)

Chorus: Here upon the village green
Crown we now our May-day Queen!

The May green maiden, yet Queen of the May, fairest and purest, elevated above all, monarch of maidens; village maiden and Queen of the May, humblest and highest; but the city calls, and danger.

George: O, beware the garb of friendship! Villainy often lurks unseen!

Rosina: Temptations will be thrown in my way—vice is there to deceive the young and innocent! The libertine is there—he pollutes the air with his pestilential breath, and like the deadly upas, destroys all that comes within its deadly circle! His presence darkens every avenue, and even the domestic fireside is not safe from his evil eye.

Vice is everywhere, lurks in every avenue, invades even the home; the libertine, pestilential, his deadly circle; but Rosina must go.

Village Chorus: Farewell to Rosina, the sweet village maiden!
The word must be spoken, farewell, O, farewell!
She goes with our prayers and our best wishes laden,
While sorrow behind her, behind her shall dwell!
God bless the sweet maid, may her pathway be fair!
God bless the sweet maid, may her pathway be fair!

Farewell, fair, fare well; God bless; but where is God in the city? and whom to trust? the woman who offers employment or the old man who interrupts?

Bartley: My dear child do you know this Mrs. Clarendon?
Rosina: I do not, sir!
Bartley: Thank Heaven, you have escaped a villain! You have been snatched from the worst woman—(no, woman is not her name)—devil that ever lived!

The devil lurks everywhere, even in the shape of woman; and whom to trust? Mendon?

Rosina: Sir, I fear you mock me, when the wealthy and beloved son of the Mendons declares his love for Rosina Meadows, a humble farmer's daughter.
Mendon: There are those in the city to whom innocence and beauty such as thine are incentives to wicked and unholy thoughts. I look with shame and pity upon the thousands who sacrifice all the purest feelings of nature upon the altar of sensuality.

The farmer's daughter, purest feelings; wealthy sensuality; mendacious.

Rosina: I believe you, Mr. Mendon, and will rely upon you.
Mendon: You may, Rosina; Let me have your confidence and you will attain all you desire. (Aside) And so will I!

Trustful innocence, subtly deceitful vice; the terror of the city and life, but the simple may walk it unhurt; one can escape the fears in laughter at their canniness; they are simple and strong and can handle the world.

Jethro: I am the sole agent, in New England, for the patent anti-appetite pills. . . . They are made by steam, out of the concentrated essence of roast beef and baked potatoes, boiled rice and macaroni pudding.

Jethro will make his way, will sell his pills; he is simple, but not to be taken in; often baffled, never abashed. (He meets a man sporting a moustache.)

Jethro: You a'nt told me what those things are on your upper lip. My father's got a terrier dog—he's darn rough and hairy about his mouth, but he a'n't a circumstance to you. He'd swing his tail between his legs and run like thunder, if he got a squint of you. How on earth do you get the vittals intu your mouth, with those things hanging over it? Du you eat meat, and such like, or du you live on spoon vittals?

246 / *Chapter 9*

(Jethro goes his way, and Rosina is led hers, to work in the shop of a milliner, a friend of Mendon.)

> *Stanley:* If she had the appellation that her deeds have won her, she would be called a procuress instead of a fashionable milliner.

A fashionable milliner, a caterer to the fashionable, a procuress; but innocence is unsuspecting, unknowing.

> *Alice:* You'll soon change the roses of your cheeks to lilies, if you keep housed up as much as your work will require you.
> *Rosina:* But if I didn't work how could I expect food and raiment?

(Mendon offers gold and position to no avail; he offers marriage.)

> *Mendon:* . . . be my beloved and honored wife, Rosina.

Marriage, the renewal of the home, shelter, the protection of the domestic fireside; but the village lessons remain and protect.

> *Rosina:* George Milton's warning seems to harrass my mind, and I strive in vain to forget. O, George, I will treasure your advice!

But evil is subtly treacherous, mendacious; letters are forged.

> *Mendon:* What news, pray, did your letter bring from your parents? Now, I'll wager the best horse in my stable against a kiss from those sweet lips, that your country lover has got another sweetheart. Ah! you sigh, and a tear glistens in your eye! Did I conjecture rightly then?
> *Rosina:* In what a dilemma do I find myself placed?
> *Mendon:* Come, dearest, say but a word, and rank, wealth, and happiness, shall be yours!.
> *Rosina:* But my parents should be consulted first.
> *Mendon:* They have been consulted, dearest! The same post that brought your letter conveyed one from your father to me; which answer to a request to your parents that I might pay my addresses to you, contained a kind affirmative.
> *Rosina:* There is a fascination in his accents. (Aside) O, George! George! have you forsaken me?
> *Mendon:* My whole existence, Rosina, shall be devoted to your happiness.
> *Rosina:* Mr. Mendon, I cannot give you riches, but if the possession of a devoted heart you can accept, in lieu of these, I give it to your keeping; and, O, remember the solemn charge you have undertaken!
> *Mendon:* Fear not, dearest! The saints above will bless our union, and strew our path with sweetest flowers.

Rosina forsaken, the solemn charge—O, remember; the path strewn with flowers, a devoted heart, crushed under foot; mendacious; pestilential; the libertine desecrates even marriage, the promise of the home.

Rosina: The recording angel has it there! There in his eternal book!
'Tis recorded with a diamond pen. He who stood before the altar,
with the habiliments of the man of God, falsely pronounced us
man and wife. And he who sits in majesty upon the high throne of
Heaven will give sentence of the convicted destroyer of honor.

*But honor is destroyed, innocence lost; the rose is blasted, discarded, left to be
picked up by whatever rough hands wilt, to die.*

Rosina: 'Tis true, I wear not now upon my cheek the ruddy glow of
innocence—the pure air of my native village has not fanned my
cheek for many a day. The dishonoured blandishments of a false
heart have driven me from the roof of virtue to the house of vice.

*From innocence to guilt, from the heighth of purity, of perfection to the depth of
vice; a house is not a home.*

Rosina: I have no home, poor, deserted, deceived Rosina! The Heaven,
whose edict you have outraged, will avenge my wrongs. Nature
will sustain no more. My limbs grow weak—I faint—who'll give
a cup of water to the lost Rosina?

*To the least of these; the limbs weaken, the petals droop; the queen of the May now
the least of these; but Heaven will avenge.*
(The father is aware of her fall.)

Old Meadows: O, my child, why would you not see the snare that was
weaving around you? Why did you not hear the loud laugh of the
libertine as he exulted over his anticipated conquests. She was the
child of innocence. She dwelt around the paradise, created by her
own holy thoughts, and saw not the serpent that lay beneath her
feet.

*Purity deafened to danger by its own perfection, and the father still loves, but he
cannot take her back.*

Old Meadows: Ay she lives, but she has lost that which alone makes life
valuable to woman—her honour! You may show me the casket,
but the jewel is gone.

*Only the casket, the coffin; when honor dies the maid is dead; but George intercedes,
leads the father to the city, to the lost sheep, the dying Rosina. (Her face veiled, she
approaches; is forgiveness, redemption possible?)*

Rosina: And may she not return to her home, and falling on her knees
as I do now, look up to you with clasped hands and contrite heart,
and implore, in the face of God, your forgiveness?

Old Meadows: Yes, let her come, if she can, and see this bleeding heart;
let her look upon these bitter, scalding tears—this hollow cheek
and death struck form; let her look upon these white hairs, dis-
graced by her—the never-sleeping agony that rends this mind with

its fearful delirium! Let her come and see the work she has wrought, and hear the curse, the terrible curse of a heart-broken father.

(Rosina throws off disguise and closely clings to Meadows. . . .)

Rosina: Father, in Heaven's name, do not curse me!—do not! I am your—O, God!.—your child! I am your once-beloved child!—your Rosina! Heaven look down, and have mercy on me!

(Tableau. Rosina falls at the feet of her father.)

(Mendon, disinherited, a drunkard and thief, is brought in by watchmen. Rosina, dying, accuses him and the confrontation wins the father's forgiveness.)

Old Meadows: Villain! Thy race of wickedness is run! Thy time is come!—seducer! murderer of my child! Look upon her father! Sweet crushed flower, I forgive you! Bless you! Bless you!

Rosina: Then I die happy. (Dies in the arms of George Milton.)

The father forgives; the rose is at peace; sin expiated by death and repentance, she now can rest in the arms of her real love. And shall vice live when victimized virtue dies?

Old Meadows: Villain! Seducer!—Murderer! Die! Die! (Music. He strangles him.)

The hands of providence; God is just, and just his rewards; the wages of sin, but the gift of God; the hands of providence. (The watchmen stand at the side of Old Meadows, who points with one hand toward Heaven and with the other toward Rosina.)

This was the heart of the dramatic form that dominated the stage in the period. Its conventions were false, its language stilted and commonplace, its characters stereotypes, and its morality and theology gross simplifications. Yet its appeal was great, and understandable. It took the lives of common people seriously and paid much respect to their superior purity and wisdom. It elevated them often into the aristocracy, always into a world charged with action, excitement and a sense of wonder. It gave audiences a chance to empathize in a direct way, to laugh and to cry, and it held up ideals and promised rewards, particularly that of the paradise of the happy home based on female purity, that were available to all. And its moral parable struggled to reconcile social fears and life's awesomeness with the period's confidence in absolute moral standards, man's upward progress, and a benevolent providence that insured the triumph of the pure. *Rosina Meadows* was the tragedy of the age.

Appendix I

POPULARITY OF PARTICULAR PLAYS

Because of their geographical range and the availability of statistics for them, Philadelphia, Charleston, New Orleans, and St. Louis are used in these tables. The half-century is divided into three parts to accord roughly with two events from which are sometimes dated intellectual or social changes—the end of the War of 1812 and the presidency of Andrew Jackson. For each city, during each period when it had a regularly functioning theater, the twenty-five dramas most frequently played have been tabulated. These lists have been broken down into "main plays" and "afterpieces," the categories into which most theatrical evenings were divided. The totals for all plays that made any of the local lists have also been compiled. Each list shows the position of the play in the totals, its title, its author, its type, the total number of performances, and the number of performances in each city with its position on the local lists in parentheses. The cities represent the three main sectional areas—the East, the South, and the West. New Orleans and St. Louis were always considered centers of the "western theater" and their leading managers, Caldwell in New Orleans and Ludlow and Smith in St. Louis, were the most important theatrical leaders in the trans-Appalachian area.

The playlists from which the following figures were derived are these: Reese Davis James, *Cradle of Culture* (Philadelphia, 1957), pp. 127–39, and *Old Drury of Philadelphia* (Philadelphia, 1932), pp. 649–76; Arthur Wilson, *A History of the Philadelphia Theatre, 1835–1855* (Philadelphia, 1935), pp. 545–672; William S. Hoole, *The Ante-Bellum Charleston Theatre* (Tuscaloosa, Ala., 1946), pp. 154–206; Nelle Smither, "A History of the English Theatre at New Orleans, 1806–1842," *Louisiana Historical Quarterly*, 28 (April, 1945): 461–541; William G. B. Carson, *The Theatre on the Frontier: Early Years on the St. Louis Stage* (Chicago, 1932), pp. 318–30 and *Managers in Distress: The St. Louis Stage, 1840–1844* (St. Louis, 1949), pp. 299–305; and Joseph P. Roppolo, "A History of the American Stage in New Orleans, 1842–1845" (Master's thesis, Tulane University, 1948), and "A History of the English Language Theatre in New Orleans, 1845–1861" (Ph.D. dissertation, Tulane University, 1950).

TABLE 1. FEATURE PLAYS, 1800–1816

Title	Author	Type	Total	Phila-delphia	Charleston
				PERFORMANCES (POSITION IN PARENS.)	
1. *Pizarro*	Kotzebue	T	69	32(2)	37(1)
2. *Blue Beard*	Colman, the Younger	M	61*	39(1)	22(3)
3. *Cinderella*	Byrne	FT	47*	32(2)	15(11)
4. *Speed the Plough*	Morton	C	46	30(4)	16(7)
5. *Mountaineers*	Colman the Younger	M	43	20(14)	23(2)
6. *Castle Spectre*	Lewis	G	42	23(8)	19(4)
7. *Children of the Wood*	Morton	FT	40*	21(12)	19(4)
7. *Hamlet*	Shakespeare	T	40	27(5)	13
7. *Macbeth*	Shakespeare	T	40	22(10)	18(6)
10. *Richard III*	Shakespeare	T	39	25(7)	14
11. *Abaellino*	Zschokke–Dunlap	M	34	18	16(7)
11. *Forty Thieves*	Sheridan–Colman the Younger	FT	34*	26(6)	8
11. *Honeymoon*	Tobin	C	34	21(12)	13
11. *Tale of Mystery*	Holcroft	G	34	22(10)	12
15. *Stranger*	Kotzebue–Dunlap	D	32	20(14)	12
16. *Exiles*	Reynolds	M	29	14	15(11)
16. *Foundling of the Forest*	Dimond	M	29	23(8)	6
16. *John Bull*	Colman the Younger	C	29	13	16(7)
19. *Romeo and Juliet*	Shakespeare	T	28	20(14)	8
20. *Alexander the Great*	Lee	T	27	19(17)	8
21. *Heir-at-Law*	Colman the Younger	C	25	10	15(11)
21. *Lover's Vows*	Kotzebue	D	25	9	16(7)

* denotes some performances in shortened form as an afterpiece

Type symbols: C—Comedy; D—Drama; FT—Fairy Tale; G—Gothic; M—Melodrama; T—Tragedy

TABLE 2. AFTERPIECES, 1800–1816

| | | | | PERFORMANCES (POSITIONS IN PARENS.) | |
Title	Author	Type	Total	Phila-delphia	Charleston
1. *Review*	Colman the Younger	F	42	23(1)	19(5)
2. *Highland Reel*	O'Keeffe	CO	39	17	22(2)
3. *Poor Soldier*	O'Keeffe	CO	38	17	21(4)
3. *Spoiled Child*	Bickerstaffe	F	38	19(8)	19(5)
5. *Agreeable Surprise*	O'Keeffe	CO	35	17	18(9)
5. *Fortune's Frolic*	Allingham	F	35	22(3)	13
5. *Rosina*	Mrs. Brooke	CO	35	11	24(1)
8. *Jew and the Doctor*	Dibdin	F	33	11	22(2)
9. *Raising the Wind*	Kenney	F	32	20(7)	12
10. *Love Laughs at Locksmiths*	Colman the Younger	CO	30	13	17(11)
10. *No Song, No Supper*	Hoare	CO	30	11	19(5)
10. *Weathercock*	Allingham	F	30	21(4)	9
13. *Adopted Child*	Birch	CO	28	10	18(9)
13. *Purse*	Cross	CO	28	11	17(11)
15. *Lock and Key*	Hoare	CO	27	8	19(5)
16. *Paul and Virginia*	Cobb	CO	25	21(4)	4
17. *Sylvester Daggerwood*	Colman the Younger	F	23	21(4)	2
17. *Three and a Deuce*	Hoare	F	23	23(1)	0

Type symbols: CO—Comic Opera; F—Farce.

TABLE 3. FEATURE PLAYS, 1816–31

PERFORMANCES (POSITION IN PARENS.)

Title	Author	Type	Total	Phila-delphia	Charles-ton	New Orleans
1. *Richard III*	Shakespeare	T	65	24(2)	22(3)	19(3)
2. *Pizarro*	Kotzebue	T	60	25(1)	20(4)	15(8)
3. *School for Scandal*	Sheridan	C	59	20(3)	23(1)	16(7)
4. *Honeymoon*	Tobin	C	56	19(5)	18(6)	19(3)
5. *Tom and Jerry*	Moncrieff	Bur	52*	9	23(1)	20(2)
6. *Rob Roy*	Pocock	M	49	20(3)	7	22(1)
6. *Hamlet*	Shakespeare	T	49	19(5)	16(9)	14(11)
8. *Othello*	Shakespeare	T	47	13	19(5)	15(8)
9. *Virginius*	Knowles	T	42	11	14	17(5)
10. *Bertram*	Maturin	T	41	16(9)	15(10)	10
10. *Devil's Bridge*	Arnold	M	41	17(7)	14	10
10. *Macbeth*	Shakespeare	T	41	14(11)	18(6)	9
13. *Broken Sword*	Dimond	M	38*	14(11)	15(10)	9
13. *Damon and Pythias*	Banim	T	38	14(11)	14	10
13. *Mountaineers*	Colman	M	38	14(11)	13	11
16. *Wandering Boys*	Noah	M	37*	12	11	14(11)
17. *Maid and Magpie*	Dibdin or Pocock	M	36*	17(7)	10	9
17. *Romeo and Juliet*	Shakespeare	T	36	11	18(6)	7
19. *The Wonder*	Centlivre	C	33	6	10	17(9)
20. *Zembuca*	Pocock	M	31*	16(9)	5	10
21. *She Would be a Soldier*	Noah	C	25	6	4	15(8)
22. *Aladdin*	——	FT	23*	14(11)	9	—
23. *Cherry and Fair Star*	——	FT	17*	—	—	17(5)

* denotes some performances in shortened form as an afterpiece.
Type symbols: Bur—Burletta; C—Comedy; FT—Fairy Tale; M—Melodrama; T—Tragedy.

TABLE 4. AFTERPIECES, 1816–31

				PERFORMANCES (POSITION IN PARENS.)		
Title	Author	Type	Total	Philadelphia	Charleston	New Orleans
1. *Spoiled Child*	Bickerstaffe	F	69	21(2)	24(3)	24(1)
2. *Of Age Tomorrow*	Dibdin	F	60	16(4)	22(5)	22(2)
3. *Turn Out*	Kenney	F	57	22(1)	20(7)	15(8)
4. *Poor Soldier*	O'Keefe	CO	56	13	25(1)	18(5)
5. *Raising the Wind*	Kenney	F	50	16(4)	22(5)	12
6. *Day after the Wedding*	Mrs. Kemble	F	49	15(9)	20(7)	14(12)
6. *Three and a Deuce*	Hoare	F	49	16(4)	17(14)	16(7)
8. *Rendezvous*	Ayton	F	46	14(10)	17(14)	15(8)
8. *Review*	Colman the Younger	F	46	13	23(4)	10
10. *Romp*	Bickerstaffe	CO	44	16(4)	15	13
11. *Irishman in London*	Macready	F	43	12	25(1)	6
12. *Rosina*	Mrs. Brooke	CO	42	11	14	17(6)
13. *Highland Reel*	O'Keeffe	CO	41	19(3)	11	11
14. *Turnpike Gate*	Knight	F	40	8	12	20(3)
15. *Fortune's Frolic*	Allingham	F	39	10	20(7)	9
15. *Forty Thieves*	Sheridan–Colman	FT	39	13	11	15(8)
17. *Liar*	Foote	F	38	5	18(11)	15(8)
18. *No Song, No Supper*	Hoare	CO	36	6	16(16)	14(12)
19. *Sleep Walker*	Oulton	F	34	10	18(11)	6
20. *Sprigs of Laurel*	O'Keeffe	CO	33	8	18(11)	7
21. *Bombastes Furioso*	Rhodes	Bur	30	8	19(10)	3
22. *Purse*	Cross	CO	28	1	8	19(4)
23. *Budget of Blunders*	Greffulhe	F	26	14(10)	8	4
24. *Adopted Child*	Birch	CO	23	16(4)	7	—

Type symbols: Bur—Burletta; CO—Comic Opera; F—Farce; FT—Fairy Tale.

TABLE 5. FEATURE PLAYS, 1831–51

PERFORMANCES (POSITION IN PARENS.)

Title	Author	Type	Total	Philadelphia	Charleston	New Orleans	St. Louis†
1. Lady of Lyons	Bulwer-Lytton	M	384	185(1)	45(1)	132(1)	22(1)
2. Richard III	Shakespeare	T	323	181(2)	33(3)	92(3)	17(5)
3. Hamlet	Shakespeare	T	252	135(4)	32(4)	75(8)	10
4. La Bayadère	Auber	B	248*	100(10)	25(9)	108(2)	15(10)
5. Stranger	Kotzebue-Dunlap	D	246	137(3)	30(5)	62(13)	17(5)
6. Hunchback	Knowles	D	240	117(8)	26(6)	80(5)	17(5)
7. Macbeth	Shakespeare	T	230	123(6)	20	80(5)	7
8. Pizarro	Kotzebue	T	221	128(5)	22(13)	61(14)	10
9. Cinderella	Rossini	O	214	91(12)	26(6)	76(7)	21(2)
10. Othello	Shakespeare	T	207	118(7)	23(11)	56(15)	10
11. Black-Eyed Susan	Jerrold	M	195	84(15)	19	71(9)	21(2)
12. Mazeppa	Milner	E	172	69	16	82(4)	5
13. Honeymoon	Tobin	C	168	90(13)	24(10)	47	7
14. Romeo and Juliet	Shakespeare	T	167	87(14)	22(13)	50	8
15. La Sonnambula	Bellini	O	166	104(9)	35(2)	22	5
15. School for Scandal	Sheridan	C	166	70	23(11)	56(15)	17(5)
17. Rob Roy	Pocock	M	162	70	16	64(11)	12
18. Damon and Pythias	Banim	D	156	80(20)	19	45	12
19. Thérèse	Payne	M	150	65	17	56(15)	12
20. Masaniello	Auber	O	144	82(17)	16	34	12
21. Norma	Bellini	O	128	93(11)	12	23	—
22. Fra Diavolo	Auber	O	117	81(19)	26(6)	10	—
22. Paul Jones	Wallack	M	117	36	1	71(9)	9
24. Guy Mannering	Terry	M	107	42	8	42	15(10)
25. Cherry and Fair Star	——	FT	100*	44	9	33	14(13)
26. Timour the Tartar	Lewis	E	96	18	10	63(12)	5
26. Tour de Nesle	Hugo	M	96	41	—	38	17(5)

28. *The Jewess*	——	M	88*	20	12	42	14(13)
29. *Cricket on the Hearth*	Smith	FT	87	83(16)	2	2	—
30. *Laugh When You Can*	Reynolds	C	83	49	1	18	15(10)
31. *Glance at Philadelphia*	——	Bur	82*	82(17)	—	—	—
32. *Belle's Stratagem*	Cowley	C	78	24	6	34	14(13)
33. *Lady of the Lake*	Dibdin	M	70	28	7	21	14(13)
34. *Ice Witch*	Buckstone	M	68	19	—	35	14(13)

* denotes some performances in shortened form as an afterpiece.

† Record for St. Louis, 1831–44.

Type symbols: B—Ballet; Bur—Burletta; C—Comedy; D—Drama; E—Equestrian; FT—Fairy Tale; M—Melodrama; O—Opera; T—Tragedy.

TABLE 6. AFTERPIECES, 1831–51

				PERFORMANCES (POSITION IN PARENS.)			
Title	Author	Type	Total	Phila-delphia	Charles-ton	New Orleans	St. Louis
1. *Perfection*	Bayly	F	263	113(2)	29(2)	100(1)	21(2)
2. *Loan of a Lover*	Planché	Bur	241	116(1)	19	82(4)	24(1)
3. *Dumb Belle*	Bernard	F	203	79(4)	21(7)	88(3)	15(8)
4. *Swiss Cottage*	Bayly	Bur	202	77(7)	19	93(2)	13
5. *Irish Tutor*	Butler	F	191	97(3)	28(3)	54(9)	12
6. *Dead Shot*	Buckstone	Bur	180	78(5)	30(1)	56(7)	16(4)
7. *Secret*	Poole	F	158	64	25(5)	58(6)	11
8. *Lottery Ticket*	Beazley	F	146	67	28(3)	44	7
8. *Robert Macaire*	Selby	Bur	146	64	8	67(5)	7
10. *Married Rake*	Selby	F	144	78(5)	11	38	17(3)
11. *Rendezvous*	Ayton	F	141	64	25(5)	36	16(4)
12. *Day after the Wedding*	Mrs. Kemble	F	138	66	21(7)	39	12
13. *Review*	Colman the Younger	F	131	61	10	48(10)	12
13. *His Last Legs*	Bernard	F	131	46	21(7)	56(7)	8
15. *Raising the Wind*	Kenney	F	125	50	21(7)	46	8
16. *Our Mary Ann*	Buckstone	F	78	36	21(7)	16	5
16. *Turn Out*	Kenney	F	78	21	8	35	14(9)
18. *Husband at Sight*	Buckstone	F	77	18	5	38	16(4)
19. *Sprigs of Laurel*	O'Keeffe	CO	76	22	8	30	16(4)

Type symbols: Bur—Burletta; CO—Comic Opera; F—Farce.

Appendix 2

PERCENTAGES OF TYPES OF PLAYS GIVEN

The figures here represent the percentage of types of plays given in particular years in Charleston, Philadelphia, New Orleans, and St. Louis. The figures in the first column under each year refer to the percentage of plays falling in the main categories, those in the second to the percentages in the sub-categories. The sources are the same as for Appendix I.

The following categories are used:

(1) Plays from the English Renaissance, all of which were Shakespearean except for an occasional performance of Beaumont and Fletcher's *Rule a Wife and Have a Wife* and Massinger's *A New Way to Pay Old Debts*. This category is subdivided into Shakespeare's comedies and tragedies. The histories are fitted into these categories—for example, *Richard III* is classified as tragedy and *Henry IV* as comedy, because these were the elements emphasized in nineteenth-century productions. Most of Shakespeare's plays were given at some time during the period. Besides the leading tragedies on the lists, *King Lear, The Merchant of Venice, Henry IV* (part 1), and *The Merry Wives of Windsor* were played often, and *Much Ado About Nothing, Coriolanus, As You Like It, Julius Caesar, A Comedy of Errors*, and *The Tempest* received regular repetitions.

(2) Seventeenth- and eighteenth-century tragedy, subdivided into the Restoration tragedy of Otway and Rowe, and the later works of Lillo, Home, and Moore, which in different ways displayed melodramatic tendencies more clearly. Although Otway, Rowe, Lillo, Moore, and Home were the most consistently popular of these dramatists, many other tragedies from the period were occasionally played. Among the most popular were Lee's *Alexander the Great; or, The Rival Queens;* Southerne's *Oronooka* and *Isabella;* Whitehead's *The Roman Father;* Murphy's *The Grecian Daughter;* Brown's *Barbarossa;* and Phillip's *The Distressed Mother.*

(3) Seventeenth- and eighteenth-century comedy, divided into (*a*) Restoration comedy and *The Beggar's Opera* with their unconventional morality, (*b*) eighteenth-century comedies by writers like Cibber, Colman the Elder, Cumberland, and Mrs. Cowley, which sentimentally and humorously exposed social follies, and (*c*) the comedies of Goldsmith, Sheridan, and Tobin,

which variously reacted against increasing sentiment and moralizing in comedy. Of the Restoration comedies, Mrs. Centlivre's plays *The Wonder, Bold Stroke for a Wife,* and *The Busybody* were played frequently, and *The Beggar's Opera* and purified versions of Wycherly's *The Country Wife* and Farquhar's *The Beaux Stratagem, The Recruiting Sargeant,* and *The Inconstant* were played from time to time. Congreve and Vanbrugh were presented rarely. The most frequently performed of the sentimental comedies included Cibber's *The Provoked Husband;* Colman's *The Clandestine Marriage* and *The Jealous Wife;* Mrs. Cowley's *The Belle's Stratagem* and *Bold Stroke for a Husband;* and Cumberland's *The West Indian. The School for Scandal* and *The Honeymoon* were frequently presented, and Goldsmith's *She Stoops to Conquer* and Sheridan's *The Rivals* were also regular stock pieces. Sheridan's *The Critic* and *The Duenna* were also played, but usually as afterpieces.

(4) "Turn-of-the-century" comedies, most of which appeared between 1790 and 1810 and emphasized the motifs and morality that was to dominate later nineteenth-century comedy and melodrama. The most successful of these many comedies were Holcroft's *The Road to Ruin;* Morton's *Speed the Plough, A Cure for the Heart-Ache,* and *Town and Country;* Colman's *The Heir-at-Law, John Bull,* and *The Poor Gentleman;* Mrs. Inchbald's *Everyone Has His Fault* and *Wives as They Were and Maids as They Are;* Reynolds' *Laugh When You Can* and *The Dramatist;* and O'Keeffe's farcical *Wild Oats.*

(5) German drama comprised of Kotzebue plays and infrequently an "adaptation" of Schiller's *The Robbers.*

(6) Nineteenth-century comedy. Of the many comedies written in the period, few achieved any great or lasting popularity. Moncreiff's burletta of *Tom and Jerry,* Payne and Irving's *Charles II,* and Boucicault's *London Assurance* were the most successful.

(7) Nineteenth-century tragedy. The period's tragedies are often hard to distinguish from melodramas. Labeled as tragedy here are those plays which have at least three of these four qualities: blank verse, an unhappy ending, a contemporary label of tragedy, and frequent performance by leading tragedians. Among the most successful of these were Shiel's *The Apostate,* Maturin's *Bertram,* Knowles's *Virginius,* Banim's *Damon and Pythias,* Payne's *Brutus,* Milman's *Fazio,* and Bulwer-Lytton's *Richelieu.*

(8) Opera and ballet.

(9) Melodrama. The most successful purveyors of melodrama in English in the period were Colman the Younger, Dibdin, Dimond, Payne, Knowles, Jerrold, Buckstone, and Bulwer-Lytton.

Although all American plays would fit into these categories, they have been segregated to give some notion of the frequency with which native plays were produced. A great many writers are represented in the American totals, but of them, John Howard Payne was by far the most frequently represented. Several of the works of Joseph S. Jones and a couple of Noah's plays were also often staged.

TABLE 7. TYPES OF PLAYS PRESENTED, CHARLESTON, S.C.

Type of Feature	1800 (57)* %	1810 (46) %	1820 (100) %	1830 (68) %	1840 (157) %	1850 (62) %
1. Renaissance	4	19	14	15	9	21
Shakespeare comedy			3		2	3
Shakespeare tragedy	4	17	10	13	7	16
2. 17th–18th-century tragedy	5	19	5	15	6	5
Otway-Rowe		4	2	4	3	2
Home-Lillo-Moore	2	4	1	4	2	3
3. 17th–18th-century comedy	13	7	15	11	10	12
Restoration	4		3		3	
18th century	4		6	4	3	
Sheridan, etc.	5	7	6	4	4	12
4. Turn-of-century comedy	25	4	12	21	12	
5. German drama	32	13	5		1	3
6. 19th-century comedy		7	3		3	11
7. 19th-century tragedy		7	6	7	3	7
8. Opera-ballet			2	1	28	7
9. Melodrama	21	13	33	19	22	29
Animal			16			
Scott			5	3	1	3
Fairy tale					6	
10. American	2	11	5	9	6	3
Tragedy		4	3		1	
Comedy				4	1	3
Melodrama	2	4	2	1	1	
Military					3	
Yankee						
Indian		2		3		

* The number in parentheses at the top of each column represents the total number of feature performances from which the percentages were tabulated.

TABLE 8. TYPES OF PLAYS PRESENTED, PHILADELPHIA

Type of Feature	1811 (135)* %	1820 (71) %	1830–31 (146) %	1840 (625) %	1850 (937) %
1. Renaissance	30	10	18	9	5
Shakespeare comedy	3	5	7	2	
Shakespeare tragedy	24	4	10	6	5
2. 17th–18th-century tragedy	16	4	6	2	4
Otway-Rowe	4		2	0	1
Home-Lillo-Moore	4	4	1	1	1
3. 17th–18th-century comedy	13	11	21	5	3
Restoration	1	3	3		
18th century	8	3	12	3	1
Sheridan, etc.	3	5	5	2	2
4. Turn-of-century comedy	10	15	11	5	2
5. German drama	8	5	3	2	3
6. 19th-century comedy	3	12	6	10	19
7. 19th-century tragedy	3	12	7	10	5
8. Opera-ballet			5	11	3
9. Melodrama	16	23	15	38	44
Animal					
Scott		5	1	2	2
Fairy tale					2
10. American	2	7	8	8	14
Tragedy		3	3	1	1
Comedy	1		1	1	1
Melodrama	1	4		2	8
Military			1	2	
Yankee			3	2	2
Indian			1	1	2

* The number in parentheses at the top of each column represents the total number of feature performances from which the percentages were tabulated.

TABLE 9. TYPES OF PLAYS PRESENTED, NEW ORLEANS AND ST. LOUIS

Type of Feature	New Orleans 1820 (77)* %		New Orleans 1830 (130) %		New Orleans 1840 (293) %		St. Louis 1840 (170) %	
1. Renaissance	16		8		5		9	
Shakespeare comedy		4		4				
Shakespeare tragedy		12		3		5		7
2. 17th–18th-century tragedy	5		3		2		1	
Otway–Rowe								
Home–Lillo–Moore		5		2		1		
3. 17th–18th-century comedy	18		15		3		4	
Restoration		1		4				
18th century		8		7				
Sheridan, etc.		9		5		2		3
4. Turn-of-century comedy	18		7		5		6	
5. German drama	4		4		2		2	
6. 19th-century comedy	4		6		6		4	
7. 19th-century tragedy	3		3		2		2	
8. Opera-ballet	4		11		20		11	
9. Melodrama	21		29		38		43	
Animal		1		1		8		4
Scott		4		3		1		2
Fairy tale		3				3		
10. American	9		13		15		16	
Tragedy		3		3		1		1
Comedy						2		3
Melodrama		5		4		3		7
Military				1		4		
Yankee				2		5		5
Indian		1		4				

* The number in parentheses at the top of each column represents the total number of feature performances from which the percentages were tabulated.

Bibliography

SELECTED BIBLIOGRAPHY

(A more extensive bibliography, as well as a more generously
annotated text, is available in the Harvard Theatre Collection.)

The three major secondary works on early nineteenth-century drama are
George C. D. Odell's fifteen-volume *Annals of the New York Stage* (New York,
1927–49), Arthur Hobson Quinn, *A History of the American Drama from the
Beginning to the Civil War* (New York, 1943), and Montrose J. Moses, *The
American Dramatist* (Boston, 1925). Odell's volumes 2 through 6 cover the
period between 1798 and 1857 with extraordinary thoroughness. As the most
extensive treatment of what came to be America's leading theatrical center,
this work conveys most strikingly the sense of the theater in that era and provides more information about it than any other source. Quinn's study, first
published in 1923, was a pioneer attempt to take the period's drama seriously.
Though not intellectually probing, Quinn's scholarship is impeccable, and his
book remains the most inclusive survey of American playwrighting in the
first half of the nineteenth century. Moses' study asks interesting and provoca-
tive questions about the course and nature of American drama in the period.
All three works draw on, but supersede, the scholarship of late nineteenth-
century stage historians, particularly Laurence Hutton and Brander Matthews.

Perhaps the most helpful of the general histories of the American stage for
the early nineteenth century is Bernard H. Hewitt, *Theatre U.S.A., 1668–1957*
(New York, 1959), in which the author has pieced together various well-
chosen primary sources with shorter bits of commentary. Other general
theatrical histories include: Mary Caroline Crawford, *The Romance of the
American Theatre* (Boston, 1913); Arthur Hornblow, *A History of the Theatre in
America From Its Beginnings to the Present Time* (2 vols.; Philadelphia, 1919);
Oral Sumner Coad and Edwin Mims, Jr., *The American Stage* (New Haven,
1929); John Anderson, *The American Theatre* (New York, 1938); Glenn
Hughes, *A History of the American Theatre* (New York, 1951); Lloyd Morris,

Curtain Time (New York, 1953); Howard Taubman, *The Making of the American Theatre* (New York, 1965); Léonie Villard, *Le théâtre américain* (Paris, 1929). Richard Moody, *America Takes The Stage: Romanticism in American Drama* (Bloomington, Ind., 1955), gives a general interpretation of American theatrical history in the nineteenth century.

All these accounts draw on histories written in the nineteenth century. The most important of these was by the manager-dramatist William Dunlap. His *History of the American Theatre* (2 vols.; London, 1833), though it concentrates predominantly on New York's stage history between 1790 and 1812, provides the liveliest introduction to the period's theater. Other important, if less substantial and interesting, accounts from the early nineteenth century are: James Rees, *The Dramatic Authors of America* (Philadelphia, 1845); Francis Courtney Wemyss, *Chronology of the American Stage from 1752 to 1852* (New York [1852]); William W. Clapp, *A Record of the Boston Stage* (Boston, 1853); Charles Blake, *Historical Account of the Providence Stage* (Providence, 1868); Joseph N. Ireland, *Records of the New York Stage from 1150–1860* (2 vols.; New York, 1866–67); William K. Northall, *Before and Behind the Curtain; or, Fifteen Years' Observations Among the Theatres of New York* (New York, 1851); Henry Dickinson Stone, *Personal Recollections of the Drama, Theatrical Reminiscences* (Albany, 1873); Charles Durang, *The Philadelphia Stage from the Year 1794 to the Year 1855* in *Philadelphia Sunday Dispatch*, 1854–60 (microfilm); Henry Irving, "Dr. Irving's Reminiscences of the Charleston Stage," ed. Emmett Robinson, *South Carolina History* and *Genealogical Magazine*, 51 (July, 1950): 125–31; (October, 1950): 195–215; 52 (January, 1951): 26–33; (April, 1951): 93–106; (July, 1951): 166–79; (October, 1951): 225–32; 53 (January, 1952): 37–47, originally appeared in *Charleston Courier*, 1857–59, 1870. Interesting for the light they shed on amateur theatricals in the period are John Gaisford, *The Drama in New Orleans* (New Orleans, 1849), and James G. Burr, *The Thalian Association of Wilmington, North Carolina, with Sketches of its Members* (Wilmington, N.C., 1871).

The most important primary source for this book has been the plays themselves, well over 250 of which I have read. Almost all are listed in Frank Pierce Hill, *American Plays Printed 1714–1830: A Bibliographical Record* (Stanford, 1934); G. William Bergquist, *Three Centuries of English and American Plays: A Checklist, England, 1500–1800; United States, 1714–1830* (New York and London, 1963); or Robert F. Roden, *Later American Plays, 1831–1900: Being A Compilation of the Titles of Plays by American Authors Published and Performed in America Since 1831*, Dunlap Society Publications, ser. 2, vol. 12 (New York, 1900). The play list appended to Quinn's book is also very helpful, as is the compilation of plays in Allardyce Nicoll's *History of English Drama*. Most readily available are those plays that have been reprinted in twentieth-century anthologies such as Alfred Bates, *American Drama*, vols. 19 and 20 of *The Drama, Its History, Literature, and Influence on Civilization* (London, 1903); Arthur Hobson Quinn, *Representative American Plays* (7th ed.; New York, 1953); Montrose J. Moses, *Representative Plays by American Dramatists* (3 vols.;

New York, 1918–25); Allan G. Halline, *American Plays* (New York, 1935); Richard Moody, *Dramas from the American Theatre, 1762–1909* (Cleveland, 1966); Barrett H. Clark, *America's Lost Plays* (20 vols.; Princeton, 1940–41).

Several manuscript collections have important materials on the theater. I have used particularly those of the theater collections at Harvard University, the New York Public Library, Princeton University, and the Folger Library.

The most important primary sources for the period's theatrical history, aside from the plays, are the numerous autobiographies of theatrical people. The most informative were written by actor-managers: William B. Wood, *Personal Recollections of the Stage, Embracing Notice of Actors, Authors, and Auditors, During a Period of Forty Years* (Philadelphia, 1855); Francis Courtney Wemyss, *Twenty-Six Years of the Life of An Actor and Manager . . . Interspersed with Sketches, Anecdotes, and Opinions of the Professional Merits of the Most Celebrated Actors and Actresses of our Day* (New York, 1847); Noah M. Ludlow, *Dramatic Life As I Found It* (St. Louis, 1880); Sol Smith, *Theatrical Management in the West and South for Thirty Years, Interspersed with Anecdotal Sketches* (New York, 1868). Also containing much material are: George S. Bryan, ed., *Struggles and Triumphs, or The Life of P. T. Barnum* (2 vols.; New York, 1927); John Bernard, *Retrospections of America*, ed. Mrs. Bayle Bernard, introduction by Laurence Hutton and Brander Matthews (New York, 1887); James Fennell, *An Apology for the Life of James Fennell Written by Himself* (Philadelphia, 1814); Frances Anne Kemble, *Journals* (2 vols.; Philadelphia, 1835); Joe Cowell, *Thirty Years Passed Among the Players in England and America* (New York, 1844); George Vandenhoff, *Leaves from an Actor's Notebook* (New York, 1860); Anna Cora Mowatt, *Autobiography of An Actress, or Eight Years on the Stage* (Boston, 1854); Walter L. Leman, *Memories of an Old Actor* (San Francisco, 1886); James Murdock, *The Stage, or Recollections of Actors and Acting from an Experience of Fifty Years* (Philadelphia, 1880); Maud and Otis Skinner, eds., *One Man in His Times: The Adventures of H. Watkins Strolling Player, 1845–1863* (Philadelphia, 1938); William G. B. Carson, ed., "The Diary of Mat Field," *Bulletin of the Missouri Historical Society*, 5 (January, April, 1949): 91–108, 157–84; Paul R. Weidner, ed., "Journal of John Blake White," *South Carolina Historical and Genealogical Magazine*, 42 (April, 1941): 55–71; (July, 1941): 99–117; (October, 1941): 169–86; 43 (January, 1942): 35–46; (April, 1942): 161–74; Robert Montgomery Bird, "A Young Dramatist's Diary: The Secret Records of R. M. Bird," ed. Richard Harris, *Library Chronicle of the University of Pennsylvania*, 25 (Winter, 1959), 8–25; Olive Logan, *Before the Footlights and Behind the Scenes* (Philadelphia, 1870); John Durang, *The Memoir of John Durang, American Actor 1785–1816*, ed. Alan S. Downer (Pittsburgh, 1966).

Less informative are: Mordecai M. Noah, *Gleanings from a Gathered Harvest* (New York, 1847); Philip H. Highfill, "Edmund Simpson's Talent Paid on England in 1818," *Theatrical Notebook*, 12 (1958), 83–90, 130–40; 13: 7–14; William Pelby, *Letters on the Tremond Theatre, Respectfully addressed to the Primitive Subscribers, its Friends and Patrons* (Boston, 1830); Louis F. Tasistro,

Random Shots and Southern Breezes (2 vols.; New York, 1842); William G. B. Carson, ed., *The Letters of Charles and Ellen Kean Relating to their American Tours* (St. Louis, 1945); William Davidge, *Footlight Flashes* (New York, 1866); James R. Anderson, *An Actor's Life* (London, 1902); Tyrone Power, *Impressions of America* (2 vols.; London, 1836); Mrs. Charles Mathews, ed., *A Continuation of the Memoirs of Charles Mathews, Including His Correspondence and An Account of His Residence In the United States* (Philadelphia, 1839); Fanny Ellsler, *Letters and Journal Written Before and After her Operatic Campaign in the United States* (New York, 1845); George Handel Hill, *Scenes from the Life of an Actor* (New York, 1853); John Gough, *Autobiography and Personal Recollections* (Springfield, Mass., 1869); Joseph Jefferson, *The Autobiography of Joseph Jefferson* (New York, 1890); Lester Wallack, *Memories of Fifty Years* (New York, 1889); Catherine Reignolds-Winslow, *Yesterdays With Actors* (Boston, 1887); Thomas Ford, *A Peep Behind the Curtain, by a Supernumerary* (Boston [1850]); Clara Fisher Maeder, *Autobiography*, ed. Douglas Taylor (New York, 1897).

Some fictional writings by people connected with the theater suggest interesting aspects of and attitudes toward the drama: William Dunlap, *Memoirs of a Water Drinker* (2 vols.; New York, 1837); Anna Cora Mowatt, *Mimic Life; or Before and Behind the Curtain* (Boston, 1856) and *Twin Roses* (Boston, 1857); Charlotte Cushman, "The Actress," *Godey's Lady's Book*, 14 (February, 1837): 70–73; Joseph Field, *The Drama in Pokerville . . . and Other Stories* (Philadelphia, 1847). Of the many travelers' accounts, the richest and most amusing in its theatrical references is Frances Trollope, *Domestic Manners of the Americans,* ed. Donald Smalley (New York, 1960).

Studies of the theater in particular localities form the bulk of the academic research on the period's drama. The books, articles, and dissertations chronicling local dramatic happenings are numerous. Clifford Hamar, "American Theatre History: A Geographical Survey," *Educational Theatre Journal*, 1 (December, 1949): 164–94, is a helpful but not complete bibliography. Many of these studies are excellent and are replete with much primary source material culled from local newspapers and from pamphlet controversies. They represent immense academic labor without which one could scarcely generalize about the period's theater. I have used them extensively and gratefully. The following are just a few of the published sources from which I have borrowed most heavily: William G. B. Carson, *The Theatre on the Frontier: The Early Years on the St. Louis Stage* (Chicago, 1932), and *Managers in Distress, the St. Louis Stage, 1840–1844* (St. Louis, 1949); Claire McGlinchee, *The First Decade of the Boston Museum* (Boston, 1940); Edward W. Mammen, *The Old Stock Company School of Acting, A Study of the Boston Museum* (Boston, 1945); James M. Barriskill, three articles published in the *Essex Institute Historical Collections,* "Newburyport Theatre in the Eighteenth Century," 91 (July, October, 1955): 211–45; 329–52, "Newburyport Theatre in the Federalist Period," 93 (January, 1957): 1–35, "Newburyport Theatre in the Early Nineteenth Century," 93 (October, 1957): 279–314, and the same author's, "The Professional Theatre in Cooperstown, New York to 1850" (MS, HTC); T.

Allston Brown, *A History of the New York Stage* (3 vols.; New York, 1903); Reese Davis James, *Old Drury of Philadelphia: History of the Philadelphia Stage 1800–1835* (Philadelphia, 1932), and *Cradle of Culture, 1800–1810* (Philadelphia, 1957); Arthur H. Wilson, *A History of the Philadelphia Theatre, 1835–1855* (Philadelphia, 1935); William Stanley Hoole, *The Ante-Bellum Charleston Theatre* (Tuscaloosa, Ala., 1946); William G. Dodd, "Theatrical Entertainments in Early Florida," *Florida Historical Quarterly*, 25 (October, 1946): 124–74; J. Max Patrick, *Savannah's Pioneer Theater from Its Origins to 1810* (Athens, Ga., 1953); John S. Kendall, *The Golden Age of the New Orleans Theater* (Baton Rouge, 1952); Nelle Smither, "A History of the English Theatre At New Orleans, 1800–1842," *Louisiana Historical Quarterly*, 28 (January, April, 1945): 85–276, 361–572; Robert L. Sherman, *Chicago Stage: Its Records and Achievements* (Chicago, 1947); Joseph S. Schick, *Early Theatre in Eastern Iowa: Cultural Beginnings and the Rise of Theatre in Davenport and Eastern Iowa, 1836–1863* (Chicago, 1939); Constance Rourke, *Troupers of the Gold Coast* (New York, 1928); G. R. MacMinn, *The Theatre of the Golden Era of California* (Caldwell, Idaho, 1941); Henry Welch Adams, *The Montgomery Theatre, 1822–1835* (Birmingham, 1955); William B. Hamilton, "The Theater in the Old South-west: The First Decade at Natchez," *American Literature*, 12 (January, 1941): 471–85; Edward G. Fletcher, "The Beginnings of the Professional Theatre in Texas," *University of Texas Bulletin*, no. 3621 (June, 1936), pp. 3–55; Joseph Gallegly, *Footlights on the Border: The Galveston Stage Before 1900* (The Hague, 1962); Lucile Gafford, *History of the St. Charles Theatre* (Chicago, 1930); Walter Moffatt, "First Theatrical Activities in Arkansas," *Arkansas Historical Quarterly*, 12 (Winter, 1953): 327–32; Elbert Bowen, *A Study of Theatrical Entertainment in Rural Missouri Before the Civil War* (Columbia, Mo., 1959); John J. Weisert, "Beginnings of the Kentucky Theatre Circuit," *Filson Club Historical Quarterly*, 34 (July, 1960): 264–85; Donald J. Rulfs, two articles published in the *North Carolina Historical Review*, "The Ante-Bellum Professional Theaters in Raleigh, 29 (July, 1952): 344–58, and "The Ante-Bellum Professional Theater in Fayetteville," 31 (April, 1954): 125–33; Alysius I. Mudd, two articles published in the *Records of the Columbia Historical Society*, "Early Theatres in Washington City," 5 (1902): 64–86, and "The Theatres of Washington from 1835 to 1850," 6 (1903): 222–66; Ophia D. Smith, two articles published in the *Historical and Philosophical Society of Ohio Bulletin*, "The Early Theater of Cincinnati," 13 (October, 1955): 231–53, and "The Cincinnati Theater (1817–1830)," 14 (October, 1956): 253–82; Douglas L. Hunt, "The Nashville Theatre, 1830–1840," *Birmingham-Southern College Bulletin*, 28 (May, 1935): 3–88; George M. Elwood, "Some Earlier Public Amusements in Rochester," *Publications of the Rochester Historical Society*, 1 (1922): 17–52 (first published, Rochester, 1894); and three articles in the *Journal of Mississippi History*: Joseph M. Free, "The Ante-Bellum Theatre of the Old Natchez Region," 5 (January, 1943): 14–27; and William Bryan Gates, "The Theatre in Natchez," 3 (April, 1941): 71–129, and "Performances of Shakespeare in Ante-Bellum Mississippi," 5 (January, 1943): 28–37.

Unpublished doctoral dissertations generally have proved as valuable as published works. Again I list only those local studies that have been particularly useful to me: Martin Staples Shockley, "A History of the Theatre in Richmond, Virginia" (2 vols.; North Carolina, 1938), from which several significant articles have been published; Joseph P. Roppolo, "A History of the English Language Theatre, New Orleans, 1845–1861" (Tulane, 1950), which is a continuation of his Tulane master's thesis "A History of the American Stage in New Orleans, 1842–1845," and from which have also been derived several significant articles, most of them published in *Tulane Studies in English;* Ruth H. McKenzie, "Organization, Production, and Management at the Chestnut Street Theatre, Philadelphia, from 1791 to 1820" (Stanford University, 1952); Edward G. Fletcher, "Records and History of Theatrical Activities in Pittsburgh, Pennsylvania from the Beginnings to 1861" (2 vols.; Harvard University, 1931); Theodore Shank, Jr., "The Bowery Theatre, 1826–1836" (Stanford University, 1956); Jack Neeson, "The Devil in Delaware: A Study of Theatre in New Castle County" (Western Reserve, 1959); Richard H. Hadley, "The Theatre in Lynchburg, Virginia, from Its Beginnings to the Outbreak of the Civil War" (University of Michigan, 1947); Joseph M. Free, "The Theatre in Southwestern Mississippi to 1840" (University of Iowa, 1941); Charles C. Ritter, "The Theatre in Memphis, Tennessee, from its Beginning to 1859" (University of Iowa, 1956); Helen Langworthy, "The Theatre in the Frontier Cities of Lexington, Kentucky, and Cincinnati, Ohio, 1797–1835" (University of Iowa, 1953); Mabel T. Crum, "The History of the Lexington Theatre From the Beginning to 1860" (University of Kentucky, 1956); Gerhard Walter Gaiser, "The History of the Cleveland Theatre from the Beginning Until 1854" (State University of Iowa, 1953); Elaine E. McDavitt, "A History of the Theatre in Detroit, Michigan, from Its Beginnings to 1862" (University of Michigan, 1947).

A number of significant biographical studies of theatrical people are also available. A few contain biographical material on several theatrical personalities: Francis C. Wemyss, *Theatrical Biography of Eminent Actors and Authors Compiled from the Standard and Minor Drama* (New York, n.d.); George Seilhammer, *An Interviewer's Album: Comprising A Series of Chats with Eminent Players and Playwrights* (New York, 1881); Robert L. Sherman, *Actors and Authors with Composers and Managers Who Helped Make Them Famous; A Chronological Record and Brief Biography of Theatrical Celebrities, 1750 to 1950* (Chicago, 1951); Laurence Hutton and Brander Matthews, eds., *Actors and Actresses of Great Britain and the United States from the Days of David Garrick to the Present Time* (5 vols.; New York, 1886); *Actors as They Are: A Series of Sketches of the Most Eminent Performers on the Stage* (New York, 1856); John Coleman, *Players and Playwrights I Have Known* (London, 1888); Lewis C. Strang, *Players and Plays of the Last Quarter Century* (Boston, 1903). Particular acting families are discussed in: Montrose J. Moses, *Famous Actor-Families in America* (New York, 1906); William Winter, *The Jeffersons* (Boston, 1881); A. S. Seer, *The Warren Family* (New York, 1893). The biographical introductions to Montrose J. Moses, *Representative Plays by American Dramatists* (3 vols.; New York, 1919–25), are very helpful, providing the most extensive accounts available for several playwrights.

Helpful biographical studies include: Edward Avery Wyatt, *John Daly Burk; Patriot, Playwright, Historian* (Charlottesville, Va., 1936); Paul H. Musser, *James Nelson Barker (1784–1858) with a Reprint of His Comedy Tears and Smiles* (Philadelphia, 1929); Isaac Goldberg, *Major Noah: American Jewish Pioneer* (New York, 1937); Paul H. Partridge, "John Blake White: The Gentleman Amateur in Republican Charleston, 1781–1859" (Ph.D. dissertation, University of Pennsylvania, 1951); Irving T. Richards, "The Life and Works of John Neal" (4 vols.; Ph.D. dissertation, Harvard University, 1933); Kendall Taft, "Samuel Woodworth" (Ph.D. dissertation, University of Chicago, 1937); Murray H. Nelligan, "American Nationalism on Stage: The Plays of George Washington Parke Custis (1781–1857)," *Virginia Magazine of History and Biography*, 58 (July, 1950): 299–323; Leola Bowie Chaplin, *Life and Works of Nathaniel Deering* (University of Maine Studies, no. 32; Orono, Me., 1934); Eric W. Barnes, *The Lady of Fashion: the Life and the Theatre of Anna Cora Mowatt* (New York, 1954); Blesi Marius, "The Life and Letters of Anna Cora Mowatt" (Ph.D. dissertation, University of Virginia, 1938); Sculley Bradley, *George Henry Boker: Poet and Patriot* (Philadelphia, 1927); David S. Hawes, "John Brougham as American Playwright and Man of the Theatre" (Ph.D. dissertation, Stanford University, 1954); Townsend Walsh, *The Career of Dion Boucicault* (New York, 1915); Elizabeth Tyler Coleman, *Priscilla Tyler and the American Scene, 1816–1889* (Tuscaloosa, Ala., 1955); *The Actor; or, A Peep Behind the Curtain, Being Passages in the lives of Booth and Some of His Contemporaries* (New York, 1846); Thomas R. Gould, *The Tragedian* (New York, 1868); Stanley Kimmel, *The Mad Booths of Maryland* (New York, 1940); William K. Northall, *Life and Recollections of Yankee Hill, together with Anecdotes and Incidents of His Travels* (New York, 1850); Margaret Armstrong, *Fanny Kemble, A Passionate Victorian* (New York, 1938); William Dunlap, *Memoirs of the Life of George Frederick Cooke* (2 vols.; New York, 1813); M. Willson Disher, *The Cowells in America* (London, 1934); Emma Stebbins, *Charlotte Cushman: Her Letters and Memories of Her Life* (Boston, 1879); James William Yeater, "Charlotte Cushman, American Actress" (Ph.D. dissertation, University of Illinois, 1959); Dorothy Eldeen Stolp, "Mrs. John Drew, American Actress-Manager, 1820–1879" (Ph.D. dissertation, Louisiana State, 1952); Morris Robert Werner, *Barnum* (New York, 1923); Jonathan F. Kelley, *Dan Marble* (n.p., 1851).

Less detailed or concerned with drama are: Lucius C. Moise, *Biography of Isaac Harby, With an Account of the Reformed Society of Israelites of Charleston, South Carolina, 1824–1833* (Columbia, S.C., 1931); Benjamin Lease, "The Literary Theory and Practice of John Neal" (Ph.D. dissertation, University of Chicago, 1949); William I. Paulding, *The Literary Life of James K. Paulding* (New York, 1867); Amos K. Herold, *James Kirke Paulding, Versatile American* (New York, 1926); Oscar Wegelin, *Micah Hawkins and the Saw-Mill: A Sketch of the*

First Successful American Opera and Its Author (New York, 1917); Mary Alice Wyman, *Two American Pioneers, Seba Smith and Elizabeth Oakes Smith* (New York, 1927); Bruce W. McCullough, *The Life and Writings of Richard Penn Smith with a Reprint of The Deformed* (Menasha, Wis., 1917); Robert E. Blanc, *James McHenry (1785–1845), Playwright and Novelist* (Philadelphia, 1939); Joseph V. Ridgely, *William Gilmore Simms* (New York, 1962); Elias Nason, *A Memoir of Mrs. Susanna Rowson* (Albany, 1870); Joseph N. Ireland, *Mrs. Duff* (Boston, 1882), and *A Memoir of the Professional Life of Thomas Abthorpe Cooper* (New York, 1888); William L. Keese, *William E. Burton* (New York, 1891); *The Life and Memories of William Warren* (Boston, n.d.); Maria Ward Brown, *The Life of Dan Rice* (Long Branch, N.J., 1901); *Sketch of the Life of George Holland* (New York, 1871); T. H. Morrell, *Sketch of the Life of James William Wallack Senior, Late Actor and Manager* (New York, 1865).

CHAPTER BIBLIOGRAPHIES

CHAPTER ONE: The standard work on Dunlap is Oral Sumner Coad, *William Dunlap, A Study of His Life and of His Place in Contemporary Culture* (New York: Dunlap Society, 1917). Also of some interpretive interest are: Charles M. Getchell, "The Mind and Art of William Dunlap, 1766–1839" (Ph.D. dissertation, Wisconsin, 1947); Mary R. Bowman, "Dunlap and the 'Theatrical Register' of New York Magazine," *Studies in Philology*, 24 (July, 1927): 413–25; Robert H. Canary, "William Dunlap and the Search for an American Audience," *Midcontinent American Studies Journal*, 4 (Spring, 1963): 45–51. In many ways suggestive of Dunlap's intellectual stance is the good biography of his close friend: James E. Cronin, "The Life of Elihu Hubbard Smith" (Ph.D. dissertation, Yale, 1946). Dunlap's own writings present by far the most telling picture of the man's point of view. Besides his history of the American theater and his theatrical novel, *Memoirs of a Water Drinker*, his most significant works are: *Diary*, ed. Dorothy Barck (3 vols.; New York, 1930); *Memoirs of George Frederick Cooke* (London, 1813); and *A History of the Rise and Progress of the Arts of Design in the United States* (3 vols.; New York, 1834), which contains a good autobiography. Of the works on Kotzebue as dramatist, A. W. Holtzmann, *Family Relationships in the Dramas of Augustus von Kotzebue* (Princeton, 1934), and Walter Sellier, *Kotzebue in England* (Leipzig, 1901), are the most helpful. Henry A. Pochman, *German Culture in America: Philosophical and Literary Influences* (Madison, Wis., 1957), gives an extraordinarily thorough survey of the German theater in America, including American translations of German plays. It supersedes the many earlier studies of German drama and adaptations in America.

The literature on French melodrama is more extensive. Of particular interest are: Paul Ginity, *Le mélodrame* (Paris, 1910); E. Jauffret, *Le théâtre révolutionnaire (1788–1799)* (Paris, 1869); George B. Daniel, *The Development of the Tragedie Nationale in France from 1552–1800* (Chapel Hill, 1964); Jean-

Alexis Rivoire, *Le patriotisme dans le théâtre sérieux de la révolution 1789–1799* (Paris, 1950); Willie G. Hartog, *Guilbert de Pixérècourt: sa vie, son mélodrame, sa technique et son influence* (Paris, 1912); Alexander Lacey, *Pixérècourt and the French Romantic Drama* (Toronto, 1928); O. G. Brockett, "Pixérècourt and Unified Productions," *Educational Theatre Journal,* 11 (October, 1959): 181–87; Lewis Patrick Waldo, *The French Drama in America in the Eighteenth Century and Its Influence on the American Drama of the Period* (Baltimore, 1942).

CHAPTER TWO: Periodicals from the early nineteenth century provided most of my material on theatrical critics. I used the very helpful *American Periodical Series, 1800–1850* (University Microfilms) predominantly, but I read the original editions for significant periodicals not yet covered by it. Well over a hundred of these periodicals yielded significant theatrical material. For newspaper sources, except for some limited culling, I relied on the material presented in the many local theatrical histories.

Several collections of theatrical criticism appeared in book or pamphlet form: Isaac Harby, *A Selection from the Miscellaneous Writings of the Late Isaac Harby, Esq., to which is prefixed a Memoir of his Life* (Charleston, 1829); James Henry Hackett, *Notes, Criticisms, and Correspondence Upon Shakespeare's Plays and Actors* (New York, 1863); Robert Ewing, *The Theatrical Contributions of "Jacques" to the "United States Gazette": Being an Account of the Performances at the New York Theatre, Philadelphia; During the Season of 1825–1826* (Philadelphia, 1826); Mathew Carey's pamphlet, *Desultory Reflections Excited by the Recent Calamitous Fate of John Fullerton Addressed to Those Who Frequent the Theatre* (Philadelphia, 1802). Some more general collections also contain theatrical observations of interest: Robert Treat Paine, *The Works in Prose and Verse to Which Are Prefixed Sketches of his Life, Character, and Writings* (Boston, 1812); Washington Irving, *The Letters of Jonathan Oldstyle, Esq.,* ed. Stanley T. Williams, facsimile ed. (New York, 1824); Joseph Rodman Drake and Fitz-Greene Halleck, "The Croaker Poems," *The Life and Works of Joseph Rodman Drake,* ed. by Frank L. Pleadwell (Boston, 1935); Edgar Allen Poe, *Works,* vols. 5 and 6 (New York, n.d.); Walt Whitman, *The Gathering of the Forces,* ed. Cleveland Rodgers and John Black (2 vols.; New York, 1920); William Gilmore Simms, *Views and Reviews in American Literature, History and Fiction* (2 vols.; New York, 1845–47); William Winter, *The Wallet of Time* (New York, 1913); Mark Twain, *Mark Twain of the Enterprise: Newspaper Articles and Other Documents, 1862–64,* ed. Henry Nash Smith (Berkeley, 1957), and *Contributions to the Galaxy, 1868–1871,* ed. Bruce McElderry, Jr. (Gainesville, Fla., 1961). *Opening Addresses Written for and Delivered at the First Performances in Many American Theatres,* ed. Laurence Hutton (New York, 1887), presents a fair selection of the arguments for drama used on these occasions. *The American Theatre as Seen By Its Critics, 1757–1934,* eds. Montrose J. Moses and John Mason Brown (New York, 1934), gives some samples of criticism written before 1850 by leading literary figures.

There are no histories of theatrical criticism in the period, but there are several studies of literary criticism. Frank Luther Mott, *A History of American Magazines, 1741–1850* (New York, 1830), is an indispensable guide to the contents and attitudes of periodicals. Other studies which were of particular use to me include: William Charvat, *The Origins of American Critical Thought, 1810–1835* (Philadelphia, 1936); John Paul Pritchard, *Criticism in America; an Account of the Development of Critical Techniques, from the Early Period of the Republic to the Middle Years of the Nineteenth Century* (Norman, Okla., 1956); Alan van Rennselaer Westfall, *American Shakespearian Criticism, 1607–1865* (New York, 1939); John Stafford, *The Literary Criticism of " Young America". A Study in the Relationship of Politics and Literature, 1837–1850* (Berkeley, 1952); Perry Miller, *The Raven and the Whale* (New York, 1956); Edd Winfield Parks, *Ante-Bellum Southern Literary Critics* (Athens, Ga., 1962) and *William Gilmore Simms as Literary Critic* (Athens, Ga., 1961); Lucile Gafford, "Transcendentalist Attitudes Towards Drama and the Theatre," *New England Quarterly*, 13 (September, 1940): 442–66; Philip Marsh, "Philip Freneau and the Theatre," *Proceedings of the New Jersey Historical Society*, 66 (April, 1948): 95– 106. Especially valuable for Dennie and his *Port-Folio* are: H. M. Ellis, *Joseph Dennie and His Circle*, in University of Texas Studies in English, no. 3 (Austin, 1915), and Randolph C. Randall, "Authors of the *Port-Folio* revealed by the Hall Files," *American Literature*, 11 (January, 1940): 379–416.

Religious periodicals provided much of the information on clerical opposition to the stage, but for this topic pamphlets were equally important. I found thirty-nine either written in the early 1800's or reprinted then. The two sources that provided the general outlines for these pamphlets were written in the eighteenth century but reprinted several times in the nineteenth: John Witherspoon, " A Serious Enquiry into the Nature and Effects of the Stage," *Essays on Important Subjects* (London, 1765), 2: 3–112; and Lindley Murray, *Extracts from the Writings of Diverse Eminent Authors of Various Religious Denominations and at Various Periods of Time, Representing the Evils and Pernicious Effects of Stage Plays and Other Vain Amusements* (Philadelphia, 1799); first published in 1789 and often reprinted until 1837 at least). There were also several pithy replies to ministerial attacks: *A Defense of the Drama Containing Mansel's Free Thoughts, Extracts from the Most Celebrated Writers, and a Discourse on the Lawfulness of Plays, by the Celebrated Father Caffaro* (New York, 1826); Thomas Barry, "Defense of Stage" (MS HTC, 1842); A. H. Pemberton, *Calumny Refuted; or, A Defense of the Drama* (Columbia, S. C., 1831); "Otway," *The Theatre Defended. A Reply to Two Discourses of the Reverend Thomas Smyth* (Charleston, 1838); "Thespis," *A Review of the Reverend Thomas Smyth's Two Sermons Against the Theatre* (Charleston, 1838). An important general defense of the stage was Frederic Sawyer, *A Plea for Amusements* (New York, 1847), which spurred some overt religious defenses of the drama: Henry Whitney Bellows, *The Relation of Public Amusements to Public Morality, Especially of the Theatre to the Highest Interests of Humanity* (New York, 1857); Moncure D. Conway, *Theatre: A Discourse Delivered in the Unitarian Church* (Cincinnati, 1857); Progressive Friends, *Amusements: Their Uses and Abuses* (New York,

1856). Two schemes for a public-supported theater were outlined in William Haliburton, *Effects of the Stage on the Manners of the People; and the Propriety of Encouraging and Establishing a Virtuous Theatre* (Boston, 1792); Edward E. Hale, *Public Amusement for Poor and Rich. A Discourse Delivered Before the Church of the Unity, Worcester, December 16, 1855* (Boston, 1857).

Three Ph.D. dissertations provide intelligent discussions of aspects of religious opposition to the stage: Harold C. Shiffler, "The Opposition of the Presbyterian Church in the United States of America to the Theatre in America 1750–1891' (University of Iowa, 1953); Janet Norberg, "From Opposition to Appropriation: The Resolution of Southern Baptist Conflict with Dramatic Forms, 1802–1962" (State University of Iowa, 1964); and William R. Reardon, "Banned in Boston: A Study of Theatrical Censorship in Boston from 1830 to 1950" (Stanford University, 1953).

CHAPTER THREE: Studies of audiences are rare. The two most significant works on this topic are Ph.D. dissertations: Ben Graf Henneke, "The Playgoer in America (1752–1952)" (University of Illinois, 1956), and more indirectly Blanche Muldrow, "The American Theatre As Seen By British Travellers, 1790–1860" (2 vols.; University of Wisconsin, 1953). Also helpful is Joseph Roppolo, "Audiences in the New Orleans Theatres, 1845–1861," *Tulane Studies in English*, 2 (1950): 121–36. Richard Moody, *The Astor Place Riot* (Bloomington, 1958), is the most recent account of that incident, but it does not fully replace the anonymous pamphlet, *Account of the Terrific and Fatal Riot at the New York Astor Place Opera House, on the Night of May 10th, 1849— With the Quarrels of Forrest and Macready, Including All the Causes that Led to that Tragedy* (New York, 1849).

Special accounts pertaining to Forrest and Macready are more numerous. Of the primary sources, the most important is William Charles Macready, *Diaries,* ed. William Toynbee (2 vols.; New York, 1912). Significant manuscript letters from both men are in the Harvard Theatre Collection and the Folger Library. The Forrest correspondence in the Princeton University Library, especially the letters to James Oakes, are particularly revealing. Other primary sources include: Edwin Forrest, "Journal" (1835) MS HTC; Forrest's *Oration Delivered at the Democratic Republican Celebration of the Sixty Second Anniversary of the Independence of the United States* (New York, 1838); the New York *Herald* published a *Report of the Forrest Divorce Case, Containing the Full and Unabridged Testimony of All Witnesses, The Affidavits and Depositions Together with the Consuelo and Forney Letters* (New York, 1852); William Charles Macready, ed., *The Replies from England, etc. to Certain Statements Circulated in this Country Respecting Mr. Macready* (New York, 1949); *Bulwer and Macready, a Chronicle of the Victorian Theatre,* ed. Charles H. Shattuck (Urbana, Ill., 1958).

Alan Downer, *The Eminent Tragedian William Charles Macready* (Cambridge, 1966), is very helpful, and Montrose J. Moses, *The Fabulous Forrest: The Record of an American Actor* (Boston, 1929), is the standard biography of Forrest, although Richard Moody, *Edwin Forrest, First Star of the American Stage* (New

York, 1960), is a more recent account. Edward Wagenknecht, *Merely Players* (Norman, Okla., 1966), has sketches of both men. The older official biographies, James Rees, *The Life of Edwin Forrest* (Philadelphia, 1874) and William R. Alger, *Life of Edwin Forrest* (2 vols; Philadelphia, 1877), have much valuable material as does Henry Wickoff, *The Reminiscences of an Idler* (New York, 1880). Interesting comments on acting styles are made in Barbara Alden, "Edwin Forrest's Othello," *Theatre Annual*, 14 (1956): 7–18, and James T. Nardin, "Forrest and Macready: A Note on Contrast," *Theatre Annual*, 15 (1957–1958): 44–54; Alan Downer, "The Making of a Great Actor—William Charles Macready," *Theatre Annual*, 7 (1948–49): 59–83.

CHAPTERS FOUR AND FIVE: The most important information about staging and costuming exists in memoirs and in local theatrical studies. Some information on American staging is to be found in: Wesley Swanson, "Wings and Backdrops: Story of American Stage Scenery from the Beginnings to 1857," *Drama*, 18 (1927): 5–7, 30, 41–42, 63–64, 78–80, 107–10; Clifford Hamar, "Scenery on the Early American Stage," *Theatre Annual*, 7 (1948–49): 84–103; Edwin Duerr, "Charles Ciceri and the Background of American Scene Design," *Theatre Arts Monthly*, 16 (1932): 983–90; Orville K. Larson, "A Commentary on the Historical Development of the Box Set," *Theatre Annual*, 12 (1954): 28–36; Theodore Shank, "Shakespeare and Nineteenth-Century Realism," *Theatre Survey*, 4 (1963): 59–75. Genevieve Richardson, "Costuming on the American Stage, 1751–1901, A Study of the Major Developments in Wardrobe Practice and Costume Style" (Ph.D. dissertation, University of Illinois, 1953), is a competent study.

Biographies provide the best introduction to acting styles, but Alan S. Downer, "Players and Painted Stage—Nineteenth Century Acting," *PMLA*, 61 (June, 1946): 522–76, and Garff B. Wilson, *A History of American Acting* (Bloomington, 1966), provide a more direct treatment of the subject. Alfred L. Bernheim, *The Business of the Theatre: An Economic History of the American Theatre, 1750–1932* (New York, 1964), is an account of theatrical financial practices. The collections of playbills and theatrical account books, particularly in the Harvard Theatre Collection, in the University of Pennsylvania Library, and in the New York Public Library also proved helpful.

Of the several accounts of various theatrical offshoots in the period, the most substantial are: Edward L. Rice, *Monarchs of Ministrelsy from "Daddy" Rice to Date* (New York, 1911); Carl Wittke, *Tambo and Bones, A History of the American Minstrel Stage* (Durham, N.C., 1930); Julian Mates, *The American Musical Stage Before 1800* (New Brunswick, N.J., 1962); Henry C. Lahee, *Grand Opera in America* (Boston, 1901); Chet Anthony Girard, "The Equestrian Drama of the Nineteenth Century" (Ph.D. dissertation, Louisiana State University, 1939); Gil Robinson, *Old Wagon Show Days* (Cincinnati, 1925); Isaac J. Greenwood, *The Circus: Its Origin and Growth Prior to 1835* (New York, 1898); Philip Graham, *Showboats: The History of An American Institution*

(Austin, 1961); Paul McPharlin, *The Puppet Theatre in America, A History* (New York, 1949).

CHAPTER SIX: The greater part of my research involved a comparison of the original texts of plays with the acting editions used predominantly in the nineteenth century in America and in England. The compilations I used most extensively were: Elizabeth Inchbald, ed., *The British Theatre* . . . (25 vols.; London, 1808); William Oxberry, ed., *New English Drama; with prefatory remarks, biographical sketches, notes, stage business, and stage directions* (20 vols.; London, 1818–20); Thomas Lacy, ed., *Lacy's Acting Edition of Plays, Dramas, Farces, Extravaganzas, etc., etc. as performed at the various Theatres* (96 vols.; London, 1835——). The prompt books in the Folger Library also proved helpful.

Besides the several "biographies" of particular plays, some studies of English drama were especially suggestive: Allardyce Nicoll, *A History of English Drama, 1660–1900* (6 vols.; Cambridge, 1955); Aline Mackenzie Taylor, *Next to Shakespeare; Otway's Venice Preserv'd and The Orphan, and Their History on the London Stage* (Durham, N.C., 1950); George C. D. Odell, *Shakespeare from Betterton to Irving* (2 vols., New York, 1920); Hazleton Spencer, *Shakespeare Improved: The Restoration Versions in Quarto and on the Stage* (Cambridge, Mass., 1927); George C. Branam, *Eighteenth Century Adaptations of Shakespearean Tragedy* (Berkeley, 1956); Allardyce Nicoll, *Dryden as an Adapter of Shakespeare* (London, 1922); Arthur Sherbo, *English Sentimental Drama* (East Lansing, Mich., 1957); Bertrand Evans, *Gothic Drama from Walpole to Shelley* (Berkeley, 1947); Ernst Bradley Watson, *Sheridan to Robertson* (Cambridge, 1926); Christopher Spencer, ed., *Five Restoration Adaptations of Shakespeare* (Urbana, Ill., 1965).

CHAPTER SEVEN: Several nineteenth-century books suggest ideas about the nature and needs of an American drama. I have used particularly: James Fenimore Cooper, *Notions of the Americans: Picked Up By A Travelling Bachelor* (2 vols.; London, 1828); Walt Whitman, *Complete Prose Works* (New York, 1914); Margaret Fuller, *Papers on Literature and Art* (New York, 1846); John Neal, *American Writers*, ed. Fred Lewis Pattee (Durham, N.C., 1937); Alexis de Tocqueville, *Democracy in America*, ed Phillips Bradley (2 vols.; New York, 1957). Benjamin T. Spencer, *The Quest for Nationality: An American Literary Campaign* (Syracuse, 1957), offers a good general survey of periodical propaganda for a more national literature.

The most important works about John Howard Payne and Robert Montgomery Bird include: Grace Overmyer, *America's First Hamlet* (New York, 1957); S. H. Blakely, "John Howard Payne's *Thespian Mirror*, New York's First Theatrical Magazine," *Studies in Philology*, 46 (October, 1949): 577–602; Vedder Morris Gilbert, "The Stage Career of John Howard Payne," *Northwest Ohio Quarterly*, 23 (Winter, 1950–51): 59–74; Lewis Leary and Arlin Turner, "John Howard Payne in New Orleans," *Louisiana Historical Quarterly*,

31 (January, 1948): 110–122; Merton E. Coulter, "John Howard Payne's Visit to Georgia," *Georgia Historical Quarterly*, 46 (December, 1962): 333–76; *A Life of Robert Montgomery Bird: Written By His Wife, Mary Mayer Bird . . . with Selections from Bird's Correspondence*, ed. C. S. Thompson (Philadelphia, 1945); Clement E. Foust, *The Life and Dramatic Works of Robert Montgomery Bird* (New York, 1919); Curtis Dahl, *Robert Montgomery Bird* (New York, 1963); Robert L. Bloom, "Robert Montgomery Bird, Editor," *Pennsylvania Magazine of History and Biography*, 76 (April, 1952): 78–92. The Luquer Collection at Columbia University is the main repository of Payne manuscripts, but there are some important documents in the Harvard Theatre Collection.

CHAPTERS EIGHT AND NINE: There have been few studies of the melodrama in English, but important material or ideas about the form can be found in: William S. Dye, *A Study of Melodrama in England from 1800 to 1840* (Philadelphia, 1919); Alan S. Downer, "A Preface to Melodrama," *Player's Magazine*, 21 (January–May, 1945); Maurice Willson Disher, *Melodrama: Plots that Thrilled* (London, 1954); Eric Bentley, *The Life of the Drama* (New York, 1964).

Some attempts have been made in dissertations to integrate early nineteenth-century plays with intellectual history. Among the more interesting of these are: Allan G. Halline, "Main Currents of Thought in American Drama" (Wisconsin, 1935); Josef Aaron Eifenbein, "American Drama 1782–1812 as An Index to Socio-Political Thought" (New York University, 1951); Norman D. Philbrick, "Democracy and Social Comedy in America from 1800 to 1830" (Cornell, 1949); Frederic L. Sederholm, "The Development of Dramatic Comic Theory in America to 1850" (State University of Iowa, 1960). Particular types of nineteenth-century plays are handled in John D. Reardon, "Verse Drama in America from 1765 to the Civil War" (Ph.D. dissertation, University of Kansas, 1957); Myron Matlow, "Persiflage on the Nineteenth Century Stage," *Educational Theatre Journal*, 11 (October, 1959): 212–21; Fred Sitton, "The Indian Play in American Drama, 1750 to 1900" (Ph.D. dissertation, Northwestern University, 1962).

Much scholarship has been devoted to the discussions of low-comedy stereotypes on the American stage. Laurence Hutton, *Curiosities of the American Stage* (New York, 1891), and Perley I. Reed, *The Realistic Presentation of American Characters in Native Plays Prior to 1870* (Columbus, Ohio, 1918), provided pioneer work in the field. The best of subsequent discussions include: Stanley L. Glenn, "Ludicrous Characterizations in American Comedy from the Beginning Until the Civil War" (Ph.D. dissertation, Stanford University, 1955); Marston Balch, "Jonathon the First," *Modern Language Notes*, 46 (May, 1931): 281–88; Richard M. Dorson, "The Yankee on the Stage—A Folk Hero of American Drama," *New England Quarterly*, 13 (September, 1940): 467–93, "Mose, the Far-Famed and World Renowned," *American Literature*, 15 (November, 1943): 288–300, and "Sam Patch, Jumping Hero," *New York Folklore Quarterly*, 1 (1945): 133–51; Francis R. Hodge, *Yankee Theatre, The Image of America on the Stage, 1825–1850* (Austin, 1964); Kent G. Gallagher,

The Foreigner in American Drama: A Study in Attitudes (The Hague, 1966);
G. C. Duggan, *The Stage Irishman* (London, 1937); Edward D. Coleman, "Plays
of Jewish Interest on the American Stage, 1752–1821," *American Jewish Historical Society Publications,* 32 (1934): 171–98; Fannin S. Belcher, Jr., "The Place
of the Negro in the Evolution of the American Theatre, 1767 to 1940" (Ph.D.
dissertation, Yale, 1945); Frederick W. Bond, *The Negro and The Drama*
(Washington, D.C., 1940).

Other character types are discussed in Blanche E. Davis, *The Hero in
in American Drama, 1787–1900: A Critical Appraisal of American Dramas
Through a Consideration of the Hero* (New York, 1950), and Georgiana J. von
Tarnow, "The Heroine in American Drama and Theatre Down to the Civil
War, and Her Relation to 'Life' and the Novels of the Time" (Ph.D. disser-
tation, Cornell, 1944). The drama's reflection of economic and urban life are
considered in: Glen H. Blayney, "City-Life in American Drama, 1825–1860,"
Studies in Honor of John Wilcox, ed. A. Doyle Wallace and Woodburn Ross
(Detroit, 1958); Charles R. Lown, "Business and the Businessman in Ameri-
can Drama Prior to the Civil War" (Ph.D. dissertation, Stanford, 1957), and
"The Businessman in Early American Drama," *Educational Theatre Journal,*
15 (March, 1963): 47–52; Monroe Lippman, "The American Playwright
Looks At Business," *Educational Theatre Journal,* 12 (May, 1960): 98–106;
Willis L. Turner, "City Low-Life on the American Stage to 1900" (Ph.D.
dissertation, Illinois, 1956). Of the several studies of particular plays, perhaps
the most important are Harry Birdoff, *The World's Greatest Hit: Uncle Tom's
Cabin* (New York, 1947), and Harold B. Obee, "A Prompt Script Study of
Nineteenth-Century Legitimate Stage Versions of Rip Van Winkle" (Ph.D.
dissertation, Ohio State, 1961).

Of the many works on general intellectual and social history, I only list
those few to which I am most conscious of my indebtedness: Meade Minni-
gerode, *The Fabulous Forties, 1840–1850: A Presentation of Private Life* (London,
1924); Constance Rourke, *American Humor, A Study of National Character*
(New York, 1931), and *The Roots of American Culture and other Essays* (New
York, 1942); Walter Blair, *Native American Humor* (San Francisco, 1960);
Richard Dorson, *American Folklore* (Chicago, 1959); Ralph L. Rusk, *The
Literature of the Middle Western Frontier* (2 vols.; New York, 1925); F. O.
Mathiesson, *American Renaissance; Art and Expression in the Age of Emerson*
(New York, 1941); Vernon Parrington, *Romantic Revolution in America, 1800–
1860* (New York, 1927); Marvin Meyers, *The Jacksonian Persuasion: Politics
and Beliefs* (Stanford, 1957); William R. Taylor, *Cavalier and Yankee: The Old
South and American National Character* (New York, 1961); Perry Miller, "The
Romantic Dilemma in American Nationalism and the Concept of Nature,"
Harvard Theological Review, 48 (October, 1955); Ernest Tuveson, *The Image As
A Means of Grace: Locke and the Aesthetics of Romanticism* (Berkeley, 1960);
Morse Peckham, *Beyond the Tragic Vision; The Quest for Identity in the Nineteenth
Century* (New York, 1962); W. Macneille Dixon, *Tragedy* (London, 1924); and
George Steiner, *The Death of Tragedy* (New York, 1963).

Index